THE SELECTED
LITERARY LETTERS *of*
Paul Laurence Dunbar

THE SELECTED
LITERARY LETTERS *of*
Paul Laurence Dunbar

EDITED BY CYNTHIA C. MURILLO
and JENNIFER M. NADER

THE UNIVERSITY OF ALABAMA PRESS
Tuscaloosa

The University of Alabama Press
Tuscaloosa, Alabama 35487-0380
uapress.ua.edu

Typeface: Adobe Caslon Pro

Cover image: Paul Laurence Dunbar seated in rocking chair near writing desk at home in Dayton, Ohio, 1900; courtesy of the Ohio History Connection
Cover design: Lori Lynch

Cataloging-in-Publication data is available from the Library of Congress.
ISBN: 978-0-8173-2078-2
E-ISBN: 978-0-8173-9334-2

CONTENTS

Figures

FIGURE 1. Dunbar (second from right) with mother, Matilda (directly behind him), and family, n.d. Courtesy of Ohio Historical Connection.

Acknowledgments

W E WOULD LIKE TO ACKNOWLEDGE and thank several individuals and institutions whose assistance aided in the production of this volume of letters. Without the help of several librarians, special collections archivists, manuscript specialists, and Dunbar scholars, this collection in its current form would not have been possible, and we are forever grateful. The Ohio Historical Society graciously lent us several microfilm reels, which included not only letters but also published and unpublished poems, stories, newspaper clippings, and other memorabilia related to Dunbar, all of which proved valuable to our work and this book. We are also grateful for contributions from the following institutions: Eberly Family Special Collections Library, Penn State University Libraries; Lilly Library, Indiana University; Houghton Library, Harvard University; Schomburg Collection, New York Public Library; James Weldon Johnson Collection, Yale University; Friends Historical Library, Swarthmore College; Special Collections and Archives, Wright State University; W. E. B. Du Bois Collection, Special Collections and University Archives, University of Massachusetts Amherst Libraries; University of Delaware Library and Special Collections; Bill Stolz with Wright State University for his meticulous high-resolution copies of Dunbar images from the gallery; and Lily Birkhimer from the Ohio Historical Society.

Special heartfelt gratitude goes to Gary Scharnhorst, whose patience, enthusiasm, generous support, and advice kept this project going and made it what it is today. Cindy would like to acknowledge Tennessee State University president Glenda Glover as well as the late Michael Catanzaro, former English Department chair, for providing a one-semester course release to help get this project off the ground. Cindy would also like to thank the TSU English Department for several small travel grants to support travel and research on Dunbar throughout her tenure there. In addition, she would like to acknowledge the generous research support provided by

Colorado State University in Fort Collins for assistance with interlibrary loans, hard-to-find newspaper clippings, and other resources that directly fed into this project. Jennifer would like to thank the Humanities and Communication Department at Embry-Riddle Aeronautical University for its excitement about this project; she would especially like to thank Liz Sterthaus, one of the interlibrary loan librarians at Embry-Riddle's Hunt Library, who readily communicated and helped deliver myriad sources. She would also like to thank Donna Barbie, associate dean of Humanities and Communication; Sally Blomstrom, Humanities and Communication chair; and Jennifer Wojton, Lindsey Ives, Leslie Salas, Taryne Taylor, and J. R. Anderson for their wonderful support and encouragement. In addition, the interlibrary loan librarians at the University of New Mexico's Zimmerman Library were invaluable in helping to locate important information in the earliest stages of this project. Finally, Jennifer would like to thank Peter Weishar of the University of Central Florida for his enthusiasm and support, as well as for fruitful and engaging discussions about the Chicago World's Fair in 1893.

Cindy would like to thank her husband, Steve Murillo; her children, Claudia and Christian; and her parents, Ken and Jenny Cupples, for their encouragement and unwavering faith. Jennifer would like to thank her husband, Josh, for his regular support, encouragement, willingness to help, and exceptional patience, and her stepdaughter Haylee for her interest and support.

And of course, both Cindy and Jennifer are thankful for and grateful to the staff at the University of Alabama Press for their guidance and assistance in organizing and finalizing the letters in this edition; specifically, we would like to thank Laurel Anderton for her meticulous editing, kindness, and dedication, Bonny McLaughlin for indexing insights, and Dan Waterman for his helpful suggestions on illustrations and his guidance through several stages of the production process.

THE SELECTED
LITERARY LETTERS *of*
Paul Laurence Dunbar

Introduction

"I KNOW WHY THE CAGED BIRD sings" opens the poem "Sympathy" by American author Paul Laurence Dunbar; this line serves as the title for Maya Angelou's famous autobiography, *I Know Why the Caged Bird Sings* (1969). When Dunbar penned that poem in 1897, he could neither have imagined the burgeoning African American literati who would revive his fame during the civil rights movement of the 1960s nor have dreamt that the "caged bird" would become a trope of oppression. Yet Dunbar's name is not often mentioned without reference to his other most well-known poem, "We Wear the Mask," which invites white readers to try to understand the complications inherent in being both an African and an American—something W. E. B. Du Bois would speak strongly about applying the psychological metaphor applied to the African American experience—double consciousness. Dunbar's "mask that grins and lies" highlights the many personas he had to assume in order to appease a voracious reading public eager to see quaint local color plantation stories and poems nostalgic for a southern past. However, what Dunbar truly wanted to sing was not dialect but verses of nostalgia and romance, songs of sorrow and contemplation in Standard English that both elegized fallen African American heroes and lamented a fractured society that embraced a covert racism. It is difficult to accurately and completely piece together Dunbar's entire life since many of the foundations of his history are based on Lida K. Wiggins's first biography of the author in 1907, a year after his death. Her language is tinged with racism that unduly prejudices the information she relays. Though much of her material can be validated, Wiggins's perspective often paints a rosier picture of Dunbar's life than he really lived; like many, she reflects the accepted ideals of her time. Beyond this, the few biographies that followed have information that has never been fully substantiated; moreover, some early biographies, in an attempt to portray Dunbar as a heroic, uplifting African American, tend to gloss over the daily literary battles he fought and the personal demons he faced. Dunbar was a public voice for many, but his private life is often missed or set aside in favor of the civic Dunbar, the iconic "poet Laureate of the Negro Race." Because of the difficulty in locating and reading the poet's personal letters, many of the exact but upsetting truths that surround Dunbar's personal life are absent from scholarship.

There are, however, a few biographies of Dunbar that help readers capture a snapshot of what his letters reveal: Virginia Cunningham's *Paul Laurence Dunbar and His Song* (Dodd, Mead, 1956), Gossie Hudson's dissertation, "A Biography of Paul Laurence Dunbar" (Ohio State University, 1970), and Felton Best's *Crossing the Color Line: A Biography of Paul Laurence Dunbar* (Kendall Hunt, 1996). Eugene Metcalf's vast dissertation, "The Letters of Paul and Alice Dunbar: A Private History" (University of California, 1973), focuses closely on the letters Dunbar and Alice wrote each other before and during their marriage, while Eleanor Alexander, in *Lyrics of Sunshine and Shadow: The Tragic Courtship and Marriage of Paul Laurence Dunbar and Alice Ruth Moore* (New York University Press, 2002), considers Dunbar's highly romantic and idyllic courtship with Alice, but with a far more realistic hue. Alexander focuses on the turbulent, dysfunctional, and troubled marriage between Dunbar and Alice. Combined, these biographies expose a genius and ambition in Dunbar that was cultivated during his childhood by a caring but demanding and needy mother, an absent father, and an intense desire, almost a compulsion, to write regularly, compounded by alcohol addiction, tuberculosis, and brutal mood swings.

However, without careful analysis of Dunbar's literary letters, we cannot fairly and fully understand the poet and his quest to be an author; we hope our section introductions, transcriptions, and detailed annotations will help clarify and provide some answers to many of the lingering questions about this famous literary genius. Through correspondence never before published, we hope to at least shed light on the gaps that biographers and scholars have encountered and even raise other questions for further study. Many of Dunbar's letters remain lost, but we anticipate that with time more of them will be recovered, answering those enduring questions we were unable to. For now, however, this is what we know.

———•——

Paul Laurence Dunbar was born in 1872 to Matilda Murphy and Joshua Dunbar of Dayton, Ohio. Both Matilda and Joshua were former slaves.

Matilda was a domestic servant until the Emancipation Proclamation, while Joshua escaped through the Underground Railroad and then later served in the Union Army during the Civil War. The couple divorced because of Joshua's continued unemployment and issues with alcoholism, but there is evidence they not only remained in contact but also continued to have a relationship. Consequently, Dunbar grew up listening to his parents tell tales of their experiences as slaves, many of which became an integral part of his writing as he created poems, short stories, and novels from their recollections. Dunbar learned about southern life and some forms of dialect from his mother and those around him, but it was Joshua who taught Dunbar about military life. Dunbar would later loosely base the protagonist of "The Ingrate" (1899) on Joshua. In fact, many of Dunbar's stories drew directly from the narratives he heard as a child.

Though he was the only African American in his class at Central High School in Dayton, Dunbar excelled and spent his days writing and publishing poetry in both the school and local papers. In 1889, Dunbar became the general assistant editor of his high school paper, the *High School Times*, where some of his earliest poems first appeared. Dunbar's hopes of being a professional writer soared when Charles W. Faber of the *Democratic Sheet* promised Dunbar a position on the condition that he solicit fifty or more subscribers. Dunbar succeeded in gaining more than the required number of subscriptions, but Faber went back on his deal. Dunbar immediately submitted his letter of resignation to Faber, whom he irately accused of "willfully and persistently failing to keep . . . the agreement" the two had made.

Dunbar's optimism for a literary career began to reshape, however, when his classmate Orville Wright started the *Westside News* in March 1889 and Dunbar became a contributor. Dunbar then served as an editor and a writer for Wright's short-lived venture with the *Dayton Tattler*, observing poetically in a scrapbook that Wright was "out of sight. In the printing business no other mind is half so bright as his'n is" (scrapbooks 1S86–1S96, box 11, Paul Laurence Dunbar Papers, Ohio Historical Society). Ultimately, the *Tattler* was unsuccessful, but Dunbar was able to look back on the enterprise with rather high spirits in an objective and realistic manner—none of the fury he felt toward Faber was present at all: "We published it as long as our financial resources permitted of it, which was not too long" (Orville Wright to Edward Johnson, January 2, 1934, in McFarland, *The Papers of Wilbur and Orville Wright*, 2:1162). But this was the beginning of Dunbar's life in the literary world, so he could not fault

Wright, and he maintained a friendship with both Wright brothers until his death.

Dunbar was not born into a family of means; this left him unable to attend college after graduation, though he had initially hoped to be a full-time writer. In a September 14, 1899, newspaper clipping, Dunbar relayed these aspirations: "I wanted to go to Harvard and study under A. S. Hill. I studied Hill's rhetoric and I wanted to study English under the man who wrote it. But I had a mother to support and I could not leave my work in Dayton" (Paul Laurence Dunbar Papers, Ohio Historical Society). To support his mother and himself, Dunbar took a position as an elevator operator in Dayton's Callahan Building, but he never stopped writing, and people would often ride the elevator just to hear him read his poetry. His name caught on, and so did his poems. Dunbar was granted an opportunity to show his skills as a writer and an orator when one of his elevator patrons invited him to attend the 1892 convention of the Western Association of Writers in Dayton. After a wildly popular address and the help of several benefactors, Dunbar self-published his first book of poems, *Oak and Ivy* (1893), shortly after. Though Dunbar initially explained to the *Detroit Free Press* on January 5, 1902, that "an advance of $100 was at first demanded, upon consideration the publisher agreed to wait for his compensation until the poems were sold." Dunbar was, if nothing else, exceedingly pleased at this turn of events.

In 1893, Dunbar attended the Chicago World's Fair. There, he met many prominent people who would have a profound influence on his literary career, most notably Frederick Douglass, who at one point employed Dunbar at the exposition. He also met such important figures and lifelong friends as Will Marion Cook, the famous composer and dramatist with whom he would later collaborate, and George Washington Cable, whose philosophies often aligned with his in their fight for equal rights for African Americans. Dunbar's youth and inexperience in a large city, however, really shine through in his letters, highlighting, perhaps, his early naiveté regarding the racial politics foregrounding the World's Fair in 1893. For many in the African American community, the Chicago World's Fair was a hotly debated topic by such well-known speakers as Ida B. Wells, who pointed out that "only one African American man was appointed to a clerical position." This, combined with being barred from exhibition halls and "left out of planning stages of the exposition" (Paddon and Turner, "African Americans," 19), caused fervent debate that seems to have either escaped

Dunbar or simply been too unpalatable for him to comment; he was, after all, there for readings, work, and networking. Yet the racism at the Chicago World's Fair was particularly potent; an all-white committee decided there would be a "Colored People's Day" but then largely ignored minorities, while African American newspapers noted the fair ought to be renamed "the white American's World's Fair" (Rudwick and Meier, "Black Man in the 'White City,'" 354). Interestingly enough, the letters Dunbar wrote during this major event reveal none of the simmering political turmoil but rather show a concerned Dunbar, who was consistently seeking work and overwhelmed with the bustling crowds.

Dunbar's literary fate was proverbially sealed, however, after James A. Herne, a well-known dramatist, ensured that a copy of *Majors and Minors* (1895), Dunbar's second book of poetry, reached William Dean Howells, the American realist and the most well-respected literary editor at the time. Howells reviewed the collection positively and enthusiastically. Though most see Howells as having rocketed Dunbar into overnight stardom, many have argued this was to Dunbar's detriment because of Howells's emphasis on Dunbar's masterly use of dialect and what the editor believed to be Dunbar's realistic representations of African Americans. In Howells's review of *Majors and Minors* in *Harper's Weekly*, he claimed Dunbar was "the first man of his color to study his race objectively, to analyze it to himself, and then to represent it in art as he felt it and found it to be; to represent it humorously, yet tenderly, and above all so faithfully that we know the portrait to be undeniably like." Despite the inherently racist foundations of Howells's claims, the American public enthusiastically embraced Dunbar, and just as quickly as Howells reviewed *Majors and Minors*, Dunbar became a literary star. Dunbar, however, would privately lament that Howells had done him an "irrevocable harm" by exhaustively praising the dialect poems at the expense of Dunbar's verses in Standard English; however, he publicly and copiously thanked Howells, and despite his penchant for romantic writing, Dunbar acknowledged in a January 5, 1902, clipping from the *Detroit Free Press* that he had "become a devotee to realism" (Arnold, "Some Personal Reminiscences," 4).

In his short life, Dunbar published prolifically and was adored by not only the American public but an international audience as well. In the span of just over fifteen years, Dunbar published hundreds of poems, short stories, and several novels as well as collections of each. By the time he published his third book of poetry, *Lyrics of Lowly Life* (1896), with Dodd and Mead, he had reached a pinnacle: he was the very first African American to earn royalties of 15 percent and be advanced several hundred dollars from a publisher. In an August 26, 1896, letter to his mother, Dunbar excitedly explained, "Dear mother: I win; My book is to be republished. I am to receive $200 at once and a royalty of fifteen percent on the first 10,000. How is this for high?" (Schomburg Collection, New York Public Library, reel 1, box 3).

In short, Dunbar's achievements as a writer were exemplary, especially considering the time in which he lived and the rampant racial prejudice he faced daily from editors, acquaintances, and sometimes even close friends. Dunbar's contemporary and sometime competitor Charles Chesnutt described these issues and the period as being at an absolute nadir, "at a lower ebb than at any time during the thirty-five years of their freedom." Chesnutt also noted that the prejudice he and others faced was "more intense and uncompromising" ("Address to the Medina Coterie"). Specifically, within the context of this historical period was the 1896 Supreme Court's landmark decision in *Plessy v. Ferguson*, which upheld the "separate but equal" doctrine. Despite this reality, Dunbar's popularity was nigh unmatched, and he was hailed as a writer and regarded as "a true singer of the people" by the *New York Times* and countless other newspapers upon his untimely death at age thirty-three. Though Dunbar was undoubtedly one of the most famous turn-of-the-century African American writers, he largely fell into obscurity less than three decades later and has struggled to remain popularly canonized since, except for a few poems sprinkled throughout anthologies. Despite small successes in recovering some of Dunbar's previously lost works, many anthologies and literary collections reproduce the same verses; as a result, readers are often unaware of what Dunbar's oeuvre truly comprises, including the diverse genres and styles to which he laid claim.

There are many reasons Dunbar has faced such difficulty in remaining canonized and studied. His sometimes problematic use of dialect during his life remains a large cause of his scholarly ostracization; on the other hand, when he was alive, dialect was wildly popular and friends, fans, and publishers praised and enjoyed his all-encompassing style of poetry. Howells, for instance, regarded Dunbar as being "among the truest of our poets" (*Atlantic Monthly* 85 [1900], 701). Upon Dunbar's passing, Brand Whitlock wrote H. A. Tobey that "Paul's range and appeal were wider than those of any other of his race; if they had not been, he would not have been a poet. For the true poet is universal as is the love he incarnates in himself, and Paul's best poetry has this quality of universality." Indeed, it was Dunbar's Standard English verses and not his dialect pieces that Whitlock quoted at the poet's funeral. However, the majority of readers and publishers during Dunbar's time wanted dialect, so that is what Dunbar wrote for them, even when he did not want to.

Critics and supporters alike often wrote of Dunbar's achievements in what would now be considered painfully racist terms, though by nineteenth-century standards some of the remarks made regarding Dunbar would have been considered progressive. Often, critics looked at Dunbar's poetry in relation to his identity as an African American or as being essentially and solely a representation of the Black experience; hence, Dunbar faced criticism when he veered from traditionally accepted areas and subjects expected of writers of color. In other words, when he dared to consider life for anyone who was not African American, no matter the portrayal of the character or realistic creation, Dunbar found himself heavily criticized by white readers. Reviews of *The Uncalled* (1898), *The Love of Landry* (1900), and *The Fanatics* (1901) reflect this. For instance, one reviewer for the *Bookman* concluded about *The Love of Landry* that "it is quite natural that Mr. Dunbar should have certain limitations when he endeavours to portray the characters of those not of his own race" (*Bookman* 12 [January 1901], 512). As such, Dunbar was largely unable to escape racist censure, doled out from multiple sources, no matter what he wrote.

Though he was widely read throughout America from the 1890s into the twentieth century and hailed by many as one who spoke for his race, Dunbar did not necessarily aim for this particular role and yet found it thrust upon him. Though he has been lambasted for his use of dialect, Gavin Jones reads this form in Dunbar's verse as not only masterful, but calculated. Jones views Dunbar as a "wily manipulator of literary conventions, a subtle overturner of racist stereotypes, and a sensitive recorder of the multiple facets of black consciousness" (*Strange Talk*, 184). Subsequent to Dunbar's death, Brand Whitlock hinted that Dunbar was harrowingly and emotionally burdened by the demand for dialect pieces. Whitlock asserted that this undue emotional stress may have contributed to Dunbar's overall failing health from alcoholism and tuberculosis. In a letter to H. A. Tobey, Whitlock confided, "You and I knew something of his deeper sufferings, something of the disease that really killed him." Indeed, perhaps Dunbar was his own speaker in "Worn Out," where the narrator confides to readers the exhaustion that comes from experiencing pain far "beyond [one's] years" after being "bid to hold [his] peace."

Dunbar's nods to the plantation tradition and his use of dialect piloted him into a controversial place within the literary canon. Mark Noonan, for example, notes that Dunbar is rightly viewed as a "complex and subtle author adept at working in a variety of literary genres and forms . . . the authenticity of his black voice and the extent to which he subverted plantation myth conventions remain at the force of criticism of his work" ("'Jump Back, Honey,'" 82). Indeed, there are several stories where Dunbar's slaves and masters have relationships: "The Last Fiddling of Mordaunt's Jim," "Dandy Jim's Conjure Scare," "A Supper by Proxy," "The Trouble about Sophiny," "Mr. Groby's Slippery Gift," "The Conjuring Contest," "The Brief Cure of Aunt Fanny," and "The Memory of Martha" are all examples of this. James Weldon Johnson highlights this complexity, noting that "not even Dunbar had been able to break the mold in which dialect poetry had" stereotypically "been set by representations made of the Negro on the minstrel stage" (*Along This Way*, 159). However, Johnson also argued that Dunbar had been able to refine the form, to add "a deeper tenderness, a higher polish, a more delicate finish to the genre." Dunbar's *cri de coeur*, as Johnson recorded it, aptly describes Dunbar's struggle: "I've got to write dialect poetry; it's the only way I can get them to listen to me" (*Along This Way*, 34). Yet even before this, Dunbar was clearly interested in the style of dialect, which burgeoned during the mid to late nineteenth century.

Many writers, from Mark Twain to Charles Chesnutt, drew on dialect, so Dunbar's use of this genre was not uncommon for the time; furthermore, Dunbar, like other writers of the day, experimented with various forms of dialect and greatly enjoyed reading stories written in this form. Dunbar explained this in a January 5, 1902, interview with the *Detroit Free Press*: "It is difficult to put any name before that of Ruth McEnery Stuart, nineteenth-century Louisiana writer, who depicts both the humorous and pathetic side of the race with such fidelity. There are, however, in the stories of Joel Chandler Harris intimate touches, which to me are absolutely marvelous. He presents the negro in an aspect in which he would scarcely exhibit himself to a white man, repeating characteristic speeches which he would hardly give utterance to except to one of his own color." Beyond simply appreciating dialect stories, Dunbar, Joanne Braxton notes, experimented with "regional language" from "German-American, Irish-American, and

Midwestern dialects" (*Collected Poetry*, xxiii). Yet Dunbar has been the most excoriated for his uses of "Negro" dialect. Besides Johnson, Robert Bone and Victor Lawson readily criticized Dunbar for his use of dialect. Not all agreed: in "Old School of Negro 'Critics' Hard on Paul Laurence Dunbar" (1924), Thomas Millard Henry argued that the writers of the *Crisis* (James Weldon Johnson, William Stanley Braithwaite, and W. E. B. Du Bois) had been unduly harsh in their criticism of Dunbar. Matthew Wilson expands on this notion, arguing, "We would quixotically (and ahistorically) like them to be unraced; we still believe that these artists should have been able to transcend the history that made the obligation for them to be representative African Americans rather than representative artists. One hundred years after their major contributions we are still enmeshed in the American racial imaginary" ("Advent of 'The Nigger,'" 43).

Though Gossie Hudson attempted to extinguish the fiery debate by arguing that Dunbar's dislike of dialect was a "myth," and that Dunbar had not been "forced to write in that vein by his editors," Matthew Wilson has asserted that "living in the era of the color line, Dunbar . . . could neither change racial discourse nor . . . the tradition of depiction of African Americans. Despite [his] artistic ambitions, [Dunbar] is an example of how minority artists a hundred years ago were circumscribed by . . . audience[s]" ("Advent of 'The Nigger,'" 43). Wilson argues, however, that despite these difficulties in success, the literary presence of Dunbar and Chesnutt "on the artistic scene helped to change, if not the discourse, the cultural climate" (43). Yet Charles Chesnutt observed a palpable, visible color line despite Howells's deepest wishes that "a color line in literature" did not exist. In response, Chesnutt explicitly explained, "On that point I take issue with him. I am pretty fairly convinced that the color line runs everywhere so far as the United States is concerned" (quoted in Helen Chesnutt, *Charles Waddell Chesnutt*, 178).

Even today, Dunbar can be difficult to teach and discuss. Criticism of Dunbar's connection to the plantation tradition and his use of dialect nearly erased his existence as an adored, cherished American writer; connecting students and readers to what is now considered a distasteful tradition can make appreciating Dunbar difficult without the appropriate resources. We intend these letters to help with that.

Prevalent and beloved as dialect was at the turn of the century, and regardless of the racial complications, Dunbar continued to experiment with this form and even appreciated it early in his career. He explained in an

1897 interview, "I must confess my fondest love is for the Negro pieces," but he simultaneously noted, "These little songs I sing because I must" (Hudson, "Paul Laurence Dunbar: Regional Heritage," 439). Indeed, Dunbar claimed he wrote dialect poems because he realized it could bring him recognition and success as a writer—the very things he urgently sought. According to James Weldon Johnson, Dunbar explained to him, "I simply came to the conclusion that I could write it as well, if not better, than anybody else I knew of, and that by doing so I should gain a hearing" (*Along This Way*, 110). Success might be an understatement in describing this tactic: Dunbar's talent was exceptional, and he gained such a hearing that he became a household name while many other writers and poets, including Richard Lew Dawson, with whom Dunbar corresponded, faded into memory. Though Dunbar could not necessarily have predicted the prolonged consequences and perils of scholarly examination and dispute regarding publishing dialect poems, he very clearly came to grasp the ramifications of his decision; as Dunbar explained, "I gained the hearing, and now they don't want me to write anything but dialect" (quoted in Johnson, *Along This Way*, 110).

Accusations regarding Dunbar's use of dialect as problematic reigned throughout the Harlem Renaissance and almost extinguished Dunbar's popularity. However, upon the republication of *The Book of American Negro Poetry* (1959), James Weldon Johnson stoked the fire anew when his astute observation reminded readers of the issue. Johnson explained that "Negro dialect is . . . a medium that is not capable of giving expression to the varied conditions of Negro life in America, and much less is capable of giving the fullest interpretation of Negro character and psychology. This is not an indictment against the dialect as dialect, but against the mold of convention in which Negro dialect in the United States has been set" (xli). Though Johnson did not openly criticize Dunbar here, within a decade of the publication of this text, he set ablaze dialect's complex history and its racial dynamics, something discussed by Dunbar's biographer Gossie Hudson, who wisely argues that Dunbar's use of dialect was not remotely representative of any but a few black communities in America: "Had Dunbar immitated [*sic*] the speech of the North Georgia Black and uttered it among the Geeches of South Georgia or the Gullahs of South Carolina, he would not have been understood. From a knowledge of many dialects he made a language or synthetic dialect that could be read with ease and pleasure by northern whites. Through this medium it was impossible for

Dunbar to speak the whole heart of a people" ("Biography," 212). Darwin
T. Turner notes that critics of a more aggressive mind-set erred in their as-
sessment of the author, as they "demanded too much of Dunbar as a symbol
for the African American population as a whole." In doing so, Turner explains that these critics had forgotten "that Negroes speak with hundreds of
different voices. Dunbar is merely one" ("Paul Laurence Dunbar: Rejected
Symbol," 13). Certainly, Dunbar understood the nuances involved in this
issue, though it greatly frustrated him: "Just think of it! literary critic and
yet doesn't know that there are as many variations of the negro [sic] dialect
as there are states in the Union! For instance an Alabama negro does not
speak any more like a Virginia colored man than a Yankee talks like a man
from Colorado" (quoted in Wiggins, *Life and Works*, 109). Published posthumously, "The Poet" reveals that struggle:

> He sang of life, serenely sweet,
> With, now and then, a deeper note.
> From some high peak, nigh yet remote,
> He voiced the world's absorbing beat.
>
> He sang of love when earth was young,
> And Love, itself, was in his lays.
> But ah, the world, it turned to praise
> A jingle in a broken tongue.

Justifiably, a debate remains centered on Dunbar's use of dialect and the
societal and institutionalized racism that people associate with this form of
speech, as well as the publishing industry and the constraints Dunbar faced
as an African American in the late nineteenth and early twentieth centuries.
In "A Personal Experience," Dunbar expressed a specific disdain for covert
racism, though noting "I have greater respect for that American entertainer
who, seeing my name at the head of a popular bureau's list of readers, said:
'Well, if you put a nigger's name first you can take mine off.' He, at least,
had the courage of his convictions" (Turpin, "Twilight Is Their Child," 166).
Regardless of the foci of Dunbar's trials and tribulations, Dunbar sought
the limelight and was determined to make a living as a writer; Howells's
review quickly provided Dunbar with that opportunity—so much so that it
caught Dunbar off guard, as his letters divulge.

   Given the rise in production of works written by African Americans at the turn of the twentieth century and the politics associated with the use of dialect, there are troubling aspects of Dunbar's writings that scholars simply cannot ignore: (1) Dunbar's portrayal of African American men in prejudicial and stereotypical ways, and (2) his participation in several minstrel shows. Even before they were married, Alice begged Dunbar not to write in dialect or participate in minstrelsy, but Dunbar insisted these performances would allow him to provide "a cozy nest for my singing bird" (Metcalf, "Letters of Paul and Alice Dunbar," 195–96). Alice responded in an October 21, 1897, letter, pleading with Dunbar: "Don't, don't write any more such truck as you've been putting in the *Journal*. Now this is between us as between husband and wife. To everyone else I champion your taste . . . I argue from all sorts of premises your right to do as you please—but to you darling, I must say—*don't*. I know it means money and a speedier union for us, but sometimes money isn't all. It is not fair to prostitute your art for 'filthy lucre,' is it? I shall be glad when the sixth story comes out. It will be such a relief, for every Sunday I find myself asking 'what next'" (quoted in Metcalf, "Letters of Paul and Alice Dunbar," 216). Dunbar, however, felt it impossible to say no to these publications because they paid him more money than he had ever earned before. For an aspiring full-time writer who agonized over money, twenty dollars for a single publication helps in understanding Dunbar's acquiescence.

Critics have long complained that Dunbar did not write enough protest literature, but just as Dunbar did not begin his career as a dialect poet, he did not begin his career as a protest writer either. It is entirely possible that critics missed Dunbar's delicate protestations and skilled use of rhetoric, which allowed him to critique politics and race issues through his pen—a talent that has led Henry Louis Gates to conclude that Dunbar actively engaged in *signifying*. Always guarded and masked in public interviews, in a January 5, 1902, piece for the *Detroit Free Press*, Dunbar explained that he was "not a controversialist," and that he "believe[d] the [race] problem . . . [would] solve itself . . . all the sooner" if those interested in it would "work more and talk and write less." Dunbar also explained his feelings on Booker T. Washington's approach to solving race issues in America. He said, "I myself should be very unhappy if I were compelled to make my living by any handicraft, and I cannot, therefore, agree with those who would doom the race to mechanical occupations. Give the negro [*sic*], I should say, thorough industrial training, and, if any among them are able to get above this, let them do it." Dunbar also never hesitated to refer to racism bluntly; he even went so far as to call out race-based pseudoscience. Dunbar did not hold back in discussing the double standards in the treatment of whites and blacks, or the terrible mistreatment of African Americans in the justice and prison systems—problems that are still pervasive today.

Careful reading of Dunbar's texts reveals several pithy attacks on racial inequality—and this includes his dialect work, which he at times used to challenge concepts of race, manipulating his readers through carefully crafted plots and rhetoric. Though Dunbar did not always write powerfully clear protest pieces, earlier in his life in the first volume of the *Dayton Tattler* (December 1890), Dunbar wrote one of his strongest statements regarding race: "You know well that the Afro-American is not one to remain silent under oppression or even fancied oppression. When kicking is needed they know how to kick." However, for quite some time, Dunbar chose a more covert style to discuss racial oppression, and his poems avert hostility to seek compassion in the reader; he created "The Haunted Oak" in memory of the lynching of four African Americans in Montgomery, Alabama. Such writing allowed him to gain an audience, a voice, and a literary presence. Later, his frustrations peaked when he journalistically protested the racially motivated mass murder of African Americans in Wilmington, North Carolina, in 1898 with "Mr. Cornelius Johnson, Office-Seeker" (*Cosmopolitan*, February 1899, 420–25). In this story, the protagonist denounced Republican politicians for manipulating innocent voters; and Dunbar's "To the South" begged for mass lynchings to stop. "The Hapless Southern Negro," published in the Sunday *Denver Post* on September 17, 1899, lambasted the living conditions of African Americans in the South, focusing on the economic problems associated with mortgage debt. In 1904, Dunbar published short stories titled "The Lynching of Jube Benson" and "The Wisdom of Silence," both of which bemoan the tragedy that ensues with racial prejudice.

Hudson's description, that Dunbar was "not a revolutionary [and] neither did he articulate propaganda," is actually quite complicated—Dunbar did not hesitate to focus on injustice but did so in a subtle, strategic manner. However, as Hudson also points out in his biography, Dunbar keenly "felt the anger and the accompanying rage of his people" ("Biography," 173) but also acknowledged that "at the turn of the century black writers, far from being radical, strove to prove to white audiences that they could be responsible and respectable" (209); this makes sense considering the host of white mentors to whom Dunbar felt a responsibility. Despite these enduring but conflicting viewpoints and arguments, it must be remembered that Dunbar was beloved by a large reading public, both domestic and international.

———•———

Dunbar's marriage to Alice Ruth Moore in 1898 signaled a change in his personality, as his letters expose. Dunbar was already prone to mood swings, had a growing alcohol addiction, and was faced with constant literary rejections; the marriage became a tumultuous one at best. Eleanor Alexander observes Alice's acquiescence to Dunbar's physical and emotional abuse but points out that when Dunbar "spread a vile story" about her, the "slander" was more than she was willing to withstand (*Lyrics of Sunshine and Shadow*, 169). Besides his marriage, Dunbar's tuberculosis and failing health contributed to several drinking bouts between 1897 and 1903, many of which left Dunbar and Alice embarrassed. Although Dunbar and Alice never divorced, they never reconciled, either, after separating in 1902; however, Dunbar's temper is clearly unveiled in both Metcalf's collection of Dunbar's private correspondence and Eleanor Alexander's monograph of Dunbar and Alice's brief courtship and marriage. Though Dunbar sought Alice's forgiveness, Sandra Archer Young writes that it was the one thing Alice would not give Dunbar: she "not only refused to respond to Dunbar's letters—she resisted even the pleas he set to poetry" ("Coercion or Concern?," 334). Most of the letters in this collection, then, do not reproduce what Metcalf and Alexander have already made available but rather unveil another, private Dunbar who struggled for money and reputation his entire life. We have, however, included selections of correspondence between the two when it is particularly illuminating and functions to highlight Dunbar's literary pursuits.

The letters in this collection also hint at several works Dunbar never published, as far as we can determine. Joanne Braxton has noted that there may be many more writings of Dunbar's that we will never recover. Only time will tell. In the meantime, several manuscripts have been found: Thomas L. Morgan recently recovered "Sue" (1892) and "A Southern Silhouette" (1899), two texts that were published but never collected. In the University of Dayton Rare Book Collection, Herbert Woodward Martin and Ronald

Primeau recently discovered the manuscript for "Ole Conjurin' [Conju'in] Joe." But Dunbar's letters often include requests for manuscripts that have never been located in any Dunbar repository. One of these is "A Race for Revenge," which Dunbar requested back from C. C. Hunt on September 13, 1892. There is also a list of stories marked as returned to Dunbar, including "A Monologue," "The Party," and "The Haunted Plantation." A deeper look into Dunbar's letters also shows missing stories, with titles including "A Detective Story," "Dialogue between Four Friends," "A Man Named Ben Adams," "Murder Story," and "Reginald Vere." On February 20, 1900, Dunbar received a letter from *The Writer: A Monthly Magazine for Literary Workers* that not only returned an unnamed story but included a note that read: "The story as you have it is not well told. Undoubtedly you would write it in much better form to-day. . . . We advise you to read it through to refresh your memory, and then lay it aside and retell it without reference to the original." It is possible that Dunbar revised this story and published it as "The Lion Tamer" in the *Smart Set*.

James Weldon Johnson's 1959 diatribe against dialect did not, however, prevent a revived interest in Dunbar in the 1970s, which led to the publication of several key works including Jean Wagner's *Black Poets of the United States: From Paul Laurence Dunbar to Langston Hughes* (University of Illinois Press, 1973), one of the earliest attempts to bring Dunbar back from scholarly oblivion; it remains formative. Wagner provides a candid evaluation of Dunbar, his use of dialect, the complicated plantation tradition, and the politics of the era, which further confounded Dunbar as a writer. Jay Martin and Gossie H. Hudson's *The Paul Laurence Dunbar Reader: A Selection of Paul Laurence Dunbar's Poetry and Prose, Including Writings Never Before Available in Book Form* (Dodd, Mead, 1975) recovers some of Dunbar's previously lost writings and adds new selections to his wide array of work. It remains an important text in studying Dunbar. Concurrently, Jay Martin's *A Singer in the Dawn: Reinterpretations of Paul Laurence Dunbar* (Dodd, Mead, 1975) offers a decisive collection of essays regarding Dunbar's significance in the literary world. Nearly two decades later, another compendium appeared, Joanne Braxton's *The Collected Poetry of Paul Laurence Dunbar* (University of Virginia Press, 1993).

Since the start of the new millennium, additional compilations of

Dunbar's short stories, poems, plays, and novels have made their way into libraries. Each of these collections offers a revival of Dunbar, arguing for his importance as a turn-of-the-century writer. Herbert Woodward Martin, Ronald Primeau, and Henry Louis Gates Jr. published *In His Own Voice: The Dramatic and Other Uncollected Works of Paul Laurence Dunbar* (Ohio University Press, 2002). In addition, Gene Andrew Jarrett, Thomas Lewis Morgan, and Shelley Fisher Fishkin gathered Dunbar's short works in *The Complete Stories of Paul Laurence Dunbar* (Ohio University Press, 2005). This particular anthology may be one of the strongest in showing the complexity of Dunbar's position as an African American writer at the turn of the century, revealing the author's problematic stories, protest literature, and the correspondence that helped inform them. Discussion and debate are key in studying Dunbar, even if the discussions are difficult, raw, and especially uncomfortable. Willie Harrell Jr.'s collection of essays, *We Wear the Mask: Paul Laurence Dunbar and the Politics of Representative Reality* (Kent State University Press, 2010), serves as a continuation of Martin's *A Singer in the Dawn* and approaches Dunbar through a twenty-first-century lens, focusing especially on minstrelsy, the use of dialect, masculinity, and politics. Most recently, Herbert Woodward Martin, Gene Andrew Jarrett, and Ronald Primeau published *The Collected Novels of Paul Laurence Dunbar* (Ohio University Press, 2009).

Each of these books illuminates Dunbar's works and provides impetus to grant his stay in the literary canon. However, none of these collections offers an intimate glimpse into Dunbar's private literary life, his authorial pursuits, successes, failures, frustrations, and how much work it took for him to be published. What is more, there is no centralized location to access Dunbar's correspondence except through microfilm and hours of deciphering nineteenth-century handwriting. We have undertaken the task of collecting and annotating Dunbar's literary letters to alleviate this issue; we believe Dunbar's literary correspondence is essential to understanding more completely Dunbar's life as a dialect writer, "elevator poet," dramatist, elocutionist, novelist, scholar, educator, journalist, and protest writer. We have spent considerable time deciphering, transcribing, and contextualizing Dunbar's literary letters, which span roughly thirteen years, so that readers can get the actual words from the author himself, while gaining a fuller picture of the circumstances that led to Dunbar's literary career as a writer and an orator. This collection aims to alleviate this gap in Dunbar scholarship by providing Dunbar's correspondence with other notable figures who influenced his life and literary choices, from his mixed feelings about dialect to the editorial decisions he made in marketing his work to publishers.

By gathering Dunbar's published and unpublished literary letters, we hope this book offers another biography in itself, as it describes a self-doubting author who urgently wanted to be a writer, and who readily communicated with publishers and friends in order to make a name for himself. The literary letters clearly reveal an intelligent, but often melancholy writer who was extremely critical of himself: as early as 1895, Dunbar explained to Alice that he was "down in the depths of despondency" and "blue" (September 21, 1895; Metcalf, "Letters of Paul and Alice Dunbar," 66). He also expressed signs of extreme jealousy in his letters and revealed to Alice in February 1896 that he had a penchant for extreme emotional states; J. N. Matthews and James Whitcomb Riley knew something of this as well, as their letters show. Dunbar described himself as "agreeable or disagreeable. Whatever my qualifications for the former are, I can be the latter with a vengeance" (Metcalf 80). On another night, Dunbar wrote Alice that not only was he "in a beastly mood" but that "all humans are cowards at heart" (Metcalf 95). Although many people in Dunbar's life were supportive and encouraging, Dunbar's letters show that not all people who knew of his sullen moods approved. On August 20, 1895, early in Dunbar's career, he received a letter from W. F. Weaver, an admirer of Dunbar's work, who admonished him for this moodiness. Weaver wrote, "I cannot imagine that you are sincere when you say that you think that was a misfortune, that you were ever born, why you of all persons should ever think that is a mystery to me. Had I your gift, I should not complain once, you, who, in a very short time will have the world at your very feet should not murmur." But Dunbar did not necessarily see it this way and at times commiserated with other struggling writers, including Walter LeRoy Fogg and James Edwin Campbell. Campbell, for instance, reassured a young Dunbar that at a similar age, he "had already failed with a newspaper and had gone from home utterly discouraged, almost broken hearted, and . . . had come from the editorial chair of the only colored paper in this state, . . . [was] paid seven dollars a month for board and slept in the loft of a log cabin where every winter night [he] would lie in bed and count through the holes of the dilapidated roof, . . . and many a morning awoke to find that the snow had spread another counterpane over [his] bed and to hide [the] bareness of [the] attic floor had covered it with a white carpet." This was the reality of Dunbar's world, and amid his many literary successes, he was able to support himself financially by writing alone for only a very short time; as he wrote, he struggled daily, with publishers, addiction, and financial woes. Most contemporary reading audiences were blind to the reality of struggling African American authors at the turn of the twentieth century and would never have known about Campbell's true labors or, as these literary letters reveal here, Dunbar's. It is with this knowledge that we delved deep into the inspirations and battles of Dunbar's literary reality to piece together a more comprehensive picture of this great artist, removing the mask that hid his deepest sentiments and unveiling a truth that vitalized his ambition.

On the surface, it would be easy to see Dunbar's fame rise and never wane until after his death; however, Dunbar's letters acknowledge the serious and varied struggles he faced in his literary life. They depict his successes and failures, his highs and lows, as well as his hopes and dreams, some of which became reality and others of which threatened to destroy Dunbar's grasps at happiness. Though his poetry reads like honey even as it reflects his hardships, his letters contain the thick, bitter molasses of Dunbar's literary life and the daily struggles he faced as a writer.

A Note on the Text

THIS COLLECTION MAKES AVAILABLE TO scholars, historians, and students a large selection of Paul Laurence Dunbar's literary letters written during his career as a struggling writer and orator, most of which have never been published. Prior to this edition, Dunbar's literary and professional letters existed only in several microfilm collections across the United States, never having been collected in a volume of any kind. Undeniably, any attempt at reading Dunbar's letters en masse leads to thorny, forked paths: in order to gain an overall understanding of Dunbar's literary pursuits, scholars must consult several different texts and biographies and then must compete with differing information or paraphrasing. After this, they must piece together the puzzle of scattered letters and, at times, must work through difficult-to-decipher handwriting. For those who are seriously interested in studying Dunbar, limited access to information is an issue. Travel to disparate locations to sift through the abundant collections is required, as is access to a microfilm reader. This is not only time consuming but can hinder the ability to research with ease.

This collection serves to alleviate this issue and add to the extant body of scholarship and collections of Dunbar's works. We have carefully selected letters that have not been widely quoted in Dunbar's biographies and literary collections to make available the full context of his publication history and literary path to success. When necessary for historical contextualization, we have reproduced letters that were originally published elsewhere, but we have annotated them meticulously to provide accurate and detailed information regarding the letters' content and necessary contextual information.

Most of the letters in this book come from two major Dunbar microfilm collections: the Schomburg Collection, housed in the New York Public Library, and Sara Fuller's indexed repository at the Ohio Historical Society. The letters reproduced in this edition were drawn from microfiche and photocopies. Questions regarding uncertain transcriptions were verified against newspaper clippings, Dunbar's biographies, and those rare interviews.

Included in this collection is selected correspondence between Dunbar and other notable literary figures, editors, and publishers between 1893 and 1906, the year of Dunbar's death. These letters first illustrate Dunbar's enthusiastic contributions to his high school paper, which eventually became the impetus to self-publish his first book of poetry in 1893. Following this, these letters reveal a creative genius marked by tuberculosis, alcoholism, and severe depression, all of which contributed to his early death at the age of thirty-three.

The role of an editor in a collection such as this is to be more objective than interpretative, and we hope we have accomplished that here. Our chapter introductions provide the necessary historical and biographical information to augment the detailed annotations at the end of each chapter. References to key events, places, people, journals, and books have been clarified and elaborated to make the letters more accessible and understandable.

Many of the annotations comment on and list additional resources should readers wish to find a more in-depth study of Dunbar and other literary figures in his circle. More to the point, we have been particularly aware of maintaining textual and historical accuracy and where necessary have indicated any places where this has been a concern. There are certain biographical details contested by Dunbar scholars, which we hope these letters correct. Dunbar was a copiously adroit speller, but when there were occasional errors, we have let them stand, so as not to obscure any notable information readers might find helpful.

We have therefore preserved as best we could Dunbar's spelling, capitalization, punctuation, line breaks, and abbreviations as he intended them, following any errors with [*sic*]. Any underlining has been changed to italics. Addresses and dates have been reformatted and edited slightly for clarity. When there was an additional comment on a letter or clarification made in another letter, we have noted that as well. In situations where the correspondence appeared damaged or water stained, we have tried to reconstruct the wording based on our research, but we have explained any difficult transcription choices in the annotations.

Dunbar corresponded with many people, so we have provided the necessary information to identify those individuals and the context that gave rise to the correspondence in the first place. Despite our best efforts, some information remains unknown, although we have managed to locate a substantial amount of material previously unavailable to scholars. We have grouped the letters in this edition chronologically, chunking correspondence that spoke to a particular time in the author's literary life.

Brief Timeline of Paul Laurence Dunbar's Life and Publications

1872–1888: Birth and Early Childhood
- June 27, 1872: Born in Dayton, Ohio, to Matilda and Joshua Dunbar.
- 1873: Joshua and Matilda Dunbar separate and later divorce. Dunbar remains with Matilda and his relationship with Joshua crumbles.
- 1878: Dunbar writes his official first poem, "An Easter Ode."
- 1884: Dunbar gives his first known public reading of "An Easter Ode."
- August 16, 1885: Joshua Dunbar dies.
- June 8, 1888: The *Dayton Herald* publishes Dunbar's poem "Our Martyred Soldiers."

1889–1891: High School Years
- Writes for and edits Dayton Central High School's *High School Times*.
- Is the president of the Philomathean Literary Society.
- Works with Orville Wright to edit and publish the *Dayton Tattler*.
- Writes a class song for the 1891 Central High School graduation.
- Secures a position at the Callahan Building as an elevator operator.

1892
- Invited to attend the Western Association of Writers conference; asked to read there.

1893
- Self-publishes first book of poems, *Oak and Ivy*, selling it for a dollar a copy.
- Attends World's Fair in Chicago, meets Frederick Douglass, and gains employment through Douglass at the Haitian Pavilion. Writes Douglass that he was charged with drunkenness, indicating an early penchant for alcoholism.

1895
- Publishes *Majors and Minors*.

1896
- June 27: William Dean Howells's review of *Majors and Minors* appears in *Harper's Weekly*.

- Obtains a literary agent and moves to New York.
- Publishes *Lyrics of Lowly Life* with an introduction by William Dean Howells.

1897

- Travels to England on a six-month literary tour.
- Works for the Library of Congress.

1898

- Publishes *Folks from Dixie*, his first collection of short stories, and *The Uncalled*, his first novel.
- Reaches his goal: resigns from the Library of Congress to make his living solely as a writer.
- Elopes with Alice Ruth Moore.

1899

- Publishes *Lyrics of the Hearthside* and *Poems of Cabin and Field*.
- Is officially diagnosed with tuberculosis and relocates to Colorado.

1900

- Publishes *The Strength of Gideon and Other Stories* and *The Love of Landry*.
- Struggles with alcoholism and must defend his behavior.

1901

- Publishes *The Fanatics* and *Candle-Lightin' Time*.

1902

- Publishes *The Sport of the Gods*, his most popular novel.
- Separates from Alice.

1903

- Publishes *Lyrics of Love and Laughter*, a collection of poems, and *In Old Plantation Days*, a short story collection, and one of his most beloved poems, "When Malindy Sings."

1904

- Publishes *The Heart of Happy Hollow*, a short story collection, *Li'l' Gal*, and *Lyrics of Sunshine and Shadow*.

1905

- Publishes *Howdy, Honey, Howdy*.

1906

- February 9: Paul Laurence Dunbar dies in Dayton, Ohio, from complications of tuberculosis.

THE LETTERS

I

Dunbar's Early Years, 1890–1895

THE LETTERS WRITTEN TO AND by Dunbar from the summer of 1890 to the end of 1895 reveal that his initial progress as a professional author was slow despite encouragement and patronage from many. As his correspondence shows, the Chicago World's Columbian Exposition in 1893 turned out to be great exposure for the gifted young writer—he recited several poems there and made many important connections through networking—but his letters also acknowledge that the exposition was not financially profitable for him; shortly after attending the event, Dunbar was back working as an elevator operator in Dayton and beginning to think he might never be able to succeed as a professional writer. Dunbar's letters reveal the mental anguish he frequently experienced. He was exceptionally hard on himself and prone to self-doubt and dark moods because of his perceived failures. Beyond this, it is clear that his financial woes frustrated him, as he was poorly compensated as an elevator operator. To further complicate his financial situation, Dunbar faced serious issues regarding his mother's home, which was in foreclosure. Additionally, a reading in Detroit had promised Dunbar a small income, but he was later told the event had been for charity, and once again, he received no compensation. It is easy to see why Dunbar lamented to Matthews: "I would that I could make my living with my pen, but it seems that I am destined never to be able to do so." Interestingly enough, however, even in these early years amid his economic woes, which would continue the rest of his life, Dunbar still chose to receive books in lieu of payment—an extraordinary choice by an extraordinary man.

Beyond support from people outside the writing community, such as Reverend Alexander Crummell, Joseph S. Cotter, and Charles A. Thatcher,

Dunbar's letters reveal that he clearly struck a chord with fellow authors, corresponding both inside and outside the African American community, even taking center stage at the once famous Western Association of Writers convention. Once his second book of poetry reached William Dean Howells in 1896, he shot to almost overnight success with the publication of *Majors and Minors*. Many scholars and critics have argued that W. D. Howells's review of this second collection of poetry immediately limited Dunbar to dialect since the poems Howells praised were in dialect, not in Standard English. However, as Dunbar's letters disclose, the problem was already there. What is not generally known is that three years prior to Howells's review of *Majors and Minors*, Dunbar found himself already pigeonholed as a dialect writer: though he had been able to publish in the *Chicago Record*, the paper was refusing to "take anything but dialect" poems from the poet. In fact, this was not Dunbar's first experience of publishers rejecting his Standard English verse in favor of his dialect, frustrating him and forcing him to feel he had "no market for anything else." Dunbar was

FIGURE 2. Central High School, Dayton, Ohio, ca. 1890. Courtesy of Special Collections and Archives, Wright State University.

acutely conscious of his audience's expectations despite his own desires and knew that in order to succeed as a writer he would have to acquiesce to their demands. Just as other authors noticed, race issues mattered even more when publishing was involved. Chesnutt, for example, railed against Howells's color-blind notions of a nonexistent "color line in literature" (Helen Chesnutt, *Charles Waddell Chesnutt*, 178). Just as this exasperated Chesnutt, Dunbar's letters reveal his own emotional turbulence and the amount of work he had to do in order to become successful and get published. His correspondence with several publishers divulges this reality but at the same time reflects the beginning of his long-lasting relationships with publishers.

Notwithstanding outside reactions to Dunbar's use of dialect and his difficulties publishing, this section of Dunbar's literary letters reveals that he became accustomed to impediments and complications from critics and the publishing industry alike. As these letters also disclose, this frustration nearly destroyed Dunbar's morale despite his popularity and the encouragement and positive feedback he regularly received from readers and critics. Before his rise to stardom in 1896, Dunbar's letters unmask desperation: he urgently wanted to make his living as a writer, but his progression was slow and hindered. When things had not improved much in April 1894, he felt serious despair and wrote of this feeling to J. Edwin Campbell. Campbell expressed surprise, writing to Dunbar, "Here I thought you were drinking to us the wine of happiness," but also noting that he understood Dunbar's discontent and commiserated with him. By November 1894, Dunbar had hit absolute rock bottom, writing, "There is but one thing left to be done," though he acknowledged he was "too big a coward" to commit suicide. Dunbar's dear friend Rebekah Baldwin noted Dunbar's depression and lamented in a July 18, 1894, letter, "If you could only throw off the cloak of skepticism that envelops you so completely and let the radiance of faith and trust enter your soul, how much happier you would be." Frederick Douglass, who took pity on Dunbar's state as well, asked Rebekah to relay the message "success must come to you," which she did on September 6, 1894. J. N. Matthews's letters also reflect encouragement, support, and dedication to Dunbar's success as a writer. Though he may have desired to give up during his extreme lows, Dunbar was able to rebound, showing a brilliant resilience to his dark moods; despite his many years of difficulties in living by his pen and publishing, he persevered, redefining the notion of "overnight success" in the process.

Letter from 1890

Letter 1: June 9, 1890, PLD to Charles Faber
Dayton, Ohio, June 9, 1890[1]
Mr. Faber[2]: Sir

After having worked the circulations of your paper up to sixty, fifty having been agreed upon, and having placed the paper in a condition to increase steadily its circulation;[3] I find that you willfully and persistently fail to keep your part of the agreement, whether your action is honest or gentlemanly is not for me to say. Suffice it to say that your action added to the fact that I have accepted the editor in chiefship of the High Sc. Times[4] causes me to resign. Make what use you please of the sixty subscribers which you, to use a very polite word, induced me to get. I heard of and knew you Mr. Faber when you were on the "record" years ago. I knew your mother and the Faber family when you were exceedingly, yes even distressingly poor. And I judge that it is no more than right that you after having struggled up through adversities to a tolerably fair place in the world should try to crush and deceive people who can ill afford to lose though not quite so poverty stricken as you were when I knew you in past years.

And by the way this reminds me that I still have in my possession a story, which you wrote when trying to gain some notice in the world. I shall always keep it to remember your kindness by.

Accept the work I did on your paper, for I worked hard, and I [illegible]. . . . With my best wishes.

Paul L. Dunbar
317 W. Washington St.

P.S. Six weeks was rather a *short* time to wait for my promised wages but I could not afford to walk and wear out my shoes getting news for nothing. Although by the middle of my June vacation I would have run the circulations of the paper up very high as in my hands your little Democratic Sheet was becoming popular.

Letter from 1891

Letter 2: December 19, 1891, A. N. Kellogg Newspaper Company to PLD
A. N. Kellogg Newspaper Company
Chicago, Dec. 19, 1891[5]

Mr. Paul L. Dunbar

Dayton, O.

Dear Sir:—

Your favor of the 13th accompanied by MSS has been received, forwarded to us from the Cincinnati House. By enclosed notice you will see that we are not now buying original stories or sketches, as we are over-stocked. We do not buy original poetry nor short ~~sketches~~ articles at any time unless by special arrangement. We will, however, take your story "The Tenderfoot"[6] and allow you $6.00 or the same if that is satisfactory to you. Will return your other matter ~~if you so wish~~ herewith.

Yours truly,

A. N. KELLOGG NEWSPAPER CO.[7]

Editors

LETTERS FROM 1892

Letter 3: July 26, 1892, PLD to J. N. Matthews

July 26, 92[8]

Dr. J. N. Matthews,[9]

Dear Sir:

Nearly a month is a long time to take in fulfilling my promises, but through your knowledge of the difficulties under which I labor,[10] you can easily forgive my negligence. You will find enclosed herewith a few of my hymns, two of which have been published—Ode for Memorial Day and the Easter poems.[11]

My hopes are no brighter than when you saw me here,[12] I am getting no better, and, what would be improbable, no worse.[13] I am nearer discouraged than I have ever yet been. Can you blame me for doubting my ability when I have never been able to sell a single poem to any paper? But enough of myself and my disappointments; suffice it that I was pleased with one thing, and that, Pfrimmer's Driftwood.[14] I found a wealth of beauty in his lines. They are like a well to do farmer. They are rich enough but still cling to a plain and homely girl that is all the more charming because so adaptable to all kinds of usage.[15] There could scarcely be a better thing than the development of a distinctly Western school of poets, such as Riley represents.[16] This may come to pass in that literary millennium, when Chicago becomes a great publishing center, as foreseen by Dr. Ridpath.[17] Until that time the nightingales and thrushes will sing so loud that the modest piping of an everyday meadow lark cannot be heard.

I want to write more, but my bell keeps ringing so I must close; With kindest regards, I am

Your friend,
Paul Laurence Dunbar

Letter 4: September 13, 1892, PLD to C. C. Hunt

American Press Association[18]
Dayton, Ohio, September 13th 1892[19]
C. C. Hunt[20]

[illegible writing for greeting]

Please find enclosed postage for the return of my manuscript "A Race for Revenge."[21] Could I make any corrections in it, so that it would stand a place of acceptance, or is it hopelessly bad? By what time do your Christmas stories have to be in? I should like to try my hand on one if there are no objections at the end of the line.

Respectfully yours,
Paul L. Dunbar
140 W Ziegler St.
Dayton, O.

Letter 5: October 12, 1892, PLD to J. N. Matthews

Dayton, Ohio, October 12th, 1892[22]
Dr. J. N. Matthews

Dear Friend:

For friend you have proven to be. Your letter found me still chained to the ropes of my dingy elevator;[23] but it came like a ray of light into the darkness of my discouragement.

I want to thank you as much for that kindly, strengthening letter as for your excellent article to the Journal.[24] I can appreciate it the more knowing as I do what little encouragement the papers of my own city give me.

They will both do me good. The letter is giving strength to my soul and this article is paving the way for me to venture which I am now about to undertake.

You could hardly have chosen a more opportune time for the publication of the letter, if you had been aware of my intentions.

I had determined to publish a number of my poems in book form[25] and try to sell them and I would not have wanted a better aid than the write up you gave me. I think it will be the means of my selling from fifty to a hundred volumes in Indianapolis; I will not print a single volume until I have written assurance of sufficient sales to cover all expenses, in the names of subscribers.[26] It will cost me two hundred dollars to sell out one thousand volumes and I will sell them at a dollar a copy. That I should make a larger profit is of less importance than that I should pave the way for better things.

The Chicago News[27] has been publishing more of my verses lately, among which was "The Ol' Tunes."[28] This was very widely copied, The American Press Association putting it in their column of "Grins in Verse."

There have been many things to encourage me but the incongruity of my work and earnings cannot have but a depressing effect. I was sorry to hear that you had sickness in your family; but it taught its lesson. It showed me that there was that generosity in the world that can lose sight of its own troubles to reach out a helping hand and aid some fellow struggler.

One thing I cannot understand is, why I have not heard from Mr. Pfrimmer.[29] I have written him twice, the last time asking for a couple of the poems I sent him which I wish to include in my book, but of which I have no copy. My letters have not yet showed any answer from him. May this one to you have a better fate. Thanking you again for the kind interest you have taken in me and my work.

I am ever

Your friend,
Paul L. Dunbar

P.S. After having sealed this I received a letter from a stranger by Valley Forts, R. I. He says he is a writer and has heard a whisper of my "sweet gift," and that if I will send him my "photo and some ten or dozen of my best poems" he will "write articles about me in New York and Boston Papers." His name is John R. Meader,[30] have you ever heard of him? Do you think it safe to send him the sketch of my life and other things he asks for? I have never heard his name and know absolutely nothing about him.

D.

Letter 6: October 19, 1892, PLD to J. N. Matthews

Dayton, Oh, Oct 19th 1892[31]

My Dear Friend[32]

I rec'd your letter several days ago, but circumstances kept me from being as prompt in answering as I should have liked to.

However, the delay brought me more to say, for yesterday's mail brought me a letter from a friend of yours, Thos. G Gentry, asking a contribution from my pen to his book of "bird poetry" and requesting me to send my photograph.[33] In the case of the latter, he says "I know your circumstances and if you have not a photo in hand, see what you can obtain a good cobruet [*sic*][34] for, and let me know, where I will make the effort to secure it," and I see no other way than to lay delicacy aside and accept his offer for I have as he says "no photo in hand."

I am receiving many letters from different parts of the country now and all through you, my friend. I do not know how I can show my gratitude to you. But just put yourself in my place with all my disadvantages and embarrassments and then bring on a benefactor such as you have proven to be, and find out how you would feel and that's just the way I feel.

Last night the Fisk Jubilee singers[35] were here and I read for them at the Y.M.C.A. hall. There was an audience of between six and seven hundred people who received my poems with an unexpected heartiness. But Doctor, with it all I cannot help being overwhelmed by self doubts. I hope there is something worthy in my writings and not merely the novelty of a black face associated with the power to rhyme that has attracted attention.

One thing I forgot to say when speaking about Mr. Gentry's letter: It is always difficult for me to write on a particular, given subject. This will be what I shall have to do in this case and I have some fears that it may fall flat.[36] I intend to do my best and in sending the verses explain the situation to Mr. Gentry.

I am going to take your advice about the editing of my poems if I can overcome the utter inability to change[37] a poem, but I am going to try very hard to do it. As soon as I have polished it up some, I am going to send you a little poem suggested by your advice to me to keep plugging away with my pen. One more thought as the ministers say: I have no books and will have *none* to sell to Dr. Matthews, please remember that. It would indeed be a pity if I couldn't take some little way of showing my gratitude to you. So say no more of putting you "down for one dollar."[38]

With Deepest regards
I am your Friend,
Paul L. Dunbar

Letter 7: October 24, 1892, PLD to C. A. Johnson
Dayton, Ohio, October 24 / 1892[39]

C. A. Johnson[40]

My Dear Sir:

Herewith I comply with your request to send you ten of my poems in manuscript, several of these are my earlier efforts while others are of quite late date. I hope after you have deciphered my writing you will not be wholly disappointed in the verses. I am preparing to publish a book of verses about Christmas,[41] if you can send me the names of any buyers, you will greatly oblige me. Its price will be one dollar. Hoping you will be satisfied with the poems sent,

I am Respt. Yours,
Paul L. Dunbar
140 W. Ziegler St.

Letter 8: November 4, 1892, PLD to J. N. Matthews
Dayton, Ohio, Nov. 4th-8th '92[42]

My Dear Friend,[43]

I received your letter and with it an influx (I was going to say of hope), but I have suffered so much since starting this letter that I don't know whether to hope or not. A ring called me from my page of stains to roll up some windows for a lady. Got my finger caught and crushed and have not been able to write any until today. This missive is written with pain and suffering. The republication of your article here has greatly inflamed my employer, especially the wage part.[44] He had just had his name in the paper for giving 2000 to charity. He is trying to make me see all in all the insult he can, and will discharge me as soon as he can find another man to work eleven hours a day for $4.00 a week. If I saw chance to get other work within two or three weeks I would quit immediately.[45] Cannot say all I want to now, but want to thank you and express my deep admiration for the two lovely pieces you sent me; they are perfect poems. When my thumb is better, I will write more.

Your friend,
Paul L Dunbar

Letter 9: November 16, 1892, PLD to J. N. Matthews

Dayton, Ohio, Nov. 16th 1892[46]

Dr. Matthews,

Dear friend:

Your letter from its nature demands an immediate response. I am sorry I spoke of so slight a matter, and indeed I fear that I painted the picture too darkly for the storm has all blown over. My employer has since probably appreciated the spirit in which the remark about the images was made. No, Doctor, it is very evident now, I am not going to lose my position. It's like bad memory, I can't lose it. I really think if I could I would get something better. I am really feeling cheerful; Mr. Gentry has kindly sent me a couple of his books and I have received a letter from the managing editor of the *Chicago News* saying that in the future he would pay me for my poetical contributions. Mr. Gentry advises that I send circulars with an appended order for my books to members of the Western Ass'n of Writers. Do you approve the idea? If so, can you send me the addresses of a few of them?

About the twenty dollars,[47] I am afraid that you will think I am unwise; but although I need the money very much, yet my great love for books will not let me lose this chance for securing some. So if you think it will be advisable I should like to have the books. While I am always compelled to regard my ordinary needs, it would be a long time before I could decree myself able to buy books and so I thought to avail myself of this kind offer.

I would like to thank you for interesting the Indianapolis Journal in me, but I owe so much to you that I know not how to thank you or make a proper return for your kindness.

I assuredly shall send Mr. Gentry a photo. He seems to be interested and has proven himself a friend.

But indeed this publicity is disturbing me. It upsets me and makes me nervous. I feel like a person walking a slick rope above thousands of spectators, who knows himself an amateur and is every moment expecting to

fall. Will be patient and try to do as you say. Have you heard anything from
Mr. Pfrimmer lately?[48] I am afraid he has entirely forgotten me. Mrs. Eva
Best[49] whom you may remember having had a poem read at the meeting of
its association, is to edit a New York women's magazine called "Humanity
and Health."[50] Pleased with her undertaking, she hopes to make a success, &
I cannot but wish that she will.

I shall write less dialect[51] after this and try to make myself worthy of
such a friend as you. If I accomplish that, truly, it will be enough.

Write to me whenever you can, I am always glad to hear from you.

Ever your friend,

Paul L. Dunbar

Letter 10: November 23, 1892, PLD to J. N. Matthews

Dayton, Ohio, Nov. 23rd [1892][52]

Dr. Matthews,

My dear friend,

It is needless to say to you, who cannot but know so well, that on the eve
of this Thanksgiving, I have much to be thankful for.[53] You seem to have been
the instrument of a special providence in my case, and from the bottom of my
heart, I thank you for what you have done, even as I thank Him that sent you.

When I think of what I owe you, it embarrasses me; for I do not know
how to show any gratitude to you. For the books which you have ordered,
I shall be so thankful, not only to my distant friend, but to you for your
excellent selection. *Crabb's Book of Synonyms* had long been one of the desires
of my heart. If there is anything in me, the fact that you have taken such
pains to help and that others are interested in my career will spur me on to
its higher cultivation.

But as I have said before, it all disturbs me, for I should feel and seem
a scoundrel and felon if I fell below the standards which my friends wish
for me.[54] I have always had the desire to go to college, but must confess to
having little faith in the "on flow'ry beds of ease" method. It would not do
me good to be able to fight my own way through a good school; but if it be
denied me, why all I can do is to resign myself and try to secure as much of a
higher education alone as I can.

I have a good foundation and instances of success in such direction have
not been exceptions.

The letters you sent me I read with feelings of gratitude and pleasure and I have kept them safe for you should you need them again. I will write my Montreal friend[55] just as soon as the books arrive and try to express the gratitude I really feel toward him. So delighted am I with the gift that I read and re-read the list to still the fever of anticipation.

I hope my conduct and life and achievements shall always be such that you will never regret the part you have acted toward me and that I shall be able to repay in measure the good you have accomplished for me. Hoping that you will spend as joyous Thanksgiving as you have made for me.

I am, Your friend,

Paul L. Dunbar

Letter 11: November 27, 1892, James Whitcomb Riley to PLD

Paul Dunbar, Esq[56]

See how your name is travelling, my chirping friend![57] And it's a good, sound name, too, that seems to imply the brave, fine spirit of a singer who should command wide and serious attention. Certainly your gift, as evidenced by this "Drowsy Day"[58] poem alone, is a superior one, and therefore its fortunate possession should bear it with a becoming sense of gratitude, and meekness,—always feeling that for any resultant good, *God's* is of the glory— the singers but His very humble instrument. Already you have many friends, and can have thousands more, being simply honest, unaffected, and just to yourself and the high source to your endowment.[59]

Very earnestly I wish you every good thing.

Your friend,

James Whitcomb Riley

Letter 12: November 29, 1892, PLD to J. N. Matthews

140 W. Ziegler St.

Dayton, OH, Nov 29th 1892[60]

Dr. Matthews,

Dear Friend:

As you requested, I write to let you know of the arrival of the books.[61] They have just come, and I am charmed with them and perfectly happy. One only that you mentioned in your list failed to come, Quackenbos' *Ancient Literature*[62] and that I suppose will come later. I thank you for these selections. Harper's *Cyclopedia of Poetry*[63] is a grand thing and will be the source of benefit and instruction as well as a pleasure to me, and of the rest I shall enjoy all equally well.

I am now going to write to Mr. Ross, just as I feel he has done a great thing for me and I want him to know that I feel grateful. I can't gush, but will tell him in as straight forward a manner as possible.

All goes on smoothly with my book,[64] and should it continue so, it will be out a week before Christmas. I received a letter Saturday from our mutual friend Mr. Pfrimmer and it is so cheerful and kind that I cannot but forgive his long silence. Sunday morning, the maid brought me my first money for a poem: two dollars for a little piece to a child's publication in New York.[65] I am beginning to hope and am going to try to improve myself more and more so that someday I may be worthy of this kindness that has been showered upon me. Hoping to hear from you soon, I am ever

Your friend,

Paul L. Dunbar

LETTERS FROM 1893

Letter 13: February 7, 1893, PLD to J. N. Matthews
Dayton, Ohio, Feb. 7th 1893[66]

Friend Matthews,

Your letter proved a very very welcome one to me, for I had been so apprehensive as to how you [would] receive my book[67] that its appearance, whether it was to contain good news, was a relief to me.

How much greater then was my relief and delight when I found out you were pleased with my work!

I have sent a copy to the *Indianapolis Journal*[68] and would send one to Riley with an answer to his letter, but he was travelling when he wrote me and I do not know where to find him.

I am so glad to hear that you have had some poems accepted by the *Ladies' Home Journal*.[69] It is a paper that I hold in high estimation. It was there that I sent my "Drowsy Day"[70] and had it returned and for about a month they have had another poem of mine called "A Nocturne,"[71] which I am expecting to be returned every day. Some time ago I got together some of my best work, so I thought and sent it off as follows: a Sonnet, *N.Y. Independent*—a Poem, *N.Y. Sun*, Poem, *Ladies Home Journal*, a story to *Washington Post*, rejected, then to *Chicago Post*, rejected; then to *Chicago News*, rejected, then A.N. Kellogg Newspaper Co., rejected, sketch to the *Cincinnati Commercial Gazette*.

Now all of these were returned except the one I mentioned to the L.H.J.[72] After this I thought I would take a rest.

I think I shall be able to send those prose pieces about the latter part of this week if you think you will find time to look over them. One of these on which I am now writing I expect to try upon the "Youth's Companion."[73]

I have acted upon your advice and am trying to work into stories the old tales of the South that I have been hearing since early childhood.[74] Whether they shall get into the papers or not I cannot foretell, for it is so hard to get a hearing for a new voice in the literary world.

I have read several times at the YMCA lately and am getting well acquainted through these readings. The idea that through this acquaintance I might find the means of securing a better situation suggested itself to me and when I have been requested to work gratis as I frequently have, I have never hesitated; but it seems vain for apparently no favorable outcome of my efforts is imminent.[75]

But I can wait and maybe if success ever does come to me, I can enjoy it more on account of this long restraint.

Hoping to hear from you soon again, I am your friend ever,

Paul L. Dunbar

Letter 14: April 21, 1893, Charles Thatcher to PLD
Law Offices of Chas. A. Thatcher[76]
Toledo, O., 21st April, 1893[77]

Paul L. Dunbar,
Dayton, Ohio—My Dear Sir:

Yours of the 20th at hand.[78] Am indeed glad to learn that you were so successful in Toledo.[79] Think you might do some more in the future?

Have talked with Mr. Murphy of the Bee.[80] He says that you are to send him a poem that has not been published and that he will publish some and make comments upon you.[81] It would be well to do this and also get something in The Blade.[82] It would pave the way for another trip.

Am sorry that I did not have much time to see you when here.

You asked for a letter from me. Enclosed find one but [I] fear it will not be what you want.

You should keep up your work [illegible] all things strive to preserve the modesty which you now possess. You know that the attention you are receiving would turn some person's heads but I do not think you will fall. You will pardon my plain talking but it is a [illegible] that we must watch and I have taken the liberty to refer to it.

Please keep me informed of your merriments. Will gladly assist you in any way I can be able.

Very truly yours,
C. A. Thatcher

Mr. Murphy wishes me to remind you of the piece. I will send you a "Bee" on Thursday.

Letter 15: April 21, 1893, Charles Thatcher to PLD
Law Offices of Chas. A. Thatcher
Toledo, O., 21st April, 1893[83]

Paul L. Dunbar,
Dayton, Ohio—My Dear Sir:

On behalf of the members of the West End Club,[84] I wish to thank you for the pleasure affected us on Wednesday evening by a rehearsal of some of your poems.[85]

I have heard a number of comments from members pleased and all express [illegible] as not only greatly pleased with your compositions and delivery but surprised that one of your years should practice such beautiful poems.

Those who purchased copies of "Oak & Ivy"[86] express a real pleasure and profit in reading the lines. I have for some time felt that since nature has endeavored you with such gifts that you should have all opportunity of acquiring a thorough education so that you may be fitted for future work.

If you find that by your own efforts that you will not be able to attend college[87] I will be one of the persons to loan you $50.00 per year during the time you may wish to spend in college.

Then I will procure from others in Toledo to do the same and do not doubt but that there are four in Dayton who would be glad to join us. Let me know how you feel about such a plan. If in the future you would wish to come to Toledo again by giving me due notice I can make your trip even more prosperous than was the first.

Trusting that you will continue your efforts and meet with the success which you merit, I remain,

Very Truly Yours,
C. A. Thatcher

Letter 16: May 2, 1893, PLD to J. N. Matthews

Chicago, Ills, May 2nd 1893[88]

Dr. J. N. Matthews

My Dear Friend: Your kind letter was received some time ago, but I thought I would not answer it until I made my next step. I am here in the World's Fair City[89] in quest of work at which I can live.[90] I make no proclamations to liking this place; there is altogether too much noise, bustle, and confusion for me,[91] but I am here to make money if I can.[92] As yet there is no opening for me, but I feel hopeful that there will be soon. I should like to tell you all about my visit to Detroit[93] and Toledo[94] if I could, but there were so many pleasures about them both that one cannot put down on paper. Financially, I was quite successful in Detroit and very successful in Toledo at which latter place I read for a very wealthy and aristocratic private club[95] who received me enthusiastically and took twenty-eight of my books, besides a small contribution which they also gave me. I had intended to try doing some world fair letters to a small syndicate of papers, but every paper to which I broach the subject seems to have made other arrangements, so I shall have to relinquish this idea.

As to coming to the meeting of the W.A.W.[96] this summer, it is the one thing that I desire and if I am not so situated that I cannot get off, I shall be there.

I am still contributing at intervals to the *Chicago News Record*.[97] I have sent my book to them and to the *Interocean* for review.[98] A write up in any of the Chicago newspapers whenever you should find it convenient, would I know, be of inestimable value to me. Especially since I am right here in the city.

The buildings at the World's Fair are indeed a wonder in themselves.[99] I spent all of my first Sunday there and for the first time in my life I must confess to having forgotten the Sabbath day, so absorbed was my mind in the places about me and there was nothing to remind one of the sacredness of the day.[100] Men were working around, the sound of file and saw and hammer was constantly in my ears. Workmen were shouting and running to and fro, no one was arrayed in Sunday attire, and there was not even the sound of a chapel bell to call my wandering mind back to the day. The fact of the matter is, things are only half ready out at Jackson Park and the person who comes to the fair now, though he will see wonderful sights, will not see near what is to be seen later on.

On Monday, opening day at the Fair, Chicago was a revelation to me.

The streets were thronged with people and the street cars and elevated roads were tested to their utmost capacity. People of every color and nationality were to be seen upon the streets, flocking toward the line of march of the great procession. I looked a little while, but I was not used to such scenes and I must confess that my brain was wheeling so with a sigh, "oh cosmopolitan Chicago, thou makes me sick." I sought my room and remained there for the rest of the day. I cannot stand crowds. At three o'clock in the afternoon there was said to have been 450,000 tickets sold to the grounds and I mutely thanked my maker that I had not gone out to be in the crush. Today a like crowd was expected but there was comparatively speaking no one at the grounds. I would that I could make my living with my pen, but it seems that I am destined never to be able to do so, but "some day" who knows what may happen. Like Mr. Micawber[101] I shall have to wait for something to turn up. The Toledo papers gave me very favorable notes. Pardon the disorganization of this letter—it's the way I feel. Believe me ever,

Your friend,

Paul L. Dunbar

Letter 17: July 17, 1893, PLD to J. N. Matthews
Chicago, Ills 7-17-93[102]

My dear Dr. Matthews,

I must drop you another line. I had intended to do it sooner but have been too busy. Was much disappointed as were many others in not seeing you at Warsaw, Ind.[103] We had a very pleasant time and your absence was the only drawback to my pleasure. The recitation which I was to give with Jennie O'Neill Potter[104] and of which I spoke to you was quite successful from an artistic stand point. But I didn't get a cent out of it. Everyone seems so willing to help me by having me recite with them for advertisement or having me give them a book to show their friends.[105] I couldn't stand the work I did when I first came here, I now have an easier place but it pays very little.

Evidently this world's goods are not for me. If you come to the fair, I should be glad to see you at the Haitian Building[106] where I am working. I have my mother here with me and she is enjoying much the sights of Chicago.

But I must be brief and close now.

With kindest regards,

I am sincerely yours,

Paul Dunbar

Letter 18: August 12, 1893, PLD to J. N. Matthews

Chicago, Ills 8-12-93[107]

Dr. James N. Matthews,

My dear friend: I must not take up my already too limited time in asking apologies for not writing sooner. I know that you will make allowances for me.

Your poem, "The Old Country Road"[108] was truly an exquisite thing and I am glad that you are into a paper where the greatest number of people will be able to read and enjoy your charming verse. I hardly know how to tell you about the W.A.W.[109] It was so altogether delightful that I cannot pretend to give you anything like an idea of it.

There were not many of the prominent numbers there.[110] The most important Hon. Ben S. Parker,[111] Mary Hartwell Catherwood,[112] hon. Eugene F. Ware,[113] Capt. Lee O. Harris,[114] and Joe Reed[115] and our W. W. Pfrimmer. Mr. Parker did not take an active part in the literary exercises as he did in pushing the other members to the front. I have just found out what a delightful man he is. He has since visited me in my working place at the Fair. I suppose you saw his poems on the Robin's song in the Ind. Journal of Sunday, July 23rd.[116] Mrs. Catherwood read part of a chapter from one of her stories and Capt. Harris gave one of his poems "The Rose-tree."[117] Pfrimmer carried off the honors with his giant dialect sketches and poems given in the very perfection of his artfully artless style. Mrs. Sawyer of St. Louis[118] gave some very pretty short poems as did Mrs. Ida May Davis.[119] Good papers were read by J. C. Ochiltree and hon. Will Cumback[120] and a strong lecture on "what shall we do with women at the universities" delivered by Dr. John of DePauw University.[121] But the best part of the pleasure of the occasion was the social side of it. There were fishing and boating parties, music and singing, kindred communities, and on the last day in lieu of a banquet a dinner was given at which toasts and speeches were made.

I spoke on two occasions giving first "The Old Country Paper" a new piece in prose English and as an encore, "The Ol' Tunes."[122]

On concert night, I gave "The Rivals" a humorous dialect sketch and responded with "My Foot and Maw."[123] I don't believe I ever enjoyed a week more in all my life and I was only sorry that you could not be there. I intended to ask you in my last letter whether you reviewed my book[124] in the Chicago News or not. Mr. Pfrimmer says you did, but I never saw it. The [Chicago] Record of Monday July 31st had a little poem[125] of mine. They won't take anything but dialect so I have no market for anything else.[126]

I was thankful for your words of encouragement, for knowing that I was really not doing anything in the world, I had begun to think I was not even learning anything. If you can come to the Fair don't fail to come and see me at the "Haitian Pavilion."

Very Sincerely Yours,
Paul L. Dunbar

2959 Dearvorro St.

Better write to the Haitian Building as I may change my address.

Letter 19: December 12, 1893, PLD to J. N. Matthews

Dayton, OH, December 12th 1893[127]

Dr. J. N. Matthews,

My Dear Friend:

Not another day shall pass without my writing you. I have been soothing my desires with promise after promise to steal time for the enjoyment of this pleasure. And I will withhold it no longer. You are surely working hard my good friend, for your silence seems to me full of labor. I saw your poem in [the] *Ladies' Home Journal*—"The Old Country Road"[128] and liked it very, very much as I did your thoughts on the close of the Fair.[129] Do you hear from Pfrimmer or Gentry? They seem both to be very busy men.

In fact, I am just beginning to realize what a busy work-a-day old world this is any way.

It used to seem all a universal holiday, even when I was drudging I thought that all beyond the limits of my elevator was rest and enjoyment, and life—ah, of that what Claude de Lorraine[130] hand painted, but alas! The pigments soon grow thin and the canvas is beginning to show through. A few more years and the canvas will crack, and also for my picture of life!

But I am feeling good in mind and body now. Would that it were always so. May I tell you just a little of what I have been doing. Well, I have become practical enough to do a little prose work. A couple of weeks ago the *Inter Ocean* took a prose article on "A Literary Colony"[131] (at Richmond, Ind.), the [*Chicago*] *Record* took an article on one of our colored leaders who recently died and the *Chicago News* took a Thanksgiving story, while the *Detroit Free Press* printed a Thanksgiving poem for which they seem to have forgotten to pay me.[132] *Munsey's Magazine* accepted a little poem and offered a year's subscription to their magazine in payment which offer I accepted, as an opening.[133] The *Youth's Companion* copied part of a little poem of mine from a child's magazine, in their issue of December.[134] I thought I would send them something soon, now as they know my name. Don't you think it a good idea?

I am beginning to feel timidly hopeful and at each step I take ahead, I thank and bless you for it, for you were the Moses that led out my enslaved powers.[135] Let me hear from you, my friend when convenient and believe me,

Most Sincerely,

Your Friend,

Paul L Dunbar

Letter 20: December 23, 1893, PLD to J. N. Matthews
Dayton O., Dec 23, 1893[136]

My Dear Dr. Matthews:

Your more than welcome letter was received a few days ago, and I heartily appreciated it coming from you in a time when all your mind must be taken up with home cares.[137] My dear friend, you have my deepest sympathy and I hope that you may find strength to bear whatever comes to you.

I am very much obliged for the interesting clippings you sent me, they were all entertaining and the one referring to your attempted assassination was a revelation and sermon to me. Especially since I returned from Chicago have I been bemoaning the fact that my own people were growing away from me, that they watched not for my success but for my failure, that they saw in my efforts—no worth, only presumption.[138] But when I see that you and others have had even harder things to bear, I feel my own burden grow lighter. I have at present no regular employment but am trying to live by my pen.

The articles published about me in Chicago were misfortunate in as much as they were copied here at home and the people to whom I would apply for employment think that I can get along with nothing beside the scanty returns of my literary and journalistic ventures.

It is not I but these people who have made up my mind for me that I must "adopt literature as a profession." *The Inter-Ocean* pays me for prose and, comparing the prices received from my last two articles, much better than the *Record*.[139]

Though I have the freest opening on the latter paper and I like them very much.

I did not see your "[The] Deserted Inn"[140] though I tried to watch the L.H.J.[141] continually after "The Old Country Road."[142] I must have missed one number.

Riley's sonnet[143] to you is beautiful but it is impossible to say even a few of the many good things you deserved to have said about you in fourteen lines.

Richard Lew Dawson[144] is staying here in Dayton and I have become quite well acquainted with him. To my mind he is a "bright, 'peculiar' star,"[145] but I like him and his clever work. I recited on the same program with him at one of the churches here not long since.

I will close now hoping that the clouds will so lift that you may see a merry Christmas and a happy new year. Will write whenever I have anything to say whether you answer or not.

Sincerely Your Friend,
Paul L. Dunbar

P.S. A couple of Rondeaux[146]

NOT THEY WHO SOAR[147]

Not they who soar, but they who plod
Their rugged way unhelped to God
Are heroes, they who higher have
And flying far the upper air
Miss all the toil that hugs the sod.
'Tis they whose backs have felt the rod,
Whose souls to sorrow have been bare,
Can smile upon defeated care,
Not they who soar.

High up there are no bones to prod
Nor boulders hiding 'neath the clod—
To him the keenness of the share,
For flight is ever free and rare—
But heroes they, the soil who've trod,
Not they who soar.

'TWIXT SMILE AND TEAR[148]

'Twixt smile and tear so wags the world—
Today are happy pinions whirled,
We tempt the blue and spirit—gay
The neighbor with the lass—today
We seek the heavens planet-pearled.

Tomorrow, oh, our wings are furled,
And Heaven seems so far away—
We lift our voices up to pray
'Twixt smile and tear

And then in eddies swiftly swirled—
Poor straws upon the current twisted,
We cling, and lose and wage this fray;
Not where we will, but where we may
No lodger, on some far shore wave-hurled.
'Twixt smile and tear.

Letter 21: December 30, 1893, PLD to Frederick Douglass
Dayton-O. Dec. 30th 1893[149]

Hon. Frederick Douglass.

My Dear Friend: Having left Chicago prior to your return I was so
unfortunate as not to be able to say goodbye to you. But you know of course
it was not neglect on my part or lack of desire. I know not how to thank you
for the many kindnesses which you showed me while at Chicago.[150] Indeed
I feel that I owe the success and pleasure of my whole summer to your
instrumentality. In my gratitude I cannot say—but will try to do,—will try to
be worthy of the kind interest which you took in me, and let it not be a vain
boast when I say, that if ever I arrive at that estate in letters which you have
so kindly wished as my destination,—if haply it should be my lot to write
some songs that posterity shall sing,[151] the name of Douglass shall not be
forgotten in my numbers.

I hope that you and Mrs. Douglass—to whom I wish to be kindly
remembered—are very well—and that you are both enjoying the rest to
which your heroic labors entitle you.

My mother is well and joins me in much love to yourselves.

For myself I am well in body but not in mind. I have learned all too
soon that the price of even meager success is much calming. The people
in my town have never encouraged my aspirations, they have done all
they could to crush me and now on my return from a summer of hard and
honest effort I find a scene of slanders afloat concerning my sojourn in
Chicago—as to my reception there, my social status and a dozen other petty
trifles, but I did not design to notice any of these until it came to my ears

that a Dayton visitor to Chicago had returned and reported here that I was *discharged* from the Haitian Building, and that the cause of said *discharge* was drunkenness and desperation.[152] I cannot overlook this, so I thought I would write and ask you to send me a few words of refutation that I can publish in the daily papers here. I am sick at heart and almost discouraged. If I ask for work I am told with a sneer that I ought to have stayed in Chicago where I got on so well. The last straw that raised so much curious antagonism against me was the republication in a Dayton Daily paper of the long complimentary article concerning me in an October Chicago Tribune.[153] There where my name appeared signed to a long article in the Inter Ocean and a poem in The Youth's Companion in the same week, it was too much and my fellow townsmen fell upon me. I can only fly to you for rescue.

Hoping you will pardon my troubling you and that I may see an early reply.

I am

Sincerely Your Friend,
Paul Dunbar

LETTERS FROM 1894

Letter 22: April 8, 1894, J. Edwin Campbell to PLD

The West Virginia Colored Institute[154]
J. Edwin Campbell, Principal[155]
Farm, W. Va, April 8, 1894[156]

Paul L. Dunbar
1406 Ziegler St.
Dayton, Ohio
My Dear Dunbar:—

Your letter was received the other day.[157]

I have concluded since reading it that there is no vale of happiness this side the mists of eternity, when a single mortal can go and be free from [illegible].

Here I thought you were drinking the wine of happiness, that you were flushed with your literary success and then the thought that you were the one Negro in the country in whom the literary talent of the race centered, raised you beyond all morbidity.

I myself for the last week or two have been a party to the deepest mental depression. Shall I tell the truth? I am tired of being a big man, tired of wearing the fool's mask of tranquility tired of running into the walls which emphasize the path in which my position makes me walk.[158]

I want to throw down the load, the nimious load of responsibility and I want to get back to boyhood. I want to roll up my trousers to the knee, push on a hat battered out of shape in a victorious battle with bumble bees, lie under the shade of a country orchard gulping June apples while the June breezes and the June grasses run over my fan legs leaving me in the sun and shade of that delicious presence while manhood is a thousand years away resting beneath the horizon away over yonder when that buzzard's wings largely cut the glorious restful blue.

In your success, you may have aroused the envy of fellow men but this envy is like the [illegible] arrows with which the Indian had to shoot. It cannot hurt you. The twice envy that my success arouses in the poisoned and flinted arrows of the full grown man, for in my position every shaft that envy directs, can maim, can kill.[159]

I tell you Dunbar, envy no man nor think any man happy from what you see of his surroundings. His smile may be the smile of the Spartan boy while the stolen fox grows out of his heart.

You are just twenty one. I am twenty six. Let me tell that the five years difference in our age means for me five years of toil, of disappointments bitter as the wild [illegible] of feeling of anguish. When I was twenty one I had already failed with a newspaper[160] and had gone back home utterly discouraged, almost broken hearted. I had come from the editorial chair of the only colored paper in this state,[161] and had opened [illegible] 6 months for $150 and made my own fees paid eight dollars a month for board and slept up in the loft of a log cabin where every winter night I would lie in my bed and count through the holes of the dilapidated roof, every star in the northern heavens and many a morning awoke to find that the snow out of [illegible] had spread another counterpane over my bed and to hide [illegible] of my attic floor had covered it with a white carpet.[162]

I then had the same talent that I have now new intense ambition, an ambition made [illegible] by *constant* denial, by *stardom*!

Pardon if I speak of my condition when at your age. God tries those whose souls essay anything in the fire and the intense heat which seems to scorch you now, is but the fire the flaming fire and from it will come the pan gold of your very soul.

I rec'd a long letter from a cousin of mine, Miss Gee who teaches in

Paris, Ky schools, and it reminded me that you knew a young lady there—"who is drawing them in Paris."

Perhaps they know each other. If anything of yours has appeared recently, send it to me.

It has been so long since anything of mine appeared that I sometimes wonder if anything did ever appear.[163]

I am doing absolutely nothing now in a literary way.[164]

The Post[165] has had in its possession for the last six weeks what I consider my first romance.[166] I do not know what they intend to do with it.

I am so glad that my [illegible] verses pleased you.

If I ever publish, I shall use them. My novel when completed will cost me above $15.00 and I am a little blue over that.

Well, I must close this long rambling letter.

> Write very soon,
> Yours ever,
> Campbell[167]

Letter 23: April 30, 1894, PLD to J. N. Matthews
Dayton, O. 4-30-'94[168]

My Dear Dr. Matthews:

Even if I thought you capable, I could not consent to let you forget me. I know and sympathize so deeply with your situation[169] as it has not improved since you wrote that—I hardly deem it right for me to take your time in asking you to read a little poem from me. But I cannot forbear a few words as you have shown such a material interest in my career.

I have watched whenever I have had the "Record"[170] all articles dated at Mason, Ill. supposing them to be yours and reading them with interest and pleasure. It has been some time now since I have seen anything, but that's probably on account of the irregularity with which I see the paper.

For myself I am doing little or nothing now and am receiving very little encouragement in a literary line.[171] Thursday I gave a successful recital at Richmond, Ind. and received a number of very complimentary poem notices, together with a little extra change. There is a possibility of my reading in Cincinnati and Indianapolis in the near future. If I go to Indianapolis, I shall call on the "Journal."[172] I am at present halting between two very fair offers for the coming autumn—neither of which fill my stomach at the present—and I want very much to ask your advice. One is from members of the club where I read in Toledo last year,[173] who makes to lend me money enough to go to college[174] if I want to go and pay it back after I graduate. The other is from J. L. Shearer[175] of the Shearer Musical and Lecture Bureau of Cincinnati, of $25.00 a week and expenses to travel with a company of musicians and recite my poems. Both things seem fair and desirable to me. Will you advise me which to take? My mother has just recovered from a very severe attack of pneumonia, I begin to feel that I want to take all responsibility as to living and providing necessities off her mind, so the latter offer has attracted me very much tho' I longed for college also.

Shall you meet the W.A.W.[176] at Warsaw this year? At present I have no outlook favorable to my being there.[177] But I am still hoping these affairs may change for the better. If it is not too great a sacrifice, let me hear from you soon.

Most sincerely yours,
Paul Dunbar

Letter 24: May 12, 1894, William Edgar Easton to PLD
San Antonio Texas, May 12th, 1894[178]

My dear Paul—

Your kind letter of various dates and places reached me today only and I answer at once. Your flattering words of commendation pleased me very much, not that I am now more susceptible to flattery than the average poor devil who gives into print for a living; but then, I appreciate your words, knowing that only those who have felt [illegible] denial first can really feel for a fellow victim inflamed. By to-day's mail I have sent Miss Davis a "Stage copy" of Dessalines.[179] I have not cut Dessalines at all, so to speak.[180] The minor characters are the parties who have suffered by my injudicious knife. The changes I have made, do not, at all, affect your role—only to make my situations more dramatic. You have no idea how well pleased I am to know you will act the part of Dessalines. I have listened entranced to your reading of your own lines. Dessalines is in good hands. The true source of eloquence is feeling. With your natural ability and training, Dessalines must be a success in your hands. Remember, he is the Negro we need in the future, loving Dessalines as I do, blinded to these faults and compromising of his virtues: Be a Negro—be a man who has wrongs to avenge and you are an ideal Dessalines. Let me hear from you soon. Excuse my apparent careless correspondence.

Your friend always,
William Edgar Easton[181]

Letter 25: May 18, 1894, Lyman C. Abbot to PLD
Richmond, Ind
May 18th, 1894[182]

Paul Laurence Dunbar,
My Dear Friend,

I some time ago said to our kind, earnest mutual friend Mrs. Selby[183] that I was going to write you some day and sitting by my "sonnet table" this lovely day of ever "inconstant spring," I thought I would send you a few lines. In the first place, to use a very original sentence and sentiment I am well and hope these few lines will find you enjoying the same blessing.

I have thought much about you and your prospects since the very enjoyable evenings your entertainment has enabled one to pass, and I have felt all the time, that we ought in this good "Quaker City"[184] to have a new remuneration over to you financially and am at all times ready to cooperate in any direction to that end, which many persons accept.

Our friend will confer with you while in Dayton and another admirer will doubtless see me and I [illegible] sincerely hope we may [illegible] a plan which will materially aid in removing the cloud which overhangs the title to your home,[185] and of course shadows your heart.

When I used to live in the South I have often heard the still fragment of [illegible] the melody of the mocking bird [illegible], and I have sometimes thought the sweetest songs of the females come singing and from the shadows, but at the same time the heart longs for some sunshine.

I hope to see the day when you will be surrounded with comfort and when unharassed by thoughts which worry, you may sing songs of pure joy— You have I think a very bright future before you if life and health are shared, and you must not let these "light afflictions which are for a moment" failing to leave out for you a "far more *exceeding* and eternal weight of glory."[186] If Mrs. Selby sees that sentence I can hear her laugh for she has often laughed at my scriptural quotations.

But I have but a moment at command and I drop you these few lines to urge you to keep safe heart and courage and to assure you I shall always be pleased to render you any service I am able.

In the beautiful language of Hyperion, "Look not mournfully into the past: it can never return. Go forth to meet the shadowy future without fear and with a manly heart."[187] This life of great possibilities is big with promise, if not mistaken faith, we do our best. Present my love and good wishes to

Mrs. Selby, and accept from me my assurance of a heartfelt interest in your welfare. With only very pleasant memories allow me to [illegible] myself,

Your Friend,
L. C. Abbott[188]

Letter 26: September 7, 1894, PLD to Frederick Douglass
Dayton, O. Sept. 7th '94[189]

Hon. Frederick Douglass

My Dear Friend: While I dislike to bother you again, I feel constrained to write and let you know that I had made application for the position of teacher of English Literature in the high school at Washington.[190] The work is in my line and I think that I could give satisfaction. I should be very grateful if you could and should use any influence in your powers to assist me in getting the place.

My high school studies in Language and Literature have, since my graduation, been supplemented by much special study along those lines, and I have been somewhat successful in practical literary work. The N.Y. Independent has lately accepted a long story from me of our own people.[191]

If you can drop a favorable word from me into the care of Mrs. Cornish[192] or any other one of the trustees, I shall be very grateful to you.

I remain as ever

Sincerely yours
Paul Dunbar

Letter 27: September 9, 1894, PLD to Alexander Crummell
Dayton, Ohio, September 9, 1894[193]

Reverend Alexander Crummell,[194]

My Dear Sir: I think there is little possibility of your remembering my name. I may be able to recall to your mind the circumstance of my delivering the ode on Negro Day[195] at the World's Fair,[196] where I had you to thank for your kind and encouraging words.

Presuming upon this brief meeting I have taken the liberty to drop you a line about a matter that concerns me deeply and wherein I believe you can greatly help me.

In a few words, the matter stands thus, hearing that the position as teacher of English literature[197] at the high school of your city was vacant I have applied to your headmaster Mr. S.A. Cornish[198] of [illegible] for appointment to the [illegible]. My high school courses have been supplemented by much special and earnest study along literary lines and the appointment to this place would be a boon to me in more ways than one.

The purpose of this letter is to ask you to use whatever influence you may conveniently employ to help me in the attainment of my work.[199] I am afraid that I have presumed much in thus addressing you, but trusting to your humanity to overlook the fault and with deepest regard for yourself and wife, whom I well remember.

Sincerely yours,
Paul Laurence Dunbar

P.S. I have just received a letter saying the Hon. BR. [illegible] has the appointing powers instead.

Letter 28: September 12, 1894, Alexander Crummell to PLD
1522 "O" St. Washington D.C., 12th of Sept /94[200]

Dear Mr. Dunbar,

It is your right + privilege to address me as you have. Every true black man, especially a man of genius + character, has t[he] right to command my sources.

I have been long wishing to write too: but I am an old man, with great limitations. I have but one eye. My correspondence, for 3 quarters of the globe, [illegible] far ahead of my persons; and my church duties have become a pressure too great for me to any longer endure.

I must say, in all candor—but [illegible] privately, that I can't give you very much encouragement in your endeavor. There are local + wicked prejudices existing here wh[ich] I fear may bar y[ou]r success: but this shall not prevent *my* best endeavors on y[ou]r behalf. I will see Mr. [illegible] + I will write to Mr. Bruce + urge y[ou]r [illegible] in wh[ich] I have great confidence.

I am sorry that I *must* postpone my endeavors a day or two; as I leave tom[orrow], this afternoon for a day or two.

Have you a volume published of y[ou]r poems? If so, lend me a copy, + I will send you the price; or, possibly, you [illegible] an exchange for a copy of my last work—"Africa + America."[201]

With regard + admiration,
Very truly y[our]s,
Alex Crummell[202]

Letter 29: September 21, 1894, Alexander Crummell to PLD
21st Sept/ 94[203]

Dear Mr. Dunbar,

I am tardy in communicating with you: + now I have t[he] unwelcome
news to send you viz, that t[he] appointment was made *before* y[ou]r letter
reached me.[204]

Can I serve you, in any other way? If I can let me know.

I am very truly y[ou]rs,

Alex Crummell

P.S. I am really distressed that I have had to keep you waiting all this
time for an answer to y[ou]r letter:—but the case is as follows.—I have been
sick:—y[ou]r letter was on my table but got misplaced:—nobody c[oul]d
find it, + so y[ou]r address was lost:—at last I have found a friend here
who knew you lived in Dayton; + so, at haphazard—ignorant of your street
+ number—I direct to Dayton. Please pardon this misadventure which
distresses me very, very, very much.

A.C.

Letter 30: October 5, 1894, Richard Lew Dawson to PLD
October 5, 1894[205]

Dear Paul,

Am glad the Shearer[206] arrangement turned out so well after all, and
hope you may make some money.

[illegible name] has evidently misrepresented the matter to you,
and I am sorry to see you apparently defend her, for she has acted in a
dishonorable way and cannot be defended. She gave my poem June 25
without even notifying me as was my due and asking my consent.[207] She
had no right on earth to use my poem, simply because I trusted it in her
hands, and as I wrote her, "she has no claim to it any more than a man
would have to the baggage I gave him to carry to the station." I had given
her an engagement at my date purely from "kindness." I repeatedly forbade
her from using this piece again until I had published it, and she as after
promised she never would. I was astonished when she violated this honor
and did [illegible] it, yet I saw nothing only to write her thanking her.
She replied and proposed that *she* should send a copy to her uncle to be
used in a Denver magazine. I told her the poem was for sale and must

not be used or published except as I directed. She did not reply, and two months afterward, to avoid any mistake, I wrote again emphasizing this. My letters were utterly courteous and friendly. But I got a sarcastic reply which I want you to read some time, sneering at my poem, and saying she would use any work of mine when she chose without credit, and closing by saying she desired no further communication from me. She got it, though, in a way she did not like, as I told her the plain facts of her conduct. Then her father replied, saying I could not get any rights, and proposing that he and his son should whip me when I was next in Dayton. Of course, I was delighted at this prospect and told him how he was defending the idea of stealing my property, and that when I was next in Dayton, as I should doubtless be some time, he could see my name announced and know where to find me. I told him I am not afraid of man, woman or devil, much less the barking of dogs.

You see the evolution of this matter, and I am not at fault in any way, but this girl is proposing to take my property without my consent.

You can show this to the Watkins family, if you desire, to whom give kind regards.

Your friend,
Richard Lew Dawson

Letter 31: November 6, 1894, Joseph S. Cotter to PLD
Louisville, Ky, Nov. 6, 1894[208]

Mr. Paul L. Dunbar,
My Dear Sir:
   I was glad to receive your letter but sorry to hear of your disappointment, for I know what it means to a person of your make-up. I hope that the law of compensation[209] will turn the balance in your favor. I would have answered your letter immediately but I was looking to see what I could do for you.[210] As yet I don't see where you would get any [illegible]. I have partly arranged with the Y.M.C.A. to have you read during Thanksgiving week. The plan is this: the Y.M.C.A. cannot run any risk. If so, the money will be divided between you and the Y.M.C.A. Now, this may be a very good thing and then it may be something else, as you see, when something may be done in Jeffersonville + New Albany. When the place is settled upon, I will write you, stating the terms as to the division of the money. Thank you for your words about the "droll gal."

I will do all I can to work it up. I hereby introduce you to "Alfred [illegible].

Yours for peace, health, & prosperity—

Joseph S. Cotter[211]

#2306—Magazine St.

Letter 32: December 1, 1894, Charles A. Thatcher to PLD
Dec. 1, 1894[212]

My Dear Mr. Dunbar,

Your letter of recent date with letter and telegram from Mr. Shearer at hand. On Sept 13—1894, Mr. Shearer wrote you a letter in which he engaged you at $25.00. If you accepted this engagement in any way, by letter or otherwise, a contract was formed between you. It is not necessary that the contract should be drawn in a formal manner. It can be made by letter as this all seems to have been done. If you desire I will write Mr. Shearer that you are ready to fulfill your part of the contract and expect your pay whether he sees fit to send [it to] you or not. You will understand that it delivers upon you to make all effort to earn what you can and deduct same from [illegible] by Shearer. The difficulty now is that his letter does not mention any fixed time you would work but says probably for [a] season. [I] Think he will be glad to pay you something to be released. What have you written since receiving this last letter?

Enclosed find a letter from Dr. Bashford.[213] Please return it to me, as [I] have not answered. When I called upon Mr. [illegible] who had agreed to be one of the number to advance $50.00 for you he said that he had just pledged $100.00 to help a colored girl and asked to be excused from his presence.

Stopped at [illegible] a few days since we talked with the president of the college. He did not offer as much encouragement as did Dr. Bashford.

Will do what I can to find others so that you may do something by [the] first of the year.

It seems as though you might make some engagements to give readings during the month.

Let me hear from you about the Shearer matter.

Truly yours,
C. A. Thatcher

Letter 33: December 8, 1894, R. U. Johnson to PLD

Editorial Department
The Century Magazine
Union Square, New York
December 8th, 1894

Mr. Paul L. Dunbar[214]
Dayton, Ohio
Dear Sir:—

We are inclined to accept the contributions[215] you are good enough to offer us for the "Lighter Vein" department. May we therefore ask you to refer us to some person known to us, which reference shall be in the nature of a voucher for your good faith, as you are a stranger to us.[216] This is in accordance with the rule of this magazine. Perhaps it would make this easier to you if I say that a note from my cousin, Mr. Charles U. Raymond of your city, vouching for you, would be sufficient. If you do not know him, some friend of yours who does know him would doubtless do you the service to speak to him of you.

Very respectfully yours,
R. U. Johnson[217]
Associate Ed.

Letter 34: December 9, 1894, Charles A. Thatcher to PLD

Dec. 9th, 1894[218]

Mr. Paul Laurence Dunbar,
Dayton's – [illegible]:[219]

Will open correspondence with Mr. Shearer as requested. I do not know when to [illegible] later [illegible] at Delaware but suppose it is soon after Jan 1st.

Have arranged for you to give [a] reading before the West End Club in Toledo, on Wednesday evening, Dec. 19th.[220] The club is in a large house there, where you were before to entertain, and will be of profit. Will try to make engagements for you at two or three other places for the 20th and 21st. You should arrange to spend two or three days here & bring a number of your books[221] with you.

If the publisher would bind a few in a neat white and gold binding I

think they would sell at this time of year. You should bring full dress suit
with you. Let me know at once if you cannot [illegible]. If you can get the
Y.M.C.A. to help you it might be well to stay at Lucas for Tuesday evening
the 18th. I have friends there who would assist.

Very truly yours,
C. A. Thatcher

Letter 35: December 10, 1894, Unknown to PLD
920 Lombard Street, Monday, Dec 10, 94[222]

Dear Mr. Dunbar,

    I have just finished your very interesting letter and thank you very
kindly for the kind reference to myself which your letter contained. I think
that our people are not too young to appreciate the dignity and worth of
the few geniuses it has been our good fortune to possess. And the "irony
of fate" to which one of your some-time critics as feelingly alludes to, or
in other words—the crude personalities of our semi-socialized-civilization
prevents our whiter[223] brothers from giving the encouragement to members
which genius should command. "Seven Cities Mourned, Homer dead—
This which the living Homer begged for bread!"[224] is a famous quotation
from which the intellectual world has never recovered. . . . I am very glad
that the fair Southland—land of my birth—should be the first to open
its doors to you and to speed you onward in your mission to conquer new
worlds and to reclaim the fair name of Ethiopia's race. You inquire in such
a half-devotional tone what does it all amount to? It was Job's inquiry and
in spite of his impetuosity he was compelled to suffer, labor and wait until
his energies bore for him its proper fruition.[225] By patience and energy
this [illegible] represented genius distinguished himself. For faith was an
essential element in his work, but it was the quality of faith which was born
of an infallible conviction that merit and merit alone would in the end
accomplish all. And by that sign, Job conquered. So mote it be with you,
humble, industrious Paul Dunbar. "The world is mine," declared Monte
Christo,[226] when he beheld the ambition of his life like a mirage spread out
before him. And then with that energy born of desperation he concentrated
his efforts to become the actual possessor of the things which Hope and
Ideal had stimulated him to work for. Set this down as inspiration. Nothing
is impossible: know thou thyself. Choose your ideal, then labour to make it
your own. Never forget the fact that you are only a part of the world. That

you have your sphere, and, that you can be King, Lord, Monarch of all you survey! But stop, I Your servant am usurping the fruition of my master. But I know by the faith I have in your friendship that your good verse will permit the mantle of charity to cover over these little friendly impertinences. And now a word to the practical. I like the suggestion of your southern admirer. It is a good idea and strikes me as being a profitable one.[227] It ought to be of great financial benefit to you. I have given the matter some thought and have about concluded that if you can make arrangements to come East I will arrange one grand reading for you in our leading Hall. I can then give one or two smaller affairs. My idea would be to have you and Miss Georgiana Kelly of Balt. Md, a young elocutionist who thus far has received very flattering comments, for her [illegible] talents appear sophisticatedly together. To have an [illegible] and I think this would make a hit. I could also arrange to have an entertainment for you in Harrisburg, the capital of the state two nights before you appeared here. What do you think about it? Let me know at once! And I will proceed to make arrangements. I enclose a circular of which I have the financial backing. I am a real-estate broker by profession, but [illegible] season manager to give two or three concerts of a heightened nature. Let me hear from you at once. Of course, I shall make arrangements for New York appearance. If you decide to try it, be sure and finish the newspaper cities [illegible] you have on hand. Also get the *Sun*[228] matter attended to.

Very sincerely,

[illegible]

P.S.

Send me a copy of your latest book, and a copy of [illegible] Journal of criticism [illegible].

Letter 36: December 12, 1894, Charles A. Thatcher to PLD
Dec. 12, 1894[229]

Mr. Paul Dunbar

Dayton, O—Dear Sir:

Yours of recent at hand, I did not intend to fix a date for you at Lucia but merely suggested it. You can arrange a date to suit your convenience and I will notify my friends of the time you may fix. I have the arrangement for you definitely for Wed. the 19th in Toledo and will try to arrange for 20th. If not I can arrange for 21st. If you will mail me ten of your books on receipt

of this, think they will help me to make engagements for you.[230] Will do
what I can.

Very truly yours,
C. A. Thatcher

Letter 37: December 12, 1894, William A. Burns to PLD
Cleveland, O., Dec. 12–94[231]

Dear Chum:

Received your note yesterday. Perfectly willing to comply with your
request. Sent the article to you today via U.S. express. Co. Please let me know
at once, whether you received it or not. Haven't time to write more. Hadn't
heard of your engagement here.

Keeping too else,
Very timely
W.A.B.[232]

Letter 38: December 17, 1894, R. U. Johnson to PLD
Editorial Department
The Century Magazine
Union Square, New York
December 17, 1894[233]

Mr. Paul L. Dunbar
Dear Sir:—

The letters[234] you send us are wholly satisfactory, and I send you herewith
for our publishers a check in payment[235] for three contributions.[236] I also
return Mr. Riley's letter and the accompanying clipping.

Very sincerely yours,
R. U. Johnson
Associate Ed.

Letter 39: December 31, 1894, Walter LeRoy Fogg to PLD
6 Columbia St., Portsmouth, NH, 12/31/94[237]

Dear Friend Paul,

I was most happy to receive your letter this morning, and I hasten to
reply. I had almost despaired of ever hearing from you again. I have thought

of you often and wondered how you were getting along. Do you see my poems in "Blue and Gray."[238] Well, your experience with that magazine is mine exactly. I sent "His Life" (as I originally called the poem) to the "B & G," long, long, long ago—so long that I forgot the date. In vain I awaited its return. Also in vain did I look for proof of its acceptance. The fate of my poor poem was unknown to me until I got your letter this morning! Such is fame! Neither have I ever been told by the editor of the acceptance of the verses, nor have I received a single coin for it, and I have never seen a copy of the magazine. I am going to write a very sharp epistle to the individual in that editorial sancture [sic]. I am well primed, and something will go off with a bang. Talk about the courtesy of the editorial class! Talk about this interest in aspiring writers! I wish you would tell me in what number of "Blue and Gray" my poem appeared. Then should they not answer my letter, as they did not yours, I will know what number to procure. I am glad you enjoyed my little remembrance in the shape of "Yule [illegible]." It was written by me when I first wooed the Muse. You say you have had many failures and few successes. That fits my case. Please tell me all about your progress. I have taken an ardent interest in my friend way out in the middle states, and I want to peek into his heart and let him look into mine, if there he cares to do. You and I, Paul, are brothers in more ways than one. I love to think that some future day, we may rise to be the most and best of our country. Is it too bright a hope? I know you have great promise in you. I cannot say that of myself, but I do know that there is something in my heart that bids me on and on. No, the muse is still faithful to me. I am writing poems continually. I saw one of yours in Munsey's some time ago, that I liked very much. I have not offered any poems to the magazine of late. I will name some that have been accepted: "Shell Song," Youth's Companion—#10; "Beneath the Birchen Trees," Good Housekeeping—#2, "At Eventide," Sunday School Times, #5; "The Song of a Breeze," Boston Transcript. "Shell Song" was the first I ever had found a market for. That was a year ago this Christmas of '94. Now, Paul, I am going to broach a subject that has struck me strongly lately. I trust I shall not offend you by mentioning it. Am I [illegible] any when I say that I long for the time when we can issue a volume of our joint selections. Perhaps I am bold in wanting to couple your name with mine. You already have a reputation that is denied me, and I am well aware of the lower position of my muse when placed with yours. But I am sincere in the belief that it would be a good arrangement. I have given this much thought. I am anxious to get your idea of it. Can we not join hands and hearts by the title page of a dainty book? I will try to tutor my timid Muse so that she will [illegible] a creditable appearance when introduced to yours. Now will it be too much to ask you concerning the cost of your "Oak and Ivy?" What was the expense of its issue, and how has it been selling? My interest is a fraternal one. I take it for granted that you have not issued another collection of your verse yet. My name has yet to appear on a title page. I am thinking, though, of putting my poetical thoughts in book form during this year of 1895. I would so delight in sharing with you the cost and labor of getting out a "partnership" volume.[239] I find that our fancy is much the same, and I am confident that we could offer a collection of poems not to be ashamed of. Please have something to say about this in your next letter. It is the [illegible] dear project of my heart, and I hope it will affect you favorably. Tomorrow I go to Manchester, this state, to reassure my position in the reportorial staff of the "Daily Union." For the [illegible] at year I have been vacillating between work and vacation. This time I hope to make it a permanent employment. Mine will be a busy life (journalism), but I assure you I shall always be able to find time for a reply to your letters, let them come two and three a week! What have you been doing all this time, Paul, and what about your mom? Tell me all about yourself. Can't you [illegible] on beyond Philadelphia when you come east? By the way, what about these readings? Write as soon as you consistently can, and address me: 50 Hanover St. Manchester, or: Daily Union. My mother and father send kind wishes. A merry New Year.

With sincerity,
Walter LeRoy Fogg[240]

Letters from 1895

Letter 40: February 15, 1895, *Independent* to PLD
The Independent
130 Fulton St.
New York
Feb. 15, 1895[241]

Mr. Paul Lawrence [*sic*] Dunbar,[242]
Dayton, O.
My dear Sir:—

I take the liberty to call your attention to one or two lines in your poem "Retrospect."[243] The line, "Wind fanned our fevered brows,"[244] lacks a foot,[245] and on the next to the last line of that page the word choir is used as a two-syllabled word.[246]

I call your attention to these little faults because this poem has been sent to our office before, and so on reading it the second time they showed possibly all the plainer. I like the spirit and movement of the poem very much and should have been glad to use it were we not very much crowded in our poetic department.

Yours very truly,
Office Editor

Letter 41: March 8, 1895, E. C. Martin to PLD

S.S. McClure, Limited
30 Lafayette Place, New York City,
CABLE ADDRESS, "Addlecamp, New York"
New York, 8th Mch., 1895[247]

Dear Mr. Dunbar:

I don't quite see how we can use any of the Ireland pieces.[248] Poetry we have as little space for that—it is about time to say we never buy it. As for the story, it has not plot enough for our use—it is too much of a sketch. All of the pieces are well written, and also well [illegible]. I'm sorry we have to return them. I hope you won't let my doing so discourage you. The most famed find the road you are on a long and hard one; and a stout heart is of perhaps more [illegible] on it—even than a divine pen.

Yours Truly,
E. C. Martin[249]

Letter 42: March 19, 1895, *Herald* to PLD

Office of the Leavenworth Herald[250]
Leavenworth, Kas. March 19, 1895[251]

Mr. Paul Laurence Dunbar:

Dayton, Ohio: Dear sir, we write to ask you if you will kindly send us your recent poem on "Frederick Douglass,"[252] of which we have heard. We have not as yet had any poem concerning the illustrious Douglass, and as we desired something good, we thought we would ask you for one, if it is not asking too much. If you cannot comply with our wish, we shall not be offended in the least, and shall look upon it as adherence to a point of professional duty in not furnishing "goods" gratis. We would willingly purchase your poems if we were financially able. Hoping that you will give this letter your consideration, we are yours for success,

"The Herald"

Letter 43: March 29, 1895, Charles Thatcher to PLD
Hurd, Brumback, & Thatcher[253]
Attorneys at Law
Mar 29, '95[254]

Dear Mr. Dunbar:

I intended writing you a few days since about a conversation I had with S.R. Gill,[255] Lakewood Ohio, Secretary of the Camp Meeting Association. In the midst of the business I have forgotten whether I wrote you or not.

I saw Mr. Gill & advised him to secure you to give [illegible] recitals during the Sunday School Encampment, which I believe cues off in July. It might be well for you to write him on the subject. I will write to Dr. Bashford and ask him to use his influence for you.

How much money would it require for you to attend the Spring [illegible] at [illegible]?

It is possible that I will be in Cincinnati during the coming month. If I am, will look up Shearer. I presumed that I am to enclose $2.00. You will find it in this.

Very truly yours,
C. A. Thatcher

You might write Shearer again.

Letter 44: April 22, 1895, S. R. Gill to PLD
Office of the Lakeside Company[256]
Lakeside, O. April 22, 1895[257]

Mr. Paul Dunbar,
Dayton, O,
Dear Sir:

Some time ago, Mr. Thatcher of Toledo spoke to me about having you come to the Lakeside and that you would do so for expenses for a week. Dr. Bashford has now written in your behalf.[258]

We are to have the Tennessee Warblers[259] here July 23rd to 30th and they will give three concerts. It occurred to me that you might be worked into these concerts. While I present this to you I will submit the matter to our program committee and will hear from them as soon as from you.[260]

Yours Truly,

S. R. Gill[261]

Letter 45: May 20, 1895, PLD to J. N. Matthews

Dayton, Ohio, May 20, 1895[262]

Dr. J. N. Matthews

My dear sir:

Your note has been just received and I was glad to hear from you again. So many letters to you have gone unanswered that I never expected this pleasure.

For the past two weeks I have been in Indianapolis reciting, and am now on the verge of returning thither. While there I met Riley and found him as delightful as his poems.

While my permanent address is the same as ever, for the next two weeks[263] mail matter may be sent to 99 Yandes St. Indianapolis.

With many thanks for your kindness,

I am

Sincerely your Friend,

Paul Dunbar

Letter 46: June 11, 1895, Richard Lew Dawson to PLD

June 11, 1895[264]

Paul Laurence Dunbar,

Dear friend:

Twenty two years ago I was a reporter, first [for the] Indianapolis *Sentinel* then [for the] Indianapolis *Journal*, and my experiences were many during that brief career. It is a pernicious work for any man who has cultivated literary style. Your work in a weekly paper[265] is not as bad for you. I should like to own an influential literary monthly, it could be a good waste-basket for all my random notes and comments. (I afterwards, by the way, was manager for a weekly paper at Indianapolis, and helped to make it a good plant—underground.) But well, well, well, well! That is what I intended to

remark when I commenced this letter—who'd 'a' thought *you'd* be locating
yourself in *my* town? Git out!²⁶⁶

One of my nieces is very ill and in a critical condition from hemorrhage.
Her sister, who married and went to Iowa, and their mother, my sister, are
now back at Indianapolis attending the sick one. Those two girls are my
favorite girls and love me as well as my own daughters. The name of the one
who is sick is Mrs. Curry, and she lives at 491 E. Truth St. I shall be grateful
if you would call on them. If you don't care to go alone, take Mr. Taylor, as he
is acquainted and they know you well through me. My sister's name is Mrs.
Thompson. You will find them at the number mentioned.

I have met a number of your people, Dr. Elbert, Mr. Christy,²⁶⁷ and many
teachers, among them W. D. McCoy, who went to Liberia, and I think died
there.²⁶⁸

Go on my "Old Covered Bridge"²⁶⁹ over the river west. It is a historic
landmark. You ought to republish my "Indianapolis."²⁷⁰ If you could get
access to files of the People and Review of 1869 to 1877, you could find
a book of my old poems. I have just finished one of my most elaborate
reminiscent poems, "The Boy in the Country," and I love it more at each
reading. It has 672 iambic feet (all triples.)²⁷¹ I am feeling *jubilant* over it.
(whoop!) I have filed it at Johnson of the *Century*, as Mr. Gilder²⁷² is in
Europe and I have Johnson [illegible]. As I finished and copied it June 9, and
it occupies 9 pages of paper, it should be accepted, if my mascot number is
worth anything. The last couplet in it pleases me as much as anything I ever
wrote;—and you may note the style of verse as this

> "O the tones of boyhood's laughter in the

> Mist of manhood's prime
> Are golden coins that jingle down the
> Stony steps of Time!"

Or this form:

> "O the tones of boyhood's laughter this the mist
> Of manhood's prime

> As golden coins come ringing down the stony
> steps of time!"

Or this:

> "O each tone of boyhood's laughter is a coin in
> Manhood's prime
>
> And rings with golden music down the
> Stony steps of time!"

The last quoted is the way I sent it and I can't decide which is best. What [do you] think?

One of my favorite haunts about there was on Fall Creek right at the head of College Ave. and on a path (opposite side) from there was on into Schefield's Mill, which is now by the new fair grounds. It used to be beautiful, was miles in the country, but now the town is building up all about there. I used to ride a "Velocipede" the first form of bicycle, along a wooded road up and down hill with grounds running across the roads and rail fences. That quiet road is now College Ave from the old university now [illegible] Home—on north to about tenth street. A wonderful change! My next poem will be "The Glen"[273] based on Watkins Glen and surroundings. It is a fairyland about there. Then I shall write a *supreme* dialect group at the *Country store*, and think I will give it a specific name, from the lecture where I use the material now, "Hoosier Hollow."[274] Another part of that lecture I will also put into verse, "The Country Hack." Then I will versify my "In De Ole Slabe Days." So I have some hard grinding labor ahead.

Say, save me one of those nice little [illegible] that you are dawdling along. I want to plant it in Virginia and build a log cabin on it by the surrounding[275]

(that is a *half-tone* [illegible]).

I always knew Indianapolis was a health resort, and now it has cured you of an awful disease: Cacoethes Scribendi![276] Mercy! What possessed you to even handle such things? Next thing you'll be going around like a bloated landholder or an Injun with war paint, from fooling with poison ivy.

'Scuse me for all this, but I'm feeling hysterical today. There was a circus procession here yesterday with three brass bands and a calliope,[277] and worse than all that, the Salvation Army is located across the street from this hotel with two or three cornets[278] that go tumbling over another with colds in their heads!

Have you seen Irvington.[279] See it and die. Cottman[280] lives there, and he is a new Thoreau and John Burroughs.[281] But he is probably camping now up at Lake Tippecanoe.

Well, durn [*sic*] it, if you can't write, then write letters. This is the way with me.

Cordially,

Richard Lew Dawson

Remarkable thing: my "poem" prose is all about the old times, but the word "old" does not occur once in it.

Letter 47: July 1, 1895, E. C. Martin to PLD

S.S. McClure, Limited
30 Lafayette Place, New York City,
Cable Address, "Addlecamp, New York"
New York, 1st Jul, 1895[282]

Mr. Paul L. Dunbar,
Dear Sir:

I have been a long time getting to your story. I was not in town when it came, and found a great accumulation for me when I returned. The story is well written and moves forward in a good swift way, and shows several virtues. But I am forced to say that it does not seem very real to me; and I don't see how we can take it. I hope you won't take this judgment to heart, however. It means at the most merely that you are to try again; for we shall be very glad to hear from you again. I saw your poem[283] in the "Century" + congratulate you on it.

Yours truly,

E. C. Martin

Letter 48: July 6, 1895, H. A. Tobey to PLD

Toledo, OH, July 6, 1895[284]

Mr. Paul Dunbar,
Dayton, Ohio
Dear Sir:

Some five or six months ago an acquaintance of mine[285] in Dayton sent me your little book of poems, which pleased me greatly. I am not a literary character, but believe I possess ordinary human instincts and emotions, and from my point of view I must compliment you enough to say that I believe you possess real poetical instinct. In these modern times, when it seems the chief aim and object of man is to obtain the "Almighty Dollar," poets and poetry are below par and by the common mass of mankind their real intrinsic value is not appreciated. This condition of society I very much deplore, as I look upon poetry as only a higher philosophy: so subtle, so ethereal, so divine, that our creator has endowed only a few of our kind with the sacred trust of translating to the masses a representation of the joys and sorrows that every heart has felt. When I first received your book I learned from the donor that, in a biblical sense, God Almighty has placed the stain of Cain[286] upon you, or, in other words, your skin is black. I knew nothing of your circumstances until some three months ago when I was in Dayton I learned from an acquaintance that your mother was a wash-woman, and that even yet you are required to earn your living by menial labor. Since then I have read your poems again and again, and the more I read them the more I recognize the divinity that stirs within you. I do not belong to any church, and the little good I may be able to do is not done in the name of Christ, but only in the name of humanity; but by this statement I would not depreciate the beautiful character of our so-called "Savior."[287] I have talked with a number of friends of mine and believe I am in a position to give you financial aid if you desire to increase your education or to travel with a view of [illegible] better [illegible] your half [illegible] to pour out your poetical songs to the world. When I was in Dayton I learned that your ambition is to become a lawyer. The world is already full of lawyers for its good, peace or welfare. What we need is more persons to interpret Nature and Nature's God.[288] I believe you are specially endowed for this world, and therefore would admonish you to continue as you have started, notwithstanding there is no popular clamor for, or perhaps much approval of what you have already done. I am so thoroughly Democratic in my sentiments that race or condition with me "cuts but little figure," in my estimation of men. Therefore I am anxious to assist or help you in any way I can. Enclosed herewith I send you a check for Five Dollars, ($5.00) and would like to have you send me the number of volumes of your poems that this amount will buy.[289] I also desire to have you write and tell me what your ambition is and what you desire to do.

Very truly yours,

H. A. Tobey

  P.S. I send you by the same mail of this letter a copy of our last annual report.

Letter 49: July 7, 1895, Charles Thatcher to PLD
Law Offices of Hurd, Brumback, & Thatcher Gardner Building
Toledo, Ohio, July 7, 1895[290]

Mr. Paul Dunbar
Dear Sir:

Dr. H.A. Tobey, superintendent of the Toledo State Hospital has become much interested in your work and would like to meet you.[291] Please let me know whether you expect to come to Toledo soon. If you go to Lakeside[292] you could come this way. Do you expect to go to Lakeside? If arrangements have not been made for you and you desire I will write Mr. Gill, the secretary. From all I can see Mr. Shearer is executive proof. Will however make further inquiry.

Very truly yours,
C. A. Thatcher

Letter 50: July 9, 1895, Joseph S. Cotter to PLD
July 9, 1895[293]

My Dear Dunbar:

Yours just at hand. Of course I am willing for you to steal as often as possible.

Glad to know you found a home for the "Pied Piper."[294] He has been a waif a long time. I have not as yet received papers. I am slightly anxious to do so. The examinations are over. They were hard indeed. Three out of 53 passed.[295]

You may have all the pleasure of editing a paper. I read your poems with much pleasure. It is unique your Century poem for July is entirely a type.[296] May you have greater success along the same line.

Mr. Watkins spoke to me the other day about you and your work. He is all praise.

Mr. McPhearson sends thanks for some manuscript you sent him. I will look after the other matter as soon as possible. It is [illegible].

All send regards to yourself and mother.

Much sincerity to the poet and editor now henceforth + forever.

Your friend,
J. S. Cotter

Letter 51: July 13, 1895, PLD to H. A. Tobey
Dayton, Ohio, July 13th, 1895[297]

My Dear Dr. Tobey:-

If it is a rule that tardiness in the acknowledgement of favors argues lack of appreciation of them, you may set it down that the rule has gone wrong in this case.[298] Your letter and its enclosure was a sunburst out of a very dark and unpromising cloud.[299] Let me tell you the circumstances and see if you do not think that you came to me somewhat in the role of a "special providence."

The time for the meeting of the Western Association of Writers was at hand. I am a member and thought that certain advantages might come to me by attending. All day Saturday and all day Sunday I tried every means to secure funds to go. I tried every known place, and at last gave up and went to bed Sunday night in despair. But strangely I could not sleep, so about half-past eleven I arose and between then and 2 A.M., wrote the paper which I was booked to read at the Association. Then, still with no suggestion of any possibility of attending the meeting, I returned to bed and went to sleep about four o'clock. Three hours later came your letter with the check that took me to the desired place. I do not think that I spent the money unwisely, for besides the pleasure of intercourse with kindred spirits which should have been sufficient motive, I believe that there were several practical advantages which I derived from the trip, whence I have just returned.[300]

I wish I could thank you for the kindness that prompted your action; I care not in whose name it was done, whether in Christ's, Mahomet's or Buddha's. The thing that concerned me, the fact that made the act a good and noble one was that it *was* done.

Yes, I am tied down and have been by menial labor,[301] and any escape from it so far has only been a brief respite that made a return to the drudgery doubly hard. But I am glad to say that for the past two or three years I have been able to keep my mother from the hard toil by which she raised and educated me. But it has been and is a struggle.

Your informant was mistaken as to my aspirations. I did once want to be a lawyer, but that ambition has long since died out before the all-absorbing desire to be a worthy singer of the songs of God and nature. To be able to interpret my own people through song and story, and to prove to the many that after all we are more human than African. And New York, Boston and Philadelphia where I might see our northern Negro at his best, before seeing his brother in the South: but it has been denied me.

I hope, if possible, to spend the coming year in college, chiefly to learn how and what to study in order to cultivate my vein. But I have my home responsibilities and unless I am to make sufficient to meet them I shall be unable to accomplish my purpose. To do this I have for some time been giving readings from my verses to audiences mostly of my own people.[302] But as my work has been confined to the smaller towns generally that result has not been satisfactory.

Perhaps I have laid my case too plainly and openly before you, but you seem to display a disposition to aid me, and I am so grateful that I cannot but be confidential. That beside, a physician does not want to take a case when there is reticence in regard to the real phase of it. And so I have been plain.

Sincerely,
Paul L. Dunbar

Letter 52: August 9, 1895, R. U. Johnson to PLD
August 9th, 1895[303]
Editorial Department
The Century Magazine
Union Square, New York

Mr. Paul Lawrence [*sic*] Dunbar
140 Ziegler St.
Dayton, Ohio
Dear Mr. Dunbar:-

There are some very nice things about these poems which you have sent us, and I am sorry that none of them takes us by the throat, so to speak. We can only print a small part of the literary output of any one poet, and we are glad to have you send us as much as you choose so that we may make our selection.

In reply to your question, let us say that we only buy the right to print contributions in "The Century," and that at a reasonable time after their appearance it is our custom to waive copyright for book publication, unless some special arrangement or another has been made. You are therefore at liberty to accept royalty for the words of your songs, but it would be well for you to let us send you a formal permission, which we will do if you will tell me which one you wish.

[illegible writing for closing]

R. U. Johnson[304]

A. E.

Letter 53: August 18, 1895, PLD to Matilda Dunbar

Dayton, O., August 18, 1895[305]

Dear Mother:

I received your card saying that you had not heard from me: I wrote you last week and mailed the letter in Toledo, it is strange you did not get it. I spent five days in Toledo and had a very good time. Dr. Tobey gave me $10.00 for my work. I paid Kuhns[306] and kept the rest except 96 cents I paid Mr. Zartman.[307]

Mr. Dustin was nominated for Judge.[308] I forgot to say, I paid Mrs. [illegible] what I owed her.

I am getting along very nicely. Julie[309] cooks for me when I don't feel like cooking, and everything is moving smoothly.

Why don't you write and tell me something about Ethel, how she is, and how she got [illegible]. I am anxious to know. I hope you are having a nice time there. Have you seen Mrs. Butler yet?[310]

Dr. Tobey and his friends moved to lend me 400 or 500 dollars to spend a year in Boston at Harvard. I am going to take it.[311]

Let me hear from you soon. Love you all.

Your affectionate son,

Paul

Letter 54: August 23, 1895, William Ellsworth to PLD

August 23rd, 1895[312]

The Century Co.

Publishers

33 East 117th St. (Union Square)

New York, NY

Mr. Paul Laurence Dunbar,

Dayton, Ohio

Dear Sir:

We give you formal permission to use with music[313] the words of the
poem, "A Negro Love Song," from the April "Century" with credit to the
author and magazine.[314]

Yours very truly,

William W. Ellsworth[315]

Letter 55: November 25, 1895, John Church Company to PLD

The John Church Company

Cincinnati, New York, Chicago

Cincinnati Office, Nov. 25th, 1895[316]

Mr. Paul L. Dunbar

Dear Sir:

Your favor of the 23rd at hand, with manuscript of your song.[317] In reply
would say, we think you have made a very happy and characteristic setting of
the words, and while of course we cannot say how the song will take with the
public, yet we shall be pleased to publish it at our own expense and pay you
a royalty of Ten per cent. of the retail price on all copies sold in excess of one
hundred.

Concerning your query as to whether you can sell the English rights
to the words without prejudicing the American rights would say that such
a thing is possible, and has been done, but in our opinion it always leaves a
chance for complications and misunderstandings through either one setting
or the other being imported into the two countries, and for this reason we
would suggest that if you are going to publish the song at all that you hold all
the rights for yourself.

If you see your way clear to accept our proposition, we will forward
paper for signature.

We return you Miss Eden's letter herewith.

Very truly yours,

The John Church Co.[318]

2

Dunbar's Meteoric Rise to Fame, 1896–1897

AFTER HIS RISE TO LITERARY stardom, Dunbar's publishing output increased drastically, especially between 1896 and 1897; fittingly, his correspondence rivals this proliferation. But, as these letters unveil, Dunbar's climb to literary success was anything but easy, and there were periods of great strife for the author; some of his correspondence reveals the necessary but exhausting and tedious lengths Dunbar still had to go in order to publish.

Dunbar's letters also show, however, that many of the early contacts he had made yielded what would have likely become lifelong friendships had he lived longer. Dunbar's correspondence with James D. Corrothers, J. N. Matthews, James Whitcomb Riley, John Richard Meader, John Clark Ridpath, Will Pfrimmer, Dr. H. A. Tobey, Brand Whitlock, and Alexander Crummell was often encouraging, even in his darkest hours. Dunbar's relationship with Howells burgeoned and the two shared an intimate friendship until the poet's death. Lyman Abbott, the famous editor, author, and theologian, supported Dunbar's pursuits and was aware of his struggles, noting he "hope[d] to see the day" when Dunbar would find happiness, while "surrounded with comfort . . . unharassed by thoughts which [caused him] worry." Abbot, like so many, simply desired Dunbar to be able to "sing songs of pure joy," and in many of Dunbar's works there are glimpses of the fleeting happiness he fervently sought to savor indefinitely.

Part of Dunbar's happiness was intricately tied to his relationship with his mother and his soon-to-be-wife, Alice Ruth Moore. Dunbar had developed an exceptionally close relationship with his mother that lasted into his adulthood and until his death; Dunbar dedicated both *Oak and Ivy* and *Lyrics of Lowly Life* to her, and there are countless letters between the

FIGURE 3. Dunbar with friend in Ohio, n.d.
Courtesy of Ohio Historical Connection.

two that reflect a deep familial love and respect. These same letters, though not the primary focus of this book, also portray a very controlling and demanding woman who sought Dunbar's constant attention. Even Alice commented on it in a 1906 letter to Lida Keck Wiggins (who subsequently chose not to include this information about the Dunbars in her biography): "There was a miserable friction between his mother and myself" (Metcalf, "Letters of Paul and Alice Dunbar," 12). An undated letter from Dunbar's older brother, Robert, described a harrowing scene involving Matilda and money: after demanding money from Robert, who refused to give it to her, Matilda "began to scream and rage and call all sort [*sic*] of bad names . . . I told her to leave the house." Apparently, Matilda did not stop there, as Robert further described the situation: Matilda "sprang on [him] like a tiger, hitting [him] in the face and clawing [him]." Matilda was, perhaps predictably, not overfond of her daughter-in-law, but she relocated from Dayton to Washington, DC, to live with the newly married couple.

Much to Dunbar's chagrin, Matilda tended to focus on monetary issues and began demanding money from her children. On November 9,

1897, Dunbar wrote his mother requesting her to "go as easy as [she] can," as Dunbar explained and admonished her: "I am not a millionaire." Yet Matilda's fixation on finances continued, and she perpetually plagued Dunbar with requests for money. Years later, on September 5, 1903, Dunbar chastised his mother for her persistent requests for money, writing, "You know I haven't got fifty dollars to my name." Dunbar struggled with financial worries until his death, but especially in his earlier years.

While in England, Dunbar expressed a similar worry about being able to provide for not only his mother but Alice as well. On May 14, 1897, he wrote Alice that he would unburden her: "I do not mean by this," Dunbar expounded, "that you care for my success only, but that I could not, in justice to you and with credit to myself take you to wife unless I had a surety of being able to make you a pleasant and easy home. However much I love you, I would rather give you up than have you struggle along with me in a life of poverty and uncertainty" (quoted in Metcalf, "Letters of Paul and Alice Dunbar," 149). Alice, too, fretted over money and her inability to earn much. Five months later, she lamented, "Paul, I don't think we *ever* will be able to marry. It takes such heaps of money—a commodity sadly lacking in this combination" (Metcalf, "Letters of Paul and Alice Dunbar," 217). Yet they married, and although Dunbar's literary fame grew, his pocketbook did not. Dunbar's financial struggles never seemed to end.

Dunbar's letters, although they reveal financial support from many, acknowledge his frustration with solidifying contracts and getting paid for the works he produced and the many recitals he attended; these literary letters help shed light on the complicated topics and issues Dunbar faced as he sought to make his living as a respected full-time writer. What we see in these next two years is that Dunbar's literary successes did not assuage his financial woes, publishing difficulties, and personal problems. At times, the letters seem superfluous, and even tedious, but they show Dunbar's dedication to his success, the minutiae he had to deal with, and the complicated nature of closing writing contracts. Perhaps more upsetting when considering the amount of time Dunbar spent on these details is that he often had to fight to receive compensation that he had been promised.

During these burgeoning years of Dunbar's success, he was also plagued with other matters, including the development of tuberculosis, which frequently left him ill and weak in constitution. What seemed to begin as a small cold would leave Dunbar fevered and bedridden for days and even weeks. This affected his ability to work, which in turn greatly upset him; he already had a growing proclivity for alcohol, inadvertently exacerbated by medical advice at the time: in order to quiet a cough, doctors recommended the consumption of alcohol. As no one understood alcoholism at that point, Dunbar drank more freely in an attempt to control his coughing. This caused him great embarrassment publicly and with Alice, as the papers sometimes reported. Despite Dunbar's best attempts, he did not stop drinking.

Although the correspondence in this section reveals that he received financial support from many sources, it also acknowledges Dunbar's frustration with solidifying contracts and receiving his due compensation. The literary letters in this section help shed light on the complicated topics and issues Dunbar faced as he sought literary success. Unfortunately, Dunbar often found that reality did not quite measure up to his dreams.

LETTERS FROM 1896

Letter 56: Undated, James A. Herne to PLD

Detroit, Mich.[1]

My Dear Mr. Dunbar,[2]

While at Toledo, a copy of your poems[3] was left at my hotel by a Mr. Childs.[4] I tried very hard to find Mr. Childs to learn more of you. Your poems are wonderful.[5] I shall acquaint William Dean Howells and other literary people with them.[6] They are new to me and may be to them.

I send you by this same mail some things done by my daughter Julia A. Herne.[7] She is in school in Boston. Her scribblings may interest you. I would like your opinion.

. . .

I am an actor and a dramatist. My latest work—"Shores Acres"[8] you may have heard of. If it comes your way, I want you to see it, whether I am with it or not. How I wish I knew you personally! I wish you all the good fortune that you can wish for yourself.

Yours very truly,
James A. Herne[9]

Letter 57: April 1896, Robert Ingersoll to H. A. Tobey

No. 220 Madison Ave.
April 1896, New York City[10]

My Dear Mr. Tobey,[11]

At last I got the time to read the poems of Dunbar.[12] Some of them are really wonderful—full of poetry and philosophy. I am astonished at their depth and subtlety. Dunbar is a thinker. "The Mystery"[13] is a poem worthy of the greatest. It is absolutely true, and proves that its author is a profound and thoughtful man. So the "Dirge" is very tender, dainty, intense, and beautiful. "Ere Sleep Comes Down to Soothe the Weary Eyes" is a wonderful poem: the fifth verse is perfect. So "He Had His Dream"[14] is very fine and many others.

I have only time to say that Dunbar is a genius. Now I ask, what can be done for him. I would like to help.

Thanking you for the book, I remain,

Yours always,

R. G. Ingersoll[15]

Letter 58: April 22, 1896, H. A. Tobey to PLD
Toledo State Hospital, H. A. Tobey, M.D., Superintendent[16]

My Dear Mr. Dunbar:

I enclose a letter that I have just received which explains itself.

I was down to the city yesterday and sold books[17] for you as follows and each one of the gentlemen said that they wanted to see you and make your acquaintance.[18] Mr. King said he would give you a number of names of persons that would buy books, that he had already spoken to several and would speak to more.

Mr. Scott, I think, is President of the Board of Trustees of the City Library.[19] He spoke of putting your book in the library.

Mr. Childs, night clerk at the Boody House,[20] told me that he had received a long and beautiful letter from Mr. Hern[e], to whom he gave a book when Mr. Hern[e] was here. He will mail me the letter today so you can see it when you can come out again. I met Mr. Knight of the Blade and he told me your poem to Louise[21] would be published either today or tomorrow. I also saw Mr. Martins who is one of the editors of the Sunday Journal, and who is in the City Engineers office in the [illegible] building, who is anxious to learn of you. He said if you would call on him, he would take pleasure in introducing you to a number of persons in the building who would probably take your books.

Don't you see your "stock in trade" is beginning to boom.[22] "Hold on to the millions" work watch and pray and "you will get there with [illegible]." Hoping that you are in better spirits and that the cuticle has thickened just a little over the [illegible] spots. I am very truly yours—let me hear from you by phone.

Very Truly Yours,
H. A. Tobey

Letter 59: April 22, 1896, Isaac D. Smead to PLD

The Smead Furnace & Foundry Co.
Isaac D. Smead, Superintendent
Toledo, O. April 22nd, 1896[23]

Paul Dunbar, Esq.,
733 Hicks St., City
My Dear Sir:

I am pleased to acknowledge receipt of yours of the 21st, which, together with enclosure has come to hand; I shall also be pleased to receive the poem when completed.

Ever since 1870 I have been much in the South and am quite familiar with the life of the colored man as it has been there for the past 200 years. As I vote the Republican ticket, you can readily understand that my sympathies are with the race, for which that party has made such great effort. While I know exactly why I asked you the question "what made you a poet," I didn't suppose that the question would suggest a poem; I am glad it has.

Yours truly,
Isaac D. Smead[24]

Letter 60: Undated, Edwin H. Keen to PLD

Birkdale
Kiddepore Avenue
Finchley Road, N.W.[25]

Dear Sir,

Your "Lyrics of Lowly Life"[26] have afforded me the greatest enjoyment. I want to thank you for them.

In conversation today with my friend the Hon. W. S. Quinby[27] of the "Detroit Free Press,"[28] I learned that there is a chance of you coming to England, and reading these charming pieces to us.—Do come—you will make them a great success.

The songs of the "Jubilee [illegible]"[29] touched our heart years ago, surely these poems could not fail to be appreciated here.

Have not your people gone wild lately over Ian McLaren and the Scotch [illegible]?[30]

Come and pay us back by reading "The Deserted Plantation" and "The Delinquent" as only their author can read them.[31]

Sincerely your friend,
Edwin Henry Keen[32]

Letter 61: July 9, 1896, Joseph S. Cotter to PLD

To Paul Laurence Dunbar
Louisville, KY
July 9, 1896[33]

Mr. Paul L. Dunbar
Dear Friend:

Mr. W.D. Howells has done you a great and just favor. Profit by it. You and Gov. McKinley are close together in Harpers.[34] Do you see the point? If he is made President, please get your friends to speak for you. It may bring you a position in Washington worth $1000 or $2000 a year.[35]

If you can get some New York House to bring out your book[36] a little fortune will be yours.

By all means arrange and give some readings in New England.

If Howells hears you read he will say some things that will mean thousands in your pocket. Don't wait on invitations. Go to New York and be your own manager.[37] Howells, in his article says you are unknown to him. When Mr. Hawkins, of the Courier Journal[38] read this, he wrote to him, speaking in the highest tones of you and your work. Now, he doubtless said something about your reading. If so, Howells will be anxious to hear you. Why not make him a visit and recite "The Party," "An Antebellum Sermon," and "Whistling Sam." "Whistling Sam" will carry New England. Don't forget the piece when the boy returns from college and so disgusts his mother.[39]

You now hold the key to your future success. Neither lose it, nor let it rust in your hands. If you can carry this point with Howells your audience will be the whole of New England. Messrs. Walker and MacPherson[40] are proud of your good fortune and both send congratulations. They want to buy the book. If you send me about two copies, I will deliver them and return the money.

Prof. McKinley has been a little slow about paying for your book I let him have. But I don't think it will last.

All send regards to you and your mother.

Respectfully,
Joseph S[41]

Letter 62: July 13, 1896, PLD to William D. Howells
2306 Magazine
Dayton Ohio
7/13-1896[42]

Dear Mr. Howells:

I have seen your article[43] in Harpers and felt its effect. That I have not written you sooner is neither the result of willful neglect or lack of gratitude. It has taken time for me to recover from the shock of delightful surprise. My emotions have been too much for me. I could not thank you without "gushing" and I did not want to "gush."

Now from the very depths of my heart I want to thank you.[44] You yourself do not know what you have done for me. I feel much as a poor, insignificant, helpless boy would feel to suddenly find himself knighted. I can tell you nothing about myself because there is nothing to tell. My whole life has been simple, obscure and uneventful. I have written my little pieces and sometimes recited them, but it seemed hardly by my volition.

The kindly praise that you have accorded me will be an incentive to more careful work. My greatest fear is that you may have been more kind to me than just.[45]

I have written to thank Mr. Herne for putting the book into your hands. I have only seen the man on the stage, but have laughed and cried with him until I love him. Again thanking you, Mr. Howells, for your more than kindness,

I am Sincerely Yours,
Paul Laurence Dunbar

Letter 63: July 31, 1896, PLD to Booker T. Washington
Dayton Ohio, July 31st 1896[46]

Dear Sir:

Yours of late date received with great pleasure. I thank you for your words of encouragement and congratulation. I think that you for one can thoroughly understand what all this means to me after a long and hard fight. I have gotten nothing without working for it and have contested every bit of the ground over which I have passed.

With Best wishes, I am Sincerely Yours,

Paul Laurence Dunbar

Letter 64: August 21, 1896, PLD to William D. Howells

August 21, 1896[47]

Dear Mr. Howells:

This note should have been written yesterday when I returned your coat[48] by the National Express. Let me thank you again for your kindness, although the circumstances brought to my mind the old fable of the ass in the lion's skin.[49]

Not withstanding all my precautions, I have taken cold. I hope that you are more fortunate and that this note will find both you and your family well.

With warmest regards,

I am Sincerely Yours,

Paul Dunbar

Letter 65: August 23, 1896, William D. Howells to PLD

Far Rockaway, L.I.

August 23, 1896[50]

Dear Mr. Dunbar:

The coat came back safely and promptly;[51] but I am sorry to learn that it did not save you from taking cold. May it cover, hereafter, as good and gifted a man as when you wore it.

We were all greatly pleased to meet you and make your acquaintance, and we shall watch your fortunes with the cordial interest of friends.[52]

Yours sincerely,

W. D. Howells[53]

Letter 66: August 25, 1896, PLD to Matilda Dunbar

James B Pond[54]

Everett House

~~New York~~

Marguerite Pier,

Aug. 25th 1896[55]

Dear Mother:

Your letter received this morning and all I can say is that I wish you would not worry as you do when I am doing for the best. If it had been best for me to come home I would have been home now.

It is the best thing that could have happened that Mr. Thatcher came here.[56] I am to give a reading[57] Thursday night in the parlors of the big house and we expect to clear about fifty dollars. He says a hundred but that is hard to believe. The very wealthy people seem much interested in me and are willing to pay fifty cents admission. I am not very wealthy yet, but I enclose you two dollars which will help you some. I cannot promise when I will be home, but [I will be] just as soon as possible, so don't let it startle you to see me walk in any time as I may not have time to write you when I am coming. I may [illegible] though if it won't [illegible] you. As things turn out as well as I hope for I shall send you to Chicago as soon as I can come. I am [illegible] very busy here giving recitals to introduce myself before the one grand recital of Thursday.[58] I recited yesterday for Mrs. Jefferson Davis[59] and she was delightful. The southern people have eaten me up wonderfully. One of them took the books, another two, & another wants five. I have order [*sic*] 200 books to be here by Thursday.

I am getting on well so don't worry.

Your affectionate son,

Paul

Letter 67: August 26, 1896, PLD to Matilda Dunbar

James B Pond

Everett House

~~New York~~

Marguerite Pier, Aug. 26th 1896[60]

Dear mother:

I win; My book is to be republished.[61] I am to receive $200 at once and a royalty of fifteen percent on the first 10,000.[62] How is this for high? Will be home soon. All continues to go well and I hope soon to get a start at last.

Keep up heart, the night has been long but the day is dawning.

No more at the present.

Your loving son,

Paul

Letter 68: September 19, 1896, PLD to William D. Howells

Paul Laurence Dunbar
Everett House, NY
C/O Major Pond
Dayton Ohio, Sept. 19th 1896[63]

Mr. W. D. Howells,
My Dear Sir:

As you see, my home holds me once more, but I have brought with me many pleasant memories of New York and the kindness I received there.[64] There are many people whom I have to thank for favors shown and none more than yourself.[65] Not the least source of my gratitude, by any means, is your excellent introduction to my new book. It was no little thing for you to introduce a book of verse by an obscure black writer and I believe that I fully appreciate the nobility of your act.[66]

You may be pleased to know that my affairs have very materially changed for the better, and entirely through your agency.[67]

Thanking you again and with regards to yourself and family,

I am Sincerely Yours,
Paul Dunbar

Letter 69: September 22, 1896, James B. Pond to PLD

James B. Pond
Everett House
318 Fourth Avenue, New York
Sept. 22nd [1896][68]

Dear Dunbar,

Sunday's *Journal* has a full page with your portrait.[69] It is excellent.

Mr. Dodd and I lunched together last Wednesday. He called to know if I would suggest anything to give the 4th coming book[70] a boom.

I am not using your books.[71] If you want them all sent to you I certainly have no objections & never had. I was under the impression that you gave Mr. Dodd—on his suggestion—to [illegible] that they would not be sent out. I sent one to Stanley and one to Sir Edwin Annabel & asked them to write you a review for their Lancaster papers.[72] You know just what I read & for what purpose. Certainly I did not use them with a [illegible] to my own acknowledgment. My purpose has been to get you before the Jubilee[73] for our mutual interest. If you think me capable of any other [illegible] it seems to me that now is about time to close up our engagement.

Mr. Edwins[74] too has a stake in my offer + is working his own business. Shall I send your books to Dayton?

Yours sincerely,

J. B. Pond

Letter 70: October 22, 1896, PLD to Helen Douglass
Washington, D.C., Oct. 22 '96[75]

Mrs. Helen Douglass,[76]

Your note of recent date has been duly received and its contents noted with surprise.

Let me say that I did not forget Mr. Douglass,[77] and that my actions will prove that I have not revered his memory less than those who have been more ostentatious in their display of loyalty. There were these considerations that kept me from giving the Douglass poem[78] the other night. First, a rather rare talent called good taste which prevents one from giving a memorial for the dead at a public entertainment of such a nature. People of good taste do not wear their hearts upon their sleeves or drag their respect on most saved emotions before the sway of the public gaze. The second consideration was my sense of the eternal falseness of things. The third a reverence for the mourning of my dear friend that would not let me drag his name into a surely commercial enterprise. My Douglass poem was a work of love, not an article of the office. I have no inclination to profit by the death of that great man.[79]

As to your remarks about my dialect, I have nothing to say save that I am sorry to find amazing intelligent people those who are unable to differentiate dialect as a philological branch from the burlesque of negro minstrelsy.[80]

I thank you for your congratulations.[81] Hopeful as I may have been I could not expect that everyone would have been satisfied; but since you admit that everyone in the house except yourself would have called the entertainment a success, I feel that the majority is as large that I shall be content with it, and not reform its good opinions.

With sincere gratitude for the thoughts you have aroused in my mind.

I am,

Very kindly yours,

Paul Laurence Dunbar

LETTERS FROM 1897

Letter 71: January 17, 1897, Charles Thatcher to PLD
Law Offices of Hurd, Brumback, & Thatcher,
Gardner Building
Toledo, Ohio Jan. 17, 1897[82]

Paul Dunbar, Esq.,
3003 Dearborn St. Chicago, Ill.
Dear Sir:

Enclosed find a statement of the receipts and expenditures of your recital, expect the following,—Dr. Tobey tells me that he has $5 collected from Mr. Detwiler, which would show a total profit to you of $21.31 instead of $16.31. He also tells me that he paid you direct the sum of $2.50 received from Mr. Wharton, and $4.50 received by the Doctor[83] himself; in all $7. The Doctor and I were also obliged to spend $2.40 for long distance telephoning to South Bend, so that there is now in my hands $16.31 less $7 which you have already received and $2.40 telephoning which leaves a balance due you of $16.31 less $9.40 or $6.91. I will let the Doctor hand me the $5 received from Detwiler, which will make in all $11.91.

Have also called upon Mr. St John, manager of the Auditorium to refund a part of the receipts which he has kept. He has taken out $40, whereas our understanding of it was that he was to share equally with you and not charge $40 for the hall unless the receipts would justify it. He claims that Mr. Fallis is now sick, so that he cannot adjust the matter at present.

Do you wish me to send you a check for the balance in my hands, or shall I credit it to you on the $15 which you borrowed from me on Nov. 5, 1896? I gave Col Smith Russell[84] the last copy of "Oak and Ivy" and "Majors and Minors" which I had. You promised to send me duplicate copies.[85] Will you please do this, as I fear that since the edition is exhausted I will not be able to get copies? You may also send me two copies of "Lyrics of Lowly Life"[86] if there will be any profit in it to you. I can buy it at the book stores at $1 per volume, but prefer giving you the profit.

Am sorry if you have cancelled the engagement at Delaware, as I had considerable trouble in making the engagement and would not like to disappoint the people. If you want to stop at Toledo the Y.M.C.A. has expressed a willingness to pay you $25 for a recital to be given to their members only. They would probably, however, give out free tickets to their friends, and make no charge at the door.

Very truly yours,
C. A. Thatcher

Letter 72: January 25, 1897, PLD to unknown recipient
Dayton, O
January 25th, 1897[87]

[illegible addressee]

Herewith, I send the correct lines, which I wrote to you.

I have rewritten things not because I thought you cared to see them but out of justice to myself.

After receiving carefully your action in making of my miserable and most deplorable mistake public property, I am in some doubt as to whom an apology is due, whether to myself or you. But I am hoping that you will explain my case to the young ladies to all of whom you made well known my blunder and before whom you placed me in false light. If I cannot entreat you to do this let your sense of justice compel you.[88]

As I have before said and I hardly know the case you request: a fakehood. No one saw or knew anything about that poem except Arthur Nixon,[89] until you showed it to [illegible]. You asked everyone if they knew anything about it in such a suspicious manner, that they were inclined to affect a knowledge & which they did not possess, in order to draw you on to tell which you know, and they were in the majority of cases successful. I have not been so foolish as to expose my own blunder by putting that poem on exhibition, but if you desire it, you have to only say the word and I will go to any extreme to please you, even to nailing it to a public wall for public inspection.

In your action in making a request of an almost total stranger to you, I have little more to say than that it was an [illegible] liberty,[90] and I cannot but regret that I did not [illegible] this on over sooner, indeed before I thought of writing any "poem." Then there could have been no chance for a "mixture" and the consequent arrogance which it has caused both of us.

I hope you will not be offended if I have tried to be very frank and plain with you and it is my earnest hope that you will feel as much pleasure in showing this letter to your confidential friends, i.e. the whole first and second year classes, as you felt in showing the others.

Yours,
In equal indignation,
Paul L. Dunbar

Letter 73: February 4, 1897, WDH to David Douglas
New York, Feb. 4, 1897[91]

My dear Mr. Douglas:[92]

Allow me to present my friend, Mr. Paul Dunbar, the first of his race to put his race into poetry.[93] I hope he will show you his book, and let it say for his worth the things he is too modest to say for himself.

Yours sincerely
W. D. Howells

Letter 74: February 10, 1897, PLD to Matilda Dunbar
At Sea—Wednesday, Feb, 10-97[94]
Fifth day out[95]
Steamship Ambrosia

My Dear Mother:

This is the first day I have felt equal to the task of working very much. I have not been throwing up much but I have gotten sick after meals and had to lie down for a good deal. So far the voyage has been pretty rough but in no wise dangerous, for our vessel is a magnificent great big ship and a fast sailor. We have already passed three ships, two French and one Spanish. I am feeling in pretty good form just now and hope to continue so. Everything has opened up auspiciously. I have a [illegible] trunk and Maj. Pond has gotten me an elegant warm overcoat. My comfort is all that you or I could ask. I think of you every day and often long to be with the family, but I cannot but feel that this trip is for the best. All [illegible] books [illegible] and Mr. Howells is to send me letters when I can get an English publisher for my book as I have the right to sell it again.[96] This will mean much even if I do something by my readings.[97] I hope you are well and happy and everything is agreeable with you. I will send something as soon as I get to work. I should like to see all of the family very much but you must keep me posted on all that happens. You will be surprised to hear that Alice Ruth Moore[98] ran off from Boston and came to New York to see me off. The half has not been told. She is the brightest and sweetest little girl I ever saw and she took everything by storm. She was very much ashamed of having run off, but she said that she could not have me gone for a year without ever seeing me. Now don't laugh, but Alice and I are engaged. You know it is what I have longed for, for a year. I know that you won't object to this.

I hope to mail this letter from [illegible] or at the latest from Liverpool.[99] Let me hear from you as soon as you get this as I shall be lonesome for a while anyhow. Take care of yourself. With love to all, I am,

Sincerely, your loving son,

Paul Laurence Dunbar

Recited on the boat this (Thursday) night for Mrs. Pond and M. Pond, and Mr. Edwards, the play wright. [illegible] it, [illegible]?

Letter 75: February 28, 1897, PLD to Matilda Dunbar
London, W.C. 28th Feb 1897[100]

My Dear Mother:

While I know it has not been long since you received my first letters I will start this one now for it will take some time to reach you. I am finally getting somewhat settled here.[101] The people all seem nice to me and we feel that our undertaking is going to be a success. It appears that I am the most interviewed man in London.[102] The best papers having sent reporters to me.[103] But the crowning of it all is that you do not know whom I met on the street Saturday and at whose house I spent yesterday, last night, and all of today.[104] If I were there, I should make you guess, but I shall have to tell you. It was no other than our old friend Dip[105] or in other words the Hon. Henry F. Downing,[106] looking like a prince, married to a white person and living at ease. He wants me to come and live with them, and I don't know but I shall.[107] His wife is charming and exceedingly well educated, and [illegible] says, she has money.[108]

Letter 76: March 15, 1897, PLD to unknown
London, W.C., 15th March '97[109]

My Dear Sir:[110]

As usual, preoccupation and a positively lazy mood compelled me to let your letters go too long unanswered. But since reaching here my mind has been so busy taking in new sights and experiences that it found little time for other efforts.

I thank you for Mr. Allen's[111] note and shall be pleased to keep it. I am so glad also that you too can see and appreciate the utter hollowness of the most of American book criticism.[112] It makes me smile and it makes me sneer. (I write the last word with some misgiving lest you should think, with good reason, it was swear).

One critic says a good thing and the rest hasten to say the same thing, in many instances using the identical words. I see now very clearly that Mr. Howells has done me an irrevocable harm in the dictum he laid down regarding my dialect verse. I am afraid that it will influence English criticism, although what notices I have had here have shown a different trend. You will be pleased to know that I have placed my book with Messrs. Chapman and Hall[113] who will soon publish it. But the returns from it here will be small unless it sells largely. At present I do not feel very sanguine of a reading success here though I have had the most excellent notices from the press and the Savage Club[114] has dined me with much enthusiasm. I am not tired of writing, but I am tired of trying to sell, and running about acting as a curiosity.[115] But enough of my griefs.

I know that you are acquainted with London and so there is nothing I can tell you about this great dingy hive. One thing, I can work here, because the constant gloom and frequent rains well accord with my mood. Away up in my high room, where my manager[116] has seen fit to place me, with a glimpse of gray sky and grimy back walls,—a prospect no brighter than my own,—I know how Thomas Chatterton[117] felt and feel as he did, only less brave and decisive.

Letter 77: April 21, 1897, William Kitching to PLD
Clevedon[118]
4, 21/TH 1897[119]

My dear Friend
Paul Laurence Dunbar,

Though we only met yesterday for the first time yet I seem to have to know you to some extent from our conversation: your attendance of our meeting for worship and your interesting recitations. I have put together a few pieces of my own composition that I think may interest you, and I shall be glad of any friendly criticism you may be able to make.

None of these pieces are contained in my little book entitled "Verses for my Friends"[120] except a few stanzas from a piece on "The Opium Burns in Asia." These are an incomplete fragment but were printed thus in a local newspaper when a lecture was given on the subject.

Did you finish the lines you began and recited to me about the silence in the meeting for worship? If so, I should be very glad of a copy & a few lines after reading some of the pieces I send. I have a great many more on a variety of subjects.

Perhaps you may like to have a copy of one I wrote on [illegible] while travelling to Glastonbury: it is entitled "Keeping in Jonah with the Maker."[121] Let us endeavor to live in this attitude? "a bridge under the shadow of the Almighty" (Ps. XCI.1).[122]

With every good wish for your future happiness and [illegible].

Your friend,
W. Kitching[123]

Letter 78: April 26, 1897, PLD to William D. Howells

3 Northumberlun [sic] Ave—
Trafalgar Sq.
London W.
Lane's Agency
26th April 1897[124]

Dear Mr. Howells:

I have been long promising myself the pleasure of writing to you. But I have forbore for lack of something really interesting to say, nor even now is this disability removed.[125]

As you possibly know Mr. Lane was in America when I reached England and did not return for nearly a month. I have not been to Edinburgh and hence have not had a chance to present your letter to Mr. Douglas. However I thank you sincerely for them both. Messrs. Chapman and Hall are to bring out my book.[126]

In the matter of reading here, I have done very little. The season was not open when we arrived here and little was to be done except in clubs and at hotel smoking concerts a sort of work which I despised. I was put in upon programs between dancing girls from the vaudeville and clowns from the varieties. At one place I went on at midnight when half or three fourths of the men were *drunk*. Miss Pond[127] cooly [sic] informed me that in such cases as this I was to *tell vulgar stories!* She has treated me in the most brutal and dishonest way.[128] Mr. Dodd kindly came to my rescue when he was here and deposited sufficient funds for my fare home. I tried to get redress from my manager by threatening to leave, but she disciplined me by going away to Paris and leaving my board bill unpaid.[129] She has scrupled at nothing to repress and annoy me, but I shall not come home without accomplishing something to keep from being marked a "failure."[130]

The Savage Club[131] entertained me at dinner and gave my work a most enthusiastic reception.[132] I shall recite next Sunday evening for Mr. Moncure D. Conway,[133] who in conversation with me the other day spoke very feelingly and affectionately of you.

Although I distrust my ability very much, I am hard at work upon a novel[134] and have made some progress with it. The press here has been uniformly kind to me, but I am wondering what they will say about my book, they are so conservative here.[135] Mr. Oswald Crawford[136] [*sic*], however, thinks very well of the work and hopes great things for it. If I once get really started in the literary line, no more readings for me—forever. I have had my fill of readings and managers. If I can make my living by my pen I will not use my voice. This will be hard I know but I have not entirely lost heart.

I hope that you and your family are well and that when you have leisure you will write to me.

Thanking you for many favors,

I am Sincerely Yours,
Paul Laurence Dunbar.

Letter 79: May 31, 1897, Edwin Keen to PLD

Birkdale,
Kidderpore Avenue,
Hampstead N.W.
May 31, 97[137]

My Dear Sir:

I am so glad to get your note—send me some tickets—I will come and bring some friends on June 5th—send me some of your programmes that I may distribute them.[138]

With regards,
In haste,
Yours truly,
Edwin H Keen

Letter 80: June 28, 1897, Unknown to PLD
Ivy Cottage
Gordon Road
Woodford
June. 28th. 97[139]

Dear Mr. Dunbar,

Your last letter until now remains unanswered. Pray, excuse me. I have just completed a Jubilee[140] week, which for engagement & pressure of business would make even some of you "go ahead" Americans "sick up."

And as I am parting thus, I borrowed the "Chronicle" to see a review of your book.[141] I have properly refrained from reading anything until I could give my own impressions. I have not done so as yet for lack of time. I was indeed sorry to hear of your loss. Yes, assuredly, I should advertise for the missing MSS.[142] I am not so fertile in ideas that I can afford to write without taking a copy.

I sincerely hope that before we meet, you will have found it. Now as to the meeting: you require some days notice. On Saturday week. IE July 10 I am free at noon & I shall be free all day on Sunday—on this day (Sunday) I should wish you to spend with me quietly in Woodford. I was thinking that we might also "[illegible]" as the Scotch would say in the Saturday presses?[143]

Anyhow, write & let me know with our united kind regards.

I am yours,

Very sincerely,[144]

[illegible]

Perhaps you could spend an evening with me, even before this. Let me know.

Letter 81: July 20, 1897, PLD to Matilda Dunbar
Street, Somerset (England)[145]
July 20, 1897[146]

Dear Mother:

While I am not very well in health all goes well with me. I have caught a cold and it has settled in my throat to some extent.[147]

I expect to sail for home one week from next Saturday.[148] I have been truly blessed with friends who are wonderfully kind to me.[149] It is an old house where I am staying with magnificent leaves and flowers and fields as far as I can see which belong to the [illegible] ladies who are entertaining me.

They are friends of Quakers and today I have been to a meeting with them, sitting in the silence.

I am the guest today of Mrs. Helen Bright Clark,[150] the daughter of the famous old John Bright.[151] They have alas a handsome home in Midfield by Somerset and are very kind to me. I shall possibly write tonight if I am well enough.

I have just received a letter from Col. Robert Ingersoll, which I copy for you. He says:

> My Dear Dunbar, the other day John Russell Young[152] was appointed librarian at Washington.[153] I know Mr. Young well and it may be that I could induce him to give you a place.[154] I will try. It seems to me that the President[155] would like to recognize your ability in some way. I will see if the library fails—what can be done in that direction. Do not become disheartened. You have already succeeded.[156] Be true to yourself—you have genius and that is enough. Better x and x with genius than x and x without. Be true to the "universal light." I met with Mr. Young today (July 5th) hoping that you are well and hopeful, I remain yours always,
> R. G. Ingersoll.

This letter is good but don't hope too much from it. We have been disappointed as often.[157] But position or no position, I hope some to prevail on Alice to set the day—one not too far in the future. I know that you will love the dear little girl as I do when you know her.[158] My books that you ask about are very beautiful and have picked up in sales now that the jubilee is over.[159] I hope that you and the family are well and that Rob and Will[160] are both at work. Tell Will that I would have written him again, but it takes him so long to answer and I would have been home before he made up his mind. The baby's picture is greatly admired here and especially today at the Bright-Clarke table. You will have time to send me another letter before I am in New York where my address will be with Dodd, Mead & Co.,[161] 149–51, Fifth Ave.

Love to all.

Your Devoted Son,

Paul L. Dunbar

Letter 82: August 7, 1897, PLD to Fisher
New York, 8/7/1897[162]

My Dear Dr. F:[163]

I am still in the "impression" business for the sake of my financial health and the satisfaction of the yellow journals.[164]

I am much better than when I visited you Sunday but am standing the heat very poorly as I have little or no strength.

This rush for London impressions seems to me a very disgusting thing[165] and I am only sorry that I am not in a position to resist the demands made upon me. A golden eagle[166] is a great corrector of the artistic sense.

I have been to order Fitzgerald's "Omar Khayyam,"[167] but did not succeed in getting it. Have also just purchased "The Damnation of Theron Ware,"[168] which my novel is said to very closely resemble. Have not yet however had the time to dip into it. That and D'Annunzio's "Triumph of Death"[169] will be my next reading. Have you read the latter? It is beastly, almost, but wonderfully striking. It is decadent and that of course spells sale.

When one is just over the first flush of youthful dreaming, how sordid and cynical and commercial we grow.[170] It reminds me of a very devilish devil, consciously contemplating: "what a devil of a devil I am!" But I think it is the condition of the atmosphere that has made me think about devils;[171] perhaps over in Jersey your thoughts are soaring. Mine are not.

Letter 83: November 25, 1897, DKB to the editor of the *Tribune*
Nov. 25th, 1897[172]

To the Editor of the Tribune,[173]

Sir; I am a daily reader of the Tribune and am greatly interested in the Sunshine society.[174] Will you allow me to correct a statement which appeared in your issue of Nov 21st[175] regarding the poet, Paul Laurence Dunbar?

Mr. Dunbar is the colored poet, who has sprung so prominently into fame during the last six months in this country and in London, but he is not blind.[176]

Knowing Mr. Dunbar to be employed in the new Library of Congress,[177] and arming myself with a copy of the Tribune, I decided upon finding the rising young poet, with whose poems of "Lowly Life,"[178] I was already familiar. Climbing four short flights of stairs in the north stack of the library, I found my poet, seated humbly at a desk, busily engaged on some special work in connection with his present position. As I approached he arose and with a kindly greeting offered me his chair, the only one, I saw on that deck. I explained my errand, I desire to correct the general publish of his blindness. "Strange," he said, "an old chum of mine, in New Jersey,[179] has just sent me the same copy of the tribune. I cannot account for such a mistake. But I should be greatly pleased if you take the trouble to write the Tribune." Whereupon, he proceeded to give me a brief outline of the origin of the poem. "Last year," said he, "while in Toledo, Ohio, I consented to recite at an entertainment given for the Insane. Before the recital, I requested the organist to play for me, Cardinal Newman's favorite hymn, "Lead Kindly Light."[180] The music and words rushed through my brain in so maddening a way, blinding me to all outside influences, surging through my soul until I could stand it no longer. I rushed off to my room, jotted down the very words of this poem, 'Lead Gently.'[181]

"When I returned to the recital to take the place assigned me on the program, I brought with me, my newly fledged poem and read it before the audience. Last summer while in London I forwarded it to the New York Independent where it was published for the first time." This short history was told by Mr. Dunbar, in a simple, unaffected way. This sincere speech, aided by a very musical voice and the entire absence of pose or pretention on his part, stamped him, to my mind as the true poet and lover of his art. Very recently, in the new Library of Congress, in the department which, that human and able librarian, Mr. John Russell Young,[182] has set aside for the use of the blind, Mr. Dunbar read and also intoned or chanted some of his poems. These were deeply enjoyed by his audience.

Poets are messengers from heaven, who bring solace to the weary-hearted and the grieved. Mr. Dunbar has a beautiful mission before him, to bring the inward and spiritual light to those who have been so long in darkness. "Lead Gently" will live long in the hearts of all true lovers of poetry.

Sincerely yours,

D.K.B.[183]

Washington, D.C.

3

Dunbar as an Established Author, 1898–1901

THE LAST QUARTER OF 1897 was emotionally trying on many levels for Dunbar, personally and professionally, though his literary letters do not express this reality. As he rose in fame and earned literary prestige and renown, Dunbar battled exhaustion and alcohol addiction. On October 29, 1897, Dunbar wrote Alice that he had been asked to be a "professor of Literature, Rhetoric, and Elocution" at Claflin University, though he expressed to Alice that he was uninterested in the position (Metcalf, "Letters of Paul and Alice Dunbar," 230). Then, in early December, Dunbar wrote Alice that *Lippincott's* had agreed to publish *The Uncalled* for a sum of $750. On December 14, Dunbar wrote Alice that he was feeling "greatly depressed . . . [and] very tired physically & mentally and spiritually" (284), though he was unable to pinpoint the cause. He even confided to her that though he had a "success[ful] reading" the night before, "it did not elate [him]" (284). Yet Dunbar persevered and finally felt in 1898 that he could officially resign from his position in Washington, DC, and "live by his pen" as a professional writer. This was a welcome change for Dunbar, whose health was slowly declining from tuberculosis and alcohol abuse.

In the interim between these high points, Dunbar's alcoholism made a public scandal in Philadelphia. In another drunken bout, this time in New York between November 16 and 19, 1897, Dunbar infamously assaulted and raped Alice, an act he expressed great remorse over. He wrote her on November 19, 1897, "I know that I have done wrong, very wrong. My course has been weak and brutal. I have dishonored you and I cannot forgive myself for it" (Metcalf, "Letters of Paul and Alice Dunbar," 242). He wrote he had been feeling "greatly depressed since [his] return from New York" and that he had "grieved for [his] escapades there" (243). Dunbar also noted he felt he "deserve[d] to suffer" and referred to himself as a "maudlin, reeling drunken libertine." Dunbar's shame seems to have been genuine, and he clearly did not want alcohol to come between him and Alice, though it would, ultimately leading to their final separation. He wrote her that he had "tried to compromise with love and share her dominion with liquor" but decided "from now on, there must be no compromise." He even went so far as to pledge sobriety to her: "When I feel like taking a drink, I will sit

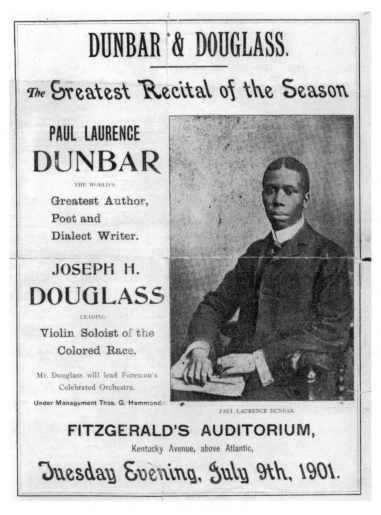

FIGURE 4. Paul Laurence Dunbar and Joseph H. Douglass recital announcement, ca. 1901. Fitzgerald's Auditorium, Atlantic City, New Jersey. Courtesy of Ohio Historical Connection.

down and write to you first, and maybe the thought of the best little woman in the word will make me strong" (244–45). Once he understood the depth of what he did to Alice, on November 22, 1897, he swore to her, "I will never drink again, so help me God!" (251).

It took Alice some time to forgive Dunbar, and despite his pledges and efforts, he never permanently stopped drinking. To top off his "damned night of folly," Dunbar explained that he had contracted gonorrhea from having sexual relations with another woman the same night, before he was with Alice. He wrote that he was "suffering bodily now but from nothing so serious that ordinary treatment may not be expected to effect a cure" (Metcalf "Letters of Paul and Alice Dunbar," 262). From Alice's reaction and need for treatments discussed over many letters, it is likely he also transmitted the disease to her. Treatments for gonorrhea at this time included urethral mercury injections, silver nitrate, and herbal mixes. By December 2, 1897, Dunbar wrote Alice that he had "only a little medicine and [had] grown worse" (266). On December 12, 1897, Dunbar claimed that his guilt at having hurt Alice so much was clouding his attempts at being a professional writer: "Success seems just within my grasp, but it means nothing to me." But he also mentioned that "I must go to Wilmington tonight to play the buffoon for a lot of grinning Negroes whom I hate" (284).

Although Dunbar was now more successful than he had been at any point before and was writing full-time, the publishing process remained a challenge. Regardless of his talents, goals, and ideas, Dunbar was never really in a position to control which of his works were selected to print. Gossie Hudson, one of Dunbar's biographers, points out that "interested as Dunbar was in sales, he usually published writings which could bring quick profits" ("Biography," 16–17). And the requests were all too often for the popular genre of dialect.

On August 1, 1900, a *Truth* editor solicited poetry from Dunbar but stated clearly that the magazine "would like best to have your characteristic dialect work." The very same editor also explained, "The poem you sent last, and which I return to you with this is too fine for *Truth*—I don't believe the average *Truth* reader would appreciate its beauty—and I know you can give me something more suited to our readers." The editor clearly did not want the Standard English verse Dunbar had sent. Indeed, despite the seeming compliment about the "fine" poem, Dunbar's letters reveal his frustration at such responses: "I am so tired of dialect. I send out graceful little poems, suited for any of the magazines but they are returned to me by editors who say, 'We would be very glad to have a dialect poem, Mr. Dunbar, but we do not care for the language compositions" (quoted in Wiggins 109). Dunbar plodded on, writing fervently, publishing as often as he could. This tactic worked, and he gained popularity and fame.

Though Dunbar strove to portray African Americans through the genre of local color, it took quite some time for him to become recognized in this area. Earlier, he had published four urban local color dialect stories in the *New York Journal and Advertiser* from September 26 to October 17, 1897. "Buss Jenkins Up Nawth: A Human Nature Sketch of Real Darkey Life in New York" appeared in September, while "Yellowjack's Game of Craps: A Character Sketch of Real Darkey Life in New York," "How George Johnson 'Won Out': A Character Sketch of Real Darkey Life in New York," and "The Hoodooing of Mr. Bill Simms: A Darkey Dialect Story" made their debut in October. The use of local color to depict setting, however, can best be seen in "Mr. Cornelius Johnson, Office-Seeker," which originally appeared in *Cosmopolitan* in 1899. However, it was not until 1901 that periodicals really began requesting local color fiction from Dunbar.

Commissioned by *Lippincott's Monthly Magazine*, Dunbar was asked to write five local color short stories; this series became known as the Ohio Pastorals, and it ran monthly from August to December. Rather than focus on specifics of dialect language, these stories center around an Ohio village and feature characters that Dunbar had included in other works he had previously published in *Lippincott's*. The first two narratives focus on two friends in a small Ohio town who grapple with the politics of marriage, powerful women, male individualism, and provincialism. "The White Counterpane," the third segment of Dunbar's Ohio Pastoral series, depicts a mother who in many ways resembles Matilda. The fourth story deals with generational conflict between older and younger townsfolk over whether to purchase an organ to modernize hymnal accompaniments for church service. The concluding fifth tale concentrates on the disagreement of two grandmothers over how to care for their grandchild, who eventually dies of an illness. Several protagonists make cameo appearances in these five stories, creating a sense of narrative continuity despite the serial format. The local color tradition was and is foundational to literary realism and naturalism with its focus on the beauty of nature as well as its limitations. Through these stories, Dunbar took his place among other well-known regional writers such as Mark Twain, Mary Wilkins Freeman, Sarah Orne Jewett, Charles W. Chesnutt, and others.

As an established author, Dunbar began writing and publishing in many other genres as well and was able to establish cordial, warm relationships with editors and publishers. He also began working with Paul R. Reynolds, credited with being the first full-time professional literary agent in the United States, in order to publish more widely and market his dramatic works. He traveled throughout the eastern and western United States and gave recitals regularly. These relationships and literary successes certainly show that Dunbar had come a long way from his days as an elevator operator; more importantly, however, these literary letters unveil the substantial efforts the author made to get there. Undoubtedly, a certain optimism permeates the letters during these years.

LETTERS FROM 1898

Letter 84: January 12, 1898, O. J. Bard to PLD
O. J. BARD,
Lawyer
Dayton, Ohio. Jany. 12, 1898[1]

Paul L. Dunbar, Washington, D.C.
Dear Sir:

Judge Dustin[2] handed me your letter and asked me to look after the matters mentioned by you. Will you please forward your contract with Sampson,[3] together with any receipts you may have from him and I will try to make some disposition of the matter at once,

Yours very respectfully,
O. J. Bard[4]

Letter 85: February 17, 1898, PLD to A. S. Lanahan
To Mrs. A. S. Lanahan[5]
Library of Congress Washington, D.C.
2-17-98

Dear Madam:

Your letter of recent date is at hand. In answer I must say that my life has been so uneventful that there is little in it to interest anyone.

I was born at Dayton, Ohio twenty-five years ago. Attended the common schools there and was graduated from the high school. This constituted my "education."

My parents and grandparents had been slaves in Kentucky. My great-grand parents on the eastern shore of Maryland.

I began writing early, when about 12, but published nothing until I was 14.[6] Then the fever took me and I wrote ream upon ream of positive trash when I should have been studying Euclid.[7] Plays, verses, stories, everything I could think or dream turned out. Fortunately, I seldom tried to publish.[8]

My school life was pleasant. I was the only Negro in my class and apparently popular. My chums encouraged me. My teachers encouraged me. Then the boys made me president of the school society, the Philomathean[9]—after that editor in chief of the school [paper].

I set earnestly to work to live up to these honors and succeeded in bringing out the paper a month late every time,[10] but agreed with such editorials as are still pointed to as marvels of schoolboy—well—audacity.[11]

I laugh at these things now but as I look back upon them, I have a fancy that they must have been very serious to me then and done much to mold my life.

After graduation, there was nothing for me to do save to go into menial employment as other Negroes did. I took the nearest thing—an elevator. A better thing could not have happened. In the nearly two years which, altogether, I spent in the place, I improved the leisure between trips in studying and writing. While working here I brought out my first book "Oak and Ivy" which was privately printed and sold well in a circumscribed plane.

Then people began to think I read well and I took engagements for recitals from my own work. While engaged thus, a copy of my second book fell into the hands of James A. Herne[12] who sent it to Mr. Howells. Through whose review, Mr. Gilder of the Century and other editors found that their contributor was a Negro.

I continued reading, published Lyrics of Lowly Life, went to England where in spite of the opposition which British sentiment offered to my having a woman-manager, I had a most enjoyable time.[13] There my book[14] was handsomely republished. And there in the heart of a typical English home among the hills of Somerset, I finished my novel "The Uncalled"[15] which is to appear in the May Lippincott's.[16] A book of short stories mostly of Kentucky life will also appear in March.[17]

I have tried to be as full as possible without being prolix.

Thanking you for your interest,
I am Sincerely Yours
Paul Laurence Dunbar

Letter 86: Undated 1898, PLD to J. N. Matthews
Washington, D.C. ——'98[18]

Dear Doctor[19]

I am almost afraid to write you, but out it must come. I am married![20]

I would have consulted you, but the matter was very quickly done.

People, my wife's parents and others—were doing everything to separate us.[21] She was worried and harassed until she fell ill. So she telegraphed me and I went to New York. We were married Sunday night by the bishop but hope to keep it a secret for a while as she does not wish to give up her school.[22]

Everything is clean and honorable save for the fear of separation there was no compulsion to the step.

I hope you will not think I have been too rash.

Sincerely yours,
Paul L. Dunbar

Letter 87: April 5, 1898, PLD to Charles W. Stoddard
Washington, Apr. 5th 98[23]

Dear Mr. Stoddard,[24]

I want to thank you for your good letter of last week and the book which accompanied it.

I shall be very happy to know you and shall take advantage of your kind invitation to visit you and make your acquaintance.[25]

I shall be pleased to have a time from you when you return from Atlantic City.

Very sincerely yours,
Paul Laurence Dunbar

Letter 88: April 6, 1898, PLD to H. A. Tobey
Washington D.C., April 6, 1898[26]

My Dear Dr. Tobey,

I was very glad to get your letter and find that you did not think ill of my step.[27] I must confess I was very anxious as to how you would take it. As to mother—I told her before it took place—she was in the secret, though not at first willing. All has come around all right now and my wife will be with me on the 18th. My announcement cards will then go out. Mother is quite enthusiastic and my new mother-in-law has yielded and gracefully accepted the situation.[28]

Aren't you saying I had better have got out of debt before taking a wife?[29] Honest, aren't you? Well, see her and know her and I won't need to make any pleas for myself. Her own personality will do that.

Letter 89: May 5, 1898, PLD to Major Pond

Library of Congress[30]

Washington, D.C., May 5th 98. [preprinted] Department

My Dear Major:

I have your very good letter and I thank you for your good wishes.

Kindly bear my regards to Mrs. Pond and your little one. As you know I am in the library[31] here and am also still doing a good deal of writing. My book of short stories[32] is proving a success and my novel[33] published in the May Lippincott's Magazine bids fair to follow its example.

With Regards,

I am as ever

Yours, P. L. Dunbar

Letter 90: May 16, 1898, PLD to Alice Ruth Moore Dunbar

May 16th 1898[34]

Gammon Theological Seminary[35]

My Dear Little Wife,

Here I am all safe and sound and would say happy if you were near me. Booker T[36] arrives tonight and speaks. I just got in in time to hear Dubois' [sic] paper.[37] It was a finely constructed article.

I am being and shall continue to be a very good boy. It's a shame—they want me to stay for the banquet but your lonesome hubby expects to start home Tuesday night by the 11:50 which ought to put me into Washington about 10:10.

I am anxious to see [my] little wife and to be at home again in my own easy nest. I hate [illegible] & people in general, although Dr. Bornan[38] with whom I am stopping is very nice.

Give mother my love. I am going upstairs to lie down on baby's picture. Au revoir—little wife of mine.

Your devoted husband.

Better have Roy[39] take my silk hat to be bleached and don't forget to have my mail for me Wednesday.

Letter 91: June 6, 1898, PLD to Paul R. Reynolds
Washington, D.C., June 6th, 1898[40]
Mr. Paul R. Reynolds,

Dear Sir:
Your letter came to [me] this morning and I am sending herewith a copy of "Folks From Dixie."[41]
I do not know what its chances for [illegible] are as it is all dialect.[42]
I shall reserve the right to reject any or all offers from the other side.

Very truly yours,
Paul L. Dunbar

Letter 92: July 28, 1898, PLD to Horace J. Rollin
Library of Congress
Washington, D.C., July 28, 1898[43]

My Dear Mr. Rollin:[44]
The delay which I have allowed in answering your letter so long ago received, does not denote me truly! It is all false in indicating that I am not greatly interested in your inquiry to the psychic phenomena of race blending.
While so far I have found the observable result of race blending less strong than either of the parent races, yet I can see how the cosmopolite of the future might be the combination of the best in all the divisions of the human family—each race supplying what all the others lacked.
Your letter has made me think, and I am glad to see such a work as yours coming from Ohio which has done too little in the scientific and literary world.
I hope your work will have the success which I really believe its importance deserves.
Thanking you for your good letter and asking your forgiveness for an unavoidable delay in answering, I am

Sincerely yours,
Paul Laurence Dunbar

Letter 93: September 10, 1898, PLD to Paul R. Reynolds
Washington, D.C., 9/10/1898[45]

Dear Mr. Reynolds,

I would advise you of disposing of "The Uncalled" on the terms you mentioned unless it is possible to get the 175.00$ or cash and a 10% royalty. Try so long as no other house publishes the book.[46]

If they will for the reason above, take it as I don't suppose the novel isn't going to set the Thames on fire.[47]

Sincerely yours,
P. L. Dunbar

Letter 94: October 2, 1898, PLD to Dr. F

Washington, D.C., Oct. 2nd, 1898[48]

My Dear Dr. F—:

I am sending you herewith a copy of "The Uncalled," which at last sees the light in book form. Even now, though I have revised and revised it, there are many things about it that I would change if I had the chance.[49]

You spoke in one of your letters about my wife's inspiring one of my poems. She inspired not only that, but is responsible for this whole novel,—a responsibility of doubtful creditability, no doubt.[50]

I still stagnate here among books on medicine and natural science in what I have come to believe the most God-forsaken and unliterary town in America.[51] I hate Washington very cordially and evidently it returns the compliment, for my health is continually poor here.

I am about finishing up the copy for a new volume of verses,[52] after which I shall go to work in real earnest on my novel[53] which will deal with the educated class of my own people. I am in love with literature and wish I could give my whole time to reading and writing, but alas, one must eat, and so I plod along making the thing that is really first in my heart, a secondary matter in life.

I shall be glad to hear from you when you have time.

Letter 95: December 5, 1898, PLD to Rev. D. J. Meese

1934 Fourth St., N.W.
Washington, D.C., Dec. 5, 1898[54]

Rev. D. J. Meese,[55]
Mansfield, O.,
Dear Sir,

I am pleased to be of assistance to your son in his work, but I hardly see how he can fill the time with the facts of my life, they are rather meager. I was born in Dayton, O., June 27, 1872. Attended the public and High Schools there and graduated from the latter in 1891. Went to work in one of the office buildings there as an elevator boy, and while doing this published the first volume of poems, "Oak and Ivy," in 1892. Later, gave readings throughout the northwest from the poems. During the World's Fair, was employed in the Haytien [*sic*] Building. Published the next volume of poems, "Majors and Minors," in 1895, continued to give readings from the poems. Was employed on some of the Chicago newspapers for a while, and had for a brief time editorial charge of the Indianapolis *World*. It was the volume of "Majors and Minors" that attracted Mr. Howells' attention and called forth that much talked of criticism of his. "Lyrics of Lowly Life" was published in New York in 1897[56] and later in the same year, in England.[57] In Feb. 1897 I went to England to read, remained for six months, and returned to take a place in the Congressional Library in this city. In April 1898 "Folks from Dixie" was published, and "The Uncalled." A new book of poems will be out in a few months.[58]

Now if this will be of any assistance to your son, I shall be pleased to have helped him a bit.

Thanking you very much for your interest,

I am,

Yours sincerely,

Paul Laurence Dunbar

Letter 96: December 12, 1898, Samuel M. Jones to PLD

Executive Department
of the City of Toledo, O.
Samuel M. Jones, Mayor[59]
December 12, 1898[60]

Dear Mr. Dunbar,

I must regret that the hoarseness has taken a turn for the worse and I am ordered by the doctor to stay in the house. My feelings plainly indicate that the order is a wise one and I therefore obey. I fully expected to have the pleasure of hearing you this evening[61] but prudence forbids—I hope you will be led to study the social question for you can be a great helper in the work of reform if you once get started. We are at a period in the work corresponding to the time 50 and 60 years ago when the antislavery agitations were denouncing African Slavery—the analogy between that reform and the present social reform is almost forefront. We need and must have a new Emancipation Proclamation. Emancipation from the slavery of our competition system that makes men argue each other as enemies instead of brothers and brings out the very worst in us instead of the best as would be the case if we lived as brethren instead of competitors.[62] I yet hope to hear you sing for the discontented and down trodden civilians black and white as Lance and Whittier[63] sung for the black slums 50 years ago. Wishing for you longest possible field of [illegible] this week.

I am ever faithfully your friend,

S. M. Jones

LETTERS FROM 1899

Letter 97: April 11, 1899, Robert E. Jones to PLD
April 11, 1899[64]

Mr. Paul Laurence Dunbar

Washington, D.C.

My dear Sir:

You will forgive this intrusion and allow me to relate an incident which thrilled my own heart, in which you were the principle character.

A few days ago I was attending the Lexington Annual Conference of the Methodist Episcopal Church[65] which met in Paris, Kentucky. Bishop J.H. Vincent, D.D., LL.D[66] presiding. The Bishop did himself and us the honor to read each morning immediately after devotion, three or four of your poems. Bishop Vincent, who is a leader of the great Chautauqua movement[67] and one of the most scholarly men of the day, said on introducing your poems that they were among the best, and that your dialects equaled those of any man of any age.

Strong resolutions were adopted by the conference expressing their high appreciation of your works, urging every member to purchase them and craving the blessings of God upon you. On the second day, a southern white woman who had heard your poems read the first day, was about to leave when the bishop announced that he would read a few selections from Dunbar. The good lady stopped and said, "I must hear them for they are fine." True merit conquers prejudice. Long live poet Dunbar!

Could you at some time favor your admirers of this city with an engagement, reading from your own writings? If so, say on what terms you would come.

Yours very truly,
Robert E. Jones[68]

Letter 98: June 5, 1899, Frederick H. Means to PLD
Windham, Conn.
June 5th, '99[69]

To Mr. Paul Laurence Dunbar
Washington, D.C.
My Dear Sir:

It gives me great pleasure, as secretary pro tem of the Annual Meeting of the Board of Trustees of Atlanta University, held in Atlanta, May 31st, to inform you of a vote passed by them, which confers upon you the Honorary Degree of "Master of Arts."[70]

The exact vote; as proposed by President Bumstead[71] & passed unanimously, was as follows:

"Voted that the Honorary Degree of Master of Arts be conferred on Mr. Paul Laurence Dunbar, of whom Mr. Wm. D. Howells has said that 'he is the only Negro of pure African extraction[72] to fill the Negro life aesthetically and to express it logically.'"

There was more from the citation from Howells, but as my full record was left in at Atlanta, I can only quote in part.

If you desire to address your acknowledgement, write to Dr. Bumstead, his Northern address is, Rev. Horace Bumstead, D.D., 22 Sawmill St. Roxbury, Mass.

Respectfully yours,
Rev. Fred'k H Means[73]

Letter 99: July 11, 1899, Kountz? to PLD
July 11, 1899[74]

My dear friend:[75]

Your letter was most welcome to us all. I assure you and my [illegible] is to your own and that if your dear girl wife who came to see me so long ago and to all appearances was shamefully [illegible]. I expected to reach you on Tuesday which Mrs. Dunbar expected and had a bundle of the most outrageous [illegible] packed up to take to you.[76] I was frustrated however from going at the very last minute and then clipped on hoping each day to do the next and awakening at last with a twinge at my heart strings to acknowledge that you had of course left for New York.[77]

Please forgive me! I was with you both in spirit if not in flesh and I need not because of you my deepest sympathy. You must brace up! You have a wonderful future before you. People say splendid things of your work. And remember this: up there in the silence so close to God that your name rings from one end of the country to the other and you have even less than charity [illegible].

I plod on. I have done two scraps[78] this morning which I send you in the rough that you may realize the beauty of your own work by comparison. I also send you this week's Literature,[79] hoping your name is in it. Do you have the Outlook and have you read [illegible]? I shall also send you the "Red Raven Sketches"[80] advertisements (the last is a slap at Mrs. Dunbar because she would not let me make fun of your literary tactic).

Write me soon both of you and order me always [illegible].

Your sincere friend,

[no signature]

Letter 100: July 24, 1899, PLD to William D. Howells

Brodhead's Bridge, Ulster Co, N.Y.[81]

July 24th 1899[82]

My Dear Mr. Howells:

I have been wanting to write and thank you for your letter to me and the personal advice it contained. Fortunately, the matter has been adjusted. *Lippincotts* retained the serial rights of the stories and relinquished the book privileges to Messrs. Dodd & Mead.[83] But more than all I want to thank you for coming and climbing away upstairs to inquire for me when I was ill.[84] The act may have meant very little to you, but it meant very much to me.[85]

I am very much better now though my health seems to be permanently impaired and my physicians forbid my return to Washington and I shall have to make a home for myself elsewhere.[86]

Thanking you again for your kindness & interest,

I am Sincerely Yours,

Paul Dunbar

Letter 101: July 25, 1899, H. A. Tobey to J. T. Eskridge

Toledo, O. July 25th, 1899[87]

Dr. J. T. Eskridge,[88]

Denver, Col,

Dear Doctor:—

I take pleasure by this letter in introducing to you Mr. Paul Laurence Dunbar. Mr. Dunbar has come to Colorado on account of his health.[89] Any consideration you can extend to Mr. Dunbar I assure you will be greatly appreciated.

Very truly yours,

H. A. Tobey

Letter 102: August 30, 1899, H. S. Morris to PLD

Lippincott's Monthly Magazine

Jamestown, R.I.

Philadelphia Aug. 30, 1899[90]

Dear Mr. Dunbar,[91]

It is difficult to express my disgust with the news of men who can act as like hogs. But, after all, the consciousness of one's own intellectual superiority is a strong and lasting satisfaction, for there is no possession as precious.[92] You can afford to laugh at their likeness. Their material circumstances sink away before the highs form [illegible]. You look down on them!

In Cooke's over the play and as I always am.[93] I feel I am fully in accord with your literary instincts and aims. You have the right road. But the payment and wages ask for [illegible] and I don't. Submit it to the publishing Dept. because you give us so short a time for its consideration.

Do come back soon from your Western Journey and then you shall have in no distant future nearly anything you want. Distinction like yours is power.

Sincerely Yours,

H. S. Morris[94]

Letter 103: September 12, 1899, PLD to H. A. Tobey

Dr. H.A. Tobey, Supt.,

State Hospital

Toledo, Ohio

Denver, Colorado, September 12, '99[95]

My Dear Doctor:

Here we[96] are, the whole "kit and bilin'" in Denver, and already I feel considerably reconciled to my fate. I am well impressed with the town, though I have been here but a few hours.

Only one thing—or really, several things in one—have bothered me—the reporters. They have taken the house[97] and I have not yet had time to rest from my journey.

. . . The *Denver Post* wishes to pay my expenses if I will travel slowly over the state and give occasionally my impressions of it.[98] They wired me at Chicago and have sent two men to interview me since I have been there. They claim the trips would be healthful that my wife could go along with the best accommodations, and that I only need do what I want in the way of writing. These people are the New York *Journal* of the west!

Letter 104: October 30, 1899, J. E. Bruce to PLD

National Afro American Council,[99]
John E. Bruce
11 Congress St.
Albany, N.Y., Oct. 30, 1899[100]

Paul Laurence Dunbar, Esq.
Toledo,
Sir:

Thank you for your polite favor of Oct 25th which conveyed some information exceedingly valuable to me which I did not possess before and for which I beg that you will accept my heartfelt grateful thanks. In view of the discourse you have made relative to the information of the matter in question it is proper that I should offer to you my humble apologies for discourteous language employed in the note to which you refer.[101] I beg also today that you are in error and do me a great injustice when you say that I had a lawyer's clerk hounding your wife[102] during your illness or that I had designs on your bank account. All of this is news to me, as before I left the city[103] some months ago I washed my hands of the whole business and told any "confidante or advocate" that I should not be a party to the persecution of a man who was reported to be so near death's door that he could bear the dealings of the things, and that I should be satisfied with the payment by having the amount advanced for transportation. On my return home recently I received a letter from this enterprising and

thoughtful gentleman saying that you had not settled. I thought over the
matter a few times and then wrote you as I did. I assure you that I did very
much regret the incident and am sincere in the expression. I realize that
I have been taken in and if you will kindly advise me to what sum, and
manner the affair was settled, I will see that my "confidante and advocate"
is taken in fiercely devilish quick. When I came to your house in New York
and told the Madam that I was satisfied I meant what I said. Throughout
this whole transaction I have acted in absolute good faith. I do not even
know the name of the attorney in the case and have never seen such a
person.[104]

I am very respectfully yours,

J. E. Bruce[105]

Letter 105: November 7, 1899, F. Z. S. Peregrino to PLD

"The Spectator"

F.Z.S. Peregrino[106]

and

Southern Help Agency

33 State St.

Albany, N.Y. 7th of Novbr, 1899[107]

Sir,

Your insolent behavior is perfect on a par with a man who would accept
by securing money for his fare from Washington to New York, then fail to
keep his appointment.[108]

You perhaps know Bruce[109] and you remember that you attended our
[illegible] as an instrument drawn by myself and which entailed also my
name. Your lawyer, oh! Well I'll contrive to give up this publication[110] in
other directions, and your lawyer[111] be damned!

F. Z. S. Peregrino

Letter 106: December 5, 1899, PLD to Paul R. Reynolds

December 5, 1899[112]

Dear Mr. Reynolds:

I am sending you herewith the manuscript of which I told you.[113] I want
you to look it over and see if you think it would go overseas, and if so try it.
I should like to dispense of both serial and book rights if it were possible.

The American end I am trying myself for the time being because I have some correspondence with several people whom I want to read the story. If it doesn't hit them, this part also will I thankfully give up to you. Many thanks for your information about "The Man with the Hoe."[114] A man is so out of it here[115] that he knows nothing of what is going on until too late, notwithstanding "The Bookman."[116]

Very truly yours,

Paul L. Dunbar

May I hear soon what you think about the story & its chances?

Letter 107: December 19, 1899, James MacArthur to PLD

Doubleday & McClure Co Publishers[117]

143–55 East 25th St., New York

December 19th, 1899[118]

Dear Mr. Dunbar,

I have just discovered your hiding place and want to say a word of goodbye before sailing on the 27th by the Teutonic[119] for London. I expect to be back for a while in the summer, but if in the meantime you should take it into your head to come with Mrs. Dunbar (whom I regret not having met yet) to London, I shall be awfully glad to see you there.

You can see, by the enclosed little tale in which I figure, that a story publishing combination has been formed and that without much bragging, will be heard from by and by. How is your work going, by the way? I understood you to say that you were engaged in a new novel.[120] Is that not so? Your next work should certainly be a novel—a book of stories might follow then; but the novel first, please, for your own sake with the public. You see I am still your old critic and adviser.

Of course, I should be delighted if you would let us be the first to read that novel and exploit it if we could come to terms.[121] I wish you would write or come in some time and see Page[122] or Doubleday.[123] You will find them splendid fellows as well as fine publishers.

Now drop me a line of God speed if you've time.

Merry Christmas to you.

Sincerely always,

[James MacArthur][124]

LETTERS FROM 1900

Letter 108: January 12, 1900, E. C. Martin to PLD

McClure's Magazine
THE S.S. MCCLURE Co.[125]
New York, Jan. 12, 1900[126]

My dear Mr. Dunbar:

I am truly sorry that you shall have been kept waiting so long for an answer about your book[127] and that is the feeling also, I can assure of those more directly responsible for the delay than I am. But have been very much against us just lately, for the Doubleday & McClure Co,[128] which have been until now a book department have been in a way separating from us and moving to new offices; and in [illegible] final decisions on such important matters, new books have been nearly impossible for the time being. I am now promised [illegible] word by tomorrow or next day.

If the Doubleday & McClure Co. should decide that they did not care to undertake the book, I should like to have the privilege of sending it under the consideration of our new company—the S.S. McClure Co[129]—which is now giving into book publication in its own account. I think I can furnish you a just treatment at our hands as at anybody's; and we'll take the matter up at once, and give you a humble answer.

I understand, of course, the importance to you of having the business settled as soon as possible, but I hope you will try to be patient with us, since it is not willful, but—unavoidable, neglect that we have to confess to.

Yours truly,
E. C. Martin[130]

Letter 109: January 13, 1900, E. C. Martin to PLD

Doubleday & Mcclure Co. Publishers
34 Union Square East
New York
January 13, 1900[131]

My dear Martin:[132]

I hope you have explained to Mr. Dunbar the reason for our long delay in giving an answer regarding "The Love of Landry." We are not yet really straightened out[133] but I've managed to get the particular matter through at last.

As you know, under ordinary circumstances we can only report that 29,000 words is hardly enough to make a book of. But we are just starting a series of "short novels"[134] (very nicely gotten up, bound in cloth, to be sold at 50 cents,) for which we anticipate a large sale. The first volume in the series—of course they will all be [illegible]—is a story by Anthony Hope.[135]

We can't pay more than 10% royalty and we are putting the price way down in order to place a whole lot of the books. Would Mr. Dunbar be willing to let us bring out *The Love of Landry* in this series with the understanding that we shall have the first chance at his next long novel?[136] If so, we will agree to do that and will bring the present book out this spring and see if we can't do something worthwhile with it.

If you'd prefer, we will write to Mr. Dunbar direct, but I suppose this letter will be all that's necessary.

Sincerely,
H. W. Laurie[137]

Dear Mr. Dunbar:

Here is Mr. Laurie's answer to you for the Doubleday & McClure Co regarding your book. I [illegible] it to you as [illegible] you can confer directly with them. But if you don't make a deal with them, I hope you'll give us a chance at the book.

Yours Truly,
E. C. Martin

Letter 110: January 22, 1900, H. W. Laurie to PLD

Doubleday & McClure Co.
Publishers
34 Union Square East
New York
January 22, 1900[138]

Mr. Paul Laurence Dunbar,
Box 263, Harmon, Colo.
My dear Sir:

Your letter of the 18th has just come to hand and while we naturally regret that you don't feel able to accept our offer, there seems to be no alternative except to return the manuscript,[139] as you request, Mr. Martin and I have done this this morning. We hope you will allow us to

say that we shall be glad to have you consider our offer still open: that
is to say, if you don't make just the arrangement you wish elsewhere and
decide that you wish to accept the proposition we made,[140] you need not
have the least hesitation about telling us. In any case, we hope you will
remember that we are much interested in your work, and that we shall
consider it a favor at any time to be allowed to consider any manuscript
of yours.[141]

Pray believe me,
Very sincerely yours,
H. W. Laurie

Letter 111: February 20, 1900, The Writer's Bureau to PLD

The Writer: A Monthly Magazine for Literary Workers[142]
282 Washington Street, Rooms 9–14 (P.O. Box 1905)
Boston, February 20,[143] 1900[144]

Paul L. Dunbar,
Congressional Library
Washington, D.C.[145]
Dear Sir:

Here is a manuscript that you put in our charge for sale so long ago that
we very likely have forgotten about it.[146] Our Commission Department at
that time offered the story to every editor who the Reader thought might
possibly accept it, but without success.

In clearing out our files we have come across the story and have given
it a rereading. The central idea—that of having the devil in the form of a
fascinating young woman tempt an impecunious young man—is capital,
but the story as you have it is not well told.[147] Undoubtedly you would
write it in much better form to-day. We advise you to read it through to
refresh your memory, and then lay it aside and retell it without reference
to the original. Told in proper style, it ought to find a place with either the
"Black Cat," Boston;[148] "The Smart Set," New York;[149] "Town Topics," New
York;[150] or the "Criterion," New York.[151]

Regretting that we were not successful in placing the story for you, and
with the best wishes we are

Yours very truly,
The Writer's Literary Bureau
Per J. J.[152]

Letter 112: July 5, 1900, PLD to Paul R. Reynolds

Brodhead's Bridge, Ulster Co., N.Y.[153]

July 5, 1900[154]

Paul R. Reynolds, Esq.,

70 Fifth Ave., New York,

Dear Mr. Reynolds,

I have your note of the 29th ult. And am glad to know the story is being looked after in England.[155] It is likely that Mr. Dodd will put it into your hands for magazine publication in America as we have decided to defer its publication until the publication of the larger novel.[156]

Very sincerely yours,

Paul Laurence Dunbar

Letter 113: July 17, 1900, PLD to Paul R. Reynolds

Brodhead's Bridge, Ulster Co., N.Y.

July 17, 1900[157]

Paul R. Reynolds, Esq.,

70 Fifth Ave., New York

Dear Mr. Reynolds,

I have your letter of the 11th in sight, and I am exceedingly sorry I missed you when I called. You are right as to Mr. Dodd. He prefers to publish this book first,[158] withholding The Love of Landry.[159] I do not know how much time you may have, but you may find out from him within a week as he will be back in that time.

I would expect for this book at least five hundred dollars, because it strikes me as a more serious work and is decidedly longer,[160] but the best price that you can get is what I want.

Hoping to have a favorable reply from you soon,

I am,

Very sincerely yours,

Paul Laurence Dunbar

Letter 114: August 1, 1900, Unsigned *Truth* editor to PLD

Truth[161]

Editorial Rooms[162]

August 1st 1900[163]

My dear Mr. Dunbar,

    Kindly pardon my delay in replying to your note. I am without assistance here just now and simply overwhelmed with work. In regard to the Christmas matter, you can make it either a story—no more than 2500 wds—or a poem—but we would like best to have your characteristic dialect work.[164] If you decide to send a story, you can have until about the middle of September to prepare it. If a poem, it will not be needed so soon. Much of the Christmas matter is already made up, and on account of the color work,[165] we have to be printed far in advance of most publications.

    If you cannot write a Christmas story in so short a time, send us a dialect poem instead and you can give us the story later on—making it suitable for any occasion—not Christmas.[166] I hope to give you better prices on your contributions [illegible] heretofore I hope you will give me something "prime" [illegible].

    The poem you sent last, and which I return to you with this is too fine for *Truth*—I don't believe the average *Truth* reader would appreciate its beauty—and I know you can give me something more suited to our readers.[167] Let me know if I can depend upon you for a contribution and that I can mention it in our holiday announcements.

    P.S. We have some fine names for the Christmas number—Stephen Crane,[168] [illegible],[169] Hamlin Garland,[170] Henry Wilton Thomas (Last Lady of Mulberry)[171] George Gissing[172] and many others—so that you will be in good company.

Letter 115: August 2, 1900, PLD to Paul R. Reynolds

Brodhead's Bridge, Ulster Co., N.Y.
August 2, 1900[173]

Paul R. Reynolds, Esq.,
70 Fifth Ave., New York
Dear Sir:

    I could not answer your letter until I had heard from Mr. Dodd to get his ideas as to the matter. He is willing that you should attempt to sell the story serially.[174] But as to how much time that would give you, you will have to find out from him as I do not know just when he intends to publish it. I should be very glad if you could see it serially. I am serious to know also what are the possibilities of "The Love of Landry." You can possibly get a copy of "The Fanatics" from Messrs. Dodd and Mead if you wish to have it now.

> Very truly yours,
> Paul Laurence Dunbar

Letter 116: August 16, 1900, PLD to Paul R. Reynolds

Brodhead's Bridge, Ulster Co., N.Y.
August 16, 1900[175]

Paul R. Reynolds, Esq.,
70 Fifth Ave., New York
Dear Mr. Reynolds,

I am sending you a couple of stories which I hope you may be able to dispose of. The Christmas story has been to "Truth" only, and the other story has been to the Saturday Evening Post only. Is it likely that they may go anywhere?

Have you heard anything about either of the two books yet?[176]

> Sincerely yours,
> Paul Laurence Dunbar

Letter 117: September 3, 1900, PLD to Paul R. Reynolds

410 Elm St., N.W., Washington, D.C.
Sept. 3, 1900[177]

Paul R. Reynolds, Esq.,
70 Fifth Ave.,
New York
Dear Mr. Reynolds,

I have your letter of the [illegible] and in reply would say that I think sixty dollars satisfactory for the story.[178] I am anxious to know where it goes. I have another Christmas story, but I hardly think it worthwhile to send another one to you now.

I regret that "The Fanatics" did not go at the Woman's Home Companion, but I hope that it may have better success elsewhere.[179]

You said nothing about poems, but do you think that the enclosed might be used? It has been to "Truth" and Lippincott's, each of whom chose another.

> Very truly yours,
> Paul Laurence Dunbar

Letter 118: September 6, 1900, PLD to Paul R. Reynolds
410 Elm St., N.W., Washington, D.C.
Sept. 6, 1900[180]

Mr. Paul R. Reynolds,
    Dear Sir—Enclosed shall find a Christmas sketch[181] for [illegible]. It will be too slight for your use. If you think it worth while I will write another, and fuller one.

Very truly yours,
Paul Laurence Dunbar

Letter 119: September 10, 1900, PLD to Paul R. Reynolds
410 Elm St., N.W., Washington, D.C.
Sept. 10, 1900[182]

Dear Mr. Reynolds,
    I have made the suggested changes to the story and send it herewith.[183] I seriously hope you may be able to use it.
    I am going to send in one more story and then give you the rest, which you deserve.[184]

Very truly yours,
Paul Laurence Dunbar

Letter 120: September 15, 1900, PLD to Paul R. Reynolds
410 Elm St., N.W., Washington, D.C.
Sept. 15, 1900[185]

Dear Mr. Reynolds,
    I send you herewith the last of the batch of stories. I do not know whether The Century would take it or not. I have so often tried them with my stories, but I only get them returned[186] and they have just taken a very long poem.[187] But I do not need to suggest to you where to send this. I leave everything to you.
    I hope soon to hear favorably from you about some of the other things.

Very sincerely yours,
Paul Laurence Dunbar

Letter 121: Unknown date (ca. fall 1900), PLD to P. M. Pearson

321 Spruce St. Washington, D.C.[188]

Professor P. M. Pearson:[189]

Dear Sir:

Now that I am at home and settled, I feel that an explanation is due you from me. I could not see you as you asked, because I was ashamed to. My brother went, but you were gone.

The clipping you sent is too nearly true to be answered. I had been drinking. This had partially intoxicated me. The only injustice lies in the writer's not knowing that there was a cause behind it all, beyond inclination. On Friday afternoon, I had a severe hemorrhage. This I was fool enough to try to conceal from my family, for, as I had had one the week before, I knew they would not want me to read. Well, I was anxious not to disappoint you, and so I tried to bolster myself up on stimulants.[190] It was the only way I could have stood up at all. But I feel now that I have rather disappointed you wholly than to have disgraced myself and made you ashamed.

As to the program, I had utterly forgotten that there was a printed one.[191] I am very sorry, and ashamed, because I do not think that the cause excuses the act.

I have cancelled all my engagements and given up reading entirely. They are trying to force me back to Denver, but I am ill and discouraged, and don't care much what happens.[192]

Don't think of this as an attempt at vindication. It is not. Try to forgive me as far as forgiveness is possible.

Sincerely yours,

Paul Laurence Dunbar

P.S. I have not told you that I was under the doctor's care and in bed up until the very day I left here for Chicago. There had been a similar flow, and I came against advice, and now I see the result.

Letter 122: October 16, 1900, PLD to Paul R. Reynolds

321 Spruce St. N.W., Washington D.C.

October 16, 1900[193]

Mr. Paul Reynolds,

70 Fifth Ave.

New York,

My Dear Sir,

I have your note of late and am pleased at the sale of "The Scapegoat."[194] I am satisfied with the price received.

Thanking you,

I am,

Very sincerely yours,

Paul Laurence Dunbar

Letter 123: October 31, 1900, PLD to Paul R. Reynolds

321 Spruce St. N.W., Washington D.C.

October 31, 1900[195]

Mr. Paul Reynolds,

70 Fifth Ave.

New York,

Dear Mr. Reynolds,

I have your note about the "Fount of Turns."[196] The amount is small, and what you say about your percentage is all right. I hope the other things that you have will do me well. The illustrations to "The Scapegoat"[197] were fine and I hope Collier's[198] will soon be coughing up as my exchequer is low.

Thanking you for your kindness,

I am,

Very truly yours,

Paul Laurence Dunbar

Letter 124: November 3, 1900, Booker T. Washington to PLD

Booker T. Washington

Tuskegee Normal and Industrial Institute

Incorporated

Tuskegee, Alabama

November 3, 1900[199]

Mr. Paul Laurence Dunbar,

Washington, D.C.

Dear Mr. Dunbar:

I thank you very sincerely for sending me a copy of the New England Magazine and more heartily for the poem which you were kind enough to dedicate to me.[200] You perhaps have noted that the Outlook for the present week reprints it from the New England Magazine. I send you under separate cover a copy which contains the first installment of an effort of mine.

Thanking you again for your very great kindness, I am,

Yours truly,

Booker T. Washington

Letter 125: November 6, 1900, PLD to Ginger R. Percy

321 Spruce St.

Washington, D.C.

Nov. 6th 1900[201]

Mrs. Ginger R. Percy[202]

Dear Madam:

The edition of the Atlantic has been kind enough to send me your excellent verses addressed to me in memory of Colonel Shaw.[203]

I want to tell you that I like them very much. I like the brave hopeful note that you put into them. But, believe me that while any sonnet was question and protest in me, I had never lost heart, and hope and faith.[204]

It has come to be almost a catch phrase to say that one believes that all things work together for good and yet I do believe all that those words mean.

Thanking you for your kind interest in many lives,

I am

Sincerely Yours,

Paul Laurence Dunbar

Letter 126: November 7, 1900, PLD to Dr. F

Washington, D.C., Nov. 7th, 1900[205]

My Dear Dr. F—:

Mine is so truant a disposition that it is hard for one to keep his finger upon me. I am here today and gone—yesterday. I doubt if you have known for some time where I am located. But the above address will tell you, I am here again. Of course, I tried to resume reading and am in consequence a reluctant invalid.

There is such a charm, though, about just lazing around in a locality that one really likes, that I do not feel very deeply my enforced idleness. Enforced idleness is good. I have been idle for just about four hours, and this is after finishing a 40,000 word novel[206] and several short stories and bits of verse since the middle of September. Do I not deserve to be lazy and to be allowed to read Van Dyke's "Fisherman's Luck,"[207] which I am now enjoying to the full! What a charming writer he is, how easy and graceful and humorous. I wonder if it is as easy writing as it seems. I don't believe. I have no doubt but that some of those lilting, musical sentences of his were carved out with deep travail.

You may look for a copy of my new book "The Love of Landry" within a week or maybe less time. It seems almost a sacrilege to mention my slight and altogether inadequate story just after "Fisherman's Luck," but we cannot all be Homers though we all may nod.

I am going to give myself a little vacation for a while right here at home. I shall smoke, and read, and play cards, and make night (and day as well) hideous with my violin. How long this will last it is hard to tell, for it takes only a short time for the bee of unrest to sting me into activity.

Will you remember me to your family please?

Letter 127: November 7, 1900, PLD to Paul R. Reynolds
321 Spruce St. N.W., Washington D.C.
November 7, 1900[208]

Dear Mr. Reynolds,

I am sending you under another cover a new story, "The Sport of the Gods," which I have done under orders for Lippincotts.[209] I am not sure, however, whether they will accept it or not, and this copy I will mind you to look after and give me your opinion whether there is any chance of [illegible] or book publication in England.[210] The other stories so far have been so unsuccessful that the effort seems hardly worthwhile, but I want to this to be at your discretion.

I will be glad if you would prod up both Ainslee's[211] and Collier's[212] a little as the [illegible] would come in very handy right now.

Let me have a line about this so try, please, as soon as possible.

Very truly yours,
Paul Laurence Dunbar

[P.S.] The story is about 40,000 words

Letter 128: November 10, 1900, PLD to Paul R. Reynolds
321 Spruce St. N.W., Washington D.C.
November 10, 1900[213]

Dear Mr. Reynolds,

I wish to also acknowledge the $12.75 for the poem "The Font of Tears."[214]

With thanks,
I am,
Sincerely yours,
Paul Laurence Dunbar

Letter 129: November 19, 1900, PLD to Paul R. Reynolds

321 Spruce St. N.W., Washington D.C.
November 19, 1900[215]

Paul Reynolds, Esq.,
New York
Dear Mr. Reynolds,

Many thanks for the $67.38, which I received Saturday[216] and good luck to you.

You did not acknowledge the receipt of the novel, "The Sport of the Gods." I suppose though, that it arrived all right.

Very sincerely yours,

Paul Laurence Dunbar

Letter 130: November 25, 1900, PLD to Paul R. Reynolds

Washington D.C., Nov. 25, 1900[217]

Dear Mr. Reynolds:

In response to your note of the 19th, I would say that I think it quite as well to give your English representative a sight of the new novel.[218] It has gone with Lippincott though I have had to cut it down some for the magazine.

I have a letter from the "Youth's Companion"[219] this morning saying that they are sending me a check for a story received through you. Has your commission been taken out yet? If not, tell me what it is and I will forward the amount as soon as it comes. I have also a note from the Century asking for some humorous work.[220] Have you any of the things you sent there? An early reply will greatly oblige.

Yours sincerely,
Paul Laurence Dunbar

Letter 131: December 30, 1900, PLD to Paul R. Reynolds
321 Spruce St. N.W., Washington D.C.
Dec 30, 1900[221]

My Dear Mr. Reynolds,

In the dearth of matter I send you two well-nigh hopeless things to
see if you think there is a chance of finding a place for them. The little play,
"Winter Roses"[222] has been to the *final* set, Munsey's, Saturday Evening
Post, Century and Lippincott's, and perhaps one or two other places. The
story "Old Elijah"[223] has been to the Cosmopolitan, N.Y. Evening Post,
Saturday Evening Post.[224] I doubt if you can do anything with these things,
but should be glad if you would try, however, I don't believe I would want
postage on them if you think they won't go. As soon as I am able I will send
you something else, but for the time being I seem pretty dry.

Thanking you for past favors,

I am, sincerely yours,
Paul Laurence Dunbar

Letter 132: December 24, 1900, PLD to Paul R. Reynolds
321 Spruce St. N.W., Washington D.C.
Dec. 24, 1900[225]

Dear Mr. Reynolds.

In reply to your note of the 18th, let me say that I hardly think it necessary
for you to send "The Fanatics" again. Will you please return it to me with the
bill for postage? Enclosed, please find two stories which Mr. Johnson[226] of the
Century did not take and which the Saturday Evening Post has also seen. Mr.
Johnson took three poems[227] and as usual sent the stories back.

Very truly yours,
Paul Laurence Dunbar

LETTERS FROM 1901

Letter 133: January 21, 1901, PLD to Paul R. Reynolds
321 Spruce St. N.W., Washington D.C.
Jan. 21, 1901[228]

Dear Mr. Reynolds,

Do you do anything in the way of handling plays for the stage?[229]
[illegible line here]

> Sincerely yours,
> Paul Laurence Dunbar

Letter 134: February 5, 1901, PLD to Paul R. Reynolds
321 Spruce St. N.W., Washington D.C.
Washington, Feb 5, 1901[230]

Dear Mr. Reynolds,

I [send] this batch of matter by Mrs. Dunbar which I asked you to look over. Each entry has on it the place to which it has been sent and should be judged by that whether or not it would be worthwhile to try them elsewhere. Of "The Stones of the Village,"[231] the editors have spoken with especial kindness, but it proved too long for the Atlantic, its length being the only objection and Mrs. Dunbar unable to cut it down without sacrificing the literary quality. Will you give it a look as soon as possible as to what you think you can do with it and also let me know how [illegible] the play[232] as I am feverish with anxiety.

> Cordially yours,
> Paul Laurence Dunbar

[written in] 5 stories

Stones of the Village
Hilma
The Pearl in the Oyster[233]
The Child is Father of the Man
False Praise

Letter 135: May 4, 1901, PLD to Paul R. Reynolds
321 Spruce St. N.W., Washington D.C.
May 4, 1901[234]

My dear Mr. Reynolds,

I know that Schwallinger[235] will be a hard thing to sell so that I think it well to close the deal at fifty dollars. Are the other stories and the play doing anything?

> Very truly yours,
> Paul Laurence Dunbar

Letter 136: May 16, 1901, PLD to Paul R. Reynolds
321 Spruce St. N.W., Washington D.C.
May 16, 1901[236]

Dear Mr. Reynolds,

After seeing Miss Kauser[237] I did not have time to visit you again but my talk with her was very clear and satisfactory and I shall do what I can to meet the requirements which she makes. Will you be kind enough to push the matter with the Chicago, Rock Island and Pacific[238] as I am going west next Wednesday and want to know whether I had better stay or not.[239]

Very truly yours,
Paul Laurence Dunbar

Letter 137: June 3, 1901, PLD to Paul R. Reynolds
321 Spruce St. N.W., Washington D.C.
June 3, 1901[240]

Dear Mr. Reynolds,

Enclosed please find another Saturday Evening Post rejection. You understand that I send them there first because I have a regular agreement with Mr. Lorimer[241] to send him so many things.

Are there any further developments in the C.R.I.P.R.R. matter?[242] I shall be glad to hear from Schwallinger and the Boy with Bayonet[243] whenever it is convenient to you, although I suppose the periodicals that have the things only pay on publication.[244]

Very sincerely yours,
Paul Laurence Dunbar

Letter 138: June 14, 1901, PLD to Grace S. Sisson
321 Spruce St., N.W., Washington, D.C.[245]
June 14, 1901,
Miss Grace S. Sisson,[246]
Potsdam, N.Y.,

Dear Miss Sisson,

I regret that I have been so long answering your letter but when you understand that I have been ill and at the same time travelling from Chicago in the North to Richmond in the South you will perhaps forgive me. Here is a list of Folk-Lore books that may help you in your studies. They are perhaps broader than your specialty, but I think you will enjoy them anyway.

Very truly yours,

[signed] Paul Laurence Dunbar

Attached:

Old Rabbit, the Voodoo, and Other Sorcerers. Mary Alicia Owen.[247]
Pub. By T. Fisher Unwin, Paternoster
Square, London.

Handbook of Folk-Lore, George Laurence Gomme.[248] (A series.)

Kaffir Folk-Lore, George McCall Theal.[249]
Pub. By T. Fisher Unwin, Paternoster
Square, London.

Voodoo Tales. Owen. Pub. By Putnam Sons, New York.[250]

Balaam and His Master. Joel Chandler Harris.[251]

Beatrice of Bayou Teche. Alice Ilgerfritz Jones[252]

Black Diamonds gathered in the Darky Homes of the South
Edward C. Pollard[253]

Letter 139: July 18, 1901, PLD to Paul R. Reynolds

321 Spruce St. N.W., Washington D.C.

July 18, 1901[254]

Dear Mr. Reynolds,

Many thanks for your kindness and promptness in advancing the money I so much needed at the time. I was foolish enough to book an entertaining scheme financially and it was a failure.[255] I should be glad if you would let this advance go on the sale of "Schwallinger" if you could do that. My wife insists right here that Schwallinger has been paid for, but I hardly think so. I think it was the "Boy and the Bayonet" for which I received a check.[256]

As to the price for the book "The Sport of the Gods"[257] I had had no idea of selling it outright, I do not think that would be a good plan as I expect the book to go well.[258] What I should prefer to do would be to follow the plan that has been followed by Dodd, Mead and Co. Get an advance of four or five hundred dollars, four hundred being the former figure from them, and then a royalty of fifteen percent.

Mrs. Dunbar wishes to thank you also for the trouble you took in dealing with her stories, and hopes for better success next time.

Very sincerely yours,
Paul Laurence Dunbar

Letter 140: August 5, 1901, PLD to Paul R. Reynolds
321 Spruce St. N.W., Washington D.C.
Aug. 5, 1901[259]

Dear Mr. Reynolds,

I find myself in somewhat of a mix-up with Messrs. Dodd, Mead and Co. They have learned through Jarrold and Sons of London[260] that the right of the "Sport of the Gods" has been offered them, and forgetting their former terms to let the novel go to Lippincott's, want to arrange for its publication.[261] Now I prefer to have another firm publish this story if possible, and I should like to know just what is going on with it, as I shall have to make immediate answer to their letter which is now a week old.

If the firm[262] who has it now should return it, will you kindly send it back to me and I will get back once more into the graces with Dodd, Mead and Co., although I am sure they will not push the book as a younger firm would do.

An early answer would greatly oblige,

Yours very sincerely,
Paul Laurence Dunbar

Letter 141: August 7, 1901, PLD to Paul R. Reynolds
321 Spruce St. N.W., Washington D.C.
Aug. 7, 1901[263]

Dear Mr. Reynolds,

I have received your letter and the manuscript for which let me thank you. In making our future accounts you will remember that there are express charges from Bowen-Bobbs-Merrill Company to you, and this later one also.

I am sorry Funk and Wagnall's[264] did not take the story as it would have settled all discussion but since Dodd and Mead forgot their promise, I shall have to bow to them. So much for being paid monthly by publishers.

I hope to send you some short stories in a little while.

Very sincerely yours,
Paul Laurence Dunbar

Letter 142: August 10, 1901, PLD to Paul R. Reynolds
321 Spruce St. N.W., Washington D.C.
Aug. 10, 1901[265]

Dear Mr. Reynolds,

I send you the remnant of my Lippincott Ohio stories.[266] It has only been there and was left over because it was one more than was to be used in the serials. Will you see what you can do with it?

I will look over "The Trouble about Sophiny"[267] which I received this morning and do what I can with it.

Very truly yours,
Paul Laurence Dunbar

Letter 143: August 13, 1901, PLD to Paul R. Reynolds
321 Spruce St. N.W., Washington D.C.
Aug. 13, 1901[268]

Dear Mr. Reynolds,

Messrs. Dodd, Mead and Co. speak of bringing the book out in the spring although at the time of their writing their readers had not yet even seen it.[269] They have wanted me to lengthen the book, but I do not see any way to do it. I am writing them to-day as to the time of publishing the book and will let you know as soon as I hear from them. I should prefer that it be published this Fall, but they seem to think it too late. What do you think about it? If necessary, and you think it safe, I will try to influence them to publish it sooner. I enclose two little sketches[270] which may help in the advertising matter for Messrs. Jarrold and Sons.[271]

Don't you think the English royalty is a little low? It is less than ten per cent.

Very truly yours,
Paul Laurence Dunbar

Letter 144: August 14, 1901, PLD to Paul R. Reynolds
321 Spruce St. N.W., Washington D.C.
Aug. 14, 1901[272]

Dear Mr. Reynolds,

Many thanks for the check which I received this morning. I was a little disturbed to hear that I had already been paid for Schwallinger's and had sent to you for money when you had no story of mine out, but your check reminds me.[273] I thank you for your many kindnesses.

Very truly yours,
Paul Laurence Dunbar

Letter 145: August 17, 1901, PLD to Paul R. Reynolds
321 Spruce St. N.W., Washington D.C.
Aug. 17, 1901[274]

Dear Mr. Reynolds,

Dodd and Mead are going to publish the "Sport of the Gods" but insist upon waiting until the Spring so that the book can be illustrated.[275] I shall be glad if you will apprise Messrs. Jarrold and Sons of this. There is to be a book of mine out this Fall, a collection of eight or ten dialect verses[276] with illustrations by the Hampton Camera Club[277] and decorations by—there the name has slipped me.[278] I did not think of offering it to you for English sale because I believe that they would hardly care for anything of that kind. It is to be a Christmas book and would sell at six shillings over there, but I do not believe that I am well enough known for a book to go as well as did a former one of the same kind here in America. The illustrations, however, are significant, all being taken from life in the South.[279] If you think there is any chance in it, let me know at once and I will try to get you the material and write Dodd and Mead about the illustrations.

Very truly yours,
Paul Laurence Dunbar

P.S. If you think it worthwhile, why not ask Dodd and Mead yourself about the [illegible]? It must [illegible].[280]

Letter 146: August 22, 1901, PLD to Paul R. Reynolds
321 Spruce St. N.W., Washington D.C.
Aug. 22, 1901[281]

Dear Mr. Reynolds,

Here are the two other little stories quite in a different vein from the usual.[282]

Do you know anything about what Miss Kauser is doing with the play "Herrick?"[283] She promised to write me two months ago about it and I am really unable to go on with it or to do anything until I hear from her. It has been four months since it was put into her hands.

Very truly yours,
Paul Laurence Dunbar

Letter 147: August 23, 1901: PLD to Paul R. Reynolds

Washington D.C., Aug. 23, 1901[284]

Mr. Paul R. Reynolds
Dear Mr. Reynolds,

I am not entirely satisfied with the story which I just sent you called "Jimmy Weedon's Contretemps."[285] If after reading it over, it strikes you as not being quite up to the mark will you send it back to me at once and I will go over it. I don't believe that I can do anything with "Sophiny."[286]

Sincerely yours,
Paul Laurence Dunbar

Letter 148: September 2, 1901, PLD to Paul R. Reynolds

321 Spruce St., N.W. Washington D.C.
Sept. 2, 1901[287]

Dear Mr. Reynolds,

I am afraid you miss the point of "Jimmy Weedon's Contretemps." There is no attempt from the first at concealing the outcome of the story. The real point of the story is as I have tried to make it, the contrast of Jimmy's honesty in having fun where he wants it and the morbid curiosity which prompts the woman to whom he is engaged but does not love, and who, by the way, is not Mrs. Weedon to go into the slums.[288] But I will go over it and see what I can do with it.

I hope you will stir Miss Kauser up and see what she has done.[289] I would have answered your letter sooner, but have been out of the city.

Very truly yours,
Paul Laurence Dunbar

Letter 149: September 3, 1901, PLD to Paul R. Reynolds
321 Spruce St., N.W. Washington D.C.
Sept. 3, 1901[290]

Dear Mr. Reynolds,

I have done the best that I could with the enclosed story, and I think now that it is something better.[291] I am sending it back to you, and hope that you may be able to do something with it.

Very truly yours,
Paul Laurence Dunbar

Letter 150: September 20, 1901, PLD to Dr. F
Washington, D.C., Sept. 20th, 1901[292]

My Dear Dr. F—:

It does seem strange to be sending a letter to you at Swiftwater,[293] but you are liking it better there I hope. The very name to me is suggestive of a delightful rural locality with a stream and the possibility of playing Isaac Walton[294] beside its banks. Maybe it's nothing of the kind. One can never count on anything in this inconsistent country.

I have been fishing down on the Chesapeake at intervals this summer and have caught many Fish and much malaria, the quality of both being above reproach.

I am glad to have you say nice things about "The Fanatics." You do not know how my hopes were planted in that book and it has utterly disappointed me.[295] Like that right wrist of yours, which I hope is better now, it went very lame upon me and, knowing it is the best thing I have done, discouragement has taken hold upon me.

There are many other things against me now to keep my cheerfulness in check. Mrs. Dunbar was injured at the President's funeral, brutally struck by a policeman in the surging crowd.[296] I returned the same day after having a nice big hemorrhage on the train. My literary reaction continues and altogether I am in a blue funk.

Letter 151: September 26, 1901, PLD to Paul R. Reynolds
321 Spruce St., N.W. Washington, D.C.
Sept. 26, 1901[297]

My Dear Mr. Reynolds,

I have your letter and the contract of the "Sport of the Gods," and I am a good deal puzzled. In the first place, I have always been in the habit of having two contracts sent, one for myself. In this case, supposed I have a kick coming, where do I come in? Again, Section 3 says that the copyright shall be vested in the publisher. This has not been done before, and pray tell me what does 433/400 copies mean?[298] Neither do I understand part of the matter written in nor the counting of thirteen copies as twelve in the reckoning of royalties. The whole agreement is very puzzling to me, and I am unwilling to sign it without further elucidation. I have penciled the points which I do not like and do not understand, and return it to you for some word. What do you yourself, think of this contract?

As to the publishing the book at any time, I do not see that Dodd, Mead and Co. have anything to do with that part of it if the book is copyrighted here in America and their rights are not injured.[299]

Hoping to have news of some short story sales.

I am,

Very sincerely yours,

Paul Laurence Dunbar

Letter 152: October 7, 1901, George B. Cortelyou to PLD

Personal.

Executive Mansion,

Washington

October 7, 1901[300]

My dear Sir:

Referring to your recent letter in regard to the case of Dr. Curtis,[301] I find upon inquiry that after a very careful investigation, the Secretary of the Interior concluded that the interest of the publish service, in connection with the administration of affairs of the Freedman's [sic] Hospital,[302] necessitated Dr. Curtis' retirement; and accordingly Dr. William A. Warfield[303] has been appointed to succeed him.

Very truly yours,

George B. Cortelyou[304]

Secretary to the President

Letter 153: October 7, 1901, PLD to Paul R. Reynolds
Oct. 7, 1901[305]

Mr. Paul R. Reynolds,
#70 5th Avenue
New York
Dear Mr. Reynolds:

I sent a story to the Metropolitan Magazine, and did not know of its acceptance, until it appeared in the October number.[306] I did not do this in order to circumvent your commission, but because I thought the thing too short and trivial to send to you.

I shall take pleasure on receiving my check in sending the usual percentage.

Truly yours,
Paul Laurence Dunbar

Letter 154: October 14, 1901, PLD to Paul R. Reynolds
321 Spruce St., N.W. Washington D.C.
Oct. 14, 1901[307]

My Dear Mr. Reynolds,

I am positively ashamed to send you your commission. The story[308] only brought six dollars, one of which I am sending you. It filled two pages, and I think the Metropolitan people rather short in their payments, trivial as it was.

In going over my letters I have just found one from you which has never been opened, with the contract returned.[309] I am perfectly willing to sign it as it is with the understanding that the eighth and tenth clauses are to be cut out. I return it to you for fear that you may not remember what those clauses are.

Very truly yours,
Paul Laurence Dunbar

Letter 155: October 21, 1901, PLD to Paul R. Reynolds
321 Spruce St., N.W. Washington D.C.
Oct. 21, 1901[310]

My Dear Mr. Reynolds,

I am returning herewith the contracts, both of them signed. I have put a caret in the places where I think something has been left out.

Hoping to hear some good news from the stories and any more from Miss Kauser.[311]

I am,
Very sincerely yours,
Paul Laurence Dunbar

Letter 156: October 23, 1901, PLD to Paul R. Reynolds

321 Spruce St., N.W. Washington D.C.
Oct. 23, 1901[312]

My Dear Mr. Reynolds,

I know you do not like to handle single poems but I am wondering if I sent you a batch of eight or ten whether or not you could handle them in a bunch.

I thank you very much for sending to Miss Kauser for the play.[313] I do now know what turn to make with it next.

Very sincerely yours,
Paul Laurence Dunbar

Letter 157: October 25, 1901, PLD to Paul R. Reynolds

321 Spruce St., N.W. Washington D.C.
Oct. 25, 1901[314]

My Dear Mr. Reynolds,

I have your letter of the 24th inst. And in answer would say that you are wrong in thinking I send my best work else-where and the second best to you. This is not true. The agreement with both Mr. Morris of Lippincott's[315] and Mr. Lorimer of the Saturday Evening Post[316] were made as far back as 1898; both are my personal friends and I should feel myself rather niggardly if I should withhold from them the first sight of the things that are in their line merely because now that my things are selling I could get better prices elsewhere.

To Mr. Morris, I have been sending but one line of work lately, these are the things in the serial of Ohio stories[317] which was begun three years ago, and when I shall have finished the novelette which is to make the book he wants of these stories. I shall be free, unless I do the serial of African stories[318] which were planned with him even before the Ohio stories. Now, do you see my position with them?

Mr. Lorimer gave me a chance on the Saturday Evening Post and dealt with me personally. Is it quite fair for me to take the things that he has suggested and offer them elsewhere or through someone else? I do not send you my second best. I send you the best I have, for as you yourself know since my health is broken I am doing very little. I should be glad if you were handling all of my work because you would get better prices for it than I can, but I feel a sense of honor and obligations towards these men which is a little beyond price. Perhaps I am unbusiness-like in this, but it is my feeling and I should be glad to hear at once from you if you do not think I am in the right.

By the way, I do not think that you can consider "The Mission of Mr. Scatters" or "The Scapegoat,"[319] neither of which had been offered elsewhere, as second best, as they are really the best short stories I have done in the last five years.

Very sincerely yours,
Paul Laurence Dunbar

Letter 158: November 10, 1901, PLD to Paul R. Reynolds

321 Spruce St., N.W. Washington D.C.
Nov. 10, 1901[320]

Dear Mr. Reynolds,

I am glad you think the poems may possibly be sold. Fifty cents alone is less than I usually get for myself, though I sell mostly but to two places, the Saturday Evening Post and The Century. For a poem the length of "The Haunted Oak"[321] the Century gave me thirty-five dollars, and for another one of twenty-four lines, fifteen dollars. This is about the way my prices run. If you can get more for its verses I shall be glad to have you try. The serious pieces usually bring higher prices.

I did not answer your letter before because I was out of the city and ill in bed ever since my return.[322] (I hope soon to get the play from Miss Kauser).

Very sincerely yours,
Paul Laurence Dunbar

Letter 159: November 10, 1901, PLD to Paul R. Reynolds

321 Spruce St., N.W. Washington D.C.
Nov. 10, 1901[323]

Dear Mr. Reynolds,

I have your letter of the 13 inst. and am exceedingly sorry that the stories won't go. However, I shall have to try again in replying to your question about the play, if you think it worthwhile to pass it over to Miss Marbury,[324] please do so. But if it is to be kept nearly half a year again while plays of a similar vein are going on, I would rather have it back in hand. I would be glad, though, if Miss Marbury would read it and read it soon.

Very truly yours,
Paul Laurence Dunbar

Letter 160: December 6, 1901, PLD to Paul R. Reynolds

321 Spruce St., N.W. Washington D.C.
Dec. 6, 1901[325]

Dear Mr. Reynolds,

Instead of answering your note of Nov. 29, I started to work at once on the story for Collier's, which is now well under way, and I expect to have it in your hands within the next day or two. It is called "The Promoter" and is somewhat in the line of "The Scapegoat" and "The Mission of Mr. Scatters," only more humorous, I think. Were you able to place "A Defender of Faith," the Christmas story?[326]

Sincerely yours,
Paul Laurence Dunbar

Letter 161: December 11, 1901, PLD to Paul R. Reynolds

321 Spruce St., N.W. Washington D.C.
Dec. 11, 1901[327]

My dear Mr. Reynolds,

In reference to "Jethro's Garden,"[328] if it is not possible to get more than twenty-five dollars for it, take it. If you can get forty, do so, by all means, as that is about the figure of that Mr. Morris of Lippincott's gives me for stories of that kind.

You did not tell me whether or not you had received "The Promoter." I hope that you have, and that Colliers will take it.[329] I am looking to you very wistfully for my Christmas money.[330]

Have you heard anything from Miss Marbury on "Herrick?"

Very truly yours,
Paul Laurence Dunbar

Letter 162: December 19, 1901, PLD to Paul R. Reynolds

321 Spruce St., N.W. Washington D.C.
Dec. 19, 1901[331]

My dear Mr. Reynolds,

I received your letter of yesterday containing a check, for which accept mine and Mrs. Dunbar's thanks. I will send contract in a day or so.

As to the story for Collier's while it is something of a disappointment, I suppose the $75.00 will do.[332]

Hoping to hear from you soon,

I am,
Sincerely yours,
Paul Laurence Dunbar

Letter 163: December 19, 1901, PLD to Booker T. Washington

To Booker T. Washington[333]
321 Spruce St., N.W., Washington, D.C.
Dec. 19, 1901

Mr. Booker T. Washington,
Crawford House, Boston, Mass.,
My dear Sir,

I have your note of the first in regard to the song,[334] and in reply would say that while I do not quite understand how much of the surroundings and object of the school you want put into the song,[335] I will try it, and let you see the result as soon as possible.

Very truly yours,
Paul Laurence Dunbar

4

Dunbar's Final Years, 1902–1906

I T IS AN ODD MISCONCEPTION that in Dunbar's entire oeuvre he did not write protest literature. Many of his poems, short stories, and novels include characters and settings that speak to an African American resistance and are blatant protest pieces. In fact, Dunbar not only wrote literature that qualifies as protest but was active in the fight for civil rights and interested in seeing the uplift of African Americans. He joined the American Negro Academy upon its formation on March 5, 1897, which worked to "be the voice of the race and to protest injustice in a period of accommodationism" (Seraile, *Bruce Grit*, 111), and published both "England as Seen by a Black Man" and his fiery "Recession Never" in support of these ideals. Dunbar also wrote Brand Whitlock on December 26, 1900, that "unless we live lives of protest, and few of us are willing to do that, we are as guilty as the lynchers of the South—we are all tarred with the same stick." Protest is not absent from Dunbar's writing in the least; in fact, as he gained more footing in the literary community and began writing longer pieces, he developed stronger rhetorical skills. Between 1900 and 1903, Dunbar published eight pieces that speak directly to civil rights and protest (see Metcalf, *Paul Laurence Dunbar*). As the letters in this section unmask, Dunbar was very much a part of the racial uplift movement headed by such leading figures as Booker T. Washington, with whom he ultimately disagreed, and W. E. B. Du Bois. Dunbar's approach was not only tactful but quite brilliant.

His private letters disclose intimate conversations dealing directly with protest writing and literature, as well as issues of racism. In one letter, Dunbar and Brand Whitlock considered the topic of white privilege—an astonishing topic for the turn of the century. Whitlock not only acknowledged the existence of his privilege but even recognized his complicity in benefiting from it. To Octavia Butler, Whitlock confided, "Paul Dunbar is the only Negro I ever met who did not remind me that he was one—and I have more than the common share of the conventional prejudice against them—I blush to confess it—the inheritance, I presume, of a Southern ancestry" (Nevins, *Letters and Journal of Brand Whitlock*, 25). Yet Whitlock came to the

FIGURE 5. Dunbar fishing, n.d. Courtesy of Ohio Historical Connection.

realization that he was wrong: in discussing race and racism with Dunbar, he conceded, "I cannot get away from the conviction that I am an unwilling participant in it all." More than this, Whitlock explained to Dunbar that he understood that this sprang "from society's trained habit of separating people into classes. Founded on various false and artificial distinctions in regarding some people not as people, but as poor people, as bad people, or black people, or some other kind of people" (Brand Whitlock to Dunbar, n.d., box 1, Paul Laurence Dunbar Papers, OHS). Perhaps most importantly, though, Whitlock recognized the issue as "the fundamental difficulty; the basic error and out of it grows all these awful deeds. Give every man a chance and life will be happy for all" (Brand Whitlock to Dunbar, n.d.).

It is one thing to read one's works and experience protest; it is something else entirely at the turn of the century to see an open and honest, frank discussion about race and the ramifications of prejudice.

During this time, Dunbar and Alice's relationship crumbled; Dunbar's alcoholism and abuse became too much for Alice to endure, and the two permanently separated. The split hit Dunbar hard: Eleanor Alexander avers that he sent Alice "forty-two letters, poems, and messages" (*Lyrics of Sunshine and Shadow*, 170) for two years after the split, but that Alice ignored them all. Matilda even attempted to help her son and Alice reconcile, writing Alice on September 18, 1902, that "Paul insisted [she] should write for him. Because he has tried so often to write himself. He has had his pen in his hand, but he can't write because he is so ashamed and remorseful. And he plead with me today between sobs and tears to write you. He sees his wrong and what he did was in a drunken passion. He wants me to tell you how he pines for you and how he still loves you, how he misses you at every turn. And he finds nothing or nobody to fill your place. Alice, wont [*sic*] you make up your mind to write him a few lines?" (Paul Laurence Dunbar Collection, box 22).

It was to no avail. Even Will Marion Cook begged Alice to take him back, noting that "if [Paul] will drop the drink, then there is nothing to fear" (April 18, 1902, Paul Laurence Dunbar Collection, box 22). Dunbar wrote Alice for the last time on January 14, 1903, noting her "brutal silence." He explained, "You have shred my telegrams, and yet, girl of my heart, I ask you to come back to me and the future shall make up for a past that was not altogether unhappy. I am not myself without you, but after this I cannot do more" (Paul Laurence Dunbar Collection, box 22). Despite Dunbar's personal grief, however, he flourished in his professional literary endeavors.

As these letters uncover, Dunbar continued his working relationship with Paul Reynolds, who managed his contracts and payments. The famous first chronicler of literary agents, William Heinemann, described these middlemen in 1893 as particularly unsavory and unscrupulous; in *The Author's Empty Purse*, James Hepburn portrays Reynolds as a "conspicuous . . . double agent" (74–75) who "served both publishers and authors" and was employed by Heinemann (86). However, Hepburn also notes "there is no evidence to suggest Reynolds used his position dishonestly" (75). The correspondence between Dunbar and Reynolds during this time not only depicts Dunbar's move away from direct contact with editors but also shows that Dunbar and Reynolds had developed a fairly close professional relationship that bordered on friendship. However, Dunbar's previous struggles with publishers who did not pay him for his work or who compensated him with free one-year subscriptions made this partnership difficult at times.

From the start of his career, Dunbar remained guarded in public interviews; he elided intimate details and information pertaining to his personal

FIGURE 6. Paul Laurence Dunbar House in Dayton, Ohio, circa 1895–1905. Courtesy of Ohio Historical Connection.

FIGURE 7. Dunbar on horseback, n.d. Courtesy
of Ohio Historical Connection.

life. The letters here disclose another side to Dunbar, revealing a complex
human being and an often misunderstood literary genius. While Dunbar
was highly driven and at times filled with energy and optimism, he was
paradoxically and simultaneously fragile, prone to extreme mood swings,
often sick with bouts of tuberculosis, and addicted to alcohol; yet he still
continued to fight for due compensation. These letters show a determined
writer who did not give up, even in his darkest moments. Dunbar, however, was ultimately undone by tuberculosis, which overwhelmed him both
mentally and physically. The downward shift in his condition is marked
by a somber tone that permeates these final letters to reveal an emotional
subtext of a rallying literary community and fan base that truly reflects the
grief and loss felt by many after Dunbar's passing. He became and remains
a forerunner of the many movements that helped shape the African American community.

LETTERS FROM 1902

Letter 164: January 7, 1902, PLD to Paul R. Reynolds
321 Spruce St. N.W., Washington, D.C.,
Jan. 7, 1902[1]

Dear Mr. Reynolds,

I had rather banked on the stories which were sold, "Jethro's Garden,"[2] "The Promoter"[3] and the two poems in some transactions which I entered.[4] Can you get hold of the cash for them, and will you let me have it as soon as possible, as my failure to receive it has rather embarrassed me?[5] Of course, you do not know it, but I have been flat off my back[6] for two weeks,[7] and the sight of a check would be as good as medicine to me.[8] Awfully sorry to trouble you.

Very truly yours,
Paul Laurence Dunbar

Letter 165: January 10, 1902, PLD to Paul R. Reynolds
321 Spruce Street., N.W., Washington, D.C.
Jan. 10, 1902[9]

Dear Mr. Reynolds,

I thank you very much for the $66.13 which came this morning just when I needed it.

I am sorry about Herrick[10] and am wondering since they all say "in this shape" if it could not be put into the hands of some experienced play wright [sic] who would collaborate.[11] What do you think about the matter? Let me hear from you at once, and greatly oblige,

Yours very sincerely,
Paul Laurence Dunbar

Letter 166: January 23, 1902, PLD to Booker T. Washington
321 Spruce St. N.W., Washington, D.C.
Jan. 23, 1902[12]

Mr. Booker T. Washington,[13]
Tuskegee, Ala.
My dear Mr. Washington,

I have your letter and note objection to the song.[14] In the first place, your objection to the line, "Swift growing South"[15] is not well taken because a song is judged not by the hundred years that it lives but from the time at which it was written, and the "swift growing" only indicates what the South has been, and will contrast with what it may achieve or any failure it may make. The "Star Spangled Banner" was written for the time, and although we may not be watching the stars and stripes waving from ramparts amid shot and shell, the song seems to be going pretty fairly still.

As to emphasizing the industrial idea,[16] I have done merely what the school itself has done, but I will make this concession of changing the fourth line of the third stanza into "Both of our minds and hands,"[17] although it is not easy to sing.

The Bible I cannot bring in. The exigencies of verse will hardly allow a paraphrase of it, or an auctioneer's list,[18] and so I am afraid that I cannot write verse up to Mr. Penney's[19] standard of it but I believe if you will look over "Fair Harvard"[20] you will note that they have not given their curriculum in the song or a list of the geological formation of the country around the school.

Very truly yours,
Paul Laurence Dunbar

Letter 167: January 25, 1902, PLD to Paul R. Reynolds
321 Spruce St. N.W., Washington, D.C.
Jan. 25, 1902[21]

My dear Mr. Reynolds,

Many thanks for the check for forty-five dollars which you were kind enough to send to me.[22] As to Herrick,[23] I hardly know what to say. Miss Kauser[24] thought it had sufficient movement, but that it needed changing, lengthening of [illegible], and shortening of the speeches. I shall write, however, to Miss Marbury,[25] as you suggest.

The names that I have thought of for the "Sport of the Gods"[26] are,

The Jest of Fate[27]
The Downward way,
The Weakest of These,
When the Gods Laugh

If these names do not suit ask them to choose a title of their own.

Very truly yours,

Paul Laurence Dunbar

Letter 168: February 20, 1902, PLD to Paul R. Reynolds

127 West 53rd St. New York City.

Feb. 20, 1902[28]

Paul R. Reynolds, Esq.

70 Fifth Ave. City

Dear Mr. Reynolds,

Please send me to the above address the following checks: $26.65 to the order of James L. Marshall[29] $13.85 to the order of The American Security and & Trust Co[30] $5.00 to the order of H. Romoiko [*sic*].[31]

Very truly yours,

Paul Laurence Dunbar

Letter 169: February 21, 1902, PLD to Paul R. Reynolds

227 West 33rd St. New York City

Feb. 21, 1902[32]

Mr. Paul R. Reynolds

70 Fifth Ave, City.

Dear Mr. Reynolds,

I have your check the other day,[33] and should have acknowledged it sooner, but I have been ill. Thank you very much for it.

I have been trying to get down to see you for several days, but I am either ill,[34] or the weather is worse than ill. I shall come, however, in a day or two, or if I find that I cannot I shall ask you to come here. There are some matters on which I wish to speak.[35]

Yours very truly,

Paul Laurence Dunbar

Letter 170: February 25, 1902, PLD to Paul R. Reynolds

127 West 53rd St. New York City.

Feb. 25, 1902[36]

Paul R. Reynolds, Esq.
70 Fifth Ave. City
My dear Mr. Reynolds,

    I pity you. Another order, if you please, and this for $50.00 to me on account.[37]

Very truly yours,
Paul Laurence Dunbar

Letter 171: March 1, 1902, PLD to Paul R. Reynolds

127 West 53rd St. New York City
March 1, 1902[38]

Paul R. Reynolds, Esq.
70 Fifth Ave. New York
Dear Mr. Reynolds,

    However much pleasure it may give you to tell me that you have sold "The Trousers,"[39] you must know that mine exceeds yours. I had faith in this story. I thought it was humorous, and at least fairly well told, and I bow to the taste of the 25th editor.[40]

    I thank you very much for your report of the facts in the case, and they have indeed interested me.[41]

    Whenever the money comes it will be acceptable. Of course, as you know, I am not in need at present. You have proven very conclusively that perseverance and a literary agent pay.

Very truly yours,
Paul Laurence Dunbar

Letter 172: March 26, 1902, PLD to Paul R. Reynolds

Harry Von Tilzer[42]
Music Publishing Co[43]
42 West 28th Street.
New York City
March 26, 1902[44]

Mr. Paul R. Reynolds,
70-Fifth Ave., City.
Dear Mr. Reynolds,

Awfully sorry that I haven't got a single other darky poem[45] and I should have taken the "Cosmopolitan's" price,[46] but since you held up to your own, I shall be awfully glad if you can sell it.

I don't remember the poem at all, as it was done on the stretch. Will you please send the manuscript of my play "Herick" [sic].[47]

With best wishes, I am,

Yours,
Paul Laurence Dunbar

Letter 173: March 26, 1902, PLD to Paul R. Reynolds

Harry Von Tilzer
Music Publishing Co
42 West 28th Street.
New York City, March 26, 1902[48]

My dear Mr. Reynolds,

I have your letter of a few days ago and in reply will say that the play "Herrick" had better be sent to the office address, 42 West 28th St., care of "Von Tilzer." At the same time, it would be a good idea to send me about $100.00, because I think my work will be sufficiently over for me to go to Chicago, about the 3rd of the month.[49] The rest of the money I shall have transferred to the Chicago Bank, after I get to that town. If you think it best to send the poem[50] back to the Cosmopolitan and let them have it at their price.

With best wishes,

Very sincerely yours,
Paul Laurence Dunbar

Letter 174: April 30, 1902, H. A. Tobey to PLD

April 30, 1902[51]

Mr. Paul Laurence Dunbar,
Dear Friend Paul:

Your letter of April 16th was duly received, and I am exceedingly sorry for my delay in writing to you because I know in your nervous conditions you would worry about anything that did not turn out just as you expected it to, and consequently would feel some apprehension that I was neglecting you. Since the date of your letter I have been away from home a good portion of the time and have been so overwhelmed with work and guests that I have been obliged to entirely neglect my correspondence. I am writing this letter just on the eve of starting to Columbus to look after our appropriations.[52] I am sorry to hear that you are so broken down but I am sure the rest and treatment is what you need.[53] I hope you will come out stronger physically, and every other way, than you have for a good while past. Physical laws must be obeyed and when we violate them long enough we have to pay the penalty. In this statement I do not speak theoretically, as you know. Let your moral resolve grow with your physical improvement, and come away strong and determined. I assure you that my sympathy goes out to you, and as Mr. Hern[e] once said to you, "I wish you all the good fortune you can wish for yourself."[54]

As soon as you feel able please write me a letter and tell me how you are physically, and about your wife and mother. I know everything looks dark to you now, but you have had some dark days before. Just keep in mind that little reference I made to your upper lip one time and it will do you good.[55]

We have larger appropriations this year than we have ever had before, which means more work for me.

When you get able to leave the Sanitarium,[56] why can't you come and make us a visit, and I am sure that you could spend two or three weeks out here with your friends very pleasantly, and make our home your headquarters.

Mrs. Tobey and Louise[57] join me in kindest regards.

Very truly yours,

H. A. Tobey

Letter 175: June 10, 1902, H. A. Tobey to PLD

June 10, 1902[58]

Mr. Paul Laurence Dunbar,

154 E. 22nd St., New York City

Dear Paul:

I received your letter along about the middle of April and immediately answered it and it has been returned,[59] therefore, I write you at your old address. I hope you are home now and well and happy, and that you have passed through the deep waters and have come out safely on the other side. We are all as well as usual.

Mrs. Tobey and Louise[60] start for Aurora, N.Y., where the girls are at college to-morrow evening.[61] They will remain there over Sunday and Monday they will all join me at Rochester and we will take the boat for Montreal where I go to attend a meeting of the Superintendents

Association.[62] We will probably be gone 8 or 10 days. Please write me so that I may have a letter from you on my return as we are all anxious to hear from you.

With kindest regards to your mother and wife, I am

Very truly yours,
H.A. Tobey

P.S. I have just read over the letter that I wrote and it has occurred to me that some of my suggestions might not be amiss now, therefore I enclose it.

Letter 176: June 17, 1902, Albert M. Read to PLD

Storage Department
American Security and Trust Company
1140 Fifteenth Street, Washington
June 17, 1902[63]

Mr. Paul Lawrence [*sic*] Dunbar
5627 Dearborn Street,
Chicago, Illinois
Dear Sir:

In reply to your esteemed favor of May 31st, just received this A.M., you are informed that your goods[64] are not in such shippable condition as is required by the railroad companies entering this city, and that it will cost something in the neighborhood of forty dollars to pack, haul to the depot, and ship them. Please inform us whether you would like this work done or not and if so enclose with it your check for the amount stated above, plus $2.50 for a half month's storage which will accrue by the time the goods are ready for shipment, and very much obliged.

Yours truly,
Albert M. Read
General Manager

Letter 177: June 26, 1902, Edward Dodd to PLD

Dodd, Mead & Company
Publishers, Booksellers, and Importers
372 Fifth Avenue
Corner Thirty-fifth St.
New York, June 26, 1902[65]

Mr. Paul L. Dunbar,
Chicago, Ill.
Dear Mr. Dunbar:

Yours of June 24th just received. Perhaps it is just as well that the illustrated book of poems is not to come out this fall since we had one last year.[66] This sort of thing can of course be overdone. As I understand it, you will have a book of general poetry ready shortly.[67] We should very much like to bring this out in January,[68] so if you can give us a copy by the end of November we can easily accomplish it, have plenty of review copies ahead, and ventilate the book thoroughly before we get it on the market. Won't you also keep in mind the illustrated book of poems for Christmas of 1903?[69] It is necessary to get the photographs for this book in the spring and early in the summer, both because the best views are to be had and because the teachers at the Hampton School go off on their vacations by the middle of summer. ~~Perhaps~~ Your lullaby poems[70] [illegible] if there are enough other than what have been used in the two books, would make a very good book of this kind.[71] However, won't you get together all the poetry that has not been used in this way and send it to us, let us make a selection, and then send it to you for approval.

I hope that your health continues to be better.

Yours truly,
Edward Dodd
EHD/G

Letter 178: October 7, 1902, Otis Skinner to PLD

Tour of Otis Skinner
St. Louis
Oct 7-02[72]

My Dear Sir:

I return the MS of "Herrick" left for me at Chicago.

I have enjoyed its perusal, for it is so atmospheric and has a fine 17th century flavor.[73]

I regret I do not find it suited to my needs—for it has much merit.

Very Truly Yours,
Otis Skinner[74]

LETTERS FROM 1903

Letter 179: January 15, 1903, PLD to W. E. B. Du Bois
W. E. B. Dubois [*sic*], Esq.,[75]
Atlanta University,
Atlanta, GA.
My Dear Prof. DuB[76]

I have had a letter from Pott & Co., N.Y.[77] about the matter of a race-book.[78] I spoke of having you assist them in the matter but they have not mentioned money. If there is any chance for cash in the matter let me know at once.

Very truly yours,
Paul Laurence Dunbar

Letter 180: January 15, 1903, W. E. B. Du Bois to PLD
#5355 Grove Ave.,
Chicago, Jan. 15, 1903[79]

My Dear Dunbar:[80]

The Potts people wrote me simply asking the privilege of using one of my unpublished magazine articles. I replied that the book rights for that article were already placed and that ended the matter.[81] I know nothing of this scheme and am suspicious of it. They write to each as tho' all the rest had consented and shall have nothing to do with the matter unless it takes more definite and tangible shape.

Meantime I am thinking of publishing in the Spring a miniature monthly magazine—small, well-formatted of limited circulation.[82] I am going to edit it & I should like to say in the announcement "with the cooperation of Mr. Paul Laurence Dunbar" and others. I am going to ask Mr. Chesnutt also. That said, "[illegible]" will consist of your good will and such contributions from you as the magazine is able to pay for. May I use your name? I think this will find you well.

Yours,
[W. E. B. Du Bois]

Letter 181: January 20, 1903, *Saturday Evening Post* editors to PLD
Editorial Rooms, The Saturday Evening Post, Philadelphia
January 20th 1903[83]

Dear Sir:

We enclose herewith for your editorial revision a galley proof of your poem, "The Plantation Child's Lullaby."[84] Kindly correct and return to us.

Yours very truly,
The Editors

Letter 182: February 3, 1903, PLD to W. E. B. Du Bois
1214 12th. St.
Kansas City, Mo. Feb. 3, 1903[85]

Prof. W. E. B. DuBois [*sic*]
Atlanta, Ga.
My Dear Sir:

I have your letter, and glad to know that you are going to do the work[86] for Potts & Co. I have had another letter from them also, I think they seem to be in earnest.

Very Sincerely,
Yours, P. L. Dunbar [signed]

Letter 183: February 20, 1903, PLD to W. E. B. Du Bois
Mr. Paul Laurence Dunbar
1214 E. 12th St.
Kansas City Mo. Feb 20 1903[87]

Mr. W. E. Burghardt Dubois [*sic*],
Dear Sir:

Will you kindly do me a favor to give me some facts about yourself which would be of interest in an article, which I am writing upon Representative Negroes?[88]

If you can find time to answer this at once, I shall be very greatly obliged.[89]

I am yours,
Very truly,
Paul Laurence Dunbar

Letter 184: April 20, 1903, Dodd, Mead & Co. to PLD
Dodd, Mead & Company
372 Fifth Avenue, Corner 35th St

New York April 20, 1903[90]

Mr. Paul Laurence Dunbar,
5355 Grove Avenue, Chicago.
Dear Mr. Dunbar:

We enclose herewith a check for $1000.00, in accordance with your letter and our telegrams, and a bill of sale for "When Malindy Sings,"[91] which please sign and return at your convenience. This completes the transaction, which we will hope will turn out to be for the best for you and for us.

Yours very truly,
Dodd, Mead & Co.

Letter 185: May 28, 1903, PLD to W. E. B. Du Bois

Prof. W. E. B. DuBois, [*sic*][92]
Atlanta, Ga.
My dear DuBois [*sic*]:

I regret that, on account of being away from my mail, I got your letter so late, but I hope my data did not come in too late for you to use it.[93] The picture I am sending direct to the magazine[94] from whom I heard yesterday. I am doing the same thing for Pott & Co., and thought you wanted the matter on some book.[95] Pardon the delay.

With best wishes I am
Yours sincerely,
Paul Laurence Dunbar

Letter 186: July 24, 1903, PLD to W. E. B. Du Bois

3209 Dearborn Street,
Chicago, Ill., July 24, 1903

Dr. W. E. B. Dubois [*sic*],[96]
Atlanta University,
Atlanta, Ga.,
My dear Dubois [*sic*]:

I have been reading your article in the Book Lovers' Magazine,[97] and thank you very much for your kindly mention of me, but I have also been doing for James Pott & Co. (the same firm with which you are now in touch) an article on the same subject, and we have said in the two articles very much the same things.[98] I am writing this so you will understand that I have not stolen your thunder. My article was done in April at Kansas City at the time that I was corresponding with you.

I have not yet got to your "Souls of Black Folk"[99] but I hope to very soon and I know just what a pleasure is in store for me there. Go on and do lots more of it.

Very sincerely yours,
Paul Laurence Dunbar

Letter 187: July 30, 1903, Brand Whitlock to PLD

629 East Winthrop St.
Toledo, Ohio, 30 July 1903[100]

Dear Paul:

The Tribune says today that you are sick,[101] and it tells a pretty story of one of your friends coming by and whistling a bugle call. I am not behind him in friendship or the desire to cheer, and I too sound a bugle call to you.[102] With all the smile and spirit I can put into it, to tell you that I am helping you all I can. Can you hear the hale [illegible] of a brother at this distance? I have wanted to tell you how much I liked that little thing you printed in the *Tribune* about our celebration on the 4th of July.[103] It brought me tears just as some of your other poems have done. The other day I saw a letter from Prof. William James[104] of Harvard at the Boston Evening Transcript and it was so good that I sent it to the editor of the Tribune asking him to reprint it. I don't suppose he will but he ought to. It is all sad and [illegible] but we must have [illegible] and above all faith. Someday, a long, long some day, no doubt, it will all come right. Meanwhile, you and I must get what press we can out of our songs and as much as you wish. [illegible] note in the harmony all the time.

I have at last got my Ohio novel[105] on paper. It lacks now but the unending work of revision. I'd like to look it over with you.

When you can, send me a line, but whether you write or not I know, and you know, that its (as old Walt says) "my spirit to thine, dear brother."[106]

Mrs. Whitlock joins in all [illegible].

as ever
Brand Whitlock

Letter 188: August 1, 1903, PLD to J. N. Matthews
3209 Dearborn St.
Chicago, Ill., Aug 1, 1903[107]

James Newton Matthews, M.D.,
Mason, Effingham, Co., Ill.,
    Are the skies ever going to fall?
My Dear old friend,
    I have never been more surprised in my life than I was this morning. I have been writing to you off and on until about three years ago and could never get a response, and here all of a sudden you come to life. I am so glad that I cannot wait until I am well enough to write you by hand but send you this little, old handshake of a machine. It is very, very good to hear from you again, though I am sorry to know that your eyes are not good. Let me hope that they will soon be better.
    If you ever come to Chicago please be sure to look me up. It must be confessed that you are wiser about the Tribune article than I because I have not even seen it, but it told quite the truth, and I am in such poor health that I am leaving very soon for the east;[108] were it not for that I could hope that I might see you some time when I was passing through your section of the state.
    With very, very grateful remembrances of all your kindness to me, I am

Sincerely your friend,
Paul Laurence Dunbar

LETTERS FROM 1904

Letter 189: September 30, 1904, PLD to Dr. F
Dayton, Ohio, September 30th, 1904[109]

Dear Dr. F:
            Long silence does not mean neglect,
            It only means
            That we may trust to friendship to reflect
            On the betweens.
    This is an apology.

Letter 190: September 30, 1904, PLD to James Corrothers

September 30, 1904[110]

Rev. James D. Corrothers,[111] South Haven, Mich.

My Dear Jim:[112]

I have your letter and was exceedingly glad to hear from you after all the years of your silence.[113] I cannot exactly write you that the report is untrue,[114] and I can only say that we hope it was exaggerated.

I sincerely wish you success in the founding of your church there and hope that you will do well in your old home and keep better health there than I have in mine. If the summer finds me still in the land of the living, I shall take pleasure in visiting you at South Haven. Shall be glad to have a line from you at any time,

> Very sincerely your friend,
> Paul Laurence Dunbar

Letter 191: October 21, 1904, PLD to Dr. F

Dayton, Ohio, Oct. 21, 1904[115]

My Dear Dr. F—:

You have turned my little poem very cleverly upon me. I insist that I meant it for an apology, and you, with the physician's subtle mind, have ferreted out a rebuke. It was nothing of the kind because I know I was entirely at fault, but it is so good to hear from you again that whether it was an apology or rebuke it has at least done me a great service.

I have indeed been very ill and am glad to be here at home where good nursing and good air ought to do me good, but I fear that I am not going to be allowed a chance to stay, as the doctors are crying California, even as before they cried Colorado.[116]

Mother joins me in very warm regards to you.

Letter 192: November 2, 1904, Theodore Roosevelt to PLD

White House, Washington[117]

Personal

November 2, 1904.

My dear Mr. Dunbar:

I am touched that you should have written me from your sick bed.

I appreciate the poem.[118] As a token of my regard, will you accept the accompanying two volumes of my speeches?[119]

    With best wishes, believe me,

Sincerely yours,

Theodore Roosevelt[120]

Mr. Paul Laurence Dunbar,

Dayton, Ohio.

Enclosures

Letter 193: November 23, 1904, PLD to Edwin Hackley

Dayton, Ohio, Nov. 23rd 1904[121]

Edw. H. Hackley, Esq.,[122]

Philadelphia, Pa.

My Dear Ed:

    I was very glad to get your letter or shall I call it a note, and your plea "Go back to Colorado," strikes me very near the bull's eye.

    I am thinking of going back, but I have transportation to California[123] and it would not be by way of Denver.

    I am so glad to hear that your mother is with you, and my mother joins me in felicitations upon that. I hope that Mrs. Hackley[124] is very well and enjoying the success which she deserves, and that your mother will continue to keep hale and hearty. You know the old stock are the real stock.

    There is a dangerous suggestion of a poem, Ed, in that line of yours, "The east for business, but the west for health."[125] Now take it up if you dare.

    As to the Mud Lake catfisher, if I go to Denver[126] and can find your old rubber boots as in the old days, look for a whole consignment of them, whether they come to me in schools or not.

Very sincerely your friend,

Paul Laurence Dunbar

Letter 194: December 20, 1904, Emmett J. Scott to PLD

Emmett J. Scott

Tuskegee Normal and Industrial Institute

Tuskegee, Alabama[127]

December 20, 1904

Mr. Paul Lawrence [*sic*] Dunbar
219 N. Summit St., Dayton, Ohio.
My dear Dunbar:

It is good to get a letter from you, and I appreciate it very much indeed. The little article which I published in The Student,[128] I clipped from a Northern newspaper, several weeks ago. I really took no note of the name of the newspaper, and am very sorry not to be able to send the information desired.[129] Certainly, however, I thought that it was entirely authentic.

I am very glad to learn that you are so much better. Our thoughts have been with you constantly during your illness.

Very truly yours,
Emmett J. Scott

LETTERS FROM 1905

Letter 195: May 23, 1905, Edward Dodd to PLD

Dodd, Mead & Company
372 Fifth Avenue, Corner 35th St
New York
May 23, 1905[130]

Mr. Paul Laurence Dunbar,
Dayton, O.
Dear Mr. Dunbar:

I am delighted to hear that you are out of bed again. I hope these warm days will quickly bring renewed health and strength. I shall, of course, be delighted to see any work of yours at any time.

I do not find that anything has been said about making the book for this year a child's book. I remember that we talked it over last year but gave it up and made "Li'l' Gal"[131] instead which was, by my way of thinking, typographically and ornamentally the prettiest illustrated book we have yet made.[132] The books and other illustrated books we have made have been imitated to such an extent that the market has been spoiled.[133] However, we shall hope for the best.

I am sorry to say that now it is too late to change it[134] into a child's book since the illustrations are made and the book is all up in type.[135] I am not at all sure that a child's book would go better. There have been poems for children in each one of the illustrated books so far[136] and I doubt whether we could have gathered enough together of purely child's poems for a book this fall. Possibly we can do it later.

I enclose a letter which is self-explanatory. I think it would be a good idea to do this.

Yours very truly,
Edward H. Dodd

Letter 196: October 4, 1905, PLD to Reginald W. Kauffman
Dayton, O., Oct. 4th, 1905.[137]

Mr. Reginald W. Kauffman[138]
Asso. Ed. Saturday Evening Post,
Philadelphia, Pa.
My Dear Mr. Kauffman:

I have your letter of recent date,[139] and as for my winter's work, it is like the core of the little poor boot-black apple, "they ain't goin' to be no work";[140] instead I am going down to North Carolina[141] to try to get in shape to work sometime in the vague misty future.

Don't ask me as to the value of verse writing[142] as a financial proposition. I have been contemplating for a long while the institution of a pension committee for ancient and decayed verse writers.[143]

As to an anecdote I don't think that I have one that is favorable to myself, except one that tells of a little occurrence down in Lexington, Ky. I had read there and my fame had spread throughout the town. Later on, in fact the next day, I was lying in a dentist's chair taking a quiet survey of the colored people who came in to the place, the dentist being my friend. Finally one old gentleman thinking that I was asleep came in and looked at me long and fixedly, then he turned with a grunt of disgust, "Is dat de Lau'ence Dunba'" he said, and being answered in the affirmative, he stumped out with the remark, "Uhm, I certainly did thing he was some big nice looking man."[144] This being taken for somebody besides myself is about the best that I have.

Thank you for your kindness and threatening you with a poem, or a short story, I am,

Very sincerely yours,
Paul L. Dunbar
219 N. Summit St.

Letter 197: November 13, 1905, PLD to Reginald W. Kauffman
Dayton, OH, Nov. 13th, 1905[145]

Reginald W Kauffman, Esq.,

Philadelphia, Pa.

My dear sir:

Tear up the little anecdote that you have of me, I have something better I think.

You may not know that I am an invalid, but lately I have had to have an attendant, and we were induced to hire an old colored preacher. He is supposed to have rather a wide knowledge, and in the arduous hours of sitting up, he looked over my books, finally he said to my mother, in a very condescending tone, "Well, my sister what does your son propose to make of himself?" and I am still wondering.

In order to spoil the point of the story I am sending you a poem "Sling along."[146] I hope you will like it, and if you don't I shall put it up in a book.[147]

Very sincerely,

Paul Laurence Dunbar

Letter 198: December 15, 1905, PLD to Dr. Fisher
219 N Summit St.

Dayton, O., Dec. 15th, 1905[148]

Dear Dr. F—:

Of course you must have known the reason that I have not answered your letter before this. I confess that I was not in a very cheerful mood and the mood has not yet come, but I must drop you a line to let you know just what a bit of good-for-nothingness I am. My life constitutes of going to bed at the beginning of the month and staying there, with the very brief intervals of half an hour or so, until the beginning of the next month. This repeated over *ad libitum* and you have my total existence.

Of course there are some friends who come in,[149] and some books that occasionally I get to read, but usually I am studying the pattern of the ceiling until I could make a very clever sketch of it from memory without the trouble of learning to draw.

I was very glad to have this word from you. It seems to put me in touch with the world again, although you say that you are up in the mountains away from the world. You are nearer to it than I. It is the proximity of the heart and mind, rather than physical nearness, that counts.

I hope that you and all the family are still very well, and I trust you will keep your health, a thing which ought to be taught in our schools if ever a branch needed teaching.

I am not going to be entirely cheerless now. I had a visit from Mrs. Eugene Field[150] this week and later she sent me her own picture of the poet[151] which has been her companion for years. Besides that, John Cecil Clay[152] was good enough to send me an exquisite book of his, "The Lover's Mother Goose."[153] So you see my cup runneth over. Add to this the expectation of an answer to this letter and I can defy a few more nights of pain and days of loneliness.

Letter 199: December 30, 1905, PLD to Dr. Fisher
Dayton, O., December 30th, 1905[154]

My Dear Dr. F—:

All greetings of the season to you and your family. And thanks for the presents which I prize very highly. Your counterfeit presentment makes me feel almost as if you were here. But will you please ask Mrs. F. where she got the card with my writing on it, "Howdy, Honey, Howdy,"[155] because it is my writing. I am burning with curiosity.

You have spent a pleasant holiday season, I know. How could you help it in the Arcadia[156] you have found for yourself?

If you do not write much poetry as the days go on I shall come to be greatly disappointed in you.

Do you ever hear from that erratic scribe, Mr. Cowan?[157] I used to come across something of his now and then but have not for a long while.

I, too, am lying fallow. I believe my soil has become greatly impoverished and it will take a good many more rains and snows to put anything into it worth coming out in blossom. But my greatest help will be the knowledge that my friends keep in touch with me, and now and then a line like an electric spark flashes from one to the other and I am new again and unafraid.

Write me when you have leisure, and believe me, with all gratitude to you and Mrs. F——.

LETTERS FROM 1906

Letter 200: February 5, 1906, H. A. Tobey to PLD

Feb. 5th/ 1906[158]

My Dear Paul!

I wrote a long letter to you and then tore it up because I found it was not in to [illegible] me and I know that is not my [illegible], the more I have come to believe I am any fool. My own analysis of myself is just, I am a fool, since I have read the papers of the last few days I have come to that conclusion. I almost wish I had not loved and had a wife, and had children, or rather that I had never had been born. Did you not read the newspapers? A poor little man who's [*sic*] name is Lamb,[159] and who by dint of circumstance was elected to the senate calls on all the bad names he can think of. Drunkard, keeper of a whorehouse, dishonest +c. + c. and says both the Democrats on any Board are not Democrats, that the whole Board stand in with me.[160] That they must all be removed in order to get into the rottenou of this situation and publishes this in great headlines in the newspapers. When the papers called me up I only say "Po little Lamb" let my friends answer for me.[161] Oh how I wish I could get from under, but now I must fight and I have read your poem over and over "Strength for the Fight."[162] Maybe I will get better although I am very weak now. I have been sick for ten days, fever, spitting blood, aching all over, but I have been better for the last two days notwithstanding I ought to have been in bed, I had to get up, had committees of people here.[163] I now have made them my friends. So have some [illegible] to help when the butter comes.

Poor boy, you are resting easy.[164] Wish you had to fight like I do. You would forget you ever had what someone called Tuberculosis.

I began my first letter to you this evening with "you poor black discouraged dying wretch, I envy you." You had the power to put on canvas stretch a picture into view. But on I plod, victim to a victim's nod. With none to see but my God.

But let this sentiment all go. If I had more of the practical, I would only be forgetting so. Yes, I am not discouraged, for if all the good I have done will not make amends for my [illegible] I will not see faults. My heart breaks, that there is no justice to say nothing of mercy. Don't let me worry you. If I were a Catholic I could go to my priest but in you my friend [illegible]. I do not know anyone closer to the thorns than you, so I [illegible] and my heart. You know [illegible]. He who steals my purse steals trash but he who filches my good name &c. &c.[165] "Poor little Lamb." I say it in putty, he knows not what he does. He thinks he can only be tall by tearing someone down.

Whatever may happen to me, don't be surprised if about next Sunday you may see me Brand Whitlock, & John Matthews down to see you. [illegible] selfishness, his [illegible] cannot break that [illegible] chord of love. But something of the practical. Three weeks ago I took Alice to New York.[166] We went to see one of the Great [illegible] there with one of his own pupils. Our friend said I want you to hear Miss Tobey play. Alice said papa what shall I play, I told her a little thing. He said is that yours. I said yes. He said that's good play some more. I then told her to play "Resignation" which is deep + difficult. He said "that's yours also," she did not hear, I said yes. He said "I [illegible] you. Why is that, there is so much talent from the Mrs." Alice smiles. He gave her [illegible] the [illegible] she pays for and in addition gives her tickets to [illegible] &c. &c. Oh says Papa, he's just like you so kind, and he is the most wonderful man, I did not say so to her, but my reply would be because she is the most wonderful girl. In this connection, what poem of yours would like of all others, rather have music set to?[167] Tell me, and Alice will do it to please you more than any you have had yet. Good night. Let me hear from you. Your mother can write a few lines for you.

H. A. Tobey

Paul, I can't read this now. You have plenty of time, so I will let you decipher it and correct the spelling and grammar.

Letter 201: February 11, 1906, Brand Whitlock to H. A. Tobey

Brand Whitlock to H. A. Tobey[168]

Toledo, Oh

February 11, 1906

I wish I could be with you all tomorrow to pay my tribute to poor Paul.[169] But I cannot, and feeling as I do his loss, I cannot now attempt any estimate of his wonderful personality that would be all worthy. If friendship knew obligation I would acknowledge my debt to you for the boon of knowing Paul Dunbar. It is one of the countless good deeds to your credit that you were among the first to recognize the poet in him and help him to a larger and freer life.

For Paul was a poet; and I find that when I have said that I have said the greatest and most splendid thing that can be said about a man. Men call this or that man great and load him with what the world holds to be honors—its soldiers and statesmen, its scholars and scientists. This may be very well, but I think we know that after all the soldiers and the statesmen and savants are not concerned with the practical things of life, the things that are really worthwhile. Nature, who knows so much better than man about everything, cares nothing at all for the little distinctions, and when she elects one of her children for her most important work, bestows on him the rich gift of poesy, and assigns him a post in the greatest of the arts, she invariably seizes the opportunity to show her contempt of rank and title and race and land and creed. She took Burns from a plow, and Paul from an elevator, and Paul has done for his own people what Burns did for the peasants of Scotland—he has expressed them in their own way and in their own words. There are many analogies between these two poets, just as there are many analogies between Paul and Shelley, and Keats, and Byron, and Pushkin.[170] They all died very young,[171] they knew little of the joys that are common to common men, but they had their griefs, their sorrows, their sufferings, far beyond the common lot.[172] But the terms on which Nature lets her darlings become poets are always obdurate. To the poet, as Whitman[173] says, agonies must become as changes of garment; he must suffer all things, hope all things, endure all things because he must know all things, and knowledge is not otherwise obtained. He must go through torments and pain, he must feel that dreadful hunger of soul, and usually he must die young—all for the sake of being a poet. And that is enough for him after all, for if the common joys and satisfactions—rest and peace and home and all that—are denied him, he has the joy of artistic creation, which is the highest man may know. It is enough for the poet that he be a poet, yet this is not his glory. His glory is that through this experience he expresses for the race all joy and grief, all the moods and emotions, exalted or depressed, of the human soul, and myriads of voiceless people, living about him and living after him, find solace and relief that come of expression, which, were it not for him, they would be compelled to go without, and suffer dumbly.[174]

I have spoken of our friend as a poet of his own people, and he was this; he expressed his own race—its hum, its kindliness, its fancy, its love of grace and melody; he expressed, too, its great sufferings, and what race has suffered more, or more unjustly, or what race has borne its sufferings with sublime patience? It is a race that has produced many great and worthy men, in the very face of that has produced many great and worthy men, in the very face of untold opposition and prejudice, but the work of these men has been more or less confined to their race. But without the least disparagement, I think I can say that Paul's range and appeal were wider than those of any other of his race; if they had not been, he would not have been a poet. For the true poet is universal as is the love he incarnates in himself, and Paul's best poetry has this quality of universality.

I am very glad that he was so thoroughly American and democratic. He might have been a poet without having been an American, but he could not have been a poet without having been democratic, and I believe I may safely add that he could not have been a poet without having at least the spirit of America. For all the poets have had this spirit; they have loved liberty, equality and fraternity. You know Browning[175] says:

> Shakespeare was of us. Milton was for us,
> Burns, Shelly were with us—they watch from their graves.[176]

There was nothing foreign in Paul's poetry, nothing imported, nothing imitated it was all original, native and indigenous. Thus he becomes the poet, not of his own race alone—I wish I could make people see this—but the poet of you and me and of all men everywhere.

You and I knew something of his deeper sufferings, something of the disease that really killed him. I can never forget the things he said about this that last evening we spent together. I know nothing anywhere so pathetic as this brave, gentle, loving spirit, with his poet's heart, moving among men who, though far his inferior in intellectual and spiritual endowment, yet claimed to be—but I must not recall such things now. The deep melancholy this caused him has been expressed over and over in his poems, "The Warrior's Prayer,"[177] "We Wear the Mask," and others veritably steeped in it. Let that suffice.

That last evening he recited—Oh! what a voice he had!—his "Ships That Pass in the Night."[178] You will remember. I sat and listened, sadly conscious that I would not hear him often again, knowing that voice would soon be mute. I can hear him now and see the expression as he said "Passing! Passing!" It was prophetic.

We shall hear that deep melodious voice no more; his humor, his drollery, his exquisite mimicry—these are gone. And tomorrow you will lay his tired body away. Fittingly enough, on Lincoln's birthday. But his songs will live and give his beautiful personality an immortality in this world, and we—we can remember that he is with Theocritus[179] tonight.

Yours very sincerely,
Brand Whitlock

Letter 202: February 24, 1906, Dodd, Mead & Company to W. E. B. Du Bois

Dodd, Mead & Company[180]
372 Fifth Avenue, Corner 35th Street
New York Feb. 24, 1906

Mr. W. E. Burghardt Du Bois,
Atlanta, G.
Dear Sir:

We are sorry to say that we have no such bibliography made up of Mr. Dunbar's works nor do we believe that a life of him would sell sufficiently well to warrant its publication.[181] We thank you, however, for writing us, and remain,

Yours very truly, Dodd. Mead Co

Letter 203: August 2, 1906, Theodore Roosevelt to Lida K. Wiggins

Oyster Bay, L. I. August 2, 1906[182]

My Dear Mrs. Wiggins,

I have your letter of the 27th. While I only had the pleasure of meeting Mr. Dunbar once or twice, I was a great admirer of his poetry and prose.[183]

I do not believe I ever spoke such a sentence as that you quote in reference to him.[184] I had been struck by the artistic merit of his work, and had not thought of what you speak of as his "philosophy" save in the sense that all really artistic work has a philosophy of application to the human race.

Sincerely yours,
Theodore Roosevelt

Notes

Chapter i

1. Ohio Historical Society (hereafter OHS), reel 1. Metcalf records this letter as written on June 7, 1890, but the letter itself is dated June 9, 1890. See Metcalf, *Paul Laurence Dunbar*.

2. Charles W. Faber (unknown–1935) ran the *Democratic Sheet*; he also managed the *Dayton Times* and *Evening News*. He published several texts on Dayton, Ohio, and was deeply involved in local organizations there.

3. Dunbar became Orville's client in December 1890 at the inception of the weekly *Dayton Tattler*, an overtly political newspaper aimed primarily at a black audience. The December 27, 1890, issue, for example, contains an article by Dunbar in which he encouraged voting for change, as well as demanding better jobs and wages. Because of an inability to maintain funding, only three issues were released. These range from December 13 to 27, 1890; Dunbar is the main contributor.

4. Dunbar published several poems in his local high school newspaper, the *High School Times*; he also served as the general assistant editor from January 1889 until the end of the school year.

5. OHS, reel 1.

6. A cowboy and Indian tale in western dialect, "The Tenderfoot" marks the sale of Dunbar's first story for publication. A. N. Kellogg bought the story and resold it to newspapers. The story appeared in a number of local papers at the time, and the sale helped boost Dunbar's morale. He made two dollars more with this publication than he did per week as an elevator attendant. Dunbar's "Little Billy," another western dialect story, appeared next, on page 2 of the *St. Landry Clarion* (Opelousas, LA) on September 3, 1892.

7. Ansel Nash Kellogg (1832–1886) founded the A. N. Kellogg Newspaper Company. Though Kellogg was originally a small-town editor in Baraboo, Wisconsin, he was responsible for creating the first independent American newspaper syndicate in 1865. See Howe, "Country Newspapers." Howe was editor of the Atchison *Globe*.

8. OHS, reel 1.

9. This is the first letter Dunbar wrote to his mentor, benefactor, and close friend Dr. James Newton Matthews (1852–1910). Dunbar was invited to the

Western Association of Writers conference on June 27, 1892, by his former teacher Mrs. Helen M. Truesdall. Dunbar presented the welcoming address and met John Clark Ridpath and Will Pfrimmer. Most notably, Matthews wrote "The Old Country Road" and was the "first student" of the University of Illinois. Matthews was an acquaintance of Mark Twain and James Whitcomb Riley. He published a collection of poems, *Temple Vale and Other Poems* (1888). Matthews was a correspondent for the *Chicago Record* and other regional papers. See "New Registrar's Office," 136.

10. Dunbar struggled to receive payment for any of his verses after his initial publication and recital at the Western Association of Writers conference, even after successfully showcasing a twenty-six-line poem, which opens "Westward the course of empire takes its way." For this address in full, see Eident and Taylor, *On Prairie Winds*, 305.

11. Also referred to as "Memorial Day" and "An Easter Ode," both poems appear in *Oak and Ivy*.

12. Dayton, Ohio; 1892 was the only year the Western Association of Writers met in Dayton. Yet this meeting helped determine the direction of Dunbar's career. Dunbar attended several other Western Association of Writers conferences. He wrote Alice Ruth Moore on July 9, 1895, that his reception at the Western Association of Writers conference in Eagle Lake, Indiana, was positive. "Although I am the only colored member, I am not allowed to feel it," Dunbar explained. Dunbar was asked to address "One Point in the Ethics of Short Story Writing" and to read "The Luck of Lazy Lang," which was never published. See Metcalf, "Letters of Paul and Alice Dunbar," 58–59.

13. According to Wiggins, Dunbar's hopes escalated when Ridpath, Matthews, and Pfrimmer approached him at his elevator position the day after Dunbar read his poem to the Western Association of Writers. They expressed great interest in Dunbar's poems, requested copies, and promised future publicity. Wiggins avers that upon arriving at the Callahan Building, Ridpath, Matthews, and Pfrimmer found Dunbar working, with a "copy of the *Century* Magazine, a writing pad with pencil, and a lexicon"—a regular habit of Dunbar's according to Joanne Braxton. Though elated by their visit, Dunbar was deeply shamed by his working conditions: he divulged to a friend, "My embarrassment was terrible. In the midst of a sentence, perhaps, a ring would come from the top of the building for the elevator, and I would have to excuse myself and run up after passengers." See Wiggins, *Life and Works*, 31. See also Braxton, *Collected Poetry*, xi.

14. William Wood Pfrimmer (1856–1935), an Indiana native, poet, educator, and lawyer, published two books of poems in dialect: *Driftwood* (1890) and *The Legend of Grape Island and Other Poems* (1907). A dear friend to Matthews and Riley, Pfrimmer titled the poem "To James Newton Matthews" in *Driftwood*. Matthews referred to Pfrimmer as "The Kentland Poet." In a December 21, 1887, letter to Riley, Matthews wrote, "Pfrimmer visited me there days last week. He is very fond of you—and I don't suppose you know how many good things he has written. He has a wonderful vigor of thought, and is the best of all imitators of you. There is

no mistake about it. I advised him sincerely to abandon dialect—for the reason that he constantly lays himself open to such a charge," see Eident and Taylor, *On Prairie Winds*, 193.

15. This comment has been taken out of context before by scholars who incorrectly assume it is Riley whom Dunbar praised.

16. James Whitcomb Riley (1849–1916), the famous American "Hoosier Poet," was a dear friend to both Dunbar and J. N. Matthews. Riley wrote a sonnet to Matthews, "In Answer to a Letter on the Anatomy of the Sonnet." The two shared a rich, deep friendship and were among the many who helped Dunbar become known. Riley read Matthews's article on Dunbar and then wrote Dunbar a letter of support that encouraged Dunbar to publish *Oak and Ivy*. See Riley to Dunbar, October 27, 1892.

17. Dr. John Clark Ridpath (1840–1900), a historian, befriended Dunbar at the Western Association of Writers conference and introduced Dunbar to the audience there. Ridpath's prediction was correct: Chicago became a publication hub by the late nineteenth century, second only to New York City.

18. Charles Johanningsmeier notes that the American Press Association (APA) was similar to many "readyprint" publishing houses that used a single area to consider publishing literary submissions (*Fiction and the American Literary Marketplace*, 46). Johanningsmeier notes that APA staff "act[ed] more like book and magazine editors and unlike readyprint editors," as the APA staff often "wrote readers' reports on the fiction manuscripts submitted to them and dealt personally with their authors" (46).

19. OHS, reel 3.

20. Charles Clyde Hunt (unknown) was the editor of the American Press Association, which was incorporated in 1886 in New York. Hunt later became the president, treasurer, editor, and manager of the *Masonic Times*. See *Moody's Manual of Investments*, 1716.

21. This story has not been recovered. On the backs of a few of Dunbar's letters, titles of several other stories (both handwritten and typed) are listed that he likely submitted for publication consideration, though they were never published in his lifetime. These include "A Monologue," "The Party," "The Haunted Plantation," and "Ole Conjurin' [Conju'in] Joe." Martin and Primeau recovered these texts in manuscript format at the Rare Book Collection at the University of Dayton and published them in their coedited collection, *In His Own Voice: Dramatic & Other Uncollected Works of Paul Lawrence Dunbar*. For more recent recovery work on Dunbar, see Thomas Morgan, "'Sue' and 'A Southern Silhouette'"; and Turpin, "Twilight Is Their Child."

22. See Martin and Hudson, *Paul Laurence Dunbar Reader*, 410.

23. Dunbar frequently expressed this feeling in these early letters while he was still an elevator attendant. See, for example, his letter to H. A. Tobey from July 13, 1895, where he bemoaned being "tied down" by "menial labor" and felt that any "escape from it" provided him with "brief respite that made a return to the drudgery

doubly hard." According to Charles W. Dustin, a Dayton lawyer and then judge who held an office in the Callahan Building where Dunbar worked, Dunbar came across the elevator attendant position after inquiring about a position in his office. Dustin recalls helping Dunbar get the job despite hard times replete with discriminatory practices. According to Dustin, Dunbar "came on a weekly errand . . . in my office, and one day applied for work. There was nothing in my control that I could give him except the position of elevator boy in the Callahan block, of which I then had charge as Mr. Callahan's agent. He took it, borrowed a law book, and went on duty." See Dustin, "Paul Laurence Dunbar," 7.

24. Matthews obtained some poems Dunbar had written after meeting him. Matthews quoted from these poems in addressing letters to various presses to help garner support for Dunbar. One such letter was published in the *Indianapolis Journal* on October 2, 1892. See, for example, "A Negro Poet: A Young Man Whose Literary Talent Shows Itself in Spite of Unfavorable Environment," *Indianapolis Journal*, October 2, 1892, 6.

25. This book would become *Oak and Ivy*. Though scholars often note that Dunbar needed an advance to begin the process, Dunbar explained that although "an advance of $100 was at first demanded . . . upon consideration the publisher agreed to wait for his compensation until the poems were sold." See *Detroit Free Press*, January 5, 1902.

26. Dunbar would eventually be advanced this money in November 1892. See Dunbar to Matthews, November 23, 1892.

27. The *Chicago Daily News* ran from 1890 to 1894.

28. "The Ol' Tunes" first appeared in the *Indianapolis Journal* in the summer of 1892.

> You kin talk about yer anthem
>   An' yer arias an' sich,
>   An' yer modern choir-singin'
>   That you think so awful rich;
>   But you orter heerd us youngsters
>   In the times now far away,
>   A-singin o' the ol' tunes
>   In the ol'-fashioned way

29. By November 29, Dunbar had heard from Pfrimmer. See Dunbar's letter to Matthews on November 29, 1892. Dunbar asked about Pfrimmer several times; it remains unclear why he asked so often.

30. John Richard Meader (1870–1921) was a New England writer most known for his contributions as Graham Hood to the *New York Globe*. Of these contributions, he is most famous for "The Ten Laws of Success." He was also known for his membership in the Society of Friends and his publication of *The Common Cause*, which discussed a wide range of social issues from child labor laws and enslavement in England to education and prison reform. Meader gained more prominence in the early twentieth century, having contributed several pieces to various

periodicals by the latter nineteenth century. For a short biography, see Scott, *History of Passaic*, 270–71. See also the entry on Meader in "Review and Comment," *Business and the Bookkeeper*, 6–7.

31. OHS, reel 3.

32. Dunbar is writing J. N. Matthews here.

33. Thomas G. Gentry (1843–1905) was a famous ornithologist from Germantown, Pennsylvania, and a frequent contributor to scientific journals during the 1870s and 1880s. His book *Nests and Eggs of Birds of the United States* (1882) was not reviewed well, and it essentially ended Gentry's already waning career. Gentry's interest in ornithology persisted, though, despite the damage the unnamed reviewer did to Gentry's career. See Folsom, "Mystical Ornithologist," 19.

34. Dunbar may be referring to a type of painting developed by Gustave Courbet (1819–1877). Courbet was known for a style that took realism literally: allegedly, Courbet would paint only what he could see and endeavored to paint things realistically. He famously painted *L'origine du monde*.

35. The Fisk Jubilee Singers are an a cappella ensemble from Fisk University in Nashville, Tennessee, who travel and perform Negro spirituals formerly sung by antebellum slaves. The original tour of vocal artists, including two former slaves and several teenagers, was created by George L. White, a Fisk University treasurer and music professor, to help raise money for the fledgling integrated university in 1871. White, drawing on the biblical reference to the year of Jubilee in the Book of Leviticus, chapter 25, named the group "The Jubilee Singers." Their first performance, on November 16, 1871, was at Oberlin College in Ohio, where they sang before a national convention of ministers. In 1882, Frederick Loudin took over White's troupe and they continued to perform nationally and internationally with wide acclaim, but they were able to avoid the trap of falling into the tradition of minstrelsy. One article in the *Centralia (WA) Daily Chronicle* observed that "there is a strange witchery in the way they render the plantation songs of the sunny south" (October 27, 1892, 3).

36. Jay Martin suggests that the poem Dunbar likely sent was "The Sparrow," later published in *Oak and Ivy*, *Majors and Minors*, and *Lyrics of Lowly Life*.

37. For some reason a myth persisted that Dunbar never edited his work and thus was an inferior poet. Clearly, this was not the case; Dunbar revised regularly. On October 2, 1898, Dunbar wrote his friend Dr. F (Fisher), noting, "I am sending you herewith a copy of 'The Uncalled,' which at last sees the light in book form. Even now, though I have revised and revised it, there are many things about it that I would change if I had the chance." Beyond this, several letters in this collection show that Dunbar revised much of his work.

38. Dunbar received pledges of one dollar for copies of his book *Oak and Ivy*. Because Dunbar had to recoup the money in order to pay back the publisher for printing costs, he marketed his work feverishly to sell copies to people in the Callahan Building, to the *High School Times*, and to other benefactors. He was able to sell eighty-five copies in three days, thus quickly recouping the $125 he owed the printer.

39. OHS, reel 1.

40. Charles A. Johnson (1865–unknown) was an African American journalist. He served as a correspondent of the *Columbus (OH) Evening Dispatch*, *Columbus (OH) Sentinel*, *Cincinnati Afro-American*, *Cleveland Globe*, and *Chicago Appeal*. Johnson also served as a clerk for the War Department. He wrote "The Dialect Story and Its Evil Influences." For more information on Johnson (though incomplete), see Penn, *Afro-American Press*, 542.

41. Although Dunbar published several Christmas poems throughout his lifetime, he never published a book of Christmas poetry while he was alive, despite his best attempts. In 1914, *Speakin' o' Christmas and Other Christmas and Special Poems* was published posthumously by Dodd, Mead. Dunbar is likely referring to *Oak and Ivy*, in which the final collection contained only one Christmas poem, "Christmas Carol."

42. OHS, reel 1.

43. Dunbar is writing Matthews here.

44. Dunbar is referring to "A Negro Poet: A Young Man Whose Literary Talent Shows Itself in Spite of Unfavorable Environment," where Matthews claimed Dunbar was not only "chained like a galley-slave to the ropes of a dingy elevator" but also endeavored to show that Dunbar was being paid "starvation wages." See the *Indianapolis Journal*, October 2, 1892, 6.

45. Shortly after, the editor of the *Herald* asked Dunbar to go to Chicago and write about the World's Fair.

46. OHS, reel 1.

47. Matthews's public proclamation of Dunbar's poetic abilities in newspapers around the country solicited fan mail, and supporters sent him money to buy books.

48. Dunbar heard from Pfrimmer: see PLD to J. N. Matthews, November 29, 1892.

49. A member of the Western Association of Writers. Little is known about her, but she is noted to have lived in Dayton, Ohio. See the *Midland Monthly*, July 1896, 416.

50. We have been unable to locate information on this journal.

51. Dialect verse was often written by well-known regionalist white poets, including Matthews and Riley, as well as Twain and countless other authors. Controversial for many reasons, dialect verse remains both immensely popular and problematic, especially when representing African Americans in a stereotypical manner such as one sees in the works of the plantation tradition. Dunbar's use of dialect has spurred more than a century of debate: arguments over his use of dialect remain even today. Regardless, requests for dialect would become one of the regular demands of Dunbar's audience and publishers alike (especially the *Century*), and it would haunt, hurt, and anger Dunbar until he died, even though he enjoyed writing dialect pieces at times. Howells may have damned Dunbar to this fate, though this is also contested, as Dunbar was publishing dialect poems before Howells's review of *Majors and Minors* (1895). Yet Howells wrote Ripley Hitchcock of Major

Pond's plan "to platform young Dunbar next winter" and predicted that "a book of entirely *black* verse from [Dunbar] would succeed." See William Dean Howells to Ripley Hitchcock, July 29, 1896, Rare Book and Manuscript Library, Columbia University; emphasis by underline in original. Criticism of Dunbar's use of dialect followed into the twentieth century, though not all critics agreed, and some viewed and still view Dunbar's use of dialect as powerful, political, and subversive. Another challenge Dunbar faced was simply based on race. While Riley was praised by Matthews, for example, for writing "humorous" dialect poems such as "When De Folks Gone" in *Afterwhiles* (Indianapolis: Bobbs-Merrill, 1887), 189, Matthews also told Riley he preferred his "non-dialect" pieces in *Green Fields and Running Brooks*, but he had been unable to "over-come [his] old prejudice in favor of [the] non-dialect poems; and in saying this, I know that I antagonize the popular taste" (Eident and Taylor, *On Prairie Winds*, 330). Dunbar faced the opposite judgment from Howells with *Majors and Minors* as well as countless others works despite the clear proof that Dunbar's poems in Standard English show that he was equally talented, and despite Dunbar's preference for writing in Standard English, as indicated in his letters. The topic of Dunbar and the use of dialect remains hotly debated. Critics accused Dunbar of being an "Uncle Tom" and of using dialect as representative of the African American population in an essentialist, plantation-style manner. Hudson argues that it was a "myth" that Dunbar disliked his dialect pieces and that Dunbar "was forced to write in that vein by his editors." Hudson continues, "It has been concluded . . . that his dialect work constituted a surrender to the racism so evident in the nation at the time. This supposition, however, badly misrepresents Dunbar's verse as well as the poet's own commitment to the black community. To an English interviewer in 1897, Dunbar remarked: 'I must confess my fondest love is for the Negro pieces. . . . These little songs I sing because I must. They have grown instinctively in me. . . . [The] poems form in my mind long before they are written on paper'" (Hudson, "Paul Laurence Dunbar: Regional Heritage," 439). But Dunbar knew that in order to maintain a public presence, he had to maintain a certain level of decorum (or, a mask). Despite Hudson's point, Dunbar's private correspondence reveals an entirely different view. As such, Jarrett has called for a "re-categorization of American literary realism" to alleviate these distractions and fallouts from these debates and to "depart from twentieth-century debates over whether or not Dunbar sold out to inherently racist mainstream literary and publishing tastes" ("'Entirely Black Verse,'" 500). It is essential to note that Dunbar also wrote in many dialects. For instance, Dunbar's first dialect poem was "Lager Beer," although he was never compensated for it. Published on December 13, 1890, it is in German dialect and appeared in the first edition of the *Dayton Tattler*. In his early years, Dunbar experimented with many dialects; this aligns him with other local color regionalist writing as seen in the local color writing of Joel Chandler Harris, William Dean Howells, and so many others in the late nineteenth century. According to Braxton, Dunbar experimented with "regional language" from "German-American, Irish-American, and Midwestern dialects" (*Collected Poetry*, xxiii). Hudson agrees, arguing that Dunbar "was part of a regional movement in literature that stressed dialect conversation. In all probability, Dunbar loved language and delighted to experiment with it" ("Paul Laurence Dunbar: Regional Heritage," 439). Dunbar's March 8, 1895, letter from E. C. Martin supports this, as Dunbar submitted pieces about Ireland (presumably written in dialect) for publication. See the August 25, 1896, letter from Dunbar to his mother, where he expresses joy at writing and performing in dialect. Indeed, Dunbar may have used dialect to gain his fame, and it clearly worked; however, it also may have pigeonholed him. Johnson quotes Dunbar: "I didn't start as a dialect poet. I simply came to the conclusion that I could write it as well, if not better, than anybody else I knew of, and that by doing so I should gain a hearing. I gained the hearing, and now they don't want me to write anything but dialect" (*Along This Way*, 110). There is more to this discussion; an intense debate followed Dunbar's choices. See Dunbar to Matthews, November 16, 1892.

52. OHS, reel 1.

53. Around this time, Dunbar decided to publish *Oak and Ivy*. After he was first rejected by the United Brethren Publishing House because he couldn't secure the funds to sell copies of his book, the business manager of the publishing house, William Lawrence Blocher (1854–unknown), gave his personal guarantee for the book, promising that it would be out in time for Christmas. Gentry's biography, *Paul Laurence Dunbar: Poet*, goes into the details of this story.

54. Much of Dunbar's unease can be attributed to some of the pressure he felt as many local friends and mentors helped drum up support to publish *Oak and Ivy*.

55. James Ross (1848–1913) was a Canadian businessman, lawyer, engineer, and philanthropist who earned his fortune in railway construction. Ross made numerous donations to various charitable and cultural institutions. When he read Matthews's newspaper article on Dunbar describing his plight as a poor African American man trying to make it in the literary world, he sent twenty dollars to Matthews to help Dunbar forward in his literary pursuits. See Eident and Taylor, *On Prairie Winds*, 328.

56. OHS, reel 1. Dated November 27, 1892, this letter was written while Dunbar was in Colorado at the Brown Palace Hotel. At the time, Riley was organizing several performances for his western lecture circuit in Colorado.

57. Riley wrote this letter to Dunbar in response to Matthews's piece "A Negro Poet: A Young Man Whose Literary Talent Shows Itself in Spite of Unfavorable Environment," *Indianapolis Journal*, October 2, 1892.

58. "A Drowsy Day" is included in *Oak and Ivy*, 7. See "Negro Poet."

59. In a letter to Matthews, Riley explains that he "picked up one of Paul Dunbar's poems 'way out here; and have just wrote him about it . . . to lend a hand, if possible, toward the initial boost you gave him. Certainly, he deserves applause, and if he can stand it, there's the making of a very novel type of poet in him—a credit not only to his own race [but] to Freedom's everywhere.'" See Eident and Taylor, *On Prairie Winds*, 324.

60. OHS, reel 1.

61. Eident and Taylor include an updated, uncited clipping for Matthews from Dunbar that reads: "The sketch of Paul Dunbar, the talented colored youth of Dayton, O, which appeared in the Journal some weeks ago from the pen of Dr. James Newton Matthews, of Mason, Ill. has attracted considerable attention and has brought the writer letters of inquiry from various parts of the country. One gentleman from Montreal manifested his interest in a practical way by sending Dr. Matthews $20 to be used in buying books for young Dunbar. This gentleman suggests that the case affords an opportunity for philanthropists and friends of the negro race to do an individual and his people a service by assisting this lad to a more congenial occupation in which he can better develop his literary and poetic abilities and that will allow him more time for study and self-improvement. He says: I consider that a colored poet of sufficient ability to take a name for himself would do more to enlighten and to encourage ambition in the multitude of the colored people in America than almost anything else that could be done for them. They would have someone to look up to—one whose pen would diffuse many wholesome truths to the people of his race and would imbue others with the desire to emulate his success." See Eident and Taylor, *On Prairie Winds*, 328. Also included with this letter is Dunbar's poem "To Dr. James Newton Matthews," which Dunbar would include in *Oak and Ivy*.

62. Quackenbos, *Illustrated History of Ancient Literature*. Eident and Taylor mistakenly transcribed this title as Inackenlos' *Ancient Literature* (*On Prairie Winds*, 326).

63. *Harper's Cyclopaedia of British and American Poetry* (New York: Harper Brothers, 1881). Epes Sargent (1813–1880) was an American newspaper editor and correspondent, biographer, poet, and dramatist. He worked as an editor for several outlets in Massachusetts and Washington and traveled in the circles of Daniel Webster, Henry Clay, and John C. Calhoun. See Nelson, *Almanac of American Letters*, 1981. Nelson includes Sargent as a part of the Knickerbocker Group.

64. *Oak and Ivy*.

65. We have been unable to identify this story.

66. OHS, reel 1.

67. *Oak and Ivy*.

68. Reviews were very positive.

69. This was an American magazine launched by the Meredith Corporation on February 16, 1883, featuring a "Ruth Ashmore advice column" written by Isabel Mallon.

70. The poem is quoted in its entirety in Matthews's essay on Dunbar, "Negro Poet."

71. We have been unable to locate this piece.

72. The *Ladies' Home Journal*. Dunbar is very likely referring to "The Old Country Road," published in the September issue.

73. The *Youth's Companion* was an illustrated weekly newspaper out of Boston

from 1827 to 1929, published by the Perry Mason Company. It was initially aimed at children, but the audience increased to half a million subscribers and widened in scope to reach a general family audience. Dunbar did publish in the *Youth's Companion*. See, for instance, "Old Abe's Conversation."

74. This remains a point of contention for many who accuse Dunbar of being insincere in his portrayal of a life he never knew and for using a dialect he did not speak himself. Dunbar was not born into slavery. However, that Dunbar was the son of former slaves must be considered; Dunbar felt this recounting of this heritage added integrity and authority to his stories. Worthy of note is the complication that dialect writing was exceptionally popular at the time. Dunbar is said to have admired white dialect authors, including Ruth McEnery Stuart (1849–1917), who wrote *Sonny: A Christmas Guest* (1894), and Joel Chandler Harris (1848–1908), author of countless texts in the plantation tradition but known mostly for his Uncle Remus tales. Samuel Chapman Armstrong's *The Southern Workman* from 1892 contains the literary note: "Paul Laurence Dunbar, speaking of dialect writers, in an interview reported in the Kansas City *Star*, says: 'It is difficult to put any name before that of Ruth McEnery Stuart, who depicts both the humorous and pathetic side of the race with such fidelity. There are however, in the stories of Joel Chandler Harris, intimate touches which to me are marvelous. He presents the Negro in an aspect in which he would scarcely exhibit himself to a white man, repeating the characteristic speeches to which the Negro would hardly give utterance except to one of his own color.'" See Armstrong, "Exchanges and Literary Notes," 125. Martin and Primeau cite Dunbar as remarking, "The white people of the south talk like they have imported many of our words into the language and you know they act like us" (*In His Own Voice*, 207).

75. Often, Dunbar's early recitations were nonpaid and earmarked as charity.

76. Charles Austin Thatcher (1862–1934) was interested in helping Dunbar attend college and be successful as a writer. Years after Dunbar's death, Thatcher was disbarred in Ohio—for what law bulletins referred to as misconduct. In reality, however, Thatcher was disbarred for "criticizing a judge." See Rabban, *Free Speech*, 48. Thatcher was reinstated after he appealed the verdict on the issue on April 18, 1911. Vinton Shepard refers to "the case [a]s perhaps the most remarkable in the history of disbarment proceedings" ("Case of Mr. Thatcher," 437). Thatcher's case is still well known in the Ohio legal world and will be "forever remembered in Ohio legal annals." See Bell, "When Zeal Becomes Trouble," 23.

77. OHS, reel 1. This is the original letter of this day. The letter that follows is the enclosed one Thatcher refers to. Dunbar expressed gratitude at Thatcher's desire to help send him to college. Dunbar remained in contact with Thatcher, and later he requested Thatcher's help to avoid foreclosure on his mother's house.

78. This letter has not been yet recovered.

79. Dunbar read at the West End Club a few nights before.

80. Thatcher may be referring to Michael P. Murphy, a member of the Toledo Press Club. Murphy became the acting editor of the Sunday *Courier Journal*. See

Harvey Scribner, ed., *Memoirs of Lucas County and the City of Toledo: From the Earliest Historical Times Down to the Present, Including a Genealogical and Biographical Record of Representative Families* (Omaha, NE: Western Historical Association, 1910), 334. A city directory does, however, list a Michael P. Murphy as the editor of the *Bee*. No other biographical data seems to be available. See *R. L. Polk & Co's Toledo City Directory* (Toledo: R. L. Polk, 1898), 954.

81. Dunbar did send a poem, although which poem he sent remains unclear. According to Cunningham, the *Bee* published its comments on Dunbar's poetry as follows: "In Paul Dunbar, the young colored poet who recited before the West End Club, Ohio has a partial genius who will be heard from in the near future if he lives. He combines the ease and grace of a Riley with the sentiment and diction of a Longfellow." See Cunningham 92, 124.

82. The *Toledo Blade*.

83. OHS, reel 1.

84. A newly formed literary organization with weekly meetings led by prominent intellects of the day, the organization held meetings at 1709 Adams Street. Thatcher sat on the board of directors. In his May 2, 1893, letter to J. N. Matthews, Dunbar described it as "a very wealthy and aristocratic private club."

85. Of particular interest to the audience were "The Ol' Tunes," "Life," "The Rivals," and "Ode to Ethiopia." See Cunningham 90–91.

86. Wiggins and Cunningham both claim that the review of *Oak and Ivy* in the *Toledo Blade* is what attracted Thatcher's attention. During this time, Dunbar had accepted a position as messenger in the Court House with the help of Judge Charles W. Dustin. See Wiggins 35; Cunningham 110.

87. This conversation may be the one initiated by Thatcher during Dunbar's visit the previous week regarding attending college. See Wiggins 36.

88. OHS, reel 1.

89. Chicago, Illinois. Dunbar went to attend and find work at the World's Columbian Exposition (also called the Chicago World's Fair) held in 1893. Designed to celebrate the four hundredth anniversary of Columbus's arrival in the New World, the fair also showed the world that Chicago had risen from the ashes of the Great Fire of 1871. Dunbar's decision to go and work at the World's Fair was strategic. When Dunbar became Frederick Douglass's personal assistant, Douglass helped to ensure that Dunbar became known in the African American community, where the young author had opportunities to perform and network. Dunbar met many figures who were interested in and supportive of his writing career, including James Weldon Johnson, Richard Berry, and William Mercer [Marion] Cook (1869–1944). In 1898, Dunbar and Cook would coauthor *Clorinda: The Origin of the Cake Walk*, which included the following songs: "Darktown Is Out Tonight," "The Hottest Coon in Dixie," "Love in a Cottage Is Best," "Dance Creole," "Who Dat Say Chicken in Dis Crowd?," and "Jump Back Honey."

90. Dunbar received an assignment from the *Herald* to write about the coming of spring at the fair's notable Soldiers' Home grounds, which featured Dunbar's

article alongside photographs and other artwork. The *Herald* had originally asked Dunbar to contribute "Dayton at the Fair," which had prompted his Chicago sojourn.

91. Dunbar's letters to his mother reveal mixed feelings regarding Chicago and the fair.

92. Dunbar stayed briefly with his brother Rob and his family. Dunbar's first job was cleaning one of the big domes. Following that, he uncrated exhibit specimens and then worked as a server in a hotel. In a letter to his mother dated May 4, 1893 (Schomburg Collection, reel 1), Dunbar noted he had secured work as a washroom attendant for $10.50 a week. He explained, "We are paid every Tuesday. I went to work Wednesday and on Tuesday . . . they keep out three dollars for a pass book and 1.00 for a badge so I will only get 2.00. But Rob says he will pay me something next Thursday and I will send you some money as soon as I can, living out here is very high with board, lodging, and laundry, and car fare. Keep and use all money for books you sell." The topic of money often caused Dunbar great stress, as his letters will continue to show.

93. Dunbar traveled to Detroit to give a reading of his poems. During this visit, Thatcher telegrammed Dunbar to say he had scheduled a recitation for him at the West End Club in Toledo the following week.

94. Dunbar returned to Toledo to give a reading at the West End Club.

95. The West End Club. The reviews following Dunbar's reading at the West End Club were favorable.

96. See Cottman, "Western Association of Writers." According to Cottman, the Western Association of Writers (WAW) sought to be an "old fashioned literary society" (187). Cottman lists Maria Louise Andrews as the creator of the WAW, but this is debated. She and Richard Lew Dawson published a "call" for the WAW in the *Chicago Current* that was "hereby extended to all writers of verse and general literature, and especially to the writers of the Wabash valley and the adjacent states . . . in June 1886." Mary Cardwill authored the "Historical Sketch" in the WAW's publication "A Souvenir of the Fourth Annual Convention at Warsaw, Indiana" in 1889, mentioning Richard L. Dawson and Mrs. Andrews's objectives "to form an association of the literary profession for mutual strength, profit and acquaintance" as well as "to discuss methods of composition, and all topics pertaining to the advancement of literature in America" (11). They wanted to "produce and publish a representative volume of western authors from the miscellaneous poems, stories and sketches read during this convention or festival" (11). Ultimately, the goal of this association was "permanent good to American literature and the welfare of its professional workers" (11).

97. Dunbar contributed two articles to the *Chicago Record* (1890–1894) during the summer of 1893: "Sunshine at Jackson Park" and "The Toy Exhibits."

98. We have been unable to locate an indexed review.

99. Designed by Daniel Burnham and Frederick Law Olmsted, the Columbian Exposition's fairgrounds covered more than six hundred acres and featured nearly

two hundred new buildings of classical architecture, canals, and lagoons; the goal was to represent peoples and cultures from around the world. Over twenty-seven million people, equivalent to about half the US population at the time, attended the exposition during its six-month run from May 1 to October 30, 1893. The exposition boasted the world's first Ferris wheel, which was erected at the center of the midway. Built by Pittsburgh bridge builder George W. Ferris, the ride was the fair's most prominent engineering marvel. The wheel rose to 264 feet, surpassing the Eiffel Tower.

100. According to Wiggins, Dunbar initially resisted attending the fair because of its perceived "wickedness" (39). It may also have been an attempt to present himself as behaving well for his mother, or it may reflect Wiggins's need to present Dunbar as a chaste, nonthreatening, devout Christian for her predominantly white audience. Despite Dunbar's penchant for alcoholism and flirtations at this early point in his life, it is likely that he did not yet suffer from the effects of alcoholism and that the city was indeed overwhelming to him.

101. A character from Charles Dickens's *David Copperfield*, Micawber represents the poor and wretched who optimistically look forward to a change in fortune.

102. OHS, reel 1.

103. Matthews did not attend the Eighth Annual Western Association of Writers conference in 1893.

104. Jennie O'Neill Potter (d. 1900) was an American elocutionist, performer, and vocalist. Cunningham claims that Dunbar wrote his mother that "Miss Jennie O'Neill Potter, the young woman who recited with Riley, wanted to see me. I went and took my book along. She was delighted with it, and I am to recite with her next week at a very aristocratic hall down in the city" (98).

105. Dunbar is likely alluding to the earlier recitations he gave for charity, although he assumed he was being paid.

106. Frederick Douglass hired Dunbar as a clerical assistant and paid him five dollars a week.

107. OHS, reel 1.

108. First published in the *Ladies' Home Journal* 10, no. 9 (September 1893): 15.

109. According to Gregory M. Pfitzer, the Western Association of Writers "was not well respected outside its own institutional and regional boundaries. Rather, it was criticized roundly by critics . . . who condemned it as an 'army of the unpublished' and an affront to the general reputation of American literature." Pfitzer notes the organization was "lampooned" by several New York magazines, referred to as the "Literary Gravel Pit Association," "The Writer's Singing Bee," and "a literary house party," whose members made "an effort to get up a corner in Spring poetry and fix the price of manuscript stories at so much per year." Riley and Ridpath found themselves attacked in this manner often, according to Pfitzer, an issue they discussed via letters containing witty insults; they also worked on shaping the Western Association of Writers to focus on "serious philosophical

discussions." See Pfitzer, *Popular History*, 154. New York magazines were not alone in their ridicule of the Western Association of Writers: Kate Chopin, for instance, referred to the group as "provincial." See Toth, "A Writer, Her Reviewers, Her Markets," 148–73.

110. The list of members may be found in several places. Richard Lew Dawson describes the foundational ideas, members, and constitution in *The Current: Politics, Literature, Science and Art* (1886): 145–47. Dawson claims that "the outgrowth of the association" originated with Matthews, which conflicts with George S. Cottman's claim that Maria Louise Andrews was the founder. See Cottman, "Western Association of Writers."

111. Benjamin Stratton Parker (1833–1911) was a US consul in Sherbrooke, Canada, from 1882 to 1885 and a poet who composed in a similar vein to Riley and Matthews. Here, he was just an early participant in the Western Association of Writers; however, he eventually became president.

112. Mary Hartwell Catherwood (1847–1902) published short stories and long serials in the *Atlantic* and *Lippincott's*. She also wrote a number of juvenile local color pieces and historical fiction. Two of her early popular serials were published in book form. See *A Woman in Armor* (New York: G. W. Carleton, 1875) and *Craque-o-Doom* (Philadelphia: Lippincott, 1881). A founding member of the Western Association of Writers, Catherwood later rejected realism in midwestern material. She had a series of published letters debating romance and realism with Hamlin Garland in Eugene Field's *Chicago News* column "Sharps and Flats." This debate reached a fever pitch during the Chicago World's Fair of 1893. Garland essentially (and not incorrectly) charged Catherwood with inauthentic, romanticized writing. See Donna Campbell, "Realism and Regionalism."

113. Eugene Fitch Ware (1841–1911) was an author, politician, poet, and Civil War soldier known fondly as Ironquill.

114. Lee O. Harris (1839–1909). The Indiana Historical Society has Harris's collected poems, manuscripts, letters, and other documents.

115. Joseph Samuel Reed (1852–unknown) of Indiana. In 1898, the *Indianan*, vols. 3–4, published by the Indiana Trustees' Association, included a brief sketch of Reed and some lines of his poetry.

116. The July 23 Sunday edition of the *Indianapolis Journal* included a poem by "The Winged Poet at Warsaw," Benjamin S. Parker, which he wrote one morning while attending the Western Association of Writers Conference at Spring Fountain Park in Warsaw, Indiana, the previous month. The poem praises a robin on an oak branch, whose chirping intruded into the day's events and entertained the WAW attendees. See *Indianapolis Journal*, July 23, 1893, 3.

117. One of Lee O. Harris's most famous poems. See *Interludes*, 180–81.

118. Harriet Adams Sawyer (b. 1859) was a poet and member of the Western Association of Writers. For a brief biographical sketch, see the *Magazine of Poetry and Literary Review*, 1895, 174.

119. Ida May De Puy Davis (1857–unknown) was a writer, poet, and member

of the Western Association of Writers. See Willard and Livermore, *Woman of the Century*, 230. Davis was also the president of the Terre Haute city school board. See the *Indiana School Journal and Teacher*, 1893, 778.

120. Will Cumback (1829–1905) was a former lieutenant governor of Indiana from 1869 to 1873. He also served as a US representative from Indiana and as minister to Portugal.

121. J. P. D. John was president of DePauw University from 1889 to 1895. August Jacob Reifel offers some background on John. See *History of Franklin County, Indiana*, 558. We have been unable to locate any information on the possible lecture Dunbar mentions. John "severed his connection with DePauw University" although he was viewed as "one of the ablest college presidents," so much so that he was asked to remain in his position. Instead, the former college president planned to "enter the lecture field." See William A. Bell, "Dr. J. P. D. John."

122. We have been unable to locate "The Old Country Paper," but "The Ol' Tunes" was published in *Oak and Ivy*.

123. "The Rivals" would later be collected in *Lyrics of Lowly Life*.

124. *Oak and Ivy*.

125. Likely "The Lawyers' Ways," reprinted in the *Wellington (OH) Enterprise* on November 29, 1893.

126. Dunbar's frustration is evident here; much to his chagrin, this frustration would become familiar.

127. OHS, reel 1.

128. This poem was later anthologized in *The Lute of Life*, 55–56.

129. Matthews published this poem originally in the *Ladies' Home Journal*, August 1893, 15. It was reprinted several more times.

130. Claude (Gellée) Lorrain (ca. 1600–1682), a French landscape painter who studied in Italy with artists including Goffredo Wals (ca. 1595–1638), Agostino Tassi (ca. 1580–1644), and Claude Déruet (ca. 1588–1660).

131. This was a Chicago newspaper that ran from 1865 to 1914. Initially founded as a Republican paper by Jacob Bunn, the paper suffered after the 1871 Chicago fire. In 1872, the paper was reimagined for a different socioeconomic audience (it remained Republican) when William Penn Nixon became editor in chief; the paper experienced several other iterations of itself including partisan and nonpartisan versions, but at the time Dunbar was publishing in it, the paper was partisan. We have been unable to locate the specific piece Dunbar refers to here.

132. Dunbar faced this issue regularly, but especially in his early years. C. W. Dustin recalls an early instance of this: "One day [Dunbar] came to me quite excitedly and said he had found in The Green Bag, a legal publication, one of his poems published without giving him credit as the author. It was a comical description of the examination of a witness and quite clever in every way. The Green Bag had copied the poem from a Kansas paper, giving credit to that publication, but not naming any author. The Kansas paper had taken it from a Dayton paper and published it without giving credit to anyone or anything. I advised him to write to

The Green Bag, asserting his authorship and complaining that credit had not been given him. In due time he received an apologetic answer, disclaiming knowledge that he was the author and inclosing $5. A like sum was offered for another poem in a similar vein" (Dustin, "Paul Laurence Dunbar").

133. This was a common practice at the time. *Munsey's* was the first national publication Dunbar was published in: he published "The Land o' Used to Be" in *Munsey's* two months before he was published in the *Century* for the first time.

134. We have been unable to locate this story.

135. Despite the scholarly debates and investigations into who may or may not have been responsible for Dunbar's success, it is clear from Dunbar's letters that he held both Matthews and Howells responsible.

136. OHS, reel 1.

137. At the time, Matthews's wife was struggling in the final stages of tuberculosis.

138. Dunbar suffered from alcoholism. It is unclear when his issues with alcohol became apparent, though this letter makes it clear that he was already falling out of favor because of it; his letters with Rebekah Baldwin reveal an early struggle (these are collected in the Schomburg Collection at the New York Public Library and by the Ohio Historical Society). To complicate this problem, Dunbar would be advised to imbibe alcohol in order to treat the bouts of active tuberculosis from which he suffered. This was standard treatment at the time and considered helpful by many. Arnold explains that Dunbar "had lung trouble. Often, he had severe hemorrhages which he concealed from his family and friends. At such times, he drank, especially if he had an engagement, with the hope that the stimulants would bolster him up and enable him to go through with his program. On several occasions this method failed him and caused a great deal of embarrassment, humiliation, and shame" ("Some Personal Reminiscences," 402). Unfortunately for Dunbar, alcohol was ineffective in treating the disease. Dunbar's drinking was so problematic that friends and even Alice beseeched him to stop at several points; however, Dunbar did attempt to quit drinking. In a letter to Alice on October 24, 1897, he explained that he had not been drinking overmuch: "Liquor seldom passes my lips" (Metcalf, "Letters of Paul," 221). But it was no use, and Alice very clearly admitted this to Wiggins in 1906, writing, "Mr. Dunbar was a heavy drinker—there were times when he was not sober for days. When in this condition he was a different man altogether, brutal, in fact." Alice concluded that "our married life would have been a happy one . . . but for that demon drink" (Metcalf, "Letters of Paul," 12). Neither Wiggins nor Cunningham included this information in their biographies.

139. The *Chicago Record* was sympathetic to the black community.

140. "The Deserted Inn" appeared in *The Lute of Life*.

141. The *Ladies' Home Journal*. Matthews contributed there on several occasions.

142. In *The Lute of Life*.

143. Dunbar is referring to Riley's poem "James Newton Matthews," published in the *Indianapolis Journal* on November 19, 1893.

144. Richard Lew Dawson (1852–1911) was a writer, poet, and founding member of the Western Association of Writers. Dawson published poetry from 1888 to 1915: "Suffer and Be Strong" appeared in the *Golden Argosy* on December 11, 1886, 28; "Ole Settlers' Meetun" appeared in the *Century* in June 1888, 319–20; and "A Thanksgiving Dozen" was published in the *Century* in November 1892, 159–60. Shortly after, "True Bravery" appeared in the *Golden Argosy* on December 31, 1892, 264. After a four-year hiatus, "Flashes" appeared in the *Century* in March 1896, 799–800. A decade later, Dawson had the poem "Mexico" published in the *National Magazine* in July 1906, 402. The final poem Dawson had published appears to be "Joaquin Miller," in the *Overland Monthly* in November 1915, 63. Information on the Richard L. Dawson Papers is available through the Rare Books and Manuscripts Division of the Indiana State Library.

145. Dunbar is referring to the tension between Dawson and Riley. Around November 1890, Riley accused Dawson of telling other authors to send their poems to Riley. Riley responded, "Dear Sir: In spite of my repeated warnings, you seem determined to involve me in the business and responsibility of your scheme of poem series for this paper [*Indianapolis Sunday Journal*], where I myself am only a contributor." See Eident and Taylor, *On Prairie Winds*, 272. The several letters that follow take the same tone.

146. A rondeau (plural, rondeaux), from medieval and Renaissance French poetry, is an octosyllabic poem that includes three stanzas comprising ten to fifteen lines with only two rhymes; the opening words are used twice in an unrhyming refrain at the end of both the second and third stanzas. Another example of this verse form would be Dunbar's famous "We Wear the Mask," published in *Lyrics of Lowly Life* in 1896.

147. Slightly revised, this poem appeared in *Majors and Minors*. This poem is included in Howells, *Complete Poems of Paul Laurence Dunbar*, 28.

148. This poem was never published. It is not indexed in *The Complete Poems of Paul Laurence Dunbar*.

149. Frederick Douglass Papers, 1841–1967, MSS11879, Manuscript Division, Library of Congress, Washington, DC, http://hdl.loc.gov/loc.mss/collmss.ms000009.

150. Dunbar is referring to Douglass's help in securing a position for him at the World's Fair.

151. Dunbar published an "Ode to Douglass" following his passing in April 1895.

152. To date, Dunbar's biographers have generally ignored this event. Only Virginia Cunningham mentions it, but her coverage glosses over the situation (107–8).

153. Though it is unclear which rejections Dunbar is referring to here, the ramifications of his drinking could have been severe enough to ruin his career.

154. The West Virginia Colored Institute became West Virginia State University.

155. James Edwin Campbell (1867–1896) was a poet, educator, journalist, and editor who was born in Pomeroy, Ohio. Hudson avers that Campbell "was the first black poet to write in plantation dialect. A close examination of Campbell's dialect pieces, probably written in the 1880s, reveals a more realistic and unliterary approach to black folk speech" ("Paul Laurence Dunbar: Regional Heritage," 436). While in Ohio, Campbell taught and participated in local Republican politics. He eventually moved to West Virginia, where he joined the staff of the *Pioneer* in Charleston. He left the paper in 1890, and then served as the principal at the Langston School and Collegiate Institute. He married Mary Champ, a teacher, in 1891. In 1892, he became the first principal of the West Virginia Colored Institute (now West Virginia State University). He later moved to Chicago, where he joined the staff of the *Chicago Times-Herald* and contributed articles and poems to several periodicals. He published two books of poetry: *Driftings and Gleanings*, comprising poems in Standard English; and *Echoes from the Cabin and Elsewhere*, which includes poems written in predominantly Black English. Research also suggests that he may have been the first African American to publish a poem about interracial love: "Pariah's Love."

156. OHS, reel 1.

157. We have been unable to locate this letter.

158. Campbell was forced to resign from his position as principal later that year and returned to newspaper writing full time. Apparently, there was strong opposition to Campbell's administration, which prompted his move to Chicago. See Wagner, *Black Poets*, 129.

159. Addison Gayle Jr. reports that Campbell wrote dialect poetry before Dunbar, but he lacked what many believed to be artistic skill. Not all critics agree; Sherman, for example, argues that "Campbell's *Echoes* contains the finest group of dialect poems of the century, praised by leading critics for their originality, hard realism, authentic dialect and spirit and aptness of phrasing rhymes, and rhythms" (*African American Poetry*, 306). James Weldon Johnson, on the other hand, asserts that Campbell was unable to get the same attention as Dunbar because his poetry spoke more toward the minstrel tradition. However, Dunbar's poetry also partly succeeded because it was more redolent of the plantation tradition (*Along This Way*, 59–60).

160. During the late nineteenth and early twentieth centuries, African American newspapers often struggled to survive, with many publishing issues for only a short time, and others publishing periodically.

161. In 1887, Campbell became the editor of the *West Virginia Enterprise*, an African American newspaper. He also edited the *Pioneer* (aka the *Pioneer Press*), the earliest black newspaper in West Virginia, in 1886. Christopher Harrison Payne (1845–1925) began the *Pioneer*.

162. Campbell's rising star was cut short: he died of either typhoid or pneumonia at the young age of twenty-eight in 1897.

163. Campbell's first book was *Driftings and Gleanings*.

164. Campbell continued to serve on the staff of the *Chicago Times-Herald* until his death in 1895; however, *Echoes from the Cabin and Elsewhere* would be published shortly after.

165. Likely the *Chicago Evening Post*.

166. In 1895, *Echoes from the Cabin and Elsewhere* was published.

167. Woodson writes that one of the reasons Campbell was appointed principal of the West Virginia Colored Institute was that the head of the board of regents had attended one of Campbell's speeches and had been very impressed with Campbell's broad literary knowledge of the best British authors (11). See "James Edwin Campbell," 11.

168. OHS, reel 1.

169. Matthews's wife, Louella (née Louella Brown), died from tuberculosis on February 11, 1894.

170. The *Chicago Record*.

171. After returning to Ohio from the Chicago Exposition at the end of 1893, Dunbar had trouble finding work. The author Charlotte Reeve Conover (1855–1940) is responsible for introducing Dunbar to Charles Dustin, who arranged for Dunbar to work as a messenger at the county courthouse. However, realizing he had no interest in the law, Dunbar returned to his former elevator position. Conover also introduced Dunbar to George Washington Cable. Dunbar would later dedicate *Lyrics of Sunshine and Shadow* (1905) to her.

172. *Indianapolis Journal*.

173. The West End Club; see Thatcher to Dunbar, December 9, 1894.

174. Charles Thatcher had originally offered to give Dunbar fifty dollars a year to attend college and had gathered several other benefactors to help, but Dunbar rejected this offer.

175. James L. Shearer and Samuel Ellis operated the Shearer Lecture and Musical Bureau of Cincinnati. Dunbar accepted the invitation to travel with them; this group had negotiated with Dunbar to tour with a musical company and give recitations for twenty-five dollars; however, they apparently reneged on the offer. Cunningham notes that "a 'Black Jenny Lind' concert company had invited him to go on tour as a reader. The manager [Shearer] had painted the prospects in dollar signs and Paul had immediately given up everything else to get ready. He had composed new poems and memorized old ones, scarcely taking time to sleep or eat. Then ten days before the tour should have started, the manager wrote Paul that the whole affair had been cancelled" (114). Dunbar took action and Thatcher advised Dunbar on his rights and wrote to Shearer directly on his behalf.

176. The Western Association of Writers.

177. Dunbar would eventually attend the WAW conference that summer and was asked by the publicity chair to send a photograph, a biographical sketch, and a poem for the paper.

178. OHS, reel 1.

179. Henrietta Vinton Davis was the director of the play *Dessalines, a Dramatic*

Tale: A Single Chapter from Haiti's History, performed at Freiberg's Opera House in Chicago in 1902. The play tells the story of Jean-Jacques Dessalines (1758–1806), the Haitian hero born into slavery who ruled second in command to Toussaint L'Ouverture during the Haitian Revolution. On April 3, 1912, Davis again staged, directed, and acted in William Edgar Easton's play *Christophe* at the Lenox Casino in Harlem, New York City.

180. Dunbar asked Easton for permission to include *Dessalines* in his recitation portfolio.

181. William Edgar Easton (1861–1936) was a prominent Republican politician in Texas as well as a writer and newspaper editor. *Dessalines* was Easton's first play; *Christophe, a Tragedy in Prose of Imperial Haiti* continues in the vein of heroic struggles, following the Haitian people's fight for a stable government. In the introduction to *Dessalines*, Easton noted that he was interested in producing positive and successful dramatic works, an area he felt African Americans had "neglected" (vi). Easton argued, "Indeed, we have had excellent caricaturists of the Negro, in his only recognized school of legitimate drama, i.e., buffoonery. But the author of this work hopes to see a happier era inaugurated by the constant production of legitimate drama" (vii). Easton dedicated *Dessalines* to his daughter, Athenais Marie Easton, with these hopes in mind. See Easton, *Dessalines*, and Easton, *Christophe, a Tragedy in Prose of Imperial Haiti*.

182. OHS, reel 1.

183. There are several references to a Mrs. Selby, but we have been unable to find any information on her.

184. "Quaker City" refers to Quaker City in eastern Ohio.

185. Dunbar contended with financial problems throughout 1894, and in one instance he asked Charles Thatcher whether, instead of money for college, he could borrow money to pay his mortgage on the Ziegler Street house. Dunbar apparently also needed to take in boarders to supplement the household income. Four tenants were listed at 140 Ziegler in the 1894–1895 city directory. Three of the individuals were listed as boarders. They include Edward S. Bundy, waiter; Jerome Haithcock, laborer; and Lewis Williams, laborer. Mary Moore, widow of William, also resided at the house, presumably as a boarder, although this was not denoted in the directory. See Brawley, *Paul Laurence Dunbar*, 33; and *Williams' Dayton City Directory* for 1894–1895.

186. 2 Corinthians 4:17, which reads in full: "For our light affliction, which is but for a moment, worketh for us a far more exceeding and eternal weight of glory."

187. Henry Wadsworth Longfellow, "Hyperion."

188. Lyman Abbott (1835–1922), an editor, author, and theologian as well as an associate editor of *Harper's Magazine*, founded the *Illustrated Christian Weekly* and coedited the *Christian Union* with Henry Ward Beecher from 1876 to 1881. Abbot was also editor in chief of the *Christian Union* (renamed the *Outlook* in 1893) and the author of *The Evolution of Christianity* and *The Theology of an Evolutionist*, in which he represented evolution in Christian terms.

189. Frederick Douglass Papers, 1841–1967, MSS11879, Manuscript Division, Library of Congress, Washington, DC, http://hdl.loc.gov/loc.mss/collmss.ms000009.

190. Dunbar decided against attending college. See Charles A. Thatcher's April 21, 1893, letter to Dunbar. Dunbar also wrote Alexander Crummell on September 9, 1894, to ask for a reference and help in obtaining this position, but the letter is largely illegible. Inevitably, Dunbar, with no college education, did not get the position.

191. Dunbar is most likely referring to "Of Negro Journals," which appeared in the *Chicago Record* on June 22, 1894. He did, however, have a short story published by the *Independent*, "Lafe Halloway's Two Fights" (September 7, 1899, 2417–22). "Of Negro Journals" examines the African American press, more specifically *Freedom's Journal* and *North Star*, as performing an invaluable service to the African American community, despite its many and repeated difficulties in regular publishing.

192. S. A. Cornish.

193. OHS, reel 3.

194. Alexander Crummell (1819–1898) was an Episcopalian clergyman, professor, abolitionist, and African nationalist. Crummell helped pioneer the concepts of Pan-Africanism and was an avid supporter of the colonization of Liberia by African Americans. In 1897 he helped found the first major scholarly society dedicated to African American scholars, education, the arts, and scholarship, the American Negro Academy (ANA). The ANA was a group of black intellectuals who would study and discuss ways in which African Americans could be integrated into mainstream America. The ANA held its inaugural meeting on March 5, 1897, in Washington, DC.

195. Also referred to as Colored Americans Day. Cunningham points out that the turnout was abysmal, as only vendors selling watermelon were there, which sparked racial tension since it was steeped in stereotyping and racism. Wiggins quotes directly from the newspapers: "Few Colored Folks There" and "Negroes Apparently Not Interested" (102).

196. According to Wiggins, "on 'Colored Folks' Day' at the fair, Dunbar was called upon to render several 'selections' before thousands of his own people" (39). Wiggins mentions "an Episocpal [*sic*] clergyman from Washington D.C." (39–40) and is most likely referring to Crummell.

197. This teaching position would have paid Dunbar one hundred dollars a month, a sizable salary increase for him. See Best, *Crossing the Color Line*, 120.

198. One of the trustees of the school, along with Frederick Douglass.

199. Crummell did help Dunbar and continued to assist in his success as evidenced by letters written in 1897 to John W. Cromwell, a former slave who inspired the formation of the Association for the Study of Negro Life and History. See Newkirk, *Letters from Black America*, 324–25.

200. This letter is in response to Dunbar's letter of September 9, 1894.

201. *Africa and America: Addresses and Discourses* is a collection of Crummell's speeches.

202. In a later letter not found in any archives but reproduced in Cunningham, Dunbar responds to Crummell, stating: "If I have been slow in answering your last kind letter, impute my tardiness to the charm of *Africa and America* which, in my leisure moments, I have been reading. I like and approve the whole tone of the book, which seems to be characterized by conservative common sense and an intelligent perception of the needs and shortcomings of our race. I was especially taken with the article Common Sense in Common Schooling, which in every particular I heartily endorse. You ask who is my favorite poet, and I feel some hesitation in answering, for at my stage of life, we have hardly developed those qualities of mind that make our judgments upon men and things secure. And I do not know whether the love of my youth shall be the love approved by my mature manhood. But, without apology for my poet, let me say that He is Shelley. That I may never change in my love for his ethereal poetry is my hope. With deep regards, I subscribe myself, Paul Dunbar" (Cunningham 116).

203. OHS, reel 1.

204. Crummell is referring to the teaching job Dunbar had asked him to supply reference for. This letter is in response to Dunbar's letter from September 9, 1894.

205. OHS, reel 1.

206. See Dunbar to J. N. Matthews, April 30, 1894.

207. Dawson is likely referring to a situation where a female elocutionist was reciting Dunbar's poetry without permission. According to Cunningham, Dunbar wrote a "letter of protest" to the elocutionist's father, but he and the elocutionist's brother argued that the elocutionist never "promised not to recite the poem" and threatened Dunbar with physical violence if he continued with the matter (117). It is unclear who this elocutionist might be. It may have been Jennie O'Neill Potter, as Dunbar had mentioned working with her earlier.

208. OHS, reel 1.

209. The "Law of Compensation" is a tenet in Emersonian Transcendentalism that appears in "Compensation," published in 1841 as part of Emerson's *Essays: First Series*. For Emerson, "It is one of the most beautiful compensations in life that no man can sincerely try to help another without helping himself," drawing on the golden rule that we will get back what we give. Emerson's Law of Compensation also argues that we will always be rewarded for our efforts and contributions; to increase compensation, we must increase the value of our contribution. See "Compensation," *The Complete Works of Ralph Waldo Emerson* (Boston: Houghton, Mifflin, 1903), 2:94.

Dunbar clearly did not feel the Law of Compensation. In a letter to a friend, written in November, he laments his inability to make ends meet and the absolute low that came with it: "There is only one thing left to do, and I am too big a coward to do that." Shortly after, Dunbar wrote to Thatcher to explain the extreme difficulty of his situation and asked about the donations for a college fund that Thatcher had previously offered him. The other potential sponsors lost interest, as Dunbar had initially rejected the offer, but Thatcher sent the money by wire immediately, which allowed the author to save his house, pay bills, and buy his mother's ticket back to Ohio. See Gayle, *Oak and Ivy*, 33.

210. Dunbar consistently struggled with money, but he had successes and was frequently invited to give recitals. Often, he was paid little (usually a percentage of the receipts), but he appeared in such places as Harrisburg, New York, as well as Washington, Detroit, Chicago, and several cities in Indiana. See Rebekah Baldwin to Dunbar, June 23, 1894, Dunbar Papers (Schomburg Collection, New York Public Library).

211. Joseph Seamon Cotter Sr. (1861–1949) was a famous poet, writer, playwright, and community leader in Kentucky who supported education for African Americans. Regarded as one of the earliest African American playwrights, Cotter was considered by many to be Kentucky's poet laureate at the time. See Ward, *Literary History of Kentucky*, 99–100. Dunbar would write a poem "To My Friend— Joseph S. Cotter" shortly after this correspondence, on December 18, 1894, a piece Herbert Woodward Martin only recently recovered (Martin, "Forgotten Manuscripts"). See also Shockley, "Joseph S. Cotter, Sr.," 327–40.

212. OHS, reel 1.

213. Bishop James Whitford Bashford (1849–1914) was the fourth president of Ohio Wesleyan University from 1889 to 1904.

214. OHS, reel 1.

215. Dunbar was an avid admirer of the *Century*. Indeed, in a January 5, 1902, *Detroit Free Press* piece, Dunbar explained, "'The Century' had always been the goal of my ambition, but it was only after nine years of persevering effort that it was reached. I began sending my youthful productions to it when I was 14 years old, and when I was 23 the editor accepted three poems from me at once. This exceeded my highest hopes, and I was so happy and so proud." The *Century* published three of Dunbar's poems: "Negro Love Song," "Curtain," and "Dilettante." See "Negro Love Song," *Century*, April 1895, 960; "Curtain," *Century*, May 1895, 159; and "Dilettante," *Century*, July 1895, 480. Reynolds J. Scott-Childress argues that Gilder and Johnson of the *Century* helped to secure Dunbar's position as a dialect poet, though he argues it was not out of a condemnation or racial bias. Scott-Childress notes that the *Century* participated in publishing *only* dialect poems from Dunbar; before succeeding in publishing in the *Century*, "Dunbar had published just over a dozen poems, of which none were in 'Negro dialect.' Ten were in standard English, two were in Hoosier dialect, and one was in German dialect. What is more, none of the so-called standard English poems had a racial theme. All were about nature, love, and other traditionally romantic subjects. In the three years following the publication of his first *Century* poem . . . Dunbar published 34 poems in national magazines. Twenty-four of these were in Negro dialect. Of the remaining 10, three were on themes related to black life. Thus, in those two years, Dunbar became a

'Negro' poet" (371). Dunbar failed to publish a nondialect poem with the *Century* until November 1898, when he published "Harriet Beecher Stowe."

216. Dunbar sent the now famous letter James Whitcomb Riley wrote about him and a copy of J. N. Matthews's letter to the press. According to Cunningham, Thomas J. Wood (1823–1906), a brigadier major general in the US Army, wrote a letter of support for Dunbar directed to the *Century* as well (118).

217. Robert Underwood Johnson (1853–1937) joined the staff of the *Century* in 1873 and succeeded Richard Watson Gilder (1844–1909) as editor, a position Johnson held until 1913.

218. OHS, reel 1.

219. The word looks like "Dianthe," although we have not been able to verify this.

220. Cf. Thatcher to Dunbar, April 21, 1893.

221. Thatcher is likely referring to copies of *Oak and Ivy*.

222. OHS, reel 1.

223. The use of "whiter" rather than "white" here is quite telling in that the former indicates mere shades of difference, while the latter clearly demarcates two separate races.

224. An ancient Greek epigram reads "Seven wealthy towns contend for Homer dead, through which the living Homer begged his bread."

225. See the book of Job in the Hebrew Old Testament.

226. Monte Cristo stopped at nothing to obtain what he felt he deserved and to dole out his revenge.

227. Possibly a reference to Dunbar's portrayal of southern blacks via dialect, which was profitable for Dunbar.

228. This matter remains unclear; it may have to do with public drunkenness.

229. OHS, reel 1.

230. Thatcher secured several readings for Dunbar.

231. This letter comes from the Ohio Historical Society.

232. William A. "Bud" Burns (1873–1905) was Dunbar's lifelong friend from high school who became Dayton's first African American medical doctor. According to Felton O. Best, Burns attended Cleveland University and often managed and arranged stage appearances for Dunbar and sent him magazine articles (*Crossing the Color Line*, 58–59). Burns treated Dunbar as his tuberculosis progressed but died after being exposed to typhoid fever in early November 1904. Honious notes that Dunbar "never seemed to recover from Bud's death," and that Burns's death had an intense impact on Dunbar's outlook on surviving tuberculosis: "After the funeral Dunbar more often seemed discouraged in his fight against tuberculosis" (*What Dreams We Have*, 75).

233. OHS, reel 1.

234. See R. U. Johnson to Dunbar, December 8, 1894.

235. After these initial publications in the *Century*, and immediately following Howells's review of *Majors and Minors*, Dunbar's literary career took off. However,

he still struggled to support himself and his family. Some of the newspapers and journals he was contributing to did not pay, and others (e.g., *Kate Field's Washington* for "The Shallows" and "Beyond the Years") traded a year's subscription for poems. See Cunningham 119.

236. "Negro Love Song," *Century*, April 1895, 960; "Curtain," *Century*, May 1895, 159; and "Dilettante," *Century*, July 1895, 480.

237. OHS, reel 1.

238. The *Blue and Gray* finally published Dunbar's "The Two Brothers" in the October 1894 issue.

239. Cunningham asserts that Fogg's suggestion did not work out because he admitted "the benefit of such a partnership" would not be in Dunbar's favor, as Dunbar was only "recognized as a poet" (122).

240. Fogg's biographical information is almost nonexistent; only his published poems survive at large. One source of information on Fogg is Fogg and Willis, *Fogg Family of America*. A poem Fogg wrote, "Verses," appears on pp. 34 and 35 in Wiggins; this volume also supports Wiggins's identification of "Walter Fagg [*sic*] a newspaperman" who originally hailed "from Portsmouth, New Hampshire" (Wiggins 122).

241. OHS, reel 1.

242. Dunbar's middle name was misspelled "Lawrence" in the first printing of *Majors and Minors* on the cover, the title page, and below his picture and accounts for the frequent misspelling of his name. Dunbar was also often criticized for agreeing to have his portrait on a book he printed himself: one reviewer called it "an editorial misdemeanor, but excusable since it established his race." See Cunningham 154.

243. "Retrospect" was later renamed "Retrospection." It was published in *Majors and Minors* (1895) and again in *Lyrics of Lowly Life* (1896).

244. Stanza 2 of this five-stanza poem was published as follows, which includes the phrase in question:

> And low the laden grape-vine swung
> With beads of night-kissed amethyst
> Where buzzing lovers held their tryst,
> When you and I were young, my boy,
> When you and I were young.
> When you and I were young, the cool
> And fresh wind fanned our fevered brows
> When tumbling o'er the scented mows,
> Or stripping by the dimpling pool,
> Sedge-fringed about its shimmering face,
> Save where we'd worn an ent'ring place.

245. Dunbar did not change his original line.

246. The published, revised version in Dunbar's collections eliminated the word "choir" altogether.

247. OHS, reel 1.

248. It is unclear which poems the office editor is referring to, but Dunbar wrote many poems in Irish dialect. Cunningham cites an unfavorable experience Dunbar had with his use of dialect when he performed a piece at the Lyceum Theater: though the review was largely favorable, ironically, the writer of one article "was annoyed to hear a Negro recite Irish dialect and wished that the particular number had been omitted" (154). Yet in "Dunbar and Dialect Poetry," Myron Simon notes that a good portion of Dunbar's poems in the *Complete Poems* are written in "white dialect" (125). Dunbar also wrote the celebratory "John Boyle O'Reilly," which is not in dialect. He included this poem in *Oak and Ivy*.

249. Edwin C. Martin (1851–1915) was an author and editor for the *Telegram* and then *McClure's Magazine*. Originally from Hamilton, Ohio, and a graduate of Dartmouth College, he also penned several small articles and books.

250. The *Daily Leavenworth Herald* (1860–1881) was a Leavenworth, Kansas, newspaper, published by William P. Fain.

251. OHS, reel 1.

252. Although Dunbar would not recite the ode until Douglass's memorial service on April 7, 1895, Cunningham reports that the ode was already very popular and quoted often (120).

253. OHS, reel 1.

254. Between this letter of March 29, 1895, and S. R. Gill's April 22, 1895, letter of invitation to Dunbar, Dunbar initiated correspondence with Alice Ruth Moore—literary interest, Dunbar insisted, was the reason. "I am drawn to write you because we are both working along the same lines and a sketch of yours in the Monthly Review so interested me that I was anxious to know more of you and your work." Dunbar introduced himself, provided Alice with an overview of his work and publications, and then asked her directly about the plantation tradition and the use of dialect: "I want to know," Dunbar wrote, "whether or not you believe in preserving by Afro-American—I don't like the word—writers those quaint old takes and songs of our fathers which have made the fame of Joel Chandler Harris, Thomas Nelson Page, Ruth McEnery Stuart, and others! Or whether you like so many others think we should ignore the past and all its capital literary materials." Alice responded positively on May 7, 1895, thanking Dunbar for sending her "dainty little verses" (Metcalf, "Letters of Paul," 37), and explained that she was indeed familiar with Dunbar and his work. She also illuminated her feelings on the use of dialect, noting, "I frankly believe in everyone following his bent. If it be so that one has a special aptitude for dialect work, why it is only right that dialect work should be made a specialty" (38). Interestingly, Alice also noted in this same letter that she was not fond of "writers that wedge the Negro problem and social inequality and long dissertation on the Negro in general into their stories," referring to this practice as "like a quinine pill in jelly" (38). Dunbar wrote back and explained he wished "to make [his] characters 'real live people'" and assured her she had not upset him (34–38).

255. Samuel R. Gill (1845–unknown). For a short biography of Gill, see Bowland, *Pioneer Recollections*, 564–5.

256. Considered to be a summer resort–like hotel on Lake Erie. See Lakeside Collection, http://www.lakeside.com.

257. OHS, reel 1.

258. The hotel agreed to pay Dunbar's expenses in return for several of his recitations throughout the week.

259. The Pugsley Brothers' Tennessee Warblers Colored Concert Company (1895–1899) was a variety troupe of African American jubilee singers out of Nashville, Tennessee. As an independent enterprise, the Warblers performed in churches and at other community events around the North and Midwest. Some portions of the proceeds were donated to charities. Other genres later engendered from this style include cat song, rooster song, and dude and character song. See *Wilkes-Barre (PA) Record*, September 1, 1890: 1; and Bernard L. Peterson, Lena McPhatter Gore, and Errol Hill, eds., *The African American Theatre Directory, 1816–1960* (Westport, CT: Greenwood, 1997), 193.

260. Dunbar's return for a week's paid trip included entertaining the hotel guests with daily recitals.

261. Gill, who grew up on the peninsula, is listed as an early member of Lakeside. He later served as a benefactor to Lakeside. Gill was the secretary of the Lakeside Company at this time.

262. OHS, reel 1.

263. This refers to Dunbar's temporary position as editor for the *Indianapolis World*, an African American newspaper based in Indianapolis, from May to July 1895, when the newspaper's owner, Alexander Manning, was on vacation. Dunbar wrote Alice of this from Indianapolis on May 23, 1895, noting, "I am . . . giving some recitals from my work and am constantly with the editor of the 'World' & after this week I shall be connected with that paper for a time" (Metcalf, "Letters of Paul," 40.) This letter to Alice marks his official request of Alice to be correspondents. Two days later, Dunbar wrote Alice again, specifically to ask whether she had "any articles or poems to spare," explaining, "I am interested in you and want all my western friends to know about you. . . . [The *World*] is at your service" (40–43).

264. OHS, reel 1.

265. Dunbar temporarily acted as the editor of the *Indianapolis World*, a small African American newspaper.

266. Two days after this, Dunbar wrote Alice for the last time on *Indianapolis World* letterhead concerning his admiration and plan to run her poem "Love for a Day" in an upcoming issue. In the same letter, he also explained, "You cannot send me too much of your work" (Metcalf, "Letters of Paul," 49).

267. We have been unable to locate information on either of these people. Presumably, they were friends of the Dunbar family.

268. William D. McCoy (1853–1893) of Indiana was appointed US minister to Liberia and died there on May 15, 1893.

269. See the *Century*, May–October 1892, 640.

270. We have been unable to locate this poem.

271. Very little remains on Dawson. Information on his poems is available via the Richard L. Dawson Papers. See the Rare Books and Manuscripts Division of the Indiana State Library for information on the contents, https://www.in.gov /library/fa_index/fa_by_letter/d/l43.html.

272. Richard Watson Gilder (1844–1909) was a poet and the editor in chief of the *Century*. See the December 8, 1894, issue for information on Johnson.

273. We have been unable to locate this piece.

274. Dawson is listed as presenting this lecture for the Indiana University Lecture Association on February 17, 1892. See *The Annual Catalogue of the Indiana University* (Bloomington, IN), 114.

275. There is a half note drawn in this letter, the note C in the G clef.

276. Latin for an unhealthy obsession with writing as if it is a bad habit. The Latin phrase, derived from Greek, comes from Juvenal's Seventh Satire and has been in use since the sixteenth century.

277. Named after the Greek muse of epic poetry, the calliope is a type of organ that uses steam to produce sound. Designed and created by Joshua C. Stoddard in 1855, the calliope was often placed at the top of American steamboats because it was easily heard; it was also used in circuses. See Espenschied, *History of the American Steam Calliope*.

278. A close relative of the trumpet. The standard cornet in brass bands is the B-flat cornet. The instrument's pitch range is the same as that of the trumpet.

279. Irvington, Marion County, Indiana.

280. George S. Cottman (1857–1937) was an Indiana historian and printer who founded and published the *Indiana Quarterly Magazine of History*. He was also a longtime member of the Western Association of Writers.

281. Henry Archibald Tobey (1852–1908) was a friend and benefactor of Dunbar. Henry C. Eyman described Tobey as "a most unusual man . . . in body, mind, and soul" (584). The memorial goes on to describe Tobey as a Mason, a "believer in the brotherhood of man the Fatherhood of God" (584), who associated closely with Dunbar, Robert G. Ingersoll, and Joseph A. Herne. See Eyman, "H. A. Tobey," 584. Dunbar dedicated *Folks from Dixie* to Tobey. Henry David Thoreau (1817–1862) was an American Transcendentalist, essayist, and abolitionist. John Burroughs (1837–1921) was a nature writer and author of *Wake-Robin*, his first published collection of essays.

282. OHS, reel 1.

283. Dunbar published three poems in the *Century* in 1895: "Negro Love Song" (later retitled "Jump Back, Honey"), "Curtain," and "Dilettante." Martin is most likely referring to "Curtain." Though the *Century* preferred to publish dialect poems from Dunbar, "Curtain" and "Dilettante" are both nondialect poems; they are also both short and humorous. The *Century* published these even before Howells praised Dunbar. Just one week before this letter, Dunbar wrote Alice of

his creation and finalization of "When Malindy Sings," a dialect poem that would shortly become one of Dunbar's most famous, cherished, and celebrated poems. See "Jump Back, Honey," *Century*, April 1895, 960; "Curtain," *Century*, May 1895, 159; and "Dilettante," *Century*, July 1895, 480.

284. OHS, reel 1.

285. Miss Mary Reeve was a book reviewer and a frequent guest of Dr. and Mrs. H. A. Tobey, mentioned in Wiggins 42–43. Brawley reports that during their conversation regarding race, Reeve mentioned to Tobey that "you would be interested in a Negro boy we have down in Dayton. I don't think much of him myself, but my sister says he has written some wonderful things" (*Negro in Literature*, 35). Reeve, according to Brawley, then sent Tobey a copy of *Oak and Ivy*. Biographers suggest that although Tobey was not initially particularly impressed with the book, he did inquire about Dunbar while they were both in Dayton. The poems then took on new meaning for him (*Negro in Literature*, 35).

286. An Old Testament biblical reference to Genesis 9:20–25, where Noah cursed his son Ham after Ham saw his father naked and drunk; Ham's descendants were also to carry the curse and were condemned to slavery. This became a common motif in American ideology from the eighteenth century well into the twentieth century.

287. As a Mason, Tobey would have believed in a supreme being and an immortal soul, but he would not have believed that Jesus Christ was the savior of humankind, as Christians do.

288. The phrase "the Laws of Nature and of Nature's God" is deist in concept and is found in America's foundational works, including the Declaration of Independence.

289. One of Dunbar's biographers, Addison Gayle Jr., reports that the five dollars allowed Dunbar to attend the yearly Western Association of Writers conference in July.

290. OHS, reel 1.

291. Thatcher's letter to Dunbar was another catalyst to Dunbar's rise to fame.

292. According to Lakesideohio.com, "Lakeside's official history began under the sponsorship of the Central Ohio Conference of the Methodist Church. Among the early organizers and financial backers were Alexander Clemons, the patriarch of one of the peninsula's leading families; the Rev. Richard P. Duvall, a local Methodist minister and ex-missionary; B. H. Jacobs, an immigrant from Denmark, civil war veteran and Port Clinton store owner; and 27-year-old Samuel R. Gill who had grown up on the peninsula."

293. OHS, reel 1.

294. Cotter published *Sequel to the "Pied Piper of Hamelin" and Other Poems*, a collection of poetry and prose, in 1939. His title poem was a response to Robert Browning's "The Pied Piper" and is most likely the reference here.

295. In 1893, Cotter founded the Paul Laurence Dunbar School; he served as the principal there until 1911.

296. "The Dilettante: A Modern Type," *Century* 50, n.s., 28 (May–October 1895): 480. According to Tony Gentry, Dunbar had been sending his poetry to the magazine for almost nine years with no success. The poem, as Gentry points out, "wryly expressed Dunbar's misgivings about his current prospects." See Gentry, *Paul Laurence Dunbar.*

297. For the original printing of this letter, see Wiggins 44, 47.

298. Dunbar sent Tobey five copies of *Oak and Ivy* before writing this letter. Upon his return from the WAW conference, Dunbar wrote to thank Tobey.

299. Tobey wrote to Dunbar with encouragement and enclosed money for copies of the book to pass along to friends. See Thatcher to Dunbar, July 7, 1895.

300. Dunbar wrote Alice on July 25, 1895, that he had been exceptionally busy with the conference and was exhausted, but his correspondence was positive, cheerful, and upbeat.

301. Dunbar had retained his position as an elevator operator.

302. Dunbar would, in August of this year, and at the invitation of H. A. Tobey, go to spend five days in Toledo, Ohio, and recite at the State Hospital for the Insane.

303. OHS, reel 2.

304. Johnson had been promoted to associate editor by this time; the initials A. E. refer to this position.

305. OHS, reel 1.

306. Ezra Kuhns (1872–1960) was a lawyer, friend, and key figure in assisting Dunbar with legal and financial matters. Dunbar would dedicate *The Heart of Happy Hollow* to Kuhns. While Dunbar's first biographer, Wiggins, does not mention Kuhns, Cunningham dates the friendship between the two men back to Dunbar's days as an elevator operator (56–57).

307. We have been unable to locate information on Zartman.

308. For more information on Dustin, see PLD to J. N. Matthews, October 12, 1892; see also C. W. Dustin, "Birth Anniversary Recalls Early Life of the Noted Poet," *Dayton Forum,* July 1918; and Dustin, "Paul Laurence Dunbar," 6–9.

309. It is unclear whom Dunbar is referring to here.

310. Family friends of the Dunbars.

311. Dunbar did not ultimately take this money or opportunity. He also wrote Alice on this day that he had "severed" his "connection with the Indianapolis World," but the reason remains unclear (Metcalf, "Letters of Paul," 64).

312. OHS, reel 2.

313. Cook set Paul's "A Negro Love Song" to music and sold it to Witmarks, a New York music publishing house, while also offering it as an all-black musical performance titled "Clorindy, the Origin of the Cakewalk." The sheet music was then published as "Jump Back, Honey."

314. By October of this year, Dunbar had become a regular contributor to several literary magazines, including the *Independent* and the *Century*; he was also, at this point, performing frequently and assembling the collection that would become

Majors and Minors. On October 28, 1895, he wrote Alice, "I am working . . . day after day to get out a new and larger collection of my verses." He voiced his difficulties in navigating the publishing world and regretted he was "not able to do more for [the] success" of *Violets and Other Tales.* Dunbar explained, "I had hoped to surprise you with a review of it in the Chicago News Record, and for nearly three months past I have been fuming with rage that my contribution should be held over until all its timelines had evaporated." Dunbar's contact, Charles Dennis, the editor of the *Chicago News Record,* had absconded to Europe. Dunbar lamented the situation, wondering whether his review of Alice's book was "in some European wastebasket or following vainly the peregrinations of this recreant editor. This is the lot of the poor quill driver." In the same letter, Dunbar confided to Alice that he was working on the poem "Ione," which he described as "a lyric narrative." He closed this letter by referring to Alice as a "friend, helper, and inspiration" (Metcalf, "Letters of Paul," 72).

315. William Webster Ellsworth (1855–1936) worked for the *Century* from 1890 to 1916. Ellsworth contributed several works to the field of publishing, including *Creative Writing: A Guide for Those Who Aspire to Authorship* (New York: Funk & Wagnalls, 1929). He also continued to give talks and present lectures after he retired. Ellsworth worked with many famous writers but noted that his relationships with them were complicated. Jerome Loving notes that Ellsworth had to "caution" Dreiser's agent, Grant Richards, against "removing too much" (*Last Titan*, 29).

316. OHS, reel 2.

317. "A Negro Love Song."

318. John Church & Company was first established in 1859 in Cincinnati, Ohio. It sold pianos and sheet music and eventually expanded to Chicago and New York.

Chapter 2

1. Although undated, this letter is likely from early 1896 when Dunbar was in Toledo.

2. Wiggins 55.

3. These poems would be collected in Dunbar's second book of poetry, *Majors and Minors,* which appeared early in 1896.

4. As per letter of April 22, 1896, H. A. Tobey to PLD, Mr. Childs was the Boody House hotel night clerk.

5. Tobey initially sent Herne a copy of Dunbar's *Majors and Minors* while Herne was promoting his play, *Shore Acres* (1892), which was playing in Toledo.

6. James A. Herne (1831–1901) was an American playwright. Herne supplied Howells with a copy of *Majors and Minors,* and Howells's review of the book in his "Life and Letters" helped launch Dunbar's national reputation, which firmly cemented his place within American literature (Howells, "Life and Letters").

Howells's influence is clear, as indicated by one reader who wrote to the publisher, "I have just noticed in Harpers Weekly a collection of poems published by you. Kindly send me word when I can obtain a couple of copies. I do not even know the name of the author, but it is the collection noticed by W. D. Howells" (see Thomas Shallcross to Hadley and Hadley, July 7, 1896, Dunbar Papers, OHS). Historically, there have been several disputes as to who "discovered" Dunbar's literary talents, but it remains clear that Dunbar was known far before Howells reviewed his book, and that many people worked to see Dunbar gain national recognition as a writer. Dunbar had met Frederick Douglass by this time, been introduced and welcomed by many Black writers, composers, and musicians, and had presented his poems at the Colored American Day Celebration at the Chicago World's Fair; this was a very successful opportunity for him, but he was still not nationally known. J. N. Matthews also worked to help Dunbar gain recognition at this point, and although he had published in *Munsey's* and the *Century*, he had little national recognition. In a July 5, 1899, letter to Octavia Roberts, Brand Whitlock argued that it was Tobey who had discovered Dunbar, and Howells who had ensured that Dunbar became a nationally recognized writer: "Dr. Tobey recognized his genius, had his verses printed in a modest little volume, which fell into the hands of Mr. Howells, and instant appreciation of the poems, set forth in a review in Harper's Weekly." See Nevins, *Letters and Journal of Brand Whitlock*, 24–25. Tobey, according to Whitlock, "assisted Dunbar in every way, financially and socially, and the love with which the poet repays him is beautiful to see" (24). Ultimately, though, Whitlock's point about Howells is accurate, though without Herne's delivery of *Majors and Minors* to Howells, Howells may never have known Dunbar's name. Howells is credited with propelling Dunbar's meteoric rise to overnight stardom because of his literary seat. Dunbar became popular so suddenly that Allen B. Fox notes that Dunbar "cast into near oblivion the works of James Madison Bell and Albery A. Whitman, the two leading black poets who preceded him" ("Behind the Mask," 7). Ultimately, though, it is clear that many people worked to help Dunbar gain literary recognition, as Dunbar's letters reveal. Joanne Braxton notes that Dunbar's struggle continued after he became known in the literary world, though he was "hailed by the black literary lions of his day as well as the white" (*Collected Poetry*, x). Braxton also notes that Dunbar struggled to meet his audience's expectations regularly, and he faced frequent battles with "racism in his search for employment" (xi) and in publishing—especially regarding expectations and acceptance largely of dialect poetry only, which these letters absolutely reflect (x–xi).

7. Julia A. Herne (1881–1955) was a performer and soprano vocalist.

8. See Clark, *British and American Drama of Today*, 231–32. The night before, Dunbar went to see a performance of Herne's *Shore Acres*.

9. James A. Herne (1839–1901) was an American director and performer.

10. See Wiggins 55–56.

11. Tobey forwarded *Majors and Minors* to Ingersoll, who had a profound influence on Dunbar. See the July 20, 1897, letter from Ingersoll.

12. At this time, Dunbar was gaining popularity. In his January 27, 1896, letter to Alice, Dunbar mentioned his excitement at her approval of *Majors and Minors*; he relayed to her that he had met with George Washington Cable, whom he described as "delightful." Dunbar noted that Cable "said some very surprising and encouraging things and invited me to contribute to a new magazine which he has bought and is to edit" (Metcalf, "Letters of Paul," 78). According to Philip Butcher, Charlotte Conover introduced Cable and Dunbar after Cable read in Dayton in 1894, noting that they "spent an hour in conversation about books and authors and social problems" ("Mutual Appreciation," 101). They then met again in the "summer of 1896 after William Dean Howells' review of *Majors and Minors*. . . . At that time Cable was editing *The Letter*" (102). The dates do not fully match up in these scholarly pieces, though the stories corroborate the details. Butcher surmises that Cable "solicited manuscripts from several writers whom he aided in their attempts to break into print, and he must have asked Dunbar for a contribution" (102). Dunbar submitted "Theology by Intuition," which was later collected in *Lyrics of the Hearthside* (1899). Butcher notes several changes to the *Lyrics of the Hearthside* publication, including a title change: Dunbar shortened it to "Theology" and "substituted *upward longing* for *yearning* and *neighbors* for *enemies*" (102).

13. This poem was collected in *Lyrics of Lowly Life*.

14. All were later collected in *Lyrics of Lowly Life*.

15. Robert Ingersoll (1833–1899), the "Great Agnostic," was an American social activist, abolitionist, Civil War veteran, active Republican, and outspoken supporter of women's and civil rights.

16. OHS, reel 1.

17. Tobey contacted Thatcher, and they devised a plan to aid Dunbar in releasing *Majors and Minors*. Cunningham reports that initially the two men agreed to give and not loan the money to Dunbar. However, the book was printed rather than formally published, so there was no regular publicity. Rather, Dunbar and those who would help him had to solicit buyers themselves (Cunningham 156–57).

18. When Tobey arranged for three gentlemen to buy copies of *Oak and Ivy*, he told Dunbar that it was on the condition that Dunbar would make their acquaintance. See Wiggins 51–52; Cunningham 139.

19. William Henry Scott (1825–1901) held this position until 1893.

20. See the undated letter from James A. Herne to PLD.

21. This would later be collected and republished in Dunbar's *Complete Works* in 1913.

22. Dunbar wrote Alice on April 19 that the *Century* had also just accepted his poem "Discover" for the June issue (Metcalf, "Letters of Paul," 90–92).

23. OHS, reel 1.

24. There is little information available about Isaac D. Smead personally, but there are records of patent applications, court cases, and other general information relating to the Smead Foundry & Furnace Company. It remains unclear what poem Dunbar may have sent back, but his response here is not typical: his

letters to fans usually exemplify a humble and shy Dunbar who is factual and to the point.

25. OHS, reel 1.

26. *Lyrics of Lowly Life* (1896) was Dunbar's third collection of poetry.

27. William S. Quinby (1835–1908) was then owner of the *Detroit Free Press*.

28. Quinby introduced the London edition of the *Free Press* in 1881, making it the first American newspaper to be published in Europe.

29. The Fisk Jubilee Singers toured England for the first time in the 1870s to advance the abolitionist cause and were well received. For an in-depth look at their tour and reception in England, see Graber, "'A Strange, Weird Effect.'"

30. Ian Maclaren was the pseudonym used by John Watson (1850–1907), a minister. Ian Maclaren's *Beside the Bonnie Brier Bush* (New York: Dodd, Mead, 1895) is a collection of stories set in the fictional village of Drumtochty.

31. Both are selections from *Lyrics of Lowly Life*.

32. Dunbar met Keen while traveling abroad in England. Dunbar wrote Alice on May 23, 1897, that Keen was a poet who was "wealthy and so seldom publishes." Despite Dunbar's enjoyable experiences in London, he was not fond of many he met there: he described London society as "the most corrupt in the world," noting there were "not two dozen that [he] would care to have [Alice] know," but he felt that Keen and his wife would be appropriate company (Metcalf, "Letters of Paul," 154). Dunbar later dedicated *The Fanatics* to Keen, and although Dunbar did respond to this letter, only Keen's response on May 13, 1897, remains in this archive.

33. OHS, reel 1.

34. Indeed, this June 27, 1896, issue of *Harper's Weekly* sold out; according to Jarrett, "even Dunbar failed to secure his own copy" of the issue ("Entirely Black Verse," 508).

35. This refers to the possible income Dunbar could earn with a position at the Library of Congress.

36. Cotter is likely referring to *Lyrics of Lowly Life*, Dunbar's third collection of poetry, which came out shortly after *Majors and Minors* and secured his literary contract with Dodd, Mead and Company, a New York–based publishing house, in 1896. He continued to publish his books of poetry with Dodd, Mead and Co. for the remainder of his life.

37. Dunbar arranged for Major Pond to act as his manager.

38. This likely refers to William Walter Hawkins. Hawkins recorded some of his achievements, but aside from this article, there is almost no other information available on him ("About People We Know," 26).

39. All are dialect poems and were published in *Lyrics of Lowly Life*.

40. It is not clear whom Cotter is referring to here.

41. Cotter.

42. The letter was first printed in Cunningham's biography (148–49), but it can also be found in William Dean Howells's Correspondence and Compositions,

1894–1917 (MS Am 1251.1–1251.3), Howells Collection, Houghton Library, Harvard University, accessed March 24, 2017, https://id.lib.harvard.edu/ead /hou01168/catalog. Cited by permission of the Houghton Library.

43. Dunbar is referring to Howells's review of *Majors and Minors*. Jarrett argues that "Howells did for Dunbar what various prefatory or concluding letters, signatures, guarantees, and/or tales had done for ex-slave authors," and his review of Dunbar helped the editor professionally: "It elevated Howells to the commercial influence of Walter Hines Page and Richard Watson Gilder, editors who encouraged African American authors to write literature in dialect in order to get published" ("Entirely Black Verse," 522).

44. Regardless of the controversy surrounding Howells's dialect use and racism, he had the power to "make or break" a career with something as small as a single review. Van Wyck Brooks acknowledged Howells's publishing power, writing, "Howells was perhaps the only critic in the history of American literature who has been able to create reputations by a single review" (*Confident Years*, 142).

45. Indeed, Dunbar clearly recognized and understood the "irrevocable harm" Howells did him.

46. Harlan et al., *Booker T. Washington Papers*, 203–4.

47. Dunbar to Howells, August 21, 1896, Dunbar Papers, OHS.

48. Dunbar, on his way to New York, paid a visit to William Dean Howells at his summer cottage in Far Rockaway Beach. Because of the cool night air, Dunbar borrowed an overcoat from Howells and returned it the following day with a brief note that read: "In wearing your coat, I felt very much like the long-eared animal in the fable of the ass clad in the lion's skin." See Wiggins 64. Brand Whitlock retold this story to Octavia Butler in a July 5, 1899, letter. Dunbar, according to Whitlock, "went to Far Rockaway with Major Pond . . . [where they] "dr[o]ve along before a row of cottages, [one of] which was Mr. Howells's . . . and down the walk came running a little fat man with white hair . . . it was Mr. Howells!" Whitlock further explained that "the pride and delight Dunbar found in the visit were most charming to witness," and that Howells generously gave his coat to Dunbar to keep warm. See Nevins, *Letters and Journal of Brand Whitlock*, 24–26.

49. This is one of Aesop's Fables about a donkey that covers itself in a lion's skin and scares away all the other animals, only to be found out by a fox: the moral of the story is essentially that clothing does not disguise a fool who is revealed through his own words.

50. OHS, reel 1.

51. While visiting Howells, Dunbar may have simply been chilled; the cold, damp ocean air may have exacerbated his tuberculosis.

52. In her biography, Wiggins observes that Howells told her, "I thought [Dunbar] one of the most refined and modest men I had ever met, and truly a gentleman" (63).

53. Before Howells's review of *Majors and Minors*, Dunbar had to solicit buyers, most of them provided in a list by Dr. Tobey. Cunningham notes that when

Dunbar appeared alone to market his book, he was often turned away from the front office of publishers because of his race (139). Shortly after Howells's review, however, Dunbar received numerous letters regarding *Majors and Minors*—thirty-six included money for the book, three New York publishers solicited an interview, and a fourth consented to bring out a volume of his poems. This would be *Lyrics of Lowly Life* (1896). See Cunningham 151.

54. Dunbar was encouraged by literary friends to obtain a lecture manager, and he selected James B. Pond, an established platform agent for such major writers as Mark Twain, Booker T. Washington, and Frederick Douglass. Brand Whitlock, "Golden Rule" Jones, and H. A. Tobey bought Dunbar a new suit and gave him cash for his trip to New York to stay with Pond (Hudson, "Biography," 83). Cunningham writes that one of Pond's goals was to get *Lyrics of Lowly Life* published by a firm that would pay for all production, printing, and sales. Pond used copies of *Majors and Minors* for publicity to secure financing for *Lyrics of Lowly Life* (Cunningham 153–54).

55. OHS, reel 1.

56. According to Wiggins, Thatcher paid for Dunbar's clothing and transportation (63).

57. Dunbar brought with him a copy of *Majors and Minors* from which he read. James Stronks notes that "Major Pond quickly booked him into readings around New York, meanwhile sending him with letters of introduction to several publishers. And soon he directed Paul out to William Dean Howells' summer home at Far Rockaway, on Long Island, for the first meeting of the two writers" (Stronks, "Paul Laurence Dunbar," 99).

58. This event could be the recital at the New Matthewson Hotel, where the proprietor secured the ballroom and orchestra for the occasion.

59. Dunbar may be referring to Varina Anne Banks Howell Davis (1826–1906), the widow of Jefferson Davis, the president of the Confederate States from 1861 to 1865. She was also the author of her husband's memoir.

60. OHS, reel 1.

61. *Lyrics of Lowly Life* was initially published on December 2, 1896, in New York, by Dodd, Mead and Company and was an immediate success—so much so that it was reprinted several times over. Dunbar would continue to publish his novels with Dodd, Mead and Co. exclusively for the remainder of his publishing career. Howells wrote the introduction to this book of poems before even reading it. According to Hudson, the book appeared in green and gold and included a fifteen-hundred-word introduction by Howells including the several points he made in his *Harper's* review, but the introduction was more "emphatic" and better written ("Biography," 85). The reference to "republished" refers to the best poems from *Majors and Minors*, which were also included in this collection. The additional poems added to *Lyrics of Lowly Life* are "Longing," "The Path," "Two Songs," "Song of Summer," "Spring Song," "Goodnight," "The Lawyers' Ways," "Discovered," and "A Coquette Conquered"; the last two had already appeared in the *Century* in June

and July. "A Coquette Conquered" included a sketch by Peter Newell, the first to be published with Dunbar's poetry.

62. Dodd, Mead and Company agreed to publish *Lyrics of Lowly Life* after Pond had pitched the book to Harper and Appleton, who also expressed interest in this new collection. Wiggins notes that Dodd, Mead and Co. agreed to advance Dunbar $400 on potential royalties, but this letter suggests $200 (66). According to Cunningham, Dunbar also agreed to receive a royalty of 17½ percent on subsequent sales following the initial ten thousand he mentions here (153).

63. William Dean Howells Correspondence and Compositions, 1894–1917 (MS Am 1251.1–1251.3), Howells Collection, Houghton Library, Harvard University, accessed March 24, 2017, https://id.lib.harvard.edu/ead/hou01168/catalog. Cited by permission of the Houghton Library.

64. On August 16, 1896, Dunbar wrote Alice that he unexpectedly cared for New York City (Metcalf, "Letters of Paul," 105). However, Dunbar's strength was failing him: three days after this, he confided to Alice that he was "worked to death and totally tired out mentally and physically." He also noted that he had "come home with the intention of resting" but that he was beleaguered with work for "Miss Ward of the N.Y. Independent and Mr. Bok of the Ladies Home Journal," observing too that D. Appleton & Co. had asked him to write a novel (109); Dunbar, however, did not think the novel would be written. Metcalf speculates that this novel could have been the beginning of *The Uncalled* (110, 136–40).

65. According to Stronks, "Major Pond quickly booked Dunbar into readings around New York, meanwhile sending him with letters of introduction to several publishers" and directing him to Howells's summer home on Long Island ("Paul Laurence Dunbar," 99).

66. In the introduction to *Lyrics of Lowly Life*, Howells writes, "I think I should scarcely trouble the reader with a special appeal in behalf of this book . . . if it had not specially appealed to me for reasons apart from the author's race, origin and condition." Howells continues, "The world is too old now, and I find myself [in] too much of its mood, to come for the work of a poet because he is black, because his father and mother were slaves."

67. Cunningham writes that Howells advised Dunbar during their initial meeting to "write what you know. Write what you feel. Analyze detail. Build the picture. Make it real" (155).

68. OHS, reel 1.

69. The *Bookman*, September 4, 1896–February 1897, published by Dodd, Mead and Company, reviewed *Majors and Minors* and included a portrait of Dunbar. The anonymous reviewer assumed Dunbar wanted his portrait printed to avoid the debacle with the white Thomas Nelson Page, who was mistakenly referred to as a black poet. The anonymous reviewer averred, "In putting out his volume of poems, entitled Majors and Minors, he has supplied a picture of himself, which can leave no one in doubt, that whatever Mr. Page may be, he, Mr. Dunbar, is a male being of the coloured race. Ordinarily, it is a mistake, of course, for a

poet—or for a prose writer—to present his portrait until he is asked for it. . . . In the case of Mr. Dunbar, however, there is some excuse for this pictorial misdemeanor; for had his photograph been lacking, and had no hint of his racial identity been given by means of an author's or publisher's note . . . it is safe to assert that the above-mentioned debonair critic of the West would have supposed him to be a white man" (18–19).

70. *Lyrics of Lowly Life* would be reprinted several times: first with the Young People's Missionary Movement of the United States and Canada (1896), then in London with Chapman and Hall Publishers (1897), and again with G. N. Morang Company (1898).

71. The tone of this letter and the mention of books illustrate the tension between Dunbar and Pond because Pond gave away copies of *Majors and Minors* for publicity and review rather than charging for them.

72. Pond was trying to expand Dunbar's audience across the Atlantic so that his work would be reviewed by well-known members of British society.

73. The Queen's Jubilee in England.

74. It is not clear whom Pond is referring to here.

75. OHS, reel 1.

76. Helen Pitts Douglass (1838–1903), wife of Frederick Douglass, was an American educator, suffragist, and abolitionist who came from a relatively wealthy, upper middle-class family in New York.

77. Frederick Douglass died on February 20, 1895; at the memorial service held at the African Methodist Episcopal Zion Church, Dunbar read "[Ode to] Ethiopia" and "Frederick Douglass," an elegy he wrote for the occasion. See the *Richmond Item*, March 5, 1895, 3. "Frederick Douglass" was not published until it was collected in *Majors and Minors* (1895–96). Several other, smaller services were held in Douglass's honor, one in Dayton, Ohio, where many attended, including Dunbar, who read "Frederick Douglass" again for the eulogy. See the *Dayton Herald*, April 8, 1895, 3. John Savoie argues that this first elegy of Dunbar's is a bit cliché and does not capture the more mature Dunbar later on ("Dunbar, Douglass, Milton.") It is difficult to say with any degree of certainty what Helen Douglass was upset about; however, we can assume it had to do with Dunbar's elegy to Douglass and his recitation of the poem for a specific audience.

78. Dunbar's second elegy, "Douglass," was written in 1903 in the form of a Petrarchan sonnet. It takes on a darker and more bitter tone. See Braxton, *Collected Poetry*.

79. Dunbar may be alluding to the fact that he did not wish to sell his poem "Frederick Douglass." Neither elegy appeared in the local or national papers.

80. Dunbar is here clarifying the role of dialect in his poetry, and although he recognizes the limitations of this genre, Morgan points out that he "recognized that dialect writing had formal conventions that could be manipulated" ("City as Refuge," 215). Dunbar, as scholars and biographers have noted, was ambivalent about his own dialect work, and in a letter to Johnson, Dunbar lamented, "You know, of

course, that I didn't start as a dialect poet. I simply came to the conclusion that I could write it as well, if not better, than anybody else I knew of, and that by doing so I should gain a hearing. I gained the hearing, and now they don't want me to write anything but dialect." Dickson Bruce notes that Alice felt the true Dunbar was in his "pure English poems" (*Black American Writing*, 59).

81. Most likely on the publication of *Majors and Minors*.

82. OHS, reel 1.

83. Dr. Tobey.

84. Colonel "Sol" Smith Russell (d. June 1908) was a comedic actor and playwright known for his play *A Bachelor's Romance*, and he had a popular following in New York.

85. Dunbar expressed excitement to Alice Ruth Moore on June 4, 1896, that the second edition of *Majors and Minors* was to be bound. Dunbar explained that the new edition was to be "much prettier" (Metcalf, "Letters of Paul," 98).

86. The profits from the sale of this book helped Dunbar pay off debts and make payments on his Ziegler Street house.

87. OHS, reel 1.

88. Felton Best extrapolates most of this letter in his biography and states that Dunbar was responding to his former English teacher Miss Coons, who found fault with a poem he submitted and pointed it out to the class. This, according to Best, was Dunbar's response to her (*Crossing the Color Line*). Hudson similarly quotes from this letter but adds that the poem Dunbar gave to Miss Coons was "an intimate poem" not meant to be shared with his classmates. Hudson also mentions that Dunbar had composed poems for Miss Coons on several other occasions ("Biography," 43–44).

89. Wiggins describes Arthur Nixon as "James O'Neill's . . . leading man in 'Monte Christo,' then being a play in Toledo." According to Wiggins, Nixon looked over a copy of *Majors and Minors* and began reading "Where Sleep Comes Down to Soothe the Weary Eyes," and "then, he gave it a dramatic rendition, his face showing his delight and surprise at the beauty and depth of the lines." Wiggins avers that Nixon read all night long and then thanked Tobey for the "opportunity" to read Dunbar's poems, which he compared to those of Poe (50).

90. This is circled in the letter with the note, "This is a falsehood." It is not clear who may have scribbled this. The reference to falsehood in the context of the letter, contrary to Best's and Hudson's interpretations, suggests an issue regarding plagiarism or inappropriate mixing of genres that embarrassed a more polished and older Dunbar.

91. OHS, reel 1.

92. Stronks observes that this letter is to "Howells' Edinburgh publisher and friend, David Douglas" ("Paul Laurence Dunbar," 103).

93. It is unclear why Howells used such language other than subtle racism or paternalism; Dunbar was certainly not the "first of his race to put his race into poetry"; however, it is possible that Howells used hyperbole here to make Dunbar

appear impressive to his friend David Douglas. It is unlikely that Howells was fully unfamiliar with other black literary figures, including James Edwin Campbell, Richard Lew Dawson, and so many more. Perhaps, however, it was Dunbar's pure African ancestry that made him more appealing to the literati. This angle is supported throughout Dunbar's correspondence.

94. OHS, reel 1.

95. It is not clear why Dunbar labeled this letter as his fifth day out unless he began writing it earlier: this ship departed on February 8.

96. Chapman and Hall, who also published Charles Dickens's work, agreed to bring out an English edition of *Lyrics of Lowly Life* (1897). A Canadian edition was also published (Toronto: G. N. Morang, 1898).

97. During the trip, Dunbar participated in a Ship Talent Night. What he refers to here, though, is the hope of becoming at least recognized, if not popular, in England, where he could also publish and make money.

98. Alice Ruth Moore (1875–1935) was an educator, author, and activist born in New Orleans, Louisiana. She published her first collection of stories, *Violets and Other Tales*, in 1895, followed by *The Goodness of St. Rocque, and Other Short Stories*. She met Dunbar in 1897, and they were married on March 6 of the following year in New York City. After a tumultuous marriage, they separated in 1902. Alice married two more times and had a very prolific literary career. See Alexander, *Lyrics of Sunshine and Shadow*.

99. The *S.S. Umbria* reached Liverpool on February 17, 1897.

100. OHS, reel 1.

101. Victoria Earle Matthews organized a going-away party for Dunbar. She also invited Alice, to whom Dunbar had become engaged that night. Dunbar left for England the next day on the *S.S. Umbria*.

102. Dunbar wrote to Matilda on February 28, 1897: "At tea with Henry M. Stanley the French waiter took off his cap to me . . . I am entirely white" (Metcalf, "Letters of Paul," 160).

103. Dunbar received a warm welcome in England, and reports of his presence and performances in England were positive. On March 2, 1897, shortly after this letter, the *Pall Mall Gazette* called for the publication of Dunbar's work in England. Additionally, the *Pall Mall Gazette* and the *Times* advertised Dunbar and his work, and a segment of *Lyrics of Lowly Life* was published by Chapman and Hall. Dunbar wrote Alice on February 20, 1897, that "the literary men and newspapers know me [in London] by name, but they invariably say, 'is this Mr. Dunbar, why I thought you were a much older man'" (Metcalf, "Letters of Paul," 118).

104. Dunbar met with Dr. Alexander Crummell and Hallie Q. Brown (c. 1845–1949), the famous African American elocutionist, activist, teacher, and active leader in women's rights. Metcalf remarks that Brown was in England at the time specifically to lecture on issues black Americans faced ("Letters of Paul," 162).

105. The word here is difficult to decipher as the ink has bled through the letter, but it is likely "Dip," clearly a nickname given to Downing.

106. Henry Francis Downing (1846–1928) introduced Dunbar to Samuel Coleridge-Taylor. Downing arranged for the two to give a joint recital that involved setting Dunbar's poems to music. The poems selected included "Comparison," "Dawn," "Starry Night," "How Shall I Woo Thee?," "Song," "Over the Hills," "A Prayer," "Ballad," and "A Corn Song." The two performed Saturday, June 5, 1898, at the Salle Erard, Great Marlborough Street. The program read: "Under the immediate patronage of His Excellency, John Hay, United States Ambassador." See Brian Roberts, "A London Legacy of Ira Aldridge: Henry Francis Downing and the Paratheatrical Poetics of Plot and Cast(e)" *Modern Drama* 55, no. 3 (2012): 396. Dunbar's financial situation was complicated by the Queen's Diamond Jubilee celebration, which attracted those who might otherwise have attended poetry recitals. Dunbar's first public recital was at Prince's Hall in West Ealing.

107. Downing invited Dunbar to stay with him in order to help Dunbar financially during the "off-season" of recitals. After arranging a reading for Dunbar, Downing assumed half the proceeds from this event, leaving Dunbar with only forty dollars. Dunbar wrote Alice that he thought he had found a "friend and companion" (Metcalf, "Letters of Paul," 128) in Mrs. Downing but confided that the Downings were unscrupulous. Dunbar then stayed with Alexander Crummell.

108. The rest of this letter has been cut off.

109. This letter appeared in the *Crisis*, June 1920, 73–74.

110. Likely J. N. Matthews.

111. James Lane Allen (1849–1925) was a local color writer, drawing on Kentucky dialect for his novels and short stories. Allen is most famous for *A Kentucky Cardinal* (1899). See also Bottorff, "James Lane Allen."

112. Dunbar is most likely referring to the American preference for his dialect pieces over England's love of his Standard English poems. The London *Mail* described the "beauty and fine philosophy of his poems," paying special attention to "The Poet and His Son," as well as other poems in Standard English. See Cunningham 161.

113. *Lyrics of Lowly Life* was also reprinted in New York by the Young People's Missionary Movement of the United States and Canada in 1896.

114. The Savage Club comprised various artistically inclined people—sculptors, actors, painters, scientists, and musicians. During his attendance at the Savage Club, Dunbar reported seeing musicians playing bagpipes and others engaging in a Scottish sword dance. During the revelry, Dunbar recited "When Malindy Sings" to an enthusiastic audience. See Wiggins 160.

115. Despite many positive experiences in England, Dunbar's early enthusiasm for the country was slowly fading. He often heard the locals yell out racial slurs and stare at his dark skin. Tired of being a spectacle, Dunbar expressed exhaustion from giving recitals and wrote of this to Alice on many occasions.

116. Edith Pond treated Dunbar rudely during the trip, even refusing to buy him a return ticket home.

117. Thomas Chatterton (1752–1770) was an English poet who committed

suicide at the young age of seventeen. Like Dunbar, he was raised in poverty and published early.

118. Close to Bristol and located on the coast, Clevedon overlooks the Severn Estuary in England and is a part of North Somerset.

119. OHS, reel 1.

120. *Verses for My Friends* (London: Edward Hicks, 1894).

121. We have been unable to locate this poem.

122. Psalms 91:1 reads: "He that dwelleth in the secret place of the Most High / Shall abide under the shadow of the Almighty."

123. William Kitching (1837–1906) was a well-known poet, Quaker, and temperance and peace advocate. See Evelyn Noble Armitage, *Quaker Poets of Great Britain and Ireland* (London: William Andrews, 1896), 160–62. See also *Ackworth Old Scholars' Association Report*, issues 23–26 (London: Headley Brothers, 1904), 94–95.

124. William Dean Howells Correspondence and Compositions, 1894–1917 (MS Am 1251.1–1251.3), Howells Collection, Houghton Library, Harvard University, accessed March 24, 2017, https://id.lib.harvard.edu/ead/hou01168/catalog. Cited by permission of the Houghton Library.

125. Dunbar wrote Alice on April 23, 1897, that despite a recent illness, he had recited the evening before and made "an astounding success" (Metcalf, "Letters of Paul," 136).

126. The 1897 English edition of *Lyrics of Lowly Life*.

127. Dunbar wrote Alice that he "hate[d]" Edith Pond (Metcalf, "Letters of Paul," 119). On May 4, 1897, Dunbar wrote Alice that he had "severed [his] connection with Miss Pond" and was, as a result, much better for the break. In this letter, Dunbar also noted he had "details" about Miss Pond that he would wait to disclose until after marriage, but he let on that Pond would "do all she can to hurt" (142) him. Dunbar wrote Alice again on May 14 and inquired about his reputation: "People are writing about this and that . . . in the American papers concerning me . . . I see none of it, and I am anxious to keep in touch with American opinion of me. It isn't egotism, it is necessity" (148).

128. Edith Pond, who left after the reading season was over, demanded a commission on the recitals Dunbar gave after she left, and when Dunbar refused to pay her, she attempted an injunction to prevent him from reading without her permission. Downing was also squeezing Dunbar financially. American newspapers caught wind of Dunbar's financial troubles, some of which he wrote Alice about on June 10, 1897: "The papers are right, I am not making a fortune; I made 17 guineas Saturday at a recital and was positively robbed of them by an unprincipled scoundrel." It is not clear whether this was Pond or Downing. In the same letter, Dunbar explained that he had "tried hard to get away from Miss Pond" but that she had "tightened her grip upon [him]" and that he was "as much in her power as ever" (Metcalf, "Letters of Paul," 160). Dunbar also mentioned his "two managers" as his "bane" (160). When Dunbar requested help from Edith Pond, she responded that

she would not buy Dunbar's return ticket home, as she considered their contract void because he recited under other sponsorship (161).

129. On April 26, 1897, Dunbar revealed to Howells that Dodd had paid for his return to the states.

130. Many Americans saw Dunbar's visit to England as a failure because of his financial problems, although clearly Dunbar enjoyed a fair share of positive publicity. He was often a guest as opposed to a paid entertainer, but he was also a victim of the scams of Henry Downing and Edith Pond. On March 16, 1897, Dunbar wrote Alice and asked, "Could you still love me and would you wed me if I returned home a failure?" He explained he was "quarreling constantly" with Edith Pond, whom he described as "beastly and I am contracting an awful disposition from her. I may take it into my head to get up and come home." Dunbar did note, however, that his readings had been "enthusiastically received" and that he "had the pleasure of attending a concert . . . given by the composer Signor Tito Mattei" among many others. Dunbar also reported that he had secured the British publication of *Lyrics of Lowly Life* with Chapman and Hall (Metcalf, "Letters of Paul," 125). In irony, Dunbar warned Alice on May 14, 1897, not to "trust anybody too far" (148).

131. Located in London, the Savage Club was a men's club for public figures, writers, and artists. To a friend in the United States, Dunbar wrote: "I have attended a banquet given by the great Savage Club of London. I was the guest of the secretary of the Royal Geological Society, and my host was more than gratified at the reception which I had when I was called upon to take part in the post-prandial program, as I received two requests to come back. The audience was very critical, and if they did not like a speaker would hiss him down." See Wiggins 68.

132. While in England, Dunbar was also the guest of the Royal Society of Painters in Water Colours.

133. Moncure D. Conway (1832–1907) was an American Unitarian minister and writer.

134. Dunbar's early biographers consider *The Uncalled* to be his first serious prose work. Disappointingly, in a number of first bindings, Dunbar's middle name was misspelled as Lawrence on the spine and front of the novel. Initially, the work appeared in the May 1898 issue of *Lippincott's*, but the novel did not share the same success as his earlier works. He began writing *The Uncalled* when he had difficulty getting recital engagements. The novel was heavily criticized because Dunbar focused on white characters, specifically on the dynamics of a white family. The novel depicts a young white man living in Dexter, Ohio, who refuses to become a minister, which his foster family tries to force upon him. The manuscript was half completed by the time Dunbar sailed back to New York. He periodically updated Alice on his progress. On May 4, 1897, Dunbar explained, "My novel grows apace, though I can hardly call that a novel which is merely the putting together of a half dozen abstract characters and letting them work out their destiny along the commonplace lines suggested by their natures and environments. It has some plot, but little incident and incident seems to be the thing nowadays" (Metcalf, "Letters of

Paul," 142). With the times, Dunbar had begun to experiment in the vein of literary naturalism, where environmental and biological factors determine a character's destiny at the expense of free will.

135. Dunbar could be referring to the fact that *The Uncalled* was a serious novel quite removed from his dialect poetry, which the reading public at this time more readily accepted.

136. Osbert Guy Stanhope Crawford (1886 –1957) was a British literary critic.

137. OHS, reel 1.

138. Keen is likely referring to a recital Dunbar gave with black English composer, performer, and violinist Samuel Coleridge-Taylor on June 5, 1897. The two made acquaintance in England after Henry F. Downing and John Hay introduced them. Downing was a famous playwright; Hay is most famous for *Pike Country Ballads*. According to Jeffrey Green in *Samuel Coleridge-Taylor: A Musical Life*, the "programme had the text of nine pieces by Dunbar, 'The Songs and Violin pieces accompanied by the composer S. Coleridge-Taylor'" (41–42). The recital had originally been planned for the Wednesday prior to June 5 but was then rescheduled. Green notes the concert was a success: the *Times* provided a positive review of the recital, as did the *Musical Times* (42).

139. OHS, reel 1.

140. In 1897, Queen Victoria celebrated her sixtieth year on the throne.

141. *Lyrics of Lowly Life* had just appeared.

142. Dunbar had lost a copy of *Lyrics of Lowly Life*.

143. The writer may be referring to the Savage Club, where artists and scientists met for drinking, eating, and conversation. Here, the entertainment often consisted of Scottish singers and bagpipe players. For more details regarding the club, see Wiggins 160.

144. This letter is unsigned, but it is obviously from a friend in England—it may have been a literary editor, perhaps, who desired a copy of Dunbar's book to review, but it is not clear whom the letter is from.

145. OHS, reel 3.

146. Dunbar wrote Alice on June 22, 1897, that he did "not care a fig" that newspapers wrote about him "breaking" his contract with Edith Pond. He also admitted that "if the making of much money means success," he had "assuredly failed" (Metcalf, "Letters of Paul," 166). Although London was a definitive financial disaster for Dunbar, he gained popularity after making several appearances and giving many recitations. While there, Dunbar networked extensively. For instance, he became reacquainted with Sidney Woodward (1823–1963), a well-known vocalist from Boston, whom Metcalf notes Dunbar had met at the Chicago World's Fair, and he also met with Alexander Crummell (1819–1898). Dunbar also read at Queen Victoria's Diamond Jubilee—this was arranged by Ambassador John Hay at the US Embassy. The most fruitful part of Dunbar's visit was his collaboration with Coleridge-Taylor on an operetta, *Dream Lovers*, for which Dunbar wrote the libretto (Metcalf, "Letters of Paul," 139).

147. General symptoms of tuberculosis include a persistent phlegmy or bloody cough that lasts for several weeks, as well as excessive fatigue, fever, weight loss, night sweats, loss of appetite, and general irritability. Dunbar's mention of the cold settling in his throat may indicate that the tuberculosis was in his lymph nodes, as those who have this form of tuberculosis often complain of a swollen throat. In his letters to Alice, Dunbar mentioned illnesses with symptoms that reveal many bouts or extended periods of active tuberculosis; Tobey would later refer to Dunbar having tuberculosis in his February 5, 1906, letter.

148. By this time, Dunbar had completed nearly half of *The Uncalled*.

149. Dunbar is likely referring to those he thought might help him financially, including Alexander Crummell, Hallie Q. Brown, and Henry F. Downing. Ultimately, however, it was Dr. Tobey and Dodd, Mead and Company who sent the money to Dunbar so he could return to the United States.

150. Helen Bright Clark (1840–1927) was a British Quaker, suffragist, and political activist.

151. John Bright (1811–1889) was a Quaker, British radical, and liberal statesman.

152. John Russell Young (1840–1899) was a journalist, diplomat, and librarian of Congress, a position he obtained in 1897. Born in Ireland, Young emigrated to America as an infant. See Broderick, "John Russell Young."

153. The Library of Congress.

154. Ingersoll secured Dunbar a position at the Library of Congress as a reading-room assistant, a job he held from October 1, 1897, until December 31, 1898. This salaried position gave Dunbar some financial security and allowed him the stability to marry Alice on March 6, 1898. His salary was reported as $720 per year. The day before he assumed his librarianship, Dunbar wrote Alice excitedly: "Tomorrow . . . is the momentous day" (September 26, 1897) (Metcalf, "Letters of Paul," 195).

155. President William McKinley was the twenty-fifth president of the United States and served from March 4, 1897, until his assassination on September 14, 1901. On March 1, 1901, Dunbar was invited to participate in the inaugural parade for William McKinley in honor of his second term as president.

156. At this time, Dunbar was still unable to make a decent income by his pen alone, although his poetry was still being published. The Library of Congress provided the necessary stability for Dunbar to marry and to publish while not relying solely on income from publishing.

157. Dunbar faced constant rejections from publishers.

158. Alice and Matilda had a complicated relationship, as many of Dunbar's letters explain. At this point, they had not met. Alice later wrote Wiggins that "there was a miserable friction between his mother and myself" (quoted in Metcalf, "Letters of Paul," 12).

159. Queen Victoria's Jubilee celebration.

160. Matilda Dunbar's sons from her first marriage.

161. Dunbar's American publisher.

162. This letter appeared in the *Crisis*, June 1920, 73–74.

163. This was likely Dr. William R. Fisher (1844–1926). There has been disagreement between Dunbar's biographers as to who Dr. F was, though it remains unclear how they reached their conclusions: Cunningham speculates that this letter is written as a poem of apology to those with whom he was unable to correspond during his illness (247). Hudson avers the letter was written to Major Charles Young, who was a military attaché to the American legation in Port-au-Prince, Haiti, from 1904 to 1907. For a biographical sketch of Young, see the National Park Service article "Colonel Charles Young," https://www.nps.gov. Hudson does not mention that Young was an attaché, but he implies Young's importance and points out that the two communicated at least once ("Biography," 145): see Charles Young to Dunbar, November 30, 1904, Dunbar Papers (OHS). Dr. F could be shorthand for the greeting Dunbar frequently used when addressing J. N. Matthews. However, it is more plausible that Dr. F is Dr. William R. Fisher from Swiftwater, Pennsylvania. Fisher was a prominent surgeon affiliated with Johns Hopkins University who served as an assistant resident physician at the Riverside Hospital in New York during the late nineteenth century and into the early twentieth. Dr. Fisher was chief of staff of the Bellevue Hospital in New York City and of St. Mary's Hospital in Hoboken, New Jersey, and at one time he was superintendent of the Inebriate Asylum on Ward's Island. Fisher once offered to give Du Bois his copy of *Oak and Ivy* (an edition out of print for several years) as a gift for the success of the *Crisis*. See William R. Fisher to W. E. B. Du Bois, February 29, 1916, W. E. B. Du Bois Papers (MS 312), Special Collections and University Archives, University of Massachusetts Amherst Libraries.

164. The enormously popular style of newspaper reporting known as yellow journalism emphasized hyperbole and crude embellishment over objective truth in order to gain a wider readership. The two major newspaper publishers at the time were Joseph Pulitzer and William Randolph Hearst, and they competed in creating sensationalism for profits. Dunbar is referring to the demand for exaggerated stories of his encounters in England, so that he could earn money.

165. Cunningham reports that newspapers were anxious for interviews with Dunbar about his observations of England from a black man's perspective, but in the vein of yellow journalism (165).

166. Issued by the US Mint from 1792 to 1933, the American Eagle was a form of coin currency valued at ten dollars.

167. In 1859, Edward Fitzgerald (1809–1883) translated a selection attributed to Omar Khayyam (1048–1131), the famous intellectual, poet, mathematician, and astronomer.

168. Harold Frederic (1856–1898) wrote *The Damnation of Theron Ware*.

169. Gabriele d'Annunzio's *Triumph of Death* (*Il trionfo della morte*) is part of the cycle of "The Novels of the Rose" and is considered one of the foundational texts of the Decadent movement in literature.

170. Dunbar wrote Alice on October 11, 1897, that he felt invaded, bitter, and even objectified by his meteoric rise to fame. He felt bombarded and cornered, writing, "They want to photograph me and my mother, and my uncle and aunt and cousin—they even want to get my little den of a work room before the camera. It makes me tired. All of my old enemies are turned friends and my friends seem to distrust me when I say I am the same old boy" (Metcalf, "Letters of Paul," 211).

171. At this time, Alice was visiting her family in Boston, which could also have contributed to Dunbar's sour mood, as Alice's family did not care for him. Dunbar was also battling a tuberculosis-induced illness or a complication of the disease. Many in the author's close circle mentioned his intense mood swings, although his depression never seemed to last for an extended period. Shortly after this letter, Dunbar wrote Alice of being very productive in his writing: he had written "a poem and an article on that Boston Hemmings girl affair . . . copied the article and two poems in my typewriter, went down town & sold them all—poem to Bookman, poem to Century . . . and the article to the N.Y. Tribune. Then I went home and copied a chapter of my novel" (Metcalf, "Letters of Paul," 189). The "Hemmings girl" refers to a multiracial student named Anita Florence Hemmings (1872–1960) who had been passing as white at Vassar College and been exposed. See Turpin, "'Twilight Is Their Child.'"

172. OHS, reel 1.

173. The *New York Tribune*.

174. The *Tribune* Sunshine Society was created by a group of journalists committed to helping secure the welfare of blind infants and children. This group's mission was to continue to expand the scope of the organization.

175. This letter appeared in the *New York Tribune* on December 8, 1897, and began as follows: "Sir: I trust my letter may have the honor of appearing in the columns of the Sunshine Society. The Tribune has been the family paper in my home for the last thirty years. I am a daily reader of the paper, and am greatly interested in the Sunshine Society."

176. The writer is referring to a situation where Dunbar read at the Library of Congress for a group of blind people as part of a new program organized by John Russell Young (1840–1899), a librarian there. A reporter from the *New York Tribune* confused the speaker with the poem when Dunbar read "Lead Gently, Lord, and Slow" and misreported in the papers that Dunbar was blind. John Russell Young introduced the Pavilion for the Blind, and Dunbar was the first poet ever to read there.

177. This position was an especially good opportunity for the young Dunbar, though it came with a demanding, rotating six-day workweek, which would eventually wear on Dunbar's already compromised health. However, Eleanor Alexander explains this fruitfulness in monetary terms—an area Dunbar very carefully considered, as he wished to marry Alice: Dunbar's income was about $130 more than the average person earned as a teacher in Washington, DC, during the 1890s (*Lyrics of Sunshine and Shadow*, 126).

178. *Lyrics of Lowly Life* (1896).

179. Dr. Fisher, perhaps, of later letters. See PLD to Dr. F (Fisher), October 2, 1898.

180. John Henry Newman (1801–1890) was an Anglican vicar and theologian. "Lead Kindly Light" was originally a poem he had written—he wrote "The Pillar of the Cloud" while abroad, ill, and shipbound. The poem was turned into a hymn in 1845.

181. This became "A Hymn," with the first line reading "Lead Gently, Lord, and Slow" after reading "Lead Kindly, Light."

182. Young served in this office from July 1, 1897, until his death on January 17, 1899. However, John Broderick notes that Young introduced several important features of libraries that persist today, including "a pavilion for the Blind" and those who are physically handicapped. He actively worked to employ women and considered introducing "a juvenile department" into the library system as well as a "binding department," while also railing against publishers' use of paper that would not last (Broderick, "John Russell Young," 140).

183. We have been unable to identify the writer of this letter.

CHAPTER 3

1. OHS, reel 1.

2. See PLD to Matilda Dunbar, August 18, 1895, for information on Dustin.

3. The content of this letter may refer to a publishing contract with Sampson Low of Sampson Low, Marston & Company (1891–1950), a London-based publishing house and bookseller known for publishing literature by Anthony Trollope, William Beckford, Louisa May Alcott, and Harriet Beecher Stowe. This situation could possibly have had to do with bringing out an English edition of one of Dunbar's works. Sampson Low, Marston and Co. published the *Nineteenth Century Review*, which printed debates by leading intellectuals. Dustin had published in literary magazines such as the *North American Review* and was an active lawyer and judge, so this idea is plausible.

4. O. J. Bard was an Ohio attorney in Montgomery County and the secretary of the Gem City Building and Loan Association of Dayton. He is briefly mentioned as an attorney in Augustus Waldo Drury's historical piece *History of the City of Dayton and Montgomery County, Ohio* and the *16th Annual Report of the Inspector of the Building and Loan Associations of the State of Ohio for the Fiscal Year Ending December 31, 1906*. There is almost no other information readily available about Bard, but it is clear he worked with Dunbar and Dustin. See Drury, *History of the City of Dayton*, 534; and Drury, *16th Annual Report*, 432.

5. We were unable to locate information on this individual. However, according to Honious, this letter appeared in the OHS archives alongside a sketch, "Paul Dunbar: The Poet in His Washington Home," box 1, MSS-659. This biographical sketch could be the result of the letter-interview to which

Dunbar is here responding. See Honious, *What Dreams We Have*, http://www
.npshistory.com.

6. Cunningham reports that as early as middle school, Dunbar was garnering
praise for his verses from some of his teachers, who encouraged him to continue
writing. All of Dunbar's biographers also write of Matilda saving his early works.

7. Euclid of Alexandria was a Greek mathematician and is considered the
founder of geometry.

8. This statement runs counter to information from Dunbar's biographers, who
mention that when he was fourteen or fifteen, Dunbar began submitting his poems
to the offices of the *Dayton Herald*, which eventually published "Our Martyred
Soldiers" in June 1888. See Cunningham 28.

9. The club's membership was based on unanimous election and met Friday
afternoons for debate and discussion.

10. The *High School Times*.

11. Many of Dunbar's contributions to his high school paper were unsigned.

12. See James A. Herne to PLD, undated.

13. Dunbar is referring to Edith Pond here, whom he had earlier described to
Alice on July 20, 1897, as "green with envy at [his] social success" (Metcalf, "Letters
of Paul," 180). Clearly, Dunbar is being political here by not mentioning his ill
treatment by Edith Pond.

14. *Lyrics of Lowly Life*, which was dedicated to Alice, was also published in
England with Chapman and Hall Publishers. In a letter to Alice on January 12,
1898, Dunbar explained, "I have just had a letter from my English publisher saying
that reviews of my book are many and *favorable*. He sends them, and if they are
what he calls favorable, I don't know where the *un* would come in. I went through
them like a wagon over a rutty road, first up and then down. Half the time I am so
discouraged I feel like throwing down the pen with a good sound 'damn.' Everything I do falls so far below what I conceive. I am only a mediocre wretch . . . all
I asked was to be allowed to work along quietly, making a living and no noise, but
here I must be pulled out into the glare of public gaze and stand where I never intended to stand on a level with criticism of men whose advantages and antecedents
have been so much greater than mine. I am sick of it" (Metcalf, "Letters of Paul,"
362). Then, in a sudden turn, Dunbar wrote Alice that "I have the plot in my head
for a new short novel. It is a wee bit racy, but striking I think. If I do anything with
it, I shall attempt to publish it anonymously. I thought perhaps you might collaborate with me on it. But, really, I've so many irons in the fire that the consideration of
any other serious literary work ought to be put off until far into the future" (362). In
her return letter Alice attempted to assuage Dunbar's worries and encouraged him.

15. *The Uncalled* sold over three thousand copies in the United States.

16. Dunbar finished writing *The Uncalled* when he left England for New York,
where he lived with Professor Kelly Miller of Howard University in Washington,
DC. Originally serialized in *Lippincott's Monthly Magazine* in May 1898, the book
was published by Dodd, Mead and Company later that year. Dodd accepted *The*

Uncalled before the manuscript was finished and also advanced Dunbar royalties. The novel was reprinted in Toronto by G. N. Morang Company in 1898 and 1899; in 1899, Service and Patton, a London firm, published an English edition. In 1901 another reprint emerged from the International Association of Newspapers and Authors, a New York firm.

17. *Folks from Dixie* (1898). The novel was illustrated by E. W. Kemble and included the following stories: "Anner 'Lizer's Stumblin' Block," "The Ordeal at Mt. Hope," "The Colonel's Awakening," "The Trial Sermons on Bull-Skin," "Jimsella," "Mt. Pisgah's Christmas 'Possum," "A Family Feud," "Aunt Mandy's Investment," "The Intervention of Peter," "Nelse Hatton's Vengeance," "At Shaft 11," and "The Deliberation of Mr. Dunkin." Cunningham notes that this collection of short stories was inspired by the stories Dunbar heard from elderly black people who lived in Howard Town in Washington and often spoke of their former days as slaves. Five stories were pre–Civil War, while seven were postbellum. See Cunningham 169–71. See also PLD to Major Pond, May 5, 1898.

18. Originally, this letter appeared in Wiggins 78–79. It was reprinted in Martin and Hudson, *Paul Laurence Dunbar Reader*, 450–51. It was undated but was sent in March.

19. Dunbar is referring to H. A. Tobey here.

20. On March 6, 1898, Dunbar and Alice were secretly married in the home of W. B. Derrick of the African Methodist Church in New York, with no attendants. Cunningham observes that their honeymoon was a mere brief night's stay in a hotel (172). Alice had been living and working as a teacher in Brooklyn during this time and was unwilling to break from her employment unless she was married.

21. The letters of Dunbar and Alice show several insecurities from the start: Dunbar did not want to reveal the dark hue of his skin to Alice, as he expected her to reject him; and he believed that even if she accepted him, her family would reject him. Additionally, the letters show a difficult relationship with Matilda and with Alice's family. Cunningham observes that "the Moores did not approve of Paul's having scraped an acquaintance with Alice through letters; they were ashamed of his having a washwoman for a mother and of his lack of college training . . . they were also ashamed of his black skin" (172), which prevented him from obtaining the advantages allowed lighter-skinned African Americans who could often pass for white. Indeed, when deciding where to buy a home, Dunbar considered not only the distance he would have to travel to work but also the neighborhood he would purchase in. On June 25, 1895, when they had first begun to correspond, Dunbar begged Alice, "Please do not ask me for my photo or express any desire to know how I look; for I fear if you knew, our budding friendship which is to me as sweet as a full-blown rose, would be checked; because women so love beauty—and I do not blame them either—though, I have not that to offer them" (Metcalf, "Letters of Paul," 51).

22. During the late nineteenth century, most working women were single and were expected to leave work once they married.

23. OHS, reel 3.

24. Charles Warren Stoddard (1843–1909) was an American author best known for his homoerotic tales *South-Sea Idyls* (1874) and *The Island of Tranquil Delight* (1904).

25. It remains unclear whether the two met, though if they communicated after this, the letters have not been recovered. However, they are both mentioned as up-and-coming writers in *Lippincott's*; see "Literary Notes," *Board of Trade Journal* 17 (1904): 553. Both authors published in the March 1905 volume of *National Magazine*: Charles Stoddard was noted for "Ouida in Her Winter City" (653–69), and Dunbar for "The Churching of Grandma Pleasant" (337–42).

26. Wiggins 79. Later reprinted in Martin and Hudson, *Paul Laurence Dunbar Reader*, 451.

27. Dunbar was anxious that his elopement would damage the "social position" he and Alice held. On March 11, 1898, he explained this worry to her and then wrote encouragingly, "Let's do all we can to obviate that danger" (Metcalf, "Letters of Paul," 498). Elopement during this time was typically viewed as "social suicide."

28. On March 9, 1898, Dunbar wrote Alice regarding their choice to elope: "The enormity of what we have done has just begun to dawn upon me. We have taken a very bold, rash step whose only vindication will be our entire happiness and well-being. I constantly reproach myself when I witness my mother's grief and disappointment . . . I feel now and then a flash of resentment at the whole business. It does not look well on cool reflection . . . we have disappointed everyone. Many looked forward to our marriage with pleasure, and it should have been an event. Instead, we sneaked away & married like a pair of criminals or two plebians [*sic*] with the fear of disgrace hanging over them . . . [however] the thing to do [now] is to carry it off with the most dignified face possible" (Metcalf, "Letters of Paul," 495). Yet he harangued Alice in several letters following this one to the point that she finally wrote, "You have told me that you regret the marriage. Let it be annulled then" (543). Metcalf speculates that the likely date was March 23, 1898. The Dunbars reconciled after this, however.

29. Dunbar was gainfully employed at the Library of Congress.

30. From Eberly Family Special Collections Library, Penn State University Libraries.

31. Library of Congress.

32. Within the first six months of his employment at the Library of Congress, Dunbar had completed all the short stories that would be included in *Folks from Dixie*, which appeared first in *Cosmopolitan*. He dedicated the book to Dr. H. A. Tobey and explained to Tobey, "I am afraid that the wish to express my gratitude to you and something of the pleasure and pride I take in our friendship has led me to take some liberties with your name. But I can only hope that you will take the dedication in the spirit in which it is offered—that of gratitude, friendship and respect for the man who has brought light to so many of my dark hours" (Wiggins 78).

33. *The Uncalled.*

34. OHS, reel 3.

35. The Gammon Theological Seminary had its roots in the Gammon School of Theology, a department of religion and philosophy at Clark University in Atlanta, until it was officially founded in 1883 by the Methodist Episcopal Church. It is the United Methodist component of a consortium of six historical African American theological schools called the Interdenominational Theological Center.

36. Interestingly, Washington makes no note of this event in any of his published letters. See Harlan, *Booker T. Washington Papers.* This meeting at Gammon was to celebrate the fifteenth anniversary of the Theological Seminary. Included among the addressees are Dunbar and Washington.

37. Dunbar could be referring to W. E. B. Du Bois's piece "The Study of the Negro Problems" in the *Annals of the American Academy of Political and Social Science.* Several responses to this paper were circulating throughout 1898. See, for example, "The Study of the Negro Problems," *American Journal of Sociology* 3 (May 1898): 864–65.

38. The writing has bled through some, making it difficult to fully decipher this physician's name.

39. It is not clear whom Dunbar is referring to here.

40. OHS, reel 1.

41. *Folks from Dixie* was published in 1898 by Dodd, Mead and Company.

42. The dialect stories collected in *Folks from Dixie* did not obscure the serious content; "At Shaft 13" considered labor issues. E. W. Kemble, considered one of the best illustrators of the day, was selected to illustrate the collection, although some objected to his tendency to draw racist caricatures. According to Cunningham, Dunbar was an admirer of the illustrator and even framed his original sketches (171).

43. From Wiggins 83. Later reprinted in Martin and Hudson, *Paul Laurence Dunbar Reader,* 451.

44. Horace J. Rollin (1845–1935) was an author, artist, and philanthropist, as well as a proponent of the positive effects of blending the races. This can be seen most prominently in the novel *Yetta Segal,* to which Dunbar is most likely referring here. Rollin had sent Dunbar a copy.

45. OHS, reel 1.

46. Ten percent was a standard royalty payment in the late nineteenth century. Dunbar, however, would be talented enough to earn 15 percent and be advanced $400 from a publisher. See Cunningham 153.

47. Dunbar is referring to the complicated start of the international publication of *The Uncalled* in England.

48. This letter appeared in the *Crisis,* June 1920, 73–74.

49. *The Uncalled* did not receive favorable reviews, mostly because the characters were white and Dunbar was not; one reviewer, arguing that Dunbar was an outsider to the white race, wrote, "Mr. Dunbar should write about Negroes" (Cunningham 183). Other critics attacked the novel's lack of character development.

50. Dunbar dedicated *The Uncalled* to Alice.

51. Dunbar had been working at the Library of Congress for a year by this point, and the hours and work were often grueling. He was working six days a week with an alternate schedule of 9 A.M. to 4 P.M. and 3:30 P.M. to 10:00 P.M.

In 1914, Alice recalled, "The iron grating of the book stacks in the Library of Congress suggested to him the bars of the bird's cage. June and July days are hot. All out of doors called and the trees of the shaded streets of Washington were tantalizingly suggestive of his beloved streams and fields. The torrid sun poured its rays down into the courtyard of the library and heated the iron grilling of the book stacks until they were like prison bars in more senses than one. The dry dust of the dry books (ironic incongruity!—a poet shut up with medical works), rasped sharply in his hot throat, and he understood how the bird felt when it beats its wings against its cage" (Alice Dunbar, "The Poet and His Song," 129). One can easily see the connection here to "Sympathy," which begins, "I know why the caged bird sings." Scholars have read this line in vastly different ways despite Alice's explanation: Peter Revel and David Nordloh argue the poem might have been an outcry "against slavery, but was probably written out of the feeling that the poet's talent was imprisoned in the conventions of his time and the exigencies of the literary marketplace" (*Paul Laurence Dunbar*, 73). Jean Wagner argues, "'Sympathy' is a heartfelt cry of a poet who finds himself imprisoned amid traditions and prejudices he feels powerless to destroy" (*Black Poets of the United States*, 119).

52. *Lyrics of the Hearthside*.

53. The next novel Dunbar published was *The Love of Landry*, which also featured white characters. Of the four novels Dunbar published, only his last novel, *The Sport of the Gods*, has African American characters who are central to the story.

54. OHS, reel 1.

55. Reverend D. J. Meese, pastor of the First Presbyterian Church of Ohio, was the president of the Chaplains' Association and chaplain of the Ohio State Reformatory in Mansfield.

56. The introduction by Howells was a slight revision of his review of *Majors and Minors*.

57. Chapman and Hall Publishers, London.

58. Dunbar also published several poems that December: "A Back-Log Song" appeared in the December 3, 1898, volume of the *Outlook* (835–36); "Christmas Is a-Comin'" and "The Conquerors: The Black Troops in Cuba" appeared in the December 1898 volume of the *Bookman* (341, 373).

59. Samuel Milton Jones (1846–1904) was a politically active and progressive member of the Republican Party in Toledo. In 1897, he was nominated for Toledo's mayoral office, and he ran on helping to improve conditions for the working class there. Jones initiated several programs to give back to the community as well. Because of his liberal policies, Jones was not favored by the wealthy; however, as a champion of the working class, he was not only able to run for mayor again in 1899 but easily won the race. After Jones died while in office, Brand Whitlock took over the position and continued to lead in the same vein as Jones.

60. OHS, reel 1.

61. Dunbar arrived in Toledo after taking a leave of absence without pay from the Library of Congress to attend various recitals, one of which was at Golden Rule Park, where he was introduced by Mayor Jones.

62. Jones is likely referring to Dunbar's article "The Race Question Discussed," which first appeared in the *Chicago Record* and then was reprinted in numerous newspapers across the country, including the *Toledo Journal* on December 11, the day before this letter was written. The article was inspired by the Wilmington, North Carolina, riots of 1898 and has sometimes been printed under the heading "Recession Never." It begins with a poem, "Negro and White Man," and outlines white atrocities committed against the black community at large. Despite challenges, the poem asserts the idea that Black Americans would succeed against all odds. For some, this challenged Washington's idea of industrial education. See "The Race Question Discussed," *Toledo Journal*, December 11, 1898.

63. This is likely John Greenleaf Whittier (1807–1892), who was a Quaker poet, essayist, and abolitionist.

64. OHS, reel 1.

65. The Methodist Episcopal Church is one of the oldest and largest Methodist denominations in the United States and is considered to be the first US religious sect to form a national organization.

66. John Heyl Vincent (1832–1920) was an American bishop of the Methodist Episcopal Church. In 1874, Vincent cofounded the Chautauqua Assembly. Religious in nature, this assembly was promoted as a Sunday school. Four years later, in 1878, he served as the chancellor of the Chautauqua Institution. For a sketch of Vincent's career and help in founding these, see Oyen, "Founder of 'Chautauquas,'" 101.

67. The progressive Chautauqua Movement was founded in part by John Heyl Vincent and Lewis Miller. The movement sought to educate people in the areas of entertainment and culture. See Vincent and Miller, *Chautauqua Movement*. Religious and exclusive to Protestants initially, the movement expanded to include summer sessions for anyone who wanted to attend.

68. Robert Elijah Jones (1872–1960), originally from Greensboro, North Carolina, was an African American Methodist Episcopalian clergyman and general superintendent of the Methodist Episcopal Church in the South. He served as editor of the *Southwestern Christian Advocate* from 1897 to 1901, where he often advocated racial equality, religion, education, and community outreach. He became one of the first African American bishops in the Methodist Episcopal Church in 1920. Because of race discrimination, he was limited to presiding over only African American churches. The Robert Elijah Jones papers can be found at the Amistad Research Center, New Orleans, Louisiana.

69. OHS, reel 1.

70. The Board of Trustees at the predominantly Black Atlanta University was made up of white individuals. Dunbar responded in a letter to a friend regarding

this honor: "To-day I received notice from the board of trustees of Atlanta University that they had conferred on me the honorary degree of Master of Arts in recognition of my literary work. Of course it is an empty honor, but very pleasant" (Wiggins 87).

71. Horace Bumstead (1841–1919) served as the Atlanta University president from 1888 to 1907. For more information, see Towns, "Phylon Profile, XVI."

72. A clear reference made by several of the white literary elite that Dunbar was fully African, which disproved the notion that his intellectual pursuits were due to his white ancestry.

73. Frederick Means (1865–1919) was a Harvard College and Yale Divinity School graduate and a practicing reverend. He temporarily served as a member of Atlanta University's Board of Trustees. For brief information, see his obituary in the *Congregationalist and Advance*, September 18, 1919, 382.

74. OHS, reel 3.

75. This is very likely from William J. Kountz Jr., whose *Billy Baxter's Letters* earned him some literary fame. The comedic sketches appeared in the form of letters written to Billy's friend Jim about the day-to-day activities experienced by a Pittsburgh gentleman, such as carousing about town, drinking, and spending money. These letters were widely distributed in 1899 to promote the Duquesne Distributing Company of Harmarville, maker of liver tonics. Kountz Sr. was a fairly popular humorist at the time, but he died at the age of thirty-two. See Kountz, *Billy Baxter's Letters*.

76. Most likely drafts of his *Billy Baxter's Letters*.

77. In late May, the Dunbars went to Brodhead's Bridge, New York, for the Catskills mountain air that the doctors prescribed to aid Dunbar's health and combat tuberculosis. During his stay in New York, Dunbar produced several works, including two stories, three poems, and a three-thousand-word article.

78. "Scraps" is a term that has been used to mean sketches, short stories, or chapters. Among others, Mark Twain mentions several scraps when referring to chapters of his autobiography.

79. We have been unable to locate this newspaper or literary journal/magazine, although it is likely one from Pennsylvania, where Kountz resided, or New York, whose society he often poked fun at. One possibility is that "Literature" could refer to *Literary Life of New York*, which interviewed Dunbar in 1899.

80. In the early 1900s, Red Raven Splits was a brand of the Red Raven Company, started by Kountz, which advertised its elixir to fight off a hangover. Its tray advertisements depicted a red raven with the slogan "Ask the Man" (likely a pharmacist/druggist); it was a huge success until Prohibition in the 1920s.

81. Research suggests that Red Raven might be a rare example of ads that were just as successful as the product. Kountz also wrote a humous booklet called *One Night in New York Society*, which was well received in bars and social clubs throughout the city and also included Red Raven ads.

Toward the close of summer, Dunbar had suffered severely from pulmonary troubles, and his doctor advised him to seek the air of the Catskills, where he resided for several months. At the writing of this letter, Dunbar and Alice were settled there, but they had their mail sent to Brodhead's Bridge in care of John Crispell. The Catskills would not benefit Dunbar, who would soon go west to Colorado at the behest of his physician. Dunbar's mother came from Washington to accompany Dunbar and Alice to Colorado. Dunbar carried several letters of introduction from Tobey.

82. Howells Collection, Houghton Library, Harvard University, accessed March 24, 2017, https://id.lib.harvard.edu/ead/hou01168/catalog. Cited by permission of the Houghton Library.

83. This fight between *Lippincott's* and Dodd, Mead caused Dunbar great apprehension. He wrote Alice of these publication troubles on several occasions, but on December 21, 1897, he explained that "there is somewhat of a hitch in the novel proceedings between Messrs Dodd & Lippincott. Dodd wants the latter to sign a contract promising not to get out a special edition of his magazine when my novel comes out. Lippincott refuses and the fight proceeds while I look on" (Metcalf, "Letters of Paul," 303). On January 4, 1898, Dunbar was hopeful, writing Alice that "things had been adjusted. Lippincott's will publish in April. They [Dodd & Mead] in Sept" (339). However, a day later, on January 5, Dunbar wrote Alice that "another letter came from Dodd & Mead. They and Lippincott's are still fighting. Lippincott's won't agree not to print more of the magazine with my story in than usual & insist that Dodd & Mead do not bring the book out until 5 months after their publication; the latter want me to decide. If I decide for Lippincott's, I lose the friendship of Dodd. If I decide for Dodd, I lose $350.00 and a big opening. I have no one with whom to advise. I am discouraged & worried to death" (343). See Metcalf 303–43.

84. See Robert E. Jones to PLD, April 11, 1899. When Dunbar had to cancel several of his readings on his way to Albany because of tuberculosis and pneumonia, he stayed with a friend who had first introduced him to Alice and was then residing in a tenement house. Howells visited, wanting to give his good wishes to Dunbar, who was resting.

85. Many of Dunbar's close literary friends were unable to travel to visit, so they sent encouraging letters. Howells and Corrothers, however, were two close friends who were able to visit during this time. For information on Corrothers, see PLD to James Corrothers, September 30, 1904.

86. Dunbar was advised to set out for Denver, Colorado; although many "cures" for tuberculosis were unsuccessful, Dunbar fared exceptionally well in Denver. See Scharnhorst and Matthews, "'Denver Took Me into Her Arms.'"

87. OHS, reel 1.

88. Jeremiah Thomas Eskridge (1848–1902) was a well-known, skilled, and honored doctor in Denver, Colorado. Upon his death in 1902, Drs. Charles K. Mills and Frank P. Norbury delivered eulogies in Eskridge's memory. For their remarks, see *Journal of the American Medical Association*, November 8, 1902, 1–2.

It is clear from this letter that Tobey wanted Dunbar to receive good care, as Dr. Eskridge was highly skilled and respected. Eskridge wrote Tobey back on July 31, 1899, and assured him that Dunbar would be well looked after. Eskridge also expressed thanks to Tobey for a book of Dunbar's poems—most likely *Majors and Minors*.

89. Dunbar's doctor insisted on this visit, as the Catskills had not aided in restoring Dunbar's health. At that time, Colorado was considered to have the best climate to help those suffering from tuberculosis, and Tobey would have been aware of this. Eskridge was considered an expert in the areas of tuberculosis and consumption, and he counseled: "When a consumptive patient finds a climate that agrees with him, he should there make his home for the remainder of his life." Eskridge further advised patients and readers alike that this "should be a rule from which there are as few exceptions as possible" ("Some Observations," 549). Dunbar and Alice settled in a small home in Harmon outside Denver in October 1899. A few years later, Eskridge would argue that it was "impossible to estimate the number of useful lives that the climate of Colorado has either saved or prolonged." See Eskridge, "Influences of the Climate of Colorado," 607.

90. OHS, reel 1.

91. Cunningham reports that Dunbar was traveling quite extensively during this time, having set up back-to-back recitals in the following cities: Lexington, Terre Haute, Lafayette, Cleveland, and Pittsburgh. At the writing of this letter, it is likely that Dunbar had just returned from these travels. The newspapers have him reading at the sixtieth anniversary of the Colored Home and Hospital in New York the day before this letter. Cunningham also explains that Dunbar canceled a recital in Albany on May 1 where he was to be introduced by Governor Theodore Roosevelt. See Cunningham 191. Wiggins reports that on his way to the recital, he was taken ill with pneumonia and had to stay at the home of a friend, where he was visited by such important figures as William Dean Howells. A later letter to Howells confirms this. See Wiggins 86.

92. Dunbar received several negative reviews of *The Uncalled* because of its focus on white characters. Overall, however, the novel received some promising feedback. "Hogs" could also refer to the fight between *Lippincott's* and Dodd, Mead. See PLD to William D. Howells, July 24, 1899. Despite the issue that caused this letter, Dunbar published extensively with *Lippincott's*, including eleven poems and twelve short stories between 1899 and 1905. The poems include "The Tryst," November 1900, 772; "To a Captious Critic," October 1901, 493; "A Roadway," January 1902, 114; "Differences," March 1902, 325; "Lyrics of Love and Sorrow," December 1902, 732; "Summer in the South," September 1903, 378; "Forever," June 1904, 670; "The Farm Child's Lullaby," August 1904, 201; "Twilight," October 1904, 497; "Compensation," December 1904, 786; "Rain-Songs," February 1905, 214; and "Day," November 1905, 629. Dunbar's short stories published in *Lippincott's* include "The End of the Chapter," April 1899, 532–34; "The Strength of Gideon," October 1899; the five stories of the "Ohio Pastorals," August–December

1901; "The Finding of Martha," March 1902, 375–84; "The Vindication of Jared Hargot," March 1904, 374–81; "The Way of Love," January 1905, 68–73; and "The Churching of Grandma Pleasant," March 1905, 337–42.

93. Likely a reference to Will Marion Cook.

94. Harrison Smith Morris (1856–1948) was an author and a historian. He was the managing director of the Philadelphia Academy of the Fine Arts, served as an art editor of the *Ladies' Home Journal*, and edited for *Lippincott's*. His poems appeared in well-known journals such as *Harper's*.

95. From Wiggins 88.

96. Dunbar had just arrived in Denver with Alice and his mother.

97. Dunbar, Alice, and Matilda lived in a cottage two and a half miles from town. See Hudson, "Biography," 89. It took Dunbar a few weeks to find "a dainty little house, pleasant and sunny," just outside Denver in Harmon. See Cunningham 199.

98. "The Hapless Southern Negro" was published in the *Denver Post* on September 17, 1899. Dunbar's article surveys Denver and suggests that African Americans could assuage their plight in the South and North by moving west.

99. The National Afro-American Council was the first national civil rights organization in the United States and was launched in Rochester, New York, in 1898. It eventually disbanded in 1908, but it served significantly as a forum for critical conversations about race relations in the early twentieth century. Thomas Fortune spearheaded this council after his earlier attempt with the National Afro-American League failed to gain momentum in the 1890s.

100. OHS, reel 3.

101. This is likely a reference to the recitals Dunbar had to cancel because of his struggle with tuberculosis. Some of the organizers demanded that Dunbar refund the money used to advertise. For example, the *Appeal* in Saint Paul, Minnesota, reported the following on May 13, 1899: "On last Tuesday a telegram was received from Mrs. Paul Laurence Dunbar stating that her husband was seriously ill in New York with pneumonia and that all engagements were canceled by order of his physician. This was quite a disappointment for the American Law Enforcement League, under whose auspices he was to appear in the Twin Cities and read from his own works. A large amount had been spent in advertising him and the outlook for a large crowd was very favorable. . . . All persons who had tickets for sale for the Dunbar reading are requested to return them to the persons from whom they obtained them at once, so that reports may be made."

102. Cunningham notes that "one day Alice was summoned out of the sick room to meet a man from the Southern Help Agency, but instead of offering help, he coldly demanded that Paul immediately refund the $150 spent for advertising the Albany recital at which the poet had failed to appear" (192). Perhaps this and the next letter speak to Cunningham's scenario; if not this, then certainly a similar situation where Bruce supposedly sent an "advocate" to Dunbar to collect money for his canceled appearance. See Cunningham 192.

103. New York.

104. Dunbar accused Bruce of hiring an attorney to recoup the lost funds from the cancellation of his appearances.

105. John Edward Bruce, also known as Bruce Grit or J. E. Bruce-Grit (1856–1924), was born a slave and eventually became an American civil rights activist, speaker, journalist, and historian. Bruce was involved in the Pan-Africanism movement. He cofounded the Negro Society for Historical Research and was part of the National Afro-American Council.

106. Francis Zacchaeus Santiago Peregrino (ca. 1851–1919) was a Ghanaian born, Pan-Africanist newspaper editor in America and South Africa who spent a decade in the United States, specifically in New York. While living in Buffalo, he published the *Fortnightly Spectator*. Peregrino then settled permanently in Cape Town, South Africa, in 1900 and founded the *South African Spectator*. For information on Peregrino, see Saunders, "F. Z. S. Peregrino."

107. OHS, reel 3.

108. A reference to Dunbar's failure to appear in Albany during his illness.

109. John E. Bruce.

110. Shortly after writing this letter, Peregrino moved to Africa and founded the *South African Spectator*, which was largely successful.

111. Most likely Charles Thatcher.

112. OHS, reel 3.

113. *The Love of Landry*. This novel never had an English edition.

114. Poem by Edwin Markham that appeared in the May 1899 issue of *Current Literature*, which is likely where Dunbar first saw it. That same year (and the year of this letter), this poem, along with several other poems of Markham's, were collected in book form and titled *The Man with the Hoe and Other Poems*. The following letters indicate that the "information" provided by Reynolds was the possibility of publishing with Doubleday & McClure. Often, Markham was referred to as the "Poet-Laureate of the West." See the "Current Opinion" section of *Current Literature: A Magazine of Record and Review*, July–December 1899.

115. Dunbar was still in Colorado at this point.

116. The *Bookman* was a literary journal begun by Dodd, Mead in New York in 1895. Harry Thurston Peck served as its first editor and worked as a staff member until 1906. At the time of this writing, the current editor was Arthur Bartlett Maurice. The magazine ceased publication in 1906.

117. Doubleday & McClure formed in partnership between Samuel S. McClure and Frank Nelson Doubleday in late 1897. Doubleday & McClure's first volume of *Tales from McClure's* sold five thousand copies during the first week in September. See the *Sioux City (IA) Journal*, September 26, 1897, 13.

118. OHS, reel 3.

119. The *Teutonic* was a White Star Line steamship and Britain's first armed merchant cruiser, which had 2,460 quarters and was one of the first modern liners to include more classes for passengers. The *Teutonic* sailed for Liverpool on

December 27, 1899 (see the *Brooklyn Daily Eagle*, 3). The letter writer would have caught a train from Liverpool to London. Among the well-known passengers were E. J. Henderson, Mrs. Kitson, D. McLean, Howard Page, Alexander A. Auld, Captain E. S. Davis, Captain M. L. Fielden, Professor Josiah Boyce, H. P. Sparks, William C. Whitney, P. H. Burton, J. R. Callender, A. G. C. Dinnick, William Geddes, E. J. Henderson, Thomas Ritchie, P. C. Stewart, Mr. and Mrs. A. M. Watt, Mr. Saiamon, and Benjamin Watkins. See the *New York Times*, December 28, 1899, 7; *Brooklyn Daily Eagle*, December 27, 1899, 3; *Newport Daily News*, December 27, 1899, 5; *New York Tribune*, December 27, 1899, 6; *New York Times*, December 27, 1899, 7.

120. *The Love of Landry* is set in the ranchlands of Colorado and is romantic in nature. The book sold for $1.25 a copy and was approximately two hundred pages long.

121. Doubleday & McClure, as the subsequent letters show, rejected the manuscript, saying it was too short, and recommended sending it to *McClure's*.

122. Walter Hines Page (1855–1918) was an American publisher and journalist but also worked as a diplomat; he became the US ambassador to the United Kingdom during World War I. Page was instrumental in forming North Carolina State University in 1885. His literary career included work with the *New York World*, *Evening Post*, and *Atlantic Monthly*, while also serving as literary adviser to Houghton Mifflin. He joined S. S. McClure in October 1899 (shortly after this, McClure canceled his contract to purchase *Harper's*). Page's biographer Noel L. Griese reports that in October, Frank Doubleday informed McClure that he and Walter Page were leaving (*Arthur W. Page*, 10). By early 1900, he had partnered with Doubleday to establish Doubleday, Page & Company, a major book publisher in New York for close to ten years.

123. Frank Nelson Doubleday (1862–1934) worked as an editor and publisher during the early nineteenth century and later partnered with Samuel S. McClure to form Doubleday & McClure in 1897. Doubleday began his career with Charles Scribner's Sons, where he served as publisher of *Scribner's Magazine*. Doubleday was also a director, along with Samuel S. McClure, John S. Philips, Oscar W. Brady, and Alfred L. Fowle, of the McClure-Tissot Company of New York, which was incorporated in May 1899 as a manufacturer and seller of books, art, and paintings. It reported $6,000 capital in 1899. See the *Buffalo Morning Express*, May 21, 1899, 14. Doubleday, while in partnership with McClure at Doubleday & McClure, also served as vice president of McClure Publishing, a position originally slated for McClure in the initial partnership with Harper & Brothers. See the *New York Times*, June 4, 1899, 1.

124. The signature is difficult to read but is likely James MacArthur, literary agent and editor for Doubleday & McClure, who was in charge of the firm's London interests. See the *Fourth Estate: A Newspaper for the Makers of Newspapers*, December 21, 1899, 1. He was also editor of the *Forum* from 1890 until 1895, when he became literary adviser for Houghton, Mifflin & Company, followed by

an editorial position with the *Atlantic Monthly*. He then became associate editor of the *Bookman* from its inception and served as literary adviser for Dodd, Mead & Company. The *New York Times* reported on December 23, 1899, that "the foreign interests of the firm [Doubleday, Page & Co.] will be looked after by Mr. James MacArthur, formerly editor of *The Bookman*, who sails next Wednesday to take up his residence in London." This is in keeping with the opening of the article, which discloses that "the Doubleday & McClure Company will shortly become Doubleday, Page & Co."

125. The S. S. McClure Company was a successful magazine and book publishing establishment and newspaper syndicate business that would later suffer its own financial hardships with in-house fighting among staff, owners, and management, leading many to go work for *American Magazine*, McClure's rival. For an analysis of McClure's struggles in the publishing business, see McClure, "My Autobiography." In 1884, S. S. McClure established the first US newspaper syndicate, the McClure Syndicate. In 1899, when *Harper's* was unable to meet its financial obligations, it sought out J. P. Morgan & Company for help, which then brought in the S. S. McClure Company since it had run a profitable international publishing syndicate. Around the time of this letter, S. S. McClure Company and Doubleday & McClure Company sought to merge into a single corporation, but Doubleday rejected the deal, and McClure was unable to purchase the Harper firm. See Kaestle and Radway, *History of the Book in America*, 58.

126. OHS, reel 1.

127. *The Love of Landry*.

128. See James MacArthur to PLD, December 19, 1899.

129. This is not entirely true because Frank Doubleday was reported as vice president of the company in 1897. See Griese, *Arthur W. Page*, 9. It is possible that Martin wrote with knowledge of an internal changeup.

130. Edwin C. Martin (1851–1915) was an author and editor for the *Telegram* and then *McClure's* magazine. Originally from Hamilton, Ohio, and a graduate of Dartmouth College, he also penned several small articles and books.

131. OHS, reel 1.

132. E. C. Martin of *McClure's*.

133. Clearly a reference to the aforementioned managerial changeups in the publishing business. At the writing of this letter, Doubleday, Page and Co. had already been formed, Doubleday having announced his intention to leave in October and making a clear break toward the end of December. However, the company continued to publish under the Doubleday & McClure imprint well into 1901. The letterhead clearly belies this change.

134. In the *Indianapolis Journal* on May 7, 1900, the editor reports that the series "is intended to present in an attractive form, cloth bound, yet at a very low price, some of the many good novelettes which are generally considered too short to make a book of by themselves, and which so often are made to carry a volume of short stories of less interest."

135. Sir Anthony Hope Hawkins (1863–1933) was a British playwright and novelist who published under the pseudonym Anthony Hope. He is most famous for his adventure novels. *Captain Dieppe* was a romance and the first of a series of "short novels" to be published by Doubleday & McClure.

136. Although Dunbar often circulated his work to try to get the best price possible, he ultimately and consistently returned to Dodd, Mead & Co., who published the remainder of his collections and novels.

137. Clearly an acquisitions editor for Doubleday & McClure; however, we have been unable to locate any additional information on Laurie.

138. OHS, reel 1.

139. *The Love of Landry*.

140. See E. C. Martin to PLD, January 13, 1900.

141. As far as we can determine, Dunbar never published with Doubleday & McClure.

142. First established in April 1887 for literary workers by two *Boston Globe* reporters, William H. Hills (1859–1930) and Robert Luce (1862–1946), the *Writer* is the oldest magazine for writers in the United States.

143. Around this same time, Booker T. Washington's letters to and from fellow writers indicate that Dunbar was being heavily criticized by the African American community for his use of dialect; Timothy Thomas Fortune (1856–1928), editor of the *New York Age*, wrote Booker T. Washington on February 10, 1900, that "if noble effort in our men is to be habitually derided in fiction and all aspiration is to be jeered at as Dunbar invariably does then it would be better for the race if it had no shining light in literature" (see Harlan et al., *Booker T. Washington Papers*). Years earlier, Dunbar wrote Alice that he had been in contact with Fortune, and according to Dunbar, Fortune "was very anxious . . . to go into the publishing business with him" (August 28, 1897). Dunbar also noted that Alice and Fortune were "good friends" (Metcalf, "Letters of Paul," 189). Eleanor Alexander describes Fortune as one of Dunbar's "drinking buddies" (169).

144. OHS, reel 1.

145. Dunbar was currently traveling in the East. Cunningham incorrectly reports the date, but Dunbar, his mother, and Alice traveled to Chicago and then on to New York to work out a business dispute with Ernest Hogan, the star of "Clorindy," over Dunbar's sketches for the comedic actor.

146. Though they remain unrecovered, several additional unpublished stories can still be found among Dunbar's correspondence, including those that were returned, such as "A Monologue," "The Party," and "The Haunted Plantation." Some other story titles remain indecipherable. Others include "A Detective Story," "Dialogue between Four Friends," "A Man Named Ben Adams," "Murder Story," and "Reginald Vere." See Jarrett and Morgan, *Complete Stories of Paul Laurence Dunbar*, introduction. Of all the titles listed here, only "Ole Conjurin' [Conju'in] Joe" has been recovered; it appears in Martin and Primeau, *In His Own Voice*.

147. This story, in its altered form, could be "The Lion Tamer" (1901), which

depicts an enchanting young woman whose charming parties draw the attention of men.

148. The *Black Cat* was an American literary magazine (1895–1922) published in Boston, specializing in short stories of mystery, horror, and science fiction.

149. The *Smart Set* was an American literary magazine (March 1900–June 1930) founded by Colonel William d'Alton Mann and later edited by H. L. Mencken. In its three decades of publication, the magazine served as a launching point for many up-and-coming authors. Mann's ultimate aim for the publication was to provide cultural and intellectual content that would uphold the social values of New York's elite. The first issue was published on March 10, 1900, under the editorship of Arthur Grissom.

150. *Town Topics* was an American literary magazine (1879–1937), founded by Colonel William d'Alton Mann, that reported on gossip concerning New York's social elite.

151. The *Criterion* was an American literary magazine (1896–1905) known for its vivid and somewhat risqué pictures, satire, and political humor.

152. It is not clear whether this letter is signed J. J. or J. D.

153. Dunbar and Alice had left Colorado for good in the summer; they returned to the Catskills.

154. OHS, reel 3.

155. This could be a reference to the serial version of "The Sport of the Gods," published in *Lippincott's Monthly Magazine* in May 1901 (515–94). The story was then published in the United States by Dodd, Mead as a novel in 1902. *The Jest of Fate: A Story of Negro Life* was retitled *The Jest of Fate: The Athenaeum* in its English edition, published by Jarrold & Sons on November 29, 1902. The reference here could not be to "The Strength of Gideon," the lead story in the collection *The Strength of Gideon and Other Stories*, because it had already been published in *Lippincott's*. See "The Strength of Gideon," in *The Strength of Gideon and Other Stories* (New York: Dodd, Mead, 1900) and "The Strength of Gideon," *Lippincott's*, October 1899, 617–25.

156. *The Fanatics* is roughly forty thousand words.

157. OHS, reel 3.

158. *The Fanatics*.

159. *The Love of Landry* did not sell as well as *The Fanatics*.

160. To put things into perspective, Major Pond, serving as the literary agent for Mark Twain at the time, offered the author $50,000 for a series of lectures in the United States.

161. *Truth* was a New York–based humor magazine, started in 1881, that originally published weekly but then published monthly from 1899 until 1905. It was widely known for its illustrative cover art. When Blakely Hall assumed editorship in 1891, he added more social satire and vivid colors and featured more women on the covers.

162. The writer of this letter could be a number of different individuals working

for *Truth* at the time, including James L. Ford (literary or "managing editor"). Hall had left by this time, and after his departure, the editor's chair was something of a revolving door.

163. Schomburg Collection, reel 1.

164. It is not clear whether Dunbar published this piece; however, he did publish "The New Slavery," in *Truth* on March 2, 1901. It exists in a clipping in the Dunbar Papers, OHS, reel 5.

165. The magazine included detailed illustrations as cover art as well as colored supplements, which took longer to produce.

166. Dunbar faced this kind of treatment regularly and understood the roots of it well. Ralph Story notes that "Dunbar did not have the opportunity to submit work to black editors and publishers" ("Paul Laurence Dunbar," 32). However, Dunbar figured out how to work with his audiences and publishers in order to gain a broad audience and therefore demand for his work (Williams, "Masking of a Novelist," 157–58). Dunbar later explained this situation to James Weldon Johnson, writing, "You know of course that I didn't start as a dialect poet. I simply came to the conclusion that I could write it as well, if not better than anybody I knew of, and that by doing so I should gain a hearing and now they don't want me to write anything but dialect" (Gayle, *Oak and Ivy*, 38). By 1904, though, Wiggins notes that Dunbar was "so tired, so tired of dialect. I sent out graceful little poems, suited for any of the magazines, but they are returned to me by editors who say, 'We would be very glad to have a dialect poem, Mr. Dunbar'" (109).

167. The readers of *Truth* expected humorous pieces—dialect would have fit this call.

168. Stephen Crane (1871–1900) was a prolific American short story writer, poet, and novelist who often wrote in the realistic and naturalistic literary traditions and is probably best known for his short story "The Open Boat," which semifictionalizes Crane's experience surviving after the *S.S. Commodore* sank off the coast between Ponce Inlet and Daytona Beach, Florida, during the Spanish-American War.

169. This may be Richard F. Outcault, who created the comic strip *The Yellow Kid*.

170. Hannibal Hamlin Garland (1860–1940) was an American author of novels, short stories, essays, and poetry who published in the vein of literary realism and naturalism; he is also well known for his local color realism in *Main Traveled Roads* (New York: Harper Brothers, 1891).

171. A relatively new writer at the time, Henry Wilton Thomas (1867–1930) was an American journalist, editor, and author who published *The Last Lady of Mulberry: A Story of Italian New York* (New York: D. Appleton, 1900).

172. George Robert Gissing (1857–1903) was a prolific English novelist who published over twenty novels between 1880 and 1903.

173. OHS, reel 3.

174. Most likely *The Fanatics*.

175. OHS, reel 3.

176. *The Fanatics* and *The Love of Landry*.

177. OHS, reel 3.

178. Perhaps a reference to "One Christmas at Shiloh," which appeared in the *Delineator*, December 1900. This poem was later collected in *The Heart of Happy Hollow*, which was illustrated by E. W. Kemble.

179. The *Woman's Home Companion* began publishing in 1874 in Cleveland, Ohio. In 1886 it was retitled the *Ladies' Home Companion* and in 1897 it again became the *Woman's Home Companion*. *The Fanatics* would be published by Dodd, Mead & Co. in 1901.

180. OHS, reel 3.

181. As indexed by Metcalf, the following are Christmas stories published by Dunbar: "One Christmas at Shiloh" (*The Heart of Happy Hollow*, 1900); "Mt. Pisgah's Christmas 'Possum" (*Folks from Dixie*, 1898); and "An Old-Time Christmas" (*Strength of Gideon and Other Stories*, 1900); we have also been able to locate one other, "The Faith Cure Man." See "The Faith Cure Man," *New York Journal and Advertiser*, December 11, 1898.

182. OHS, reel 3.

183. It is not clear which story or publication this might be. *Uncle Eph's Christmas* is a one-act play he wrote with Will M. Cook, and *Candle-Lightin' Time* was not published until 1901 by Dodd, Mead and Company. This letter serves as another example to combat the myth that Dunbar did not revise his work.

184. It is not clear which story this might be.

185. OHS, reel 3.

186. Over the years, Dunbar never published a short story in the *Century*, though he regularly published dialect verse in its pages.

187. This is very likely "The Haunted Oak," in the *Springfield (MA) Republican*, January 6, 1901; reprinted in *Lyrics of Love and Laughter*. In 1900, Dunbar had published the following other poems with *Century*: "Dinah Kneading Dough," January 1900, 483; "Dat Ol' Mare o' Mine," May 1900, 159–60; and "A Spiritual," September 1900, 800.

188. In the early fall of 1900, Dunbar moved his family to this address, located in an attractive suburban neighborhood near LeDroit Park. The date of this letter remains contested. Wiggins and Catherine Reef place it in the fall of 1900, while Hudson dates it to February 1900, although he could be confusing the Evanston event with a similar one that occurred in February 1900 when Dunbar was asked to report the proceedings of black farmers at the Tuskegee Institute but was not in good enough shape to attend (Arnold, "Some Personal Reminiscences," 402). Gary Scharnhorst and Kadeshia Matthews locate this letter to shortly before Dunbar's death in 1905 ("'Denver Took Me into Her Arms,'" 23).

189. Paul Martin Pearson (1871–1938) became a professor of elocution at Swarthmore College in 1902. He supported the Chautauqua Movement, which Dunbar had been involved with earlier in his career. According to Wiggins and Hudson, Dunbar had been drinking excessively for years and had earned a reputation. At

one event (the one mentioned in this letter), Dunbar was reported to have shown up at a recital intoxicated. The fiasco reached the national newspapers and tarnished Dunbar's reputation. In a March 1906 article for *Talent*, a magazine edited by Pearson, the editor pays tribute to the poet, observing that "it has been frequently reported in the public prints that Dunbar was a drunkard. Though it was founded on truth, it was not the whole truth. With a friend I had engaged Dunbar to give an evening of readings at Evanston, Illinois. We had thoroughly advertised the event, and a large audience from the University and the city were present to hear him. At eight o'clock, a messenger brought me word that he had broken a dinner engagement at the Woman's College, and that no word had been received from him. After an anxious delay he arrived a half hour late and with him were a nurse, a physician and his half-brother, Mr. Murphy. The first number or two could not be heard, but not until he had read one poem the second time did we suspect the true cause of his difficulty in speaking. His condition grew steadily worse, so that most of the people left in disgust" (reprinted from *Talent* in Pearson, *Paul Laurence Dunbar*, 8–9. Best notes that the *Chicago [Evening] Post* printed the details of this event in its October 1900 issue (see *Crossing the Color Line*, 198). Hudson quotes from the same article, pointing out the author's obtuseness in his speech: "I am now going to read the 'Party,'" Dunbar said, "and I hope there has been no requests for it, for I would not read it if there had" (quoted in "Biography," 111). At the time of this incident, Pearson would have been a doctoral student and instructor at Northwestern University. According to Cunningham, Pearson had attempted to contact Dunbar, but it was three days before Dunbar responded with this letter.

190. Alcohol.

191. Preprinted programs and advertisements had already been paid for.

192. Dunbar was in Denver from the end of summer 1899, after failed attempts to recover from his illness in the Catskills, until the spring of 1900, when he returned home to Washington, DC, where he had been residing in a boardinghouse. Dunbar would revisit the Catskills for his health in the early summer of 1900, returning to Washington in the fall of that same year to take up residence with Alice at 321 Spruce Street, which they would call home for the next two years. Denver had become the center of a new approach to treating tuberculosis. For Dunbar, Colorado was miraculous. He argued he had been "restored to health" in Denver, "with her clear skies, her wine-like air and her great all-holding heart" (Scharnhorst and Matthews, "'Denver Took Me into Her Arms,'" 23).

193. OHS, reel 3.

194. "The Scapegoat," *Collier's*, October 27, 1900, 8–9. The poem was reprinted in *The Heart of Happy Hollow* (1904), Dunbar's last short story collection.

195. OHS, reel 3.

196. The poem appeared first in the *Montreal Star* and was then collected in *Lyrics of Love and Laughter*.

197. *The Heart of Happy Hollow*, in which "The Scapegoat" appeared, was illustrated by E. W. Kemble.

198. *Collier's* would publish both "The Mission of Mr. Scatters" and "The Scapegoat."

199. OHS, reel 1.

200. Dunbar's poem "Booker T. Washington," was first published in the *New England Magazine*, October 1900, 227.

201. Reproduction in Special Collections, University of Delaware, MS 99, box 66, folder 65.

202. We have not been able to locate any information on this individual.

203. Robert Gould Shaw (1837–1863) was appointed by Massachusetts governor John A. Andrew to found one of the first African American infantry troops fighting for the Union. In 1863, this group would become the Fifty-Fourth Massachusetts Infantry. Historical accounts allege that Shaw found the men to be able-bodied soldiers who could fight just as well as white soldiers, despite stereotypes that argued otherwise. Upon learning that soldiers of color would be paid less than white soldiers, Shaw led a famous boycott of all wages. After leading a charge on Batter Wagner in Charleston, Shaw was killed in action. General Johnson Hagood, a Confederate leader, buried Shaw in a common grave after refusing to return his body to the Union army. It is for this act alone that Shaw is portrayed as both hero and martyr. Gary Scharnhorst notes that "Shaw's corpse was desecrated—stripped of its uniform and interred without regard for rank or station," an action that "sealed Shaw's reputation as a martyr to the cause of abolition. By the close of the nineteenth century, he would be canonized a saint in the pantheon of American heroes." According to Scharnhorst, "No less than nine bombastic poems specifically devoted to Robert Shaw's burial . . . appeared in Northern newspapers and popular magazines over the next several months." However, Scharnhorst contests Shaw's martyrdom, arguing that he was "not an abolitionist," but notes that Shaw's burial brought him posthumous attention and fame until the 1940s. Shaw's burial struck hope in the hearts of many: the creation of the Shaw Memorial in 1897 "soon inspired a new wave of poetry, particularly on the theme of racial justice. Much as Shaw's burial with his troops had typified the brotherhood of men to an earlier generation of abolitionists, the bronze effigy of the colonel and his marching men seemed an innocent reminder of the unfilled promise of equality under the law." Even Richard Watson Gilder became involved. See Scharnhorst, "From Soldier to Saint."

204. Dunbar published "Robert Gould Shaw" in the *Atlantic Monthly* 86 (October 1900): 516. While so many of the poems written about Gould reflect "Shaw's mission as divine, his sacrifice successful, his martyrdom assured," Allen Flint argues Dunbar's poem to be "startling" because Dunbar presents Shaw's sacrifice as "in vain" ("Black Response to Colonel Shaw," 212). Dunbar's response to Percy fits here. Flint also notes that of the more than fifty poems he could find about Shaw, only four had been written by African Americans. For more information about popular poems on Shaw, see Axelrod, "Colonel Shaw in American Poetry," 523–37. Turpin recently recovered a pithy response from Dunbar years later to an

unsympathetic, likely racist reader: "As to the spirit of my Robert Gould Shaw poem I do not believe that you are able to judge. I see from the point of view of the 'Under Dog,' and it is a much broader view than you can possibly have. I see the disfranchisement of my people in the South, their murders North and South, the curtailment of their chance for education, the abridgment of their opportunity to do any but the most menial labor. I stand up for the truth of every line in the poem" (Turpin, "Twilight Is Their Child," 178).

205. This letter appeared in the *Crisis* 20, no. 2 (June 1920): 73–74.

206. *The Fanatics*.

207. Henry Van Dyke (1852–1933) was an American author, educator, and Presbyterian minister. "Fisherman's Luck" is the first short story in the collection *Fisherman's Luck and Some Other Uncertain Things*.

208. OHS, reel 3.

209. *The Sport of the Gods* was first serialized in *Lippincott's Monthly Magazine* (May 1901) and then published in book form by Dodd, Mead in 1902. It is Dunbar's fourth and final novel, and it was received well.

210. *The Sport of the Gods* would be published in England by Jarrold & Sons under the title *The Jest of Fate* in the same year.

211. Originally called the *Yellow Kid* after a popular comic strip character, *Ainslee's Magazine* was an American humor literary journal published from 1897 until 1926.

212. *Collier's Once a Week* was an American magazine founded by Peter Fenelon Collier in 1888, eventually becoming *Collier's* in 1905. It focused on areas of social reform, using a muckraking style of journalism.

213. OHS, reel 3.

214. This poem was published in *Ainslee's Magazine*, August 8, 1901, 67, and was later collected in *Lyrics of Love and Laughter*.

215. OHS, reel 3.

216. Dunbar may be referring to the money received for his poem "Booker T. Washington."

217. OHS, reel 3.

218. Dunbar is referring to *The Sport of the Gods*; Dunbar and Reynolds were interested in publishing with the London-based Jarrold & Sons again.

219. We have been unable to locate this story.

220. Likely "Long To'ds Night," which appeared in the *Century*, February 1901, 639.

221. OHS, reel 3.

222. Though *Winter Roses* was never produced, it is likely Dunbar's third play according to Brawley (85). *Herrick* was Dunbar's second play (*Robert Herrick* was his first); he wrote it in 1898. None of Dunbar's plays were ever produced. Unlike other Dunbar works, *Herrick* was written in the tradition of an eighteenth-century English comedy of manners. Speculation remains that it was inspired by the life of poet Robert Herrick. Despite early claims about the plot, this text remained

unrecovered until recently; Herbert Woodward Martin and Ronald Primeau recovered it in 2002. See *In His Own Voice: The Dramatic and Other Uncollected Works of Paul Laurence Dunbar*.

In "Paul Laurence Dunbar's Overlooked Play," Leuchtenmüller reports that a copy of the drama was sent to Richard B. Harrison (1864–1935), who had helped Dunbar earlier in his career; Harrison looked for a producer, but he had no luck and in 1908 returned the manuscript to Alice. Following this, Alice sent the drama to well-known author and publisher Carter Woodson (1875–1950).

223. This unpublished play was written by Dunbar in 1900. It is likely that he also sent this play to Harrison.

224. This play was never published. Unfortunately, Dunbar wrote only a few dramas during his lifetime, none of which were ever published despite his best efforts.

225. OHS, reel 3.

226. Robert Underwood Johnson (1853–1937) was the associate editor of the *Century* at the time of this letter. See also Scott-Childress, "Paul Laurence Dunbar," 367–75.

227. The reference here is likely to "Long To'ds Night" and "Itching Heels," both of which appeared in the *Century*, March 1901, 639.

228. OHS, reel 3.

229. Dunbar is likely referring to *Winter Roses* and *Old Elijah*, neither of which succeeded in being published.

230. OHS, reel 3.

231. Despite the attempts of both Dunbars, Alice's short story "The Stones of the Village" was never published. See Ewell, Menke, and Humphrey, *Southern Local Color*, liii–liv. This would be discussed over several letters.

232. Most likely a reference to Dunbar's unpublished "Herrick."

233. "The Pearl in the Oyster" was published in the *Southern Workman* in 1900. Perhaps Dunbar was trying to help Alice publish another book of short stories.

234. OHS, reel 3.

235. "Schwallinger's Philanthropy," *Metropolitan*, August 1901. It was later collected in *The Heart of Happy Hollow* (1904).

236. OHS, reel 3.

237. Alice Kauser (1872–1945) was a theatrical agent and play broker, playwright, and author's representative, as well as one of the leading dramatist's agents in New York during the late nineteenth and early twentieth centuries. Kauser was born in the American consulate in Budapest, Hungary, where her father, Joseph Kauser, was consul. Her mother was Berta Gerster, a well-known Hungarian opera singer with many connections to the European world of the arts. For more information on her, see Witham, *Theatre in the United States*, 188–89.

238. A now defunct rail line. Blair L. M. Kelley writes that "Dunbar traveled in an age of increasing restrictions on black travelers; state by state, southern legislatures demanded the segregation of black passengers from whites." Kelley explains, "Dunbar did not record his recollections of riding in a Jim Crow car," although

"restrictions on black travelers were formally set aside by state laws during Republican Reconstruction, informally, segregation and mistreatment continued . . . [and] African Americans had increasing difficulty receiving equitable treatment, and could not predict whether they would encounter discrimination on any given journey" ("Right to Ride," 348).

239. On October 15, 1896, long before Dunbar was diagnosed with tuberculosis, he wrote his mother that his travel through Virginia was "very delightful" and that he "could look out . . . from a luxurious coach all the way and did not once have to take a 'Jim Crow' car." Later, and once he was officially diagnosed with tuberculosis, this would become an even more important privilege for Dunbar. Sheila Rothman notes that "although scientists had discovered that tuberculosis passed from person to person through contact with bodily fluid and was not caused by genetic weaknesses . . . they still believed African Americans were more frequent carriers. They considered black communities hotbeds for the spread of TB, and black people responsible for the spread of the disease to otherwise healthy white victims. While Dunbar received good care from doctors in Ohio and Washington, DC, public perceptions of the disease—particularly in the close quarters of a train car—were shaped by fear and prejudice. In fact, fear of black disease was one of many arguments segregationists made to exclude blacks from public accommodations. A sick black passenger verified whites' worst fears about the virulence of the black body. Dunbar's physical need for a sleeping car or comfortable first-class seating put him in a precarious position" (Rothman, *Living in the Shadow of Death*, 351–52). There was a movement in 1900 to "restrict the interstate travel of persons with tuberculosis" (190–91). It ultimately failed for obvious reasons, but there were definite efforts to keep sick people off trains and out of hotels.

240. OHS, reel 3.

241. George Horace Lorimer (1867–1937) was an American journalist, author, and editor who started as a journalist for the *Saturday Evening Post* before assuming temporary editorship while Cyrus Curtis was abroad. Lorimer was then made editor in chief of the paper. Lorimer and Dunbar had a long-standing relationship that was fruitful and yet hurtful to Dunbar—one that was not unlike his relationship with Howells. For as much as Lorimer encouraged and supported Dunbar, he also hindered Dunbar's subject material by requesting mainly dialect poems from him (Revell and Nordloh, *Paul Laurence Dunbar*, 107–8). Yet Dunbar published several pieces in the *Saturday Evening Post* from 1899 to 1902 and worked well with Lorimer. Matt Sandler examines the complicated relationship between Dunbar and Lorimer in "The Glamour of Paul Laurence Dunbar."

Dunbar presented a copy of *In Old Plantation Days* and inscribed it to those "out of whose suggestion these stories were born, and by whose kindness they first saw light." Many of the stories Dunbar published in the *Saturday Evening Post* were collected in this edition. Lorimer is included in this reference.

242. Chicago Rock Island Pacific Railroad. See PLD to P. Reynolds, May 16, 1901.

243. "Schwallinger's Philanthropy" and "The Boy with the Bayonet" were both collected in *The Heart of Happy Hollow*.

244. Dunbar is likely referring to the practice of periodicals at the time of paying an author after his work was published, because of lax copyright laws. Although the 1891 manufacturing clause of the US Copyright Act was created to protect authors so they would receive royalties on all publications of their works, nevertheless, literary piracy laws were not strictly enforced; publishers might often pay for an author's novel, story, or poem only to see it appear in another publication that never paid for it. Dunbar circumvented this system by receiving advances on his work.

245. Eberly Family Special Collections Library, Penn State University Libraries.

246. Grace S. Sisson (b. 1864) was the daughter of a prominent Potsdam, New York, family. For information on her family, see *Potsdam, NY*, edited by the Potsdam Public Museum (2004), 60–62. Upon the marriage of Grace's parents in 1854, "A Golden Wedding" appeared in a Wisconsin periodical, the *Owl*; the article lists a "Miss Grace" of Potsdam (New York). See "A Golden Wedding," *Owl*, March 1904, 252–53.

247. Mary Alicia Owen (1850–1935) was a writer and a collector of folklore from Missouri. She is most famous for her compilations of local legends, especially those pertaining to voodoo. Published in 1893, *Old Rabbit, the Voodoo, and Other Sorcerers* is based on cultural and religious traditions of African Americans in Missouri. She served as the president of the Missouri Folklore Society.

248. George Laurence Gomme (1853–1916) was a British folklorist and public servant. Gomme's *Handbook of Folk-Lore* (1890) attempted not only to define folklore for readers but to look at it via a scientific, objective method.

249. Known more politely now as *Xhosa Folklore*, this 1890 publication includes several Xhosa folktales, proverbs, cultural information, and translations of Xhosa words. Theal is said to have collected and verified the information personally. The Xhosas are the second largest ethnic group in South Africa (next to the Zulus). As a language, Xhosa is a Nguni Bantu language that employs click consonant sounds. It is one of the official languages of South Africa today.

250. Also by Mary Alicia Owen, this text seems to be the American version of *Old Rabbit, the Voodoo, and Other Sorcerers* (London: T. Fisher Unwin, 1893).

251. Joel Chandler Harris (1848–1908), perhaps most well known for his Uncle Remus tales, published *Balaam and His Master* in 1891. Predictably, this book was well received, as it was based in the plantation tradition.

252. Alice Ilgenfritz Jones (1846–1905); with Beatrice of Bayou Têche (1895), Jones is said to have been the first white woman to consider the junction of race, gender, and creativity.

253. Edward C. Pollard (1831–1872) was a white supremacist and Confederate sympathizer most famous for writing *The Lost Cause* (1866) and *The Lost Cause Regained* (1868). The two texts offer disparate analyses as to the cause of the Civil War and attempt to defend southern culture and society while asserting the argument of states' rights. Originally published in 1859 under the title *The Southern Spy:*

or, Curiosities of Negro Slavery in the South, the book was republished in 1860 with the title *Black Diamonds Gathered in the Darky Homes of the South*, which consists of letters in the vein of apology for slavery.

254. OHS, reel 3.

255. It is not clear what Dunbar is referring to here. However, he was certainly swindled out of money on many occasions—publishers did not always provide payment; people reprinted his work and did not pay him; and he performed for audiences and would not see any of the profit, especially when he was just beginning to perform.

256. Both texts appeared in *The Heart of Happy Hollow*; as far as we know, neither text was published elsewhere; it is unclear why the Dunbars believed there had been payment for either short story.

257. In a letter, Dunbar mentioned that when *Lippincott's* asked him for a story, he considered this just another prose piece until he found that he had written fifty thousand words in thirty days, concluding, "But I have never recovered from the strain of it." See William Andrews, introduction to *The Sport of the Gods* (New York: Penguin, 2011).

258. The early criticism of *The Sport of the Gods* was fairly negative, although it did achieve some modicum of success in its depiction of urban American black life in the North. The novel today is mostly regarded as one of his most significant works.

259. OHS, reel 3.

260. Dodd, Mead published *The Sport of the Gods* in March 1902, and it was republished in England as *The Jest of Fate: A Story of Negro Life* in December. Dunbar did not publish with Jarrold & Sons again.

261. Clearly, this establishes that Jarrold & Sons had first rights to the novel's publication in England. Originally Dodd, Mead and Co. passed on the American edition, but as indicated by this letter and the one that follows, it quickly changed its mind once the novel had a London publisher. A contract supplied by the Library of Congress shows an interesting renewal history for *The Sport of the Gods*: on August 15, 1911, attorneys Craighead & Kuhn wrote the following to Dodd, Mead & Co.: "Replying to your favor of August 11th, 1911, in regard to an Agreement for distribution of royalties due to Paul Lawrence Dunbar's legatees, we beg to say that we have prepared such an Agreement and have had it signed by Mrs. Matilda Dunbar. The same has been forwarded to Mrs. Alice Dunbar and she will send to you. Upon receipt of the same will you kindly send Mrs. Matilda Dunbar's share to her direct and accompany same with the customary statement." On August 21, 1929, the copyright office at the Library of Congress wrote to Dodd, Mead & Co. noting that renewal registration for *The Sport of the Gods* must go in the name of the author's widow, Alice. It pointed out that "there is no provision under which a 'mother of an author' is authorized to make renewal." In a postscript, it acknowledged that "an author's mother would be regarded as 'next of kin,' but this is not before us at the present time." The renewal was made on behalf of Alice on August

26, 1929. Contract and letters provided by the University of Delaware Special Collections Department, Dodd, Mead & Company Archive, series V.

262. Originally a small bookstore in Indianapolis, the company became the Bobbs-Merrill Company in 1883. For more information, see O'Bar, *Origins and History of the Bobbs-Merrill Company*.

263. OHS, reel 3.

264. Funk and Wagnalls was an American publisher known for publishing reference works such as *A Standard Dictionary of the English Language* (1st ed., 1893–95) and *Funk & Wagnalls Standard Encyclopedia* (1st ed., 1912).

265. OHS, reel 3.

266. In the fall of 1901, Dunbar agreed to write a series of five short stories for *Lippincott's* under the title "Ohio Pastorals." These stories ran from August until December and included the following: "The Mortification of the Flesh," August 1901, 250–56; "The Independence of Silas Bollender," September 1901, 375–81; "The White Counterpane," October 1901, 500–508; "The Minority Committee," November 1901, 617–24; and "The Visiting of Mother Danbury," December 1901, 746–51.

267. Published in *In Old Plantation Days* (1903).

268. OHS, reel 3.

269. *The Sport of the Gods*.

270. This could be poems or a picture and short biographical note.

271. English publisher for *The Sport of the Gods*.

272. OHS, reel 3.

273. Dunbar originally typed "you check settles me." He hand-corrected the typographical error and augmented the sentence to read "your check reminds me." Dunbar made this request almost a month previously. See July 18, 1901.

274. OHS, reel 3.

275. *The Sport of the Gods* was not illustrated.

276. Dodd, Mead published *Candle-Lightin' Time*, a collection of poetry, in fall 1901.

277. See Sapirstein, "Out from Behind the Mask." Sapirstein argues, "The photographs in Dunbar's works were created explicitly to reconceive pictorial representations of African Americans, and to subtly discredit any reductive conventional perception of racial character altogether. By depicting their subjects photographically, the members of the Hampton Camera Club sought to undermine essentialist characterizations—both derogatory and sentimental—by presenting their subjects as self-determining and multifaceted individuals" (vii). See also Saperstein, "Picturing Dunbar's Lyrics," 327–39.

278. Margaret Neilson Armstrong (1867–1944) was known for her artistic book design covers. She decorated several hundred books and worked with Chicago-based publisher A. C. McClurg, as well as Scribner's and Dodd, Mead.

279. Sapirstein further asserts that the photographs taken for Dunbar's book by the Hampton Camera Club between 1899 and 1906 "represent a counterpoint

to the much-emphasized publicity photographs made concurrently for the school by Frances Benjamin Johnston; this further complicates such simplistic conclusions about the nature of Hampton Institute and the industrial education movement" ("Out from Behind the Mask," vii). Although "nearly forgotten today, Dunbar's illustrated volumes were among Hampton's most visible publicity instruments" (Sapirstein, "'Original Rags,'" 33).

280. Handwritten by Dunbar, this section is illegible.

281. OHS, reel 3.

282. "Jimmy Wheedon's Contretemps" and possibly "The Trouble about Sophiny."

283. See PLD to Paul R. Reynolds, December 30, 1900.

284. OHS, reel 3.

285. "Jimmy Weedon's Contretemps" is a nine-page manuscript signed by Dunbar; it can be found in the Paul Laurence Dunbar Papers, roll 4, box 12, frames 258–61. This story remained unpublished until 2002, when Herbert Woodward Martin and Ronald Primeau published it in *In His Own Voice*, 238–43.

286. "The Trouble about Sophiny" appeared in *In Old Plantation Days*.

287. OHS, reel 3.

288. For a summary of this short story, see Martin and Primeau, *In His Own Voice*, xxxix.

289. Dunbar is referring to what she had done, if anything, with the play *Herrick*.

290. OHS, reel 3.

291. Dunbar refers here to an updated version of "Jimmy Weedon's Contretemps," which Reynolds's handwritten note verifies receipt of.

292. This letter comes from the *Crisis* 20, no. 2 (June 1920): 73–74.

293. Mount Pocono, Pennsylvania.

294. Izaak Walton (1593–1683) was the author of *The Compleat [sic] Angler*.

295. *The Fanatics* was a commercial failure. Dunbar received several harsh reviews and criticism of the novel, which many felt reinforced black stereotypes, especially through the character "Nigger Ed." Brawley points out that the reception of the novel greatly disturbed and disappointed Dunbar because he had spent so much time on it (*Paul Laurence Dunbar*, 93). Near Dunbar's proof version of *The Fanatics* is a note about a novel-in-progress titled *The Copperheads*. See also Long, *Rehabilitating Bodies*, 286.

296. The *Evening Star* reported on this incident on January 13, 1902. Alice was injured during a crowded gathering for President McKinley's funeral when she was hit over the head with a police club.

297. OHS, reel 3.

298. Clearly, this agreement was not beneficial to Dunbar. As per Philip V. Allingham, "In the nineteenth century, publishers on both sides of the Atlantic had five ways of paying authors: 1. Commission (the author retained his or her copyright, but had to bear the costs of printing, binding, and advertising the work);

2. Half or three-quarter profits (the publisher bore production costs, which he then charged against the book; since liability for losses was split between publisher and author, so were the profits); 3. Outright purchase of an author's copyright, the practice of the House of Tauchnitz in acquiring Continental rights for supplying British novels for railway station bookstands; 4. Short lease or short run (the publisher bought the right to print the work for a definite period of time, or for a specified number of copies); 5. Royalty system of varying percentages to the author for different editions—perhaps 25 per cent for a triple-decker, 10 per cent for an American cheap edition, 15 per cent for a London cheap edition, and as little as 3d. a copy for a colonial edition." See Philip V. Allingham, "How Did Nineteenth-Century British and American Authors Get Paid?," The Victorian Web, http://www.victorianweb.org; see also the University of Delaware Special Collections Department, Dodd, Mead & Company Archive, series V, Paul Laurence Dunbar, 1896–1969. A variety of material related to Dunbar is included in this series, specifically Dunbar's contracts with Dodd, Mead; copyright renewals; and correspondence concerning original publications and reprints.

299. Here Dunbar is referring to the publication of the book in London by Jarrold & Sons under the title *The Jest of Fate: A Story of Negro Life*. Copyright was tricky at this time: though Benjamin Rudd notes that the 1834 case of *Wheaton v. Peters* was a landmark ruling "that an author has perpetual rights in his unpublished works, but that after publication his rights are limited by the statutory provisions imposed by the Congress, including deposit requirements. The case is to be regarded as laying the groundwork for modern U.S. copyright jurisprudence." See Benjamin Rudd, "Notable Dates in American Copyright, 1783–1969," *Quarterly Journal of the Library of Congress*, April 1971, 140. However, in England, the 1838 International Copyright Act granted foreign authors the same rights as British writers publishing there. This practice was slow to catch on in America. Rudd notes that the Chace Act of 1891 (also known as the International Copyright Law of 1891) offered "protection for works of foreign origin . . . for the first time" (140).

300. OHS, reel 1.

301. Austin Maurice Curtis (1868–1939) was the surgeon in chief from 1898 to 1902. For a brief professional sketch of Dr. Curtis, see Nichols and Crogman, *Progress of a Race*, 359–60. This letter most likely has to do with Curtis's treatment of tuberculosis patients.

302. Founded during the Civil War, the Freedmen's Hospital (now Howard University Hospital) is in Washington, DC.

303. William Alonza Warfield (1866–1951) was a doctor and surgeon at the Freedmen's Hospital. For a brief sketch, see Nichols and Crogman, *Progress of a Race*, 444.

304. George Bruce Cortelyou (1862–1940) was an adviser to President Theodore Roosevelt. For a brief sketch, see Manweller, *Chronology of the U.S. Presidency*, 791.

305. OHS, reel 3.

306. Dunbar is referring to the short story "In a Circle," which appeared in the *Metropolitan*, October 14, 1901, 460–62.

307. OHS, reel 3.

308. "In a Circle," *Metropolitan*, October 14, 1901, 460–62.

309. The contract for *The Sport of the Gods*.

310. From the Schomburg Collection Calendar of Manuscripts, specifically the Paul Laurence Dunbar Section, reel 3.

311. She had *Herrick* and perhaps another of Dunbar's unpublished plays.

312. From the Schomburg Collection Calendar of Manuscripts, specifically the Paul Laurence Dunbar Section, reel 3.

313. Most likely *Herrick*.

314. OHS, reel 3.

315. Harrison S. Morris (1856–1957) was an editor of *Lippincott's*, art editor of the *Ladies' Home Journal*, and chair of the Ways and Means Committee of the National Academy of Design. See the Harrison S. Morris Papers, 1895–1935, in Princeton University Library, Department of Rare Books and Special Collections. Dunbar had agreed to write a series of Ohio pastoral stories for Morris. See PLD to Reynolds, August 10, 1901.

316. Although the specifics of any contract cannot be found, Dunbar published several stories over the years with the *Saturday Evening Post*. See PLD to Paul R. Reynolds, June 3, 1901.

317. Dunbar used characters that had previously appeared in his other stories published by *Lippincott's*, and these sketches directly informed *The Uncalled* (1898).

318. Dunbar never published a series of African stories for *Lippincott's*; however, his next collection of short stories, *In Old Plantation Days*, reverberates with antebellum old plantation life in its depiction of the South.

319. Both stories were initially published in *Collier's*: "The Mission of Mr. Scatters," March 30, 1901, 14–16; and "The Scapegoat," October 27, 1900, 8–9. Both were also later collected in *The Heart of Happy Hollow*.

320. OHS, reel 3.

321. Brawley avers that this poem was based on a story Dunbar heard from an older black man, whose nephew was hanged on an oak tree by a group of white men in Alabama, having been wrongly accused of a "grave crime" (*Paul Laurence Dunbar*, 88).

322. Dunbar's tuberculosis is the likely cause of the illness he mentions here.

323. OHS, reel 3.

324. Elizabeth Marbury (1856–1933) was a dramatist's agent and Alice Kauser's mentor.

325. OHS, reel 3.

326. "The Promoter" was first published in *Collier's* on February 1, 1902, and then republished in *The Heart of Happy Hollow* (1904). "The Scapegoat" and "The Mission of Mr. Scatters" were initially published in periodicals and then

republished in *The Heart of Happy Hollow*. See PLD to Paul R. Reynolds, October 25, 1901. "A Defender of Faith" was first published in the *San Francisco Chronicle* on December 22, 1908. It too was later collected in *The Heart of Happy Hollow*.

327. OHS, reel 3.

328. "Jethro's Garden" appeared in *The Era: An Illustrated Monthly Magazine*, July 1902, 78–80.

329. *Collier's* did take the "The Promoter," but not until February 1902 (10–11). It was later collected in *The Heart of Happy Hollow* (1904), 163–90.

330. Indeed, Dunbar was unsuccessful in publishing anything or in obtaining any money at that specific time. On December 31, 1901, he wrote Reynolds to wish him "a Merry Christmas and a Happy New Year. Both should be abolished. I am broke!" See the Schomburg Collection Calendar of Manuscripts, specifically the Paul Laurence Dunbar Section, reel 3.

331. OHS, reel 3.

332. Dunbar is referring to "The Promoter" here. See "The Promoter," *The Heart of Happy Hollow*, 163–88. Dunbar wrote Reynolds shortly after, on December 19, that he had been under the impression that "'The Promoter' was one of the best things" he had ever written, "but you yourself know that the author is notoriously unable to judge his own work and that he must have a hard-handed business man to do it for him. So go right ahead with what you think best and I shall be satisfied as usual."

333. From the Schomburg Collection Calendar of Manuscripts, specifically the Paul Laurence Dunbar Section, reel 3.

334. Shortly after Dunbar's visit to Tuskegee, Washington asked him to write a song for the school; this resulted in "Tuskegee Song."

335. See Dunbar's letter to Washington on January 23, 1902, where Dunbar discusses the response of the Tuskegee authorities to this song.

CHAPTER 4

1. OHS, reel 3.

2. "Jethro's Garden," *The Era Magazine: An Illustrated Monthly*, July 1902, 77–80.

3. "The Promoter," *Collier's*, February 1902, 10–11.

4. It is not certain which poems Dunbar refers to here.

5. Dunbar's embarrassment may have been due to his many successes at the time and his annoyance at not being paid on time, as other successful authors were. In fact, Dunbar's work was so valued that Dodd, Mead kept him on retainer for first chance at publishing rights.

6. By this time, Dunbar's illness was becoming severe, and he was plagued with constant coughing and bleeding, which was popularly referred to as hemorrhaging.

7. Just the week before, Dunbar had attended the public presidential reception

at the White House, where he met Theodore Roosevelt. For details regarding this introduction, see Cunningham 229, and Brawley, *Paul Laurence Dunbar*, 90–91.

8. Even with all his financial success, Dunbar's medical bills were increasing.

9. OHS, reel 3.

10. See PLD to Paul R. Reynolds, December 30, 1900.

11. For a detailed history of the play and its evolution, see Leuchtenmüller, "Paul Laurence Dunbar's Overlooked Play."

12. This letter was reproduced in Newkirk, *Letters from Black America*, 272–73.

13. Dunbar's relationship with Booker T. was often strained, but their correspondence over the years reflects a high degree of respect between the two men.

14. In 1902, Booker T. Washington commissioned Dunbar to write the school song for the Tuskegee Institute. Dunbar wrote the lyrics to the tune of "Fair Harvard," but Washington was not pleased with the "Tuskegee Song." He objected to Dunbar's covert avoidance of "the industrial idea" and the exclusion of biblical references. In this letter to Washington, Dunbar defended his artistic sensibility. More to the point, in a letter to Emmett Jay Scott on August 23, 1898, Washington criticized an article Dunbar had published in the *Independent* about the downfalls of industrial education, pointedly arguing that "anyone who has visited the school at Tuskegee, Ala., and seen the efficiency of the work being done there, can have no further doubt of the ability and honesty of purpose of its founder and president. But I do fear that this earnest man is not doing either himself or his race full justice in his public utterances." See "Our New Madness," *Independent*, September 15, 1898, 469–71. Washington's response was sharp and biting: "I am very sorry that he has suffered himself to fly off in this way, not because it will do Tuskegee or the cause of industrial education any harm but I regret to see a man discuss something about which he knows nothing. In matters of poetry and fiction Dunbar is a master; in matters of industrial education and the development of the Negro race he is a novice" (Harlan, *Booker T. Washington Papers*, 456).

15. The final version of the song is as follows:

> Tuskegee, thou pride of the swift growing South
>   We pay thee our homage to-day;
> For the worth of thy teaching, the joy of thy care,
>   And the good we have known 'neath thy sway.
> Oh, long striving mother of diligent sons,
>   And of daughters, whose strength is their pride,
> We will love thee forever, and ever shall walk
>   Thro' the oncoming years at thy side.
>
> Thy hand we have held up the difficult steeps,
>   When painful and slow was the pace,
> And onward and upward, we've labored with thee
>   For the glory of God and our race.

The fields smile to greet us, the forests are glad,
   The ring of the anvil and hoe
Have a music as thrilling and sweet as a harp
   Which thou taught us to hear and to know.

Oh, Mother Tuskegee, thou shinest to-day
   As a gem in the fairest of lands;
Thou gavest the Heav'n-blessed power to see
   The worth of our minds and our hands.
We thank thee, we bless thee, we pray for thee years
   Imploring with grateful accord,
Full fruit for thy striving, time longer to strive,
   Sweet love and true labor's reward.

See the *Tuskegee Student*, February 15, 1902, 2.

16. Close friends of Washington often criticized the severity with which Dunbar attacked industrial education.

17. Clearly, Dunbar did not make the change.

18. A catalog of important items up for bid.

19. Reverend Edgar J. Penney was a faculty member at Tuskegee and dean of the Bible School. In 1907, a student accused him of sexual misconduct, and Penney resigned. He was an alumnus and trustee of Atlanta University.

20. "Fair Harvard" was composed by the Reverend Samuel Gilman (1791–1858) for the university's two hundredth anniversary. Tuskegee set its university anthem to the tune of "Fair Harvard"; Dunbar's 1906 contribution was lyrical only.

21. OHS, reel 3.

22. Reynolds, as Dunbar's literary agent, would market Dunbar's poems to various publishers and also seek payment for those published.

23. See PLD to Paul R. Reynolds, December 30, 1900.

24. See PLD to Paul R. Reynolds, May 16, 1901.

25. Elisabeth Marbury (1856–1933) began her career as a dramatic agent in connection with Mrs. Hodgson Burnett's play *Little Lord Fauntleroy*. As reported by *Theatre Magazine*, women were often the pioneers in play brokering, and Marbury "was practically the first to act as 'middleman' between author and manager," followed closely by Alice Kauser. Marbury ran the American Play Company, which was formed in 1914. See *Theater Magazine*, 1905, 163–64.

26. *The Sport of the Gods* (1902), often referred to as a protest novel, first appeared in *Lippincott's* in May 1901. Brawley points out that the novel offered itself up for debate as Dunbar's first real attempt to depict the harsh realities of the black experience, as seen through a family who moves from the South to Harlem (*Paul Laurence Dunbar*, 94–95). As biographers and scholars have pointed out over the years, many of Dunbar's previous works had centered around white families. This novel, indeed, was new territory for him. Addison Gayle Jr. mentions that this

novel was written during a time when Dunbar's illness was becoming debilitating, quoting a letter Dunbar wrote to a friend lamenting how his illness had stifled his ability to write: "When I first began my career, I wrote rapidly, accomplishing without difficulty five thousand words a day. Now I write slowly—oh! So slowly. I sometimes spend three weeks on a chapter and then am not satisfied with the result. . . . Last spring, when filling an order for a prose composition for *Lippincott's* magazine, I wrote fifty thousand words in thirty days, but I have never recovered from the strain of it" (Gayle, *Oak and Ivy*, 151). *The Sport of the Gods* was Dunbar's last published novel.

27. See PLD to Paul R. Reynolds, November 7, 1900.

28. OHS, reel 3. This letter was handwritten by Alice for Dunbar.

29. Dunbar is likely referring to an unpaid tab at Marshall's Hotel. James L. Marshall was the owner and proprietor of Marshall's Hotel, which not only provided accommodations but also featured jazz, music, and food and was located in the center of the Tenderloin district in New York. As James Weldon Johnson notes, Marshall's Hotel was one of "the centres of a fashionable sort of life that hitherto had not existed" (*Along This Way*, 209). Many well-known white and black celebrities visited the hotel, including "Rosamond Johnson, James Reese Europe, Paul Laurence Dunbar, Florenz Ziegfeld, and W. E. B. Du Bois." Being located in the Tenderloin district led to negative stereotypes, but Fronc shows "it was not a gin-soaked, rat-infested, honky tonk" but instead was "an important gathering place for New York's black cultural elite" See Fronc, *New York Undercover*, specifically chapter 4, "Race Mixing, Investigation, and the Enforcement of Jim Crow."

30. The American Security and Trust Company was a major Washington bank. It incorporated in 1889 as the city's second trust company. Dunbar held a line of credit there.

31. Henry Romeike (1855–1903) was the originator of a press-clipping service known as Romeike's. Dunbar used this service as his fame grew to track his publicity, which also allowed him to catch plagiarists and see what was being written about him. Cunningham briefly touches on this (201). For detailed information on Romeike and his business, see *The Trade-Mark Reporter*, vol. 7 (US Trademark Association, 1917). For the service's relationship to Dunbar, see "Jack Frost at Bedtime," unidentified newspaper clipping, Henry Romeike clipping service, New York City, 1884. Copy courtesy of Paul Laurence Dunbar Collection, MSS 659, series 1, box 1, OHS.

32. OHS, reel 3.

33. Dunbar at this time was still publishing prolifically and regularly received funds from Reynolds, having stayed on in New York after his separation from Alice. He was writing songs for several New York song publishers, most notably for the show *In Dahomey*, a musical comedy completely written and performed by African Americans; this play was extremely successful both in the States and in England, where it made theater history. It opened at the Globe Theatre in Boston on September 12, 1902. As Cunningham reports, it also enjoyed a command

performance at Buckingham Palace in England for the birthday of the Prince of Wales (Cunningham 232). Dunbar moved to Chicago after his work on *In Dahomey* was finished.

34. Dunbar was experiencing frequent bouts of tuberculosis at this time.

35. Very likely, Dunbar is referring to the investment properties he purchased in New Jersey prior to his move to Chicago in the spring. See PLD to W. E. B. Du Bois, May 28, 1903. Cunningham notes very briefly in her biography that Dunbar and Reynolds discussed going into business together, but they could not come to terms as to the nature of the business. Dunbar did, however, make a down payment in Whitesboro, New Jersey, on five lots (Cunningham 133).

36. OHS, reel 3.

37. Dunbar by this time was letting Reynolds handle most of his sales. This money is from either the songs he wrote or funds from his Dodd, Mead royalty check. Dunbar was most likely requesting funds for his real estate investment in New Jersey.

38. OHS, reel 3.

39. "The Trousers" was first published in the *St. Louis Mirror*, March 2, 1902. It was later collected in *In Old Plantation Days*.

40. Dunbar may be referring to William Marion Reedy (1862–1920), the African American editor of the *St. Louis Mirror* (1893–1920). The *St. Louis Mirror*, as it was originally named, was considered a scandal sheet when Reedy first assumed the position of editor. Shortly after, the paper went bankrupt, and the owner gave it to Reedy, who renamed it *The Mirror*. After another paper bankruptcy, and with help from a friend who gave the editorship back to Reedy, the newspaper returned to expose government corruption and introduce some of the most influential writers of the twentieth century. Reedy ran the paper until his death.

41. It is not clear what Dunbar is referring to here.

42. Harry Von Tilzer (born Harry Gumm, 1872–1946) came from a theatrical family (his brother Albert was the lyricist of "Take Me Out to the Ball Game") and was one of the best-known Tin Pan Alley songwriters at the turn of the twentieth century. Born in Detroit, Michigan, to Polish Jewish immigrants, Tilzer joined the Cole Brothers Circus at the age of fourteen, and shortly thereafter he was successfully playing the piano, acting, and composing in a repertory company. In 1892 he landed in New York and worked as a saloon pianist. His first published song was "My Old New Hampshire Home." In 1902, Von Tilzer's success led to the formation of the Harry Von Tilzer Music Company in New York.

43. After splitting with Alice, Dunbar stayed here.

44. OHS, reel 3.

45. Dunbar is referring either to his dialect pieces here or to a specific genre poem similar to "Darkie's Rainy Day" (also sometimes referred to as "Fishing"). See "Darkie's Rainy Day," *Current Literature*, January 1901, 673.

46. It is difficult to ascertain from this brief letter and the one before it which poem Dunbar is referring to. He had, however, been successful in placing "The

Poet" with *Cosmopolitan* just a month before; the only other poem of Dunbar's published by *Cosmopolitan* after this letter was "Joggin' Erlong." See "The Poet," *Cosmopolitan*, February 1902, 376; and "Joggin' Erlong," *Cosmopolitan*, June 1902, 227.

47. See PLD to Paul R. Reynolds, December 30, 1900.

48. From the Schomburg Collection Calendar of Manuscripts, specifically the Paul Laurence Dunbar Section, reel 3.

49. Dunbar is referring to his semipermanent move to Chicago.

50. The poem referenced here is very likely "Joggin' Erlong."

51. OHS, reel 1.

52. "Appropriations" here most likely refers to a medical initiative to create a sanatorium for sufferers of tuberculosis in Columbus, Ohio. Dr. Tobey served as one of the trustees for the State Tuberculosis Commission in Ohio, which was formed by a joint resolution prepared by the Legislative Committee of the Ohio Society. The commission's enactment was secured on April 23, 1902, and the group became known as the Ohio Society for the Prevention of Tuberculosis. Tobey and his group of doctors had published articles at this time seeking to secure a state sanatorium for the cure of consumption. In 1911, Ohio opened its first tuberculosis hospital.

53. Dunbar was ill after Alice left, a few weeks previously. In a personal letter to Booker T. Washington on February 1, 1902, T. Thomas Fortune wrote, "Saturday night [January 25] Dunbar went home and tried to kill his wife. He left Washington on the 12 o'clock train, and had not been heard from when I left Washington Thursday morning. He is a high class brute, and I will tell you what led up to it when we meet. His family has left his home, on the advice of friends, but I do not know their address. I am sorry, for them, as they are helpless" (see Harlan et al., *Booker T. Washington Papers*).

54. Herne said this in an undated letter to Dunbar before Dunbar's rise to fame. See chapter 2, letter 56: Undated, James A. Herne to PLD.

55. Very likely, Tobey is referring to a remark Dunbar made about himself in January 1897 after preparing to travel to England with Major Pond's daughter. Dunbar, understandably upset regarding the meager terms of his sojourn, pointed out that "they are going to make it hard for me, but I need the training, and I shall try to keep my upper lip well starched" (Wiggins 62). In another letter, dated July 27, 1902, Dunbar wrote to a friend after the breakup of his marriage to Alice that "you will be seriously shocked to hear that Mrs. Dunbar and I are now living apart, and the beautiful home I had at Washington is a thing of the past. . . . I am greatly discouraged and if I could do anything else, I should give up writing. Something within me seems to be dead. There is no spirit or energy left in me. My upper lip has taken on a droop." Dunbar wrote this letter from Chicago, where he traveled, accompanied by his mother, after his divorce from Alice (96).

56. Dunbar checked himself into a sanatorium in March. Cunningham surmises the reasons for this, but it was likely the culmination of his separation from Alice, tuberculosis, alcoholism, and exhaustion that forced him to seek help.

Dunbar likely sought help for his alcoholism, which he had been battling for years. Sanatoriums for alcoholism had become popular in the 1890s as a valid method of treatment, though physicians continued to debate approaches to treatment.

57. Tobey's daughter.

58. OHS, reel 1.

59. Clearly this is a falsehood, though it is not clear why he wrote it; as noted in the previous letter, Tobey was unable to respond to Dunbar's letter until April 30. This note suggests that Dunbar may not have received the letter from Tobey.

60. Tobey's daughter.

61. Wells College, founded by Wells Fargo pioneer Henry Wells in 1869, was a small liberal arts college for women located in Aurora, New York.

62. The Association of Medical Superintendents of American Institutions for the Insane, also referred to as the Superintendents' Association, was the first professional medical specialty organization in the United States. It held its first meeting in Philadelphia in October 1844, with thirteen superintendents present. The medical group was formed to share experiences and trade data in working with the insane, while also collaborating on better treatments for patients. The association's name was changed to the American Medico-Psychological Association in 1892, and it eventually became the American Psychiatric Association in 1921.

63. OHS, reel 1.

64. This refers to Dunbar's belongings after his separation from Alice. Dunbar did not really need many of his furnishings, as he made no major permanent living arrangements, taking only a furnished flat in Chicago with his mother.

65. OHS, reel 1.

66. *Candle-Lightin' Time*, illustrated with photographs by the Hampton Institute Camera Club and decorated by Margaret Armstrong. Poems included in this volume are "Dinah Kneading Dough," "Dat Ol' Mare o' Mine," "A Spring Wooing," "The Old Front Gate," "Fishin'," "When Dey Listed Colored Soldiers," "Lullaby," "Song of Summer," and "At Candle-Lightin' Time." Dunbar dedicated this collection to fellow Ohioan and benefactor Mrs. Fitzgerald.

67. *Lyrics of Love and Laughter* (1903). The book was dedicated to Miss Catherine Impey, an Englishwoman the poet had befriended while abroad.

68. The book was not published until March.

69. *When Malindy Sings*, illustrated with photographs by the Hampton Institute Camera Club and decorated by Margaret Armstrong.

70. Dodd is referring to "Lullaby" in *Candle-Lightin' Time* (1901). Reprinted in *Chris'mus Is A-Comin' and Other Poems* (1905). The poem first appeared in the *Bookman*, October 1896, 121. There are no "Lullaby" poems indexed in the other book to which Dodd refers here, *Lyrics of Love and Laughter*.

71. Dunbar never published a book of lullaby poems, although he did publish "The Plantation Child's Lullaby" in *Li'l' Gal*.

72. OHS, reel 1.

73. It is unclear why Skinner would refer to the play as seventeenth century in

nature, as Dunbar wrote *Herrick* in the tradition of an eighteenth-century English comedy of manners.

74. Otis Skinner (1858–1942) was an American stage actor from Massachusetts who had a successful thirty-year career in the theater.

75. William Edward Burghardt Du Bois (1868–1963) was an African American civil rights activist, Pan-Africanist, sociologist, author, historian, and editor who was most known for his metaphor of the "veil" and the appropriation of the psychological term "double consciousness" to understand the plight of the black individual in America. Du Bois is also well known as the founder and editor of the Crisis in 1910 (the home journal of the NAACP), as well as the cofounder of the Niagara Movement, the NAACP, and the Pan-African Congress. Many of his ideas that still resonate today first appeared in the first chapter, "Of Our Spiritual Strivings," in *The Souls of Black Folk* (1903). As shown in these letters, the relationship between Dunbar and Du Bois was complicated. Like Du Bois, however, Dunbar favored a philosophy counter to industrial education, and their correspondence reveals a bond in their shared hope for quicker advancement for people of color.

76. From the W. E. B. Du Bois Papers (MS 312), Special Collections and University Archives, University of Massachusetts Amherst Libraries.

77. James Pott & Co. of New York was known for its religious publications.

78. The race book refers to *The Negro Problem: A Series of Articles by Representative American Negroes of To-day* (1903), a collection of essays written by leading African Americans, edited by Booker T. Washington, and published by Pott & Co. Its contents include Booker T. Washington's "Industrial Education for the Negro," W. E. B. Du Bois's "The Talented Tenth," Charles W. Chesnutt's "The Disfranchisement of the Negro," Wilford H. Smith's "The Negro and the Law," H. T. Kealing's "The Characteristics of the Negro People," Dunbar's "Representative American Negroes," and T. Thomas Fortune's "The Negro's Place in American Life at the Present Day."

79. From the W. E. B. Du Bois Papers (MS 312), Special Collections and University Archives, University of Massachusetts Amherst Libraries.

80. Du Bois's response was fairly immediate to the previous letter (PLD to W. E. B. Du Bois, January 15, 1903) and handwritten on the typed correspondence from Dunbar.

81. Du Bois is referring to "Strivings of the Negro People," which appeared in the August 1897 *Atlantic* (194–98). This piece extended Du Bois's influence to an international audience and served as the opening chapter of his most well-known work, *The Souls of Black Folk* (1903). In this collection of essays, Du Bois argues that, given the opportunity to cultivate and educate themselves, African Americans would demonstrate that they have their own distinctive and worthy contributions to make to American life and culture. Du Bois predicted that "two world races may give each to each those characteristics which both so sadly lack." *The Souls of Black Folk* at this time was under contract with A. C. McClure and Co. This collection remains a seminal work in the history of sociology, and it is a cornerstone

of African American literary history in its breakthrough discussions of race in the United States. Some of the essays in the book had previously been published in the *Atlantic*; these are the essays Du Bois refers to here.

82. At this time, correspondence was circulating regarding the need to start a national African American magazine that would address race issues directly to a white audience. See, for example, the letters between Du Bois and Charles W. Chesnutt in Aptheker, *Correspondence of W. E. B. Du Bois*, 55–58. In 1906, Du Bois started a weekly publication called the *Moon*, which lasted until 1907, when he launched the *Horizon*; this gave way to the *Crisis* in 1910.

83. OHS, reel 1.

84. "The Plantation Child's Lullaby" was never published by the *Saturday Evening Post* or independently with any other journal, paper, or magazine. The poem did appear, however, in the collections *Li'l' Gal* and *Lyrics of Sunshine and Shadow*. Another poem by Dunbar, "Two Little Boots," appeared in the *Saturday Evening Post*, April 1902, 3.

85. W. E. B. Du Bois Papers (MS 312), Special Collections and University Archives, University of Massachusetts Amherst Libraries.

86. Du Bois contributed "The Talented Tenth" to Washington's *The Negro Problem*, 31–75.

87. W. E. B. Du Bois Papers (MS 312), Special Collections and University Archives, University of Massachusetts Amherst Libraries.

88. "Representative American Negroes" would be one of several articles published in *The Negro Problem*, 187–210.

89. Du Bois responded by noting, "There isn't much to be read. My biography can be found in 'Who's Who' and I sent a list of my writing—those starred are books." Du Bois typically responded to Dunbar by typing on the letters Dunbar sent him.

90. OHS, reel 1.

91. "When Malindy Sings," a recollection of Dunbar's mother's frequent singing of hymns and spirituals, first appeared in *Majors and Minors*. The letter here, however, refers to Dunbar's collection *When Malindy Sings*, which introduces several new poems as well as older ones, including "When Malindy Sings," which opens the collection. *When Malindy Sings* was illustrated with photographs by the Hampton Institute Camera Club and decorated by Margaret Armstrong.

92. From the W. E. B. Du Bois Papers (MS 312), Special Collections and University Archives, University of Massachusetts Amherst Libraries. This letter is written on Toledo State Hospital stationery. Here, Dunbar included a biographical sketch, which he also sent to Pott & Co.

93. Dunbar's biographical sketch for Du Bois's "Possibilities of the Negro: The Advance Guard of the Race," *Booklover's Magazine*, July 1903, 2–15.

94. Dunbar is referring to the *Booklover's Magazine*.

95. Dunbar may be referring to a biography Du Bois was considering publishing on Douglass before Washington was contracted to do so.

96. W. E. B. Du Bois Papers (MS 312), Special Collections and University Archives, University of Massachusetts Amherst Libraries.

97. Mentioned in Du Bois's discussion were Washington, Granville T. Woods, Edward H. Morris, Henry O. Tanner, Daniel H. Williams, Kelly Miller, and Chesnutt. The article also included photographs of these writers and leaders.

98. Du Bois's "The Talented Tenth" and Dunbar's "Representative American Negroes."

99. *The Souls of Black Folk* remains an extreme success; it was initially reprinted as many as twenty-four times from the first set of plates, and between its first publication in 1903 and 1940 it sold more than twenty thousand copies.

100. OHS, reel 1.

101. The headline ran, "Poet Dunbar Is Ill Again. Negro Author Seriously Affected with a Recurrence of Pulmonary Trouble." The article appeared in the *Chicago Tribune* on July 30, 1903.

102. The last paragraph of the short piece reads: "During the evening one of the colored poet's friends, a member of the Eighth regiment passed the house, whistling a bugle call. Dunbar sent back the call as clearly as his condition would permit, but the effort brought on another spell of coughing."

103. Likely the *New York Tribune*. Dunbar wrote a scathing letter to the *New York Times* (which was reprinted in several newspapers) on July 10, responding to the increase in lynchings and the disenfranchisement that bred destruction: "With citizenship discredited and scorned, with violated homes and long unheeded prayers, with bleeding hands uplifted, still sore and smarting from long beating at the door of opportunity, we raise our voices and sing, 'My Country, 'Tis of Thee.'" See "The Fourth of July and Race Outrages: Paul Laurence Dunbar's Bitter Satire on Independence Day," *New York Times*, July 10, 1903, 5.

104. Professor William James of Harvard (1842–1910), often referred to as the founder of modern psychology, was the brother of American novelist Henry James. Here, Whitlock is referring to a "commencement dinner address" on "the need of spiritual education to supplement book learning." William James argued that Harvard, as an institution, could fill that void. The transcript of this speech was recorded in the *Boston Evening Transcript* on June 27, 1903, 18. William James's focuses included pragmatism and phenomenology; his seminal text is *The Principles of Psychology* (1890). It may be, however, that the illegible name refers instead to William Stanley Beaumont Braithwaite (1878–1962), a self-taught African American author, editor, publisher, and literary critic who regularly contributed to the *Boston Evening Transcript* and eventually became its literary editor from 1906 to 1931. However, Braithwaite was not a professor. See the William Stanley Braithwaite Papers at the New York Public Library Archives and Manuscripts for additional biographical information.

105. Whitlock wrote several novels during his lifetime, but he may be referring here to his unpublished manuscript "The Buckeyes," a historical novel about antebellum Ohio, based on his grandfather Brand and the governor of Ohio.

106. Whitlock's reference here is to Walt Whitman's *Leaves of Grass* #33: "To Him That Was Crucified." It is an allusion from line 1, which reads "My spirit to yours, dear Brother."

107. Schomburg Collection, reel 1.

108. Dayton, Ohio, is not far from Dunbar's boyhood home. Dunbar and his mother moved from Chicago to Dayton in the fall of 1903. While looking for a new home, Dunbar rented a house at 118 Sycamore Street, two doors away from one of his childhood homes. Ezra Kuhns helped Dunbar find a house, and he purchased lots 12448 and 12449 at 219 North Summit Street on June 3, 1904, for $4,100. Buying the house for his mother, Dunbar put the deed in her name. See Deed Records, book 263, p. 157, Montgomery County Records Commission; Paul Laurence Dunbar House, HABS No. OH-218, Historic American Buildings Survey Collection, Prints and Photographs Division, LC; and *Williams' Dayton City Directory* for 1904–1905, 423.

109. This letter first appeared in the *Crisis*, 1920, 74.

110. Published in Corrothers and Baker, *In Spite of the Handicap*, 146–47.

111. James David Corrothers (1869–1917) was an African American journalist, poet, and minister from South Haven, Michigan. He attended Northwestern University but eventually left to become a newspaper reporter for several of the Chicago daily papers, most notably the *Daily Record* and the *Daily News*. Corrothers worked with Frederick Douglass and was revered by many. He first met Dunbar while at the 1893 World's Columbian Exposition, and they continued their friendship. In 1912, he published the tribute "Paul Laurence Dunbar" in *Century* magazine. In his autobiography, *In Spite of the Handicap*, Corrothers avers he attempted to bring Dunbar to Howells's attention. He recalls how he wrote about Dunbar a year before Howells reviewed *Majors and Minors*: "once in the '*Chicago Journal*' and another in the '*Record-Herald*.'" Moreover, Dunbar allegedly "acknowledged the appearance of the articles with a grateful note" (*In Spite of the Handicap*, 144).

112. In his autobiography, Corrothers reports that "a little prior to the Fair I had become acquainted with Paul Laurence Dunbar, the poet, who acted as Douglass's secretary during the Fair" (*In Spite of the Handicap*, 126). Corrothers had originally been sent to the Fair to interview Douglass.

113. Corrothers reports that prior to receiving this letter from Dunbar, he had written the author, who he learned was ill, to come stay with him in Michigan so he could help Dunbar recover. Corrothers never saw Dunbar again. In his reminisces, Corrothers playfully acknowledges that Dunbar at times referred to him as his "friend, the poet," and "rival."

114. This could refer to rumors that Dunbar was nearing death due to tuberculosis, or to Dunbar's public drunken behavior, or to his attack on Alice.

115. This letter comes from the *Crisis*, 1920, 74–76.

116. Despite their best efforts, doctors could not prevent tuberculosis from worsening, though they did recommend traveling west. Jeanne Abrams explains Dunbar's exact frustration and complaint: "No single accepted standard for

tuberculosis treatment prevailed in American medicine in the early years. Various experimental medications, surgical procedures, and folk remedies competed with the 'open air' method of therapy" ("On the Road Again," 272). Additionally, Abrams notes that "tuberculosis became a regional pre-occupation in the American West, as well as the source of a robust economy, perhaps nowhere more visibly than in Colorado, New Mexico, and California," and that "despite multiple approaches among physicians to treat consumptives, by the 1850s medical opinion began to emphasize a 'healthful' climate as a central ingredient, and many American physicians sent their patients west to take advantage of 'nature's remedy.' Thus, in the absence of a 'magic pill' to cure the disease, traveling often became an essential part of the search for a cure, although the undertaking produced mixed results" (272). Dunbar discussed this at length. See PLD to Edward Hackley, November 23, 1904.

117. OHS, reel 1.

118. Roosevelt was in the midst of his second campaign for president. The poem, which was never published, is included here in its entirety:

> Here's a mighty sound a comin,'
> From the East and there's a hummin'
>   And a bumtnin' from the bosom of the West,
> While the North has given tongue,
> And the South will be among
>   Those who holler that our Roosevelt is best.
>
> We have heard of him in battle
> And amid the roar and rattle
>   When the foemen fled like cattle to their stalls:
> We have seen him staunch and grim
> When the only, battle hymn
>   Was the shrieking of the Spanish Mauser balls.
>
> Product of a worthy sireing,
> Fearless, honest, brave, untiring—
>   In the forefront of the firing, there he stands:
> And we're not afraid to show
> That we all revere him so,
>   To dissentients of our own and other lands.
>
> Now, the fight is on in earnest,
> And we care not if the sternest
>   Of encounters try our valor or the quality of him,
> For they're few who stoop to fear
> As the glorious day draws near,
>   For you'll find him hell to handle when he gets in fightin' trim.

This poem can be found in full in Cunningham 250 and Wiggins 112–13.

119. Wiggins reports that the two volumes were inscribed "To Paul Laurence Dunbar from Theodore Roosevelt, Christmas, 1903" (112). Cunningham (250) records the following inscribed on the flyleaf:

> To Paul Laurence Dunbar, Esquire
> With the regards of
> Theodore Roosevelt
> Nov. 2d, 1904

120. Roosevelt later wrote about meeting Dunbar. See his August 2, 1906, letter to Wiggins, who records Roosevelt as writing, "I only had the pleasure of meeting Mr. Dunbar once or twice, [but] I was a great admirer of his poetry and prose" (20).

121. From Eberly Family Special Collections Library, Penn State University Libraries.

122. Edwin H. Hackley (1859–1940), onetime editor of the *Denver Statesman*, was an attorney, playwright, and songwriter and was considered one of Denver's black elite. Hackley attended the University of Michigan and was a county clerk in the recorder's court in Detroit. For detailed information about his life, see Brevard, *Biography of Edwin Henry Hackley*.

123. Cunningham reports that although the doctors urged Dunbar to go to California for his health, he could not afford to make the trip and continue with payments on his Dayton house. A friend of Dunbar's could get only one railroad pass, and Dunbar did not want to travel alone (247).

124. Azalia Hackley was the first African American to graduate from the University of Denver School of Music. She later taught in the school's extension program and toured with the Denver Choral Society. Eventually settling in Philadelphia, she founded the one-hundred-voice People's Chorus, which was later renamed the Hackley Choral Society. She also held a class in oratorio at the Hampton Institute summer school, which also served as the location for the illustrations that accompanied Dunbar's collections. She and Edwin separated in 1909.

125. This letter has been republished in Brevard, *Biography of Edwin Henry Hackley*, 16. As Brevard reports, Hackley, like Dunbar, suffered lung ailments from an early age and could speak to the health benefits of the western winter air. Hackley moved to Denver in May 1885 after accepting the position of county clerk, and he remained in the city until 1900 when he and his wife, Azalia, relocated east to Philadelphia. Hackley met Dunbar in Denver in 1899 when Dunbar moved there for his health, and they continued a correspondence and friendship.

126. Dunbar could be alluding to his poem "Fishing," which reveals his appreciation of the sport: "Jes' a slew o' new-ketched catfish sizzlin' / daih fu huh an' me. / . . . Needn't wriggle, Mistah Catfish, case I / got you jes' de same." See Wiggins 259 and Brawley, *Paul Laurence Dunbar*, 16–17. Also, photographs in the Wright State University Special Collections gallery show Dunbar fishing with several friends.

127. OHS, reel 3.

128. *The Tuskegee Student: Devoted to the Interests of Students and Graduates of the Tuskegee Normal and Industrial Institute* was the bimonthly school newspaper of the Tuskegee Institute that ran from 1884 to 1924.

129. Scott followed Washington's ideology, which advocated for constructive accommodation over immediate social integration.

130. OHS, reel 3.

131. All of the poems in *Li'l' Gal* had appeared in previous collections except "Charity," which would be omitted from the final collection. Dunbar inscribed a copy of the book he sent to Tobey: "This is my seventeenth book; that's what you get for encouraging youthful ambition—and you did, you can't deny it. Gratefully yours, Paul" (Cunningham 249).

132. The last few collections that Dunbar published were decorated by Margaret Armstrong and included illustrations and photographs by the Hampton Institute Camera Club. According to Ray Sapirstein, it is uncertain who selected the poems to be illustrated. The meeting minutes from the club note that "a three-member editorial committee drew up a schematic plan" to create "images that would correspond to outstanding imagery in Dunbar's poem. After a suitable interval, allowing for the images to be staged, photographed, and developed, the group selected illustrations for poems from members' submissions to a weekly critique" (Sapirstein, "Picturing Dunbar's Lyrics," 330).

133. Only one other collection of poetry following *Howdy, Honey, Howdy* would be illustrated and include photos from the Hampton Institute Camera Club: *Joggin' Erlong*.

134. *Howdy, Honey, Howdy*.

135. The collection was illustrated with photographs by Leigh Richmond Miner (of the Hampton Institute Camera Club) and decorated by Will Jenkins. According to Emily Oswald, "The Camera Club, at least in its work prior to Leigh Richmond Miner's influence, was primarily concerned with producing images of blacks that would strike a nostalgic chord with its audience because of the easy popularity of these images already established through plantation fiction" ("Imagining Race," 222). Oswald focuses specifically on the relationship between Dodd, Mead and the Camera Club and the racist undercurrents in the illustrations.

136. *Poems of Cabin and Field* (1899), *Candle-Lightin' Time* (1901), *When Malindy Sings* (1903), and *Li'l' Gal* (1904).

137. MSS 099, F948, Paul Laurence Dunbar letters to Reginald Wright Kauffman, Special Collections, University of Delaware Library, Newark.

138. Reginald Wright Kauffman (1877–1959) was an American writer and editor who served as associate editor of the *Saturday Evening Post* during his correspondence with Dunbar. Kauffman wrote several works of fiction as well as screenplays, including several produced by Hollywood, such as *The House of Bondage* (1914) and *School for Girls* (1934), both of which are based on his fiction.

139. Dunbar was responding to Kauffman's solicitation of his poems for a future publication.

140. During the winter, Dunbar's literary output was considerably low, and there was no book published as in previous years. As indexed by Metcalf, Dunbar did, however, publish the following poems between the writing of this letter and February 1906: "Day," *Lippincott's*, November 1905, 639; "The Photograph" and "Po' Little Lamb" in *Werner's Readings and Recitations*, ed. Pauline Phelps and Marion Short (New York: Edgar S. Werner, 1906), 123, 156; "Alexander Crummel[i]—Dead," "Conscience and Remorse," "Life," "Mortality," "The Path," and "The Warrior's Prayer," *Alexander's*, February 1, 1906, 14–18; "Howdy, Honey, Howdy!," and "For Theodore Roosevelt," *Dayton News*, February 10, 1906. The short story "The Way of Love" was published in *Lippincott's*, January 1905, 68–73. Cunningham alleges that a poem to Bud (in memoriam) and another called "Denied" were found in Dunbar's desk following his death, though these texts have yet to be recovered (259).

141. Dunbar never left Ohio after this letter.

142. Dunbar is very likely referring to the political implications of his dialect verse, which often pigeonholed him at the expense of his personally preferred Standard English poetry. This issue had plagued him for years: in 1899, he expressed his hesitancy to write for the *Century*, one of his most desired publications, arguing that "they hold me down too much to one style" in an interview with *Literary Life*, October 16, 1899.

143. Interestingly, five months after this letter was written, Dunbar published an article on this very subject. See "Is There a Slump in Poetry?," *Literary Digest*, March 18, 1905, 391.

144. This anecdote, as taken from this letter, was published in *Our Day*, December 24, 1905, 20; it appeared under "Disappointed in Him" in "Snapshots at Notables," a section within *Our Day* that focused on witticisms.

145. Reproduction in Special Collections, University of Delaware, MS 99, box 66, folder 948.

146. "Sling Along" was the last known poem Dunbar composed aloud. According to Wiggins, Dunbar's stenographer Miss Mundhenk recorded the poem as Dunbar rehearsed it. The full poem can be found in Wiggins (118). Cunningham reports that at this point in Dunbar's life, most of his work was dictated (253).

147. "Sling Along" appears as the second poem in the collection *Joggin' Erlong*, which was dedicated to William Blocher from the United Brethren Publishing House, who helped Dunbar initially publish. Dunbar's inscription reads: "To William Blocher, Who Aided Me Financially In The Publication Of My First Book."

148. This letter first appeared in the *Crisis*, 1920, 74.

149. Dunbar's biographers note that throughout the final months of his life, he was visited by several family members and friends.

150. Julia Sutherland Comstock Field (1856–1936); Dunbar had written to her at the time of her husband's death. Aware of Dunbar's sickness, she came to pay her respects.

151. Eugene Field Sr. (1850–1895) was a poet, journalist, and humorist most known for his poems for and about children. He began his professional writing career as a journalist for the *St. Louis Evening Journal*, serving as its editor after only six months. He became city editor of the *Gazette* and earned his living writing gossip and humorous-style articles in such newspapers as the *Morning Journal* and *Times-Journal*, eventually serving as managing editor of the *Kansas City Times* and editor of the *Denver Tribune*. Eventually, he was given a regular column, "Sharps and Flats," to which he contributed for the *Chicago Daily News*.

152. John Cecil Clay (1875–1930) was an American illustrator who worked for well-known magazines such as *Life*, *Frank Leslie's Popular Monthly*, *Century*, *Saturday Evening Post*, and *Good Housekeeping*; he is best known for his caricature painting.

153. Clay's version adapts Mother Goose rhymes for adults. According to Cunningham, Clay also included a line from one of Dunbar's poems that read: "And hand in hand we shall walk up the hill." Enclosed with these lines was a short note from Clay that read: "You have committed yourself by saying you have enjoyed my drawings. I want to try the full bottle on you—not in the hope that it will kill or cure, but intensify the trouble. I thank you very much for permission to use the verse." See Cunningham 259.

154. This letter first appeared in the *Crisis*, 1920, 74.

155. *Howdy, Honey, Howdy*, a book of poems, was published in 1905 by Dodd, Mead and was illustrated with photographs by Leigh Richmond Miner. Decorations were by Will Jenkins. The collection was reprinted the same year by the Musson Book Company in Toronto.

156. The ever-unattainable but desired literary place of pastoral utopian life where humans live in full harmony with nature.

157. This could be a reference to the well-known Scottish writer Samuel Cowan, whose reviewed work sometimes appeared next to Dunbar's. See, for example, *Publisher's Weekly*, September 24, 1904, 558.

158. OHS, reel 1.

159. Senator Lamb was the Independent member from Toledo and was often at odds with the Democrats who stood in the way of his temperance measures. See, for example, "Shown Up by Lamb," *Mansfield (OH) News-Journal*, March 20, 1906, 6.

160. This was not Tobey's first scandal. On May 14, 1891, the *Democratic Northwest*, an Ohio paper, ran an article pointing to an incident so great that Tobey was replaced. The accusations included misappropriation of funds and other dishonest financial dealings. However, Tobey was reinstated in this position in 1892. Unfortunately, at some point, Tobey began to have an alcohol problem that led to a second scandal and then culminated in his forced resignation in July 1907; the local papers at the time were not gentle in their descriptions of Tobey's alcoholism. The *Cincinnati Enquirer* (July 4, 1907) shows that Tobey was admitted to a hospital for an alcohol problem in 1907. For a historical overview of Tobey and the

Toledo State Hospital (now the Northwest Ohio Psychiatric Hospital), as well as an in-depth overview of Tobey's involvement there, see Emily Ruckwell, "A Room for History: Professionalizing the Archives Room at Northwest Ohio Psychiatric Hospital to Create the Toledo State Hospital Museum" (master's thesis, University of Toledo, 2014).

161. Brand Whitlock served as Tobey's lawyer. In a July 5, 1899, letter to Octavia Roberts, Whitlock looked back on the time he spent with Dunbar as "delightful" and described Dunbar as one whose poems had a "pathetic note in them. The boy has suffered much because of the accident of his birth. He is a rare and delicate soul." See Nevins, *Letters and Journal of Brand Whitlock*, 24–25.

162. Tobey is likely referring to "The Warrior's Prayer."

163. Tobey also suffered from tuberculosis.

164. It is clear Tobey did not realize the severity of Dunbar's condition; Dunbar had been bedridden several times before.

165. Tobey is referencing the villain Iago's words from act 3, scene 3 of *Othello*.

166. Alice Tobey was the daughter of Tobey and Minnie Conklin of Sidney, New York, who married in 1881 and had three children: Helen, Alice, and Louise.

167. Dunbar set his poetry to music on several occasions, most notably in collaboration with Will Marion Cook.

168. This letter appears in both Wiggins 133–35 and Nevins 49–52.

169. Dr. Tobey read this letter out loud at Dunbar's funeral because Whitlock, then mayor of Toledo, was tending to his critically ailing mother.

170. Robert Burns (1759–1796) is not only Scotland's national poet but also perhaps the most famous poet in Scotland's history; even today, people know *Auld Lang Syne*, even if they do not know Burns's name. A Romantic poet, Burns wrote poetry in Scottish dialect as well as British English. Percy Bysshe Shelley (1792–1822) was one of the major second-generation English Romantic poets of the nineteenth century. John Keats (1795–1821) was also a second-generation English Romanticist, as was George Gordon Byron (1788–1824). Alexander Sergeyevich Pushkin (1799–1837) was a major Russian novelist, poet, and dramatist of the Romantic period.

171. Shelley was twenty-nine when he died; Keats was twenty-five; Byron was twenty-six; and Pushkin was thirty-seven. Dunbar was thirty-three upon his death.

172. Whitlock shows here that all these authors were considered revolutionary in their vision, which transcended traditional boundaries, but they also suffered the consequences of it.

173. Walt Whitman (1819–1892) was an American poet and essayist, most known as a key figure among the second-generation American Romantics.

174. Whitlock is referring to Whitman's "Song of Myself," with fifty-two sections that catalog disparate subjects and perspectives in an attempt to create a "democratic poem."

175. Robert Browning (1812–1889) was an English poet famous for his dramatic monologues.

176. These lines come from Browning's poem "The Lost Leader," published in 1845. This poem appeared in *Dramatic Romances and Lyrics* and heavily criticizes William Wordsworth for deserting his ideal hopes and liberal cause.

177. "The Warrior's Prayer," after appearing in individual papers, was collected in *Lyrics of the Hearthside* (1899).

178. "Ships That Pass in the Night" appeared in *Lyrics of Lowly Life* (1896). All the poems Whitlock mentions explicitly acknowledge the racism experienced by African Americans. Dunbar wrote none of them in dialect.

179. Theocritus (ca. 300 BCE–ca. 260 BCE) is usually attributed as the creator of pastoral poems known as *eidyllia*, or "little poems." Dunbar did not write many pastoral pieces, but "Cahoots," "The Wisdom of Silence," and "The Lynching of Jube Benson," all of which appear in *The Heart of Happy Hollow*, generally adhere to the genre. In true Dunbar fashion, he also wrote stories that encapsulate the antithesis of the pastoral, including "The Stanton Coachman" and "Who Stand for the Gods," which appeared in *In Old Plantation Days*; "The Intervention of Peter," which appeared in *Folks from Dixie*; and "The Last Fiddling of Mordaunt's Jim," which was originally published in the *Saturday Evening Post*, August 30, 1902, but was later was re-collected in *In Old Plantation Days*.

180. From Eberly Family Special Collections Library, Penn State University Libraries.

181. Wiggins would publish Dunbar's first biography in 1907 with Nichols and Company.

182. See Wiggins 20.

183. See Theodore Roosevelt to PLD, November 2, 1904.

184. Wiggins refers to the accusation that Roosevelt had spoken ill of Dunbar (19). However, in the October 1, 1901, letter, Theodore Roosevelt wrote E. A. Hitchcock, then secretary of the interior: "My dear Mr. Secretary: Referring to the enclosed papers in the case of Dr. A. N. Curtis, of Freedmen's Hospital. Paul Laurence Dunbar is a man for whom I have a high regard on account of his literary ability. Would you look into this case, and report to me!" See the Letters from President Theodore Roosevelt to Secretary of the Interior Ethan Allen Hitchcock (1900–1906); Series: Communications with the Executive Department, 1900–1907; Collection: Papers of Ethan Allen Hitchcock, 1835–1909; National Archives.

BIBLIOGRAPHY

Abrams, Jeanne. "On the Road Again: Consumptives Traveling for Health in the American West, 1840–1925." *Great Plains Quarterly* 30, no. 4 (Fall 2010): 271–85.

Aldrich, Abigail J. "The Hamilton Family and the Trials of Job: The Clash of Faith and Fate in Paul Laurence Dunbar's *The Sport of the Gods.*" *CLA Journal* 50, no. 2 (2006): 219–37.

Alexander, Eleanor. *Lyrics of Sunshine and Shadow: The Tragic Courtship and Marriage of Paul Laurence Dunbar and Alice Ruth Moore.* New York: New York University Press, 2002.

Allen, Caffilene. "The Caged Bird Sings: The Ellison-Dunbar Connection." *CLA Journal* 40, no. 2 (1996): 178–90.

Ampadu, Lena. "The Poetry of Paul Laurence Dunbar and the Influence of African Aesthetics: Dunbar's Poems and the Tradition of Masking." In Harrell, *We Wear the Mask*, 3–16.

Aptheker, Herbert, ed. *The Correspondence of W. E. B. Du Bois.* Amherst: University of Massachusetts Press, 1997.

Armstrong, Samuel Chapman, "Exchanges and Literary Notes." *Southern Workman* 31 (1892): 125.

Arnold, Edward F. "Some Personal Reminiscences of Paul Laurence Dunbar." *Journal of Negro History* 17 (October 1932): 400–408.

Axelrod, David. "Colonel Shaw in American Poetry: 'For the Union Dead' and Its Precursors," *American Quarterly* 24, no. 4 (October 1972): 523–37.

Baker, Houston A., Jr. *Blues, Ideology, and American Literature: A Vernacular Theory.* Chicago: University of Chicago Press, 1984.

———. "The 'Limitless' Freedom of Myth: Paul Lawrence Dunbar's *The Sport of the Gods* and the Criticism of Afro-American Literature." In *The American Self: Myth, Ideology, and Popular Culture,* edited by Sam B. Girgus, 124–43. Albuquerque: University of New Mexico Press, 1981.

———. "Paul Laurence Dunbar: An Evaluation." *Black World* 21, no. 1 (1971): 30–37.

———. "Report on a Celebration: Dunbar's One-Hundredth Year." *Black World* 22, no. 4 (1973): 81–85.

———. *Singers of Daybreak: Studies in Black American Literature.* Washington, DC: Howard University Press, 1974.

Balestrini, Nassim W. "National Memory and the Arts in Paul Laurence Dunbar's War Poetry." In Harrell, *We Wear the Mask*, 17–31.

Barbour, James. "Nineteenth Century Black Novelists: A Checklist." *Minority Voices: An Interdisciplinary Journal of Literature and the Arts* 3, no. 2 (1980): 27–43.

Bausch, Susan. "Inevitable or Remediable? The Historical Connection between Slavery, Racism, and Urban Degradation in Paul Laurence Dunbar's *The Sport of the Gods*." *CLA Journal* 45, no. 4 (June 2002): 497–522.

Bearss, Linda. "Dunbar's Fiction: Transgressing the Limits of Realism to Breach the Horizon of Modernism." *Midwestern Miscellany* 34 (2006): 69–77.

Bell, Albert. "When Zeal Becomes Trouble," *Ohio Lawyer* 5 (1991): 23.

Bell, William A., ed. "Dr. J. P. D. John." *Indiana School Journal* 40, no. 1 (1895): 439.

Bender, Bert. "The Lyrical Short Fiction of Dunbar and Chesnutt." In Martin, *A Singer in the Dawn*, 208–22.

Bennett, Paula Bernat. "Rewriting Dunbar: Realism, Black Women Poets, and the Genteel." In *Post-Bellum, Pre-Harlem: African American Literature and Culture*, edited by Barbara McCaskill and Caroline Gebhard, 146–61. New York: New York University Press, 2006.

Best, Felton O. *Crossing the Color Line: A Biography of Paul Laurence Dunbar*. Dubuque, IA: Kendall Hunt, 1996.

———. "Paul Laurence Dunbar's Protest Literature: The Final Years." *Western Journal of Black Studies* 17, no. 1 (1993): 54–63.

Black, Daniel P. "Literary Subterfuge: Early African American Writing and the Trope of the Mask." *CLA Journal* 48, no. 4 (2005): 387–403.

Blount, Marcellus. "Caged Birds: Race and Gender in the Sonnet." In *Engendering Men: The Question of Male Feminist Criticism*, edited by Joseph A. Boone and Michael Cadden, 225–38. New York: Routledge, 1990.

———. "The Preacherly Text: African American Poetry and Vernacular Performance." *PMLA: Publications of the Modern Language Association of America* 107, no. 3 (1992): 582–93.

Boesenberg, Eva. "Sex and the City: Gender and Consumption in Late Nineteenth-Century Fiction." In "Literature and Consumption in Nineteenth-Century America," edited by Nicole Maruo-Schröder and Christoph Ribbat, special issue, *Anglistik und Englischunterricht* 82 (2014): 153–69.

Bontemps, Arna. "The Relevance of Paul Laurence Dunbar." In Martin, *A Singer in the Dawn*, 45–53.

Bottoms, Pam. "The Controversial, Subversive 'Broken Tongue' of Paul Lawrence Dunbar." *Midwestern Miscellany* 34 (2006): 6–26.

Bottorff, William K. "James Lane Allen (1849–1925)." *American Literary Realism* 2, no. 2 (Summer 1969): 121–24.

Bowland, James Mitchell. *Pioneer Recollections of the Early 30's and 40's in Sandusky County, Ohio*. Chicago: J. H. Beers, 1896.

Brawley, Benjamin G. *The Negro in Literature and Art in the United States*. New York: Duffield, 1918.

———. *Paul Laurence Dunbar: Poet of His People*. Chapel Hill: University of North Carolina Press, 1937.

Braxton, Joanne M. *The Collected Poetry of Paul Laurence Dunbar*. Charlottesville: University of Virginia Press, 1993.

———. "Dunbar, the Originator." *African American Review* 41, no. 2 (2007): 205–13.

Brevard, Lisa Pertillar. *A Biography of Edwin Henry Hackley: African American Attorney and Activist*. Lewiston, NY: Edwin Mellen Press, 2002.

Brezina, Jennifer Costello. "Public Women, Private Acts: Gender and Theater in Turn-of-the-Century American Novels." In *Separate Spheres No More: Gender Convergence in American Literature, 1830–1930*, edited by Monika M. Elbert, 225–42. Tuscaloosa: University of Alabama Press, 2000.

Briggs, Cordell Augustus. "A Study of Syntactic Variation in the Dialect Poetry of Paul Laurence Dunbar." *Dissertation Abstracts International* 44 (1982): 157A.

Broderick, John. "John Russell Young: The Internationalist as Librarian." *Quarterly Journal of the Library of Congress* 33, no. 2 (April 1976): 116–49.

Brooks, Van Wyck. *The Confident Years, 1885–1915*. New York: Dutton, 1952.

Brothers, Thomas Davison. "Is Inebriety Curable?" *North American Review*, 1891, 359–60.

Brown, E. M. "'What Shall We Do with the Inebriate?': Asylum Treatment and the Disease Concept of Alcoholism in the Late Nineteenth Century." *Journal of the History of the Behavioral Sciences* 2, no. 1 (January 1985): 48–69.

Bruce, Dickson D., Jr. "Identity and Ambiguity: The Literary Career of Paul Laurence Dunbar, 1892–1906." In *Black American Writing from the Nadir: The Evolution of a Literary Tradition, 1877–1915*, edited by Dickson D. Bruce, 56–98. Baton Rouge: Louisiana State University Press, 1989.

———. "On Dunbar's 'Jingles in a Broken Tongue': Dunbar's Dialect Poetry and the Afro-American Folk Tradition." In Martin, *A Singer in the Dawn*, 94–113.

Burroughs, John. *Wake-Robin*. Boston: Houghton Mifflin, 1871.

Butcher, Philip. "Mutual Appreciation: Dunbar and Cable." *CLA Journal* 1 (1958): 101–2.

Campbell, Donna. "Realism and Regionalism." In *A Companion to the Regional Literatures of America*, edited by Charles Crow, 107–8. Malden, MA: John Wiley & Sons, 2008.

Campbell, James Edwin. *Driftings and Gleanings*. Charleston, WV: State Tribune, 1887.

———. *Echoes from the Cabin and Elsewhere*. Chicago: Donohue & Henneberry, 1895.

———. "Pariah's Love." Philadelphia: A. M. E. Church Review, 1889.

Candela, Gregory Louis. "Melodramatic Form and Vision in Chesnutt's *The House behind the Cedars*, Dunbar's *The Sport of the Gods*, and Toomer's *Cane*." *Dissertation Abstracts International* 42.11 (1982): 4826A.

———. "We Wear the Mask: Irony in Dunbar's *The Sport of the Gods*." *American Literature: A Journal of Literary History, Criticism, and Bibliography* 48, no. 1 (1976): 60–72.

Cardwill, Mary E. "Historical Sketch." *Western Association of Writers: Proceedings of the Annual Convention* 4 (1890): 11.

Carr, Elston L., Jr. "Minstrelsy and the Dialect Poetry of Paul Laurence Dunbar." In Harrell, *We Wear the Mask*, 49–58.

Carter, Marva Griffin. "Removing the 'Minstrel Mask' in the Musicals of Will Marion Cook." *Musical Quarterly* 84, no. 2 (2000): 206–20.

Catherwood, Mary Hartwell. *Craque-o-Doom*. Philadelphia: Lippincott, 1881.

———. *A Woman in Armor*. New York: G. W. Carleton, 1875.

Cavaioli, Frank J. "Phillis Wheatley and Paul Laurence Dunbar Discover Christopher Columbus." *VIA: Voices in Italian Americana* 10, no. 1 (1999): 47–55.

Chandonia, Ronald Paul. "The New South in Black and White: Afro-American Fiction from the End of Reconstruction until the First World War." *Dissertation Abstracts International* 35 (1975): 4506A.

Chesnutt, Charles W. "Address to the Medina Coterie." In *Charles W. Chesnutt: Essays and Speeches*, edited by Joseph R. McElrath Jr., Robert C. Leitz III, and Jesse S. Crisler, 308–21. Stanford, CA: Stanford University Press, 1999.

Chesnutt, Helen M. *Charles Waddell Chesnutt: Pioneer of the Color Line*. Chapel Hill: University of North Carolina Press, 1952.

Clark, Barrett H. *The British and American Drama of Today*. New York: Henry Holt, 1915.

Cohen, Michael. "Paul Laurence Dunbar and the Genres of Dialect." *African American Review* 41, no. 2 (2007): 247–57.

Cole, Jean Lee. "Coloring Books: The Forms of Turn-of-the-Century American Literature." *Papers of the Bibliographical Society of America* 97, no. 4 (2003): 461–93.

Cook, William W. "I Greet the Dawn: Poems by Paul Laurence Dunbar." *New English Review* 1 (1978): 241–46.

Corrothers, James David, and Ray Stannard Baker. *In Spite of the Handicap: An Autobiography*. New York: George H. Doran, 1916.

Cottman, George S. "The Western Association of Writers: A Literary Reminiscence." *Indiana Magazine of History* 29, no. 3 (1933): 187–97.

Crabb, George. *English Synonyms: Explained in Alphabetical Order with Copious Illustrations and Examples Drawn from the Best Writers*. New York: Harper and Brothers, 1892.

Crummell, Alexander. *Africa and America: Addresses and Discourses*. Springfield, MA: Wiley, 1891.

Cummins, Amy. "'We Know de Time Is Ouahs': The Power of Christmas in the Literature of Paul Laurence Dunbar." In Harrell, *We Wear the Mask*, 138–53.

Cunningham, Virginia. *Paul Laurence Dunbar and His Song*. New York: Dodd, Mead, 1947.

Daigle, Jonathan. "Paul Laurence Dunbar and the Marshall Circle: Racial Representation from Blackface to Black Naturalism." *African American Review* 43, no. 4 (2009): 633–54.

D'Annunzio, Gabriele. *The Triumph of Death*. Translated by Arthur Hornblow. New York: George H. Richmond, 1895.

Davis, Alonzo Hilton. *Poems of Alonzo Hilton Davis*. Omaha, NE: Omaha Print Company, 1892.

Denny, Sheena. "'The Province of the Poet': Biographical Themes in Paul Laurence Dunbar's *Herrick*." *Midwestern Miscellany* 34 (2006): 53–60.

De Santis, Christopher C. "The Dangerous Marrow of Southern Tradition: Charles W. Chesnutt, Paul Laurence Dunbar, and the Paternalist Ethos at the Turn of the Century." *Southern Quarterly: A Journal of the Arts in the South* 38, no. 2 (2000): 79–97.

Drury, Augustus Waldo. *16th Annual Report of the Inspector of the Building and Loan Associations of the State of Ohio for the Fiscal Year Ending December 31, 1906*. Springfield, OH: Springfield Publishing, 1907.

———. *History of the City of Dayton and Montgomery County, Ohio*. Vol. 2. Chicago: S. J. Publishing, 1909.

Du Bois, William Edward Burghardt. *The Souls of Black Folk*. Oxford: Oxford University Press, 1903.

———. "The Study of the Negro Problems." *Annals of the American Academy of Political and Social Science* 11 (January 1898): 1–23.

Dunbar, Alice. "The Poet and His Song." *A. M. E. Review* 12 (October 1914): 121–35.

———. *Violets and Other Tales*. Boston: Monthly Review, 1895.

Dunbar, Paul Laurence. (works listed chronologically)

———. "The Case of Cadwallader." Unpublished manuscript. Paul Laurence Dunbar Papers, roll 4, box 12. Library of Congress, Washington, DC.

———. "From Impulse." *Dayton Tattler*, December 13, 1890.

———. "His Bride of the Tomb." *Dayton Tattler*, December 13, 1890.

———. "His Failure in Arithmetic." *Dayton Tattler*, December 20, 1890.

———. "His Little Lark." *Dayton Tattler*, December 20, 1890.

———. "The Tenderfoot." A. N. Kellogg Newspaper Co., 1891–1892.

———. "Little Billy." A. N. Kellogg Newspaper Co., 1891–1893.

———. *Oak and Ivy*. Dayton, OH: Press of the United Brethren Publishing House, 1893.

———. "Sunshine at Jackson Park." *Chicago Record*, Summer 1893.

———. "The Toy Exhibits." *Chicago Record*, Summer 1893.

———. "Of Negro Journals." *Chicago Record*, June 22, 1894.

———. *Majors and Minors*. Toledo, OH: Hadley and Hadley, 1895.

———. *Lyrics of Lowly Life*. New York: Dodd, Mead, 1896.

———. "Mt. Pisgah's Christmas 'Possum." In *Werner's Readings and Recitations*, no. 25, edited by Rachel Bauman, 127–32. New York: Edgar S. Werner, 1896.

———. "Some London Impressions." *Chicago Record*, April 14, 1897.

———. "England as Seen by a Black Man." *Independent* 48 (September 16, 1897): 4.

———. "Buss Jenkins Up Nawth: A Human Nature Sketch of Real Darkey Life in

New York." *New York Journal and Advertiser*, September 26, 1897, 18.

———. "How George Johnson 'Won Out': A Character Sketch of Real Darkey Life in New York." *New York Journal and Advertiser*, October 9, 1897, 22.

———. "Yellowjack's Game of Craps: A Character Sketch of Real Darkey Life in New York." *New York Journal and Advertiser*, October 9, 1897, 22.

———. "The Hoodooing of Mr. Bill Simms: A Darkey Dialect Story." *New York Journal and Advertiser*, October 16, 1897, 21.

———. *Folks from Dixie*. New York: Dodd, Mead, 1898.

———. *The Uncalled*. New York: Dodd, Mead, 1898.

———. "The Deliberation of Mr. Dunkin." *Cosmopolitan* 24 (April 1898): 678–85.

———. "A Family Feud." *Outlook* 58 (April 23, 1898): 1016–20.

———. "Jimsella." *Current Literature* 24 (July 1898): 15.

———. "Our New Madness." *Independent* 50 (September 15, 1898): 469–71.

———. "The Race Question Discussed." *Toledo Journal*, December 11, 1898.

———. "The Faith Cure Man: A Pathetic Story of a Colored Mammy." *New York Journal and Advertiser*, December 11, 1898.

———. *Lyrics of the Hearthside*. New York: Dodd, Mead, 1899.

———. *Poems of Cabin and Field*. New York: Dodd, Mead, 1899.

———. "Mr. Cornelius Johnson, Office-Seeker." *Cosmopolitan* 26 (February 1899): 420–24.

———. "The End of the Chapter." *Lippincott's Monthly Magazine* 63 (April 1899): 532–34.

———. "The Conjuring Contest." *Saturday Evening Post* 172 (July 8, 1899): 30.

———. "The Ingrate." *New England Magazine* 20 (August 1899): 676–81.

———. "The Finish of Patsy Barnes." *Saturday Evening Post* 172 (August 12, 1899): 98–99.

———. "Lafe Halloway's Two Fights." *Independent* 51 (September 7, 1899): 2417–22.

———. "The Defection of Maria Ann Gibbs." *Saturday Evening Post* 172 (September 9, 1899): 172.

———. "The Hapless Southern Negro." *Denver Post*, September 17, 1899.

———. "The Strength of Gideon." *Lippincott's Monthly Magazine* 64 (October 1899): 617–25.

———. "A Mess of Pottage." *Saturday Evening Post* 172 (December 16, 1899): 516–17.

———. *The Love of Landry*. New York: Dodd, Mead, 1900.

———. *The Strength of Gideon and Other Stories*. New York: Dodd, Mead, 1900.

———. "Johnsonham, Junior." *Saturday Evening Post* 172 (January 6, 1900): 597.

———. "Negro Life in Washington." *Harper's Weekly* 44 (January 13, 1900): 32.

———. "Silas Jackson." *New York Evening Post*, February 10, 1900, 8.

———. "The Emancipation of Evalina Jones." *People's Monthly* 1, no. 2 (April 1900): 8–9.

———. "Is Higher Education for the Negro Hopeless?" *Philadelphia Times*, June 10, 1900.

———. "Silent Sam'el." *Saturday Evening Post* 172 (June 16, 1900): 1181.

———. "How Brother Parker Fell from Grace." *Saturday Evening Post* 173 (July 21, 1900): 11.

———. "A Lady Slipper." *Saturday Evening Post* 173 (September 15, 1900): 11, 19.

———. "Aunt Temple's Revenge." *New York Evening Post* 173 (November 10, 1900): 27.

———. "Ash-Cake Hannah and Her Ben." *Saturday Evening Post* 173 (December 8, 1900): 16–17.

———. *Candle-Lightin' Time*. New York: Dodd, Mead, 1901.

———. *The Fanatics*. New York: Dodd, Mead, 1901.

———. "The Lion Tamer." *Smart Set* 3 (January 1901): 147–50.

———. "Old Abe's Conversation." *Youth's Companion*, January 1901, 40–44.

———. "The Walls of Jericho." *Saturday Evening Post* 173 (April 8, 1901): 14–15.

———. "The Mortification of the Flesh." *Lippincott's Monthly Magazine* 68 (August 1901): 250–56.

———. "Nathan Makes His Proposal." *Pittsburgh Chronicle Telegraph* 10 (August 10, 1901): 10.

———. "The Independence of Silas Bollender." *Lippincott's Monthly Magazine* 68 (September 1901): 375–81.

———. "In a Circle." *Metropolitan Magazine* 14 (October 1901): 460–62.

———. "The White Counterpane." *Lippincott's Monthly Magazine* 68 (October 1901): 500–508.

———. "The Minority Committee." *Lippincott's Monthly Magazine* 68 (November 1901): 746–51.

———. "A Defender of the Faith." *San Francisco Chronicle*, December 22, 1901, 8.

———. *The Jest of Fate: A Story of Negro Life*. London: Jarrold & Sons, 1902.

———. *The Sport of the Gods*. New York: Dodd, Mead, 1902.

———. "The Finding of Martha." *Lippincott's Monthly Magazine* 69 (March 1902): 375–84.

———. "The Trousers." *St. Louis Mirror*, March 2, 1902, 2.

———. "A Judgment of Paris." *Saturday Evening Post* 174 (May 24, 1902): 3–4.

———. "Jethro's Garden." *Era* 10 (July 1902): 78–80.

———. "The Last Fiddling of Mordaunt's Jim." *Saturday Evening Post* 175 (August 30, 1902): 11.

———. *In Old Plantation Days*. New York: Dodd, Mead, 1903.

———. *Lyrics of Love and Laughter*. New York: Dodd, Mead, 1903.

———. "Representative American Negroes." In *The Negro Problem: A Series of Articles by Representative American Negroes*, edited by W. E. B. Du Bois, 187–211. New York: James Pott, 1903.

———. *When Malindy Sings*. New York; Dodd, Mead, 1903.

———. "Possibilities of the Negro: The Advance Guard of the Race." *Booklover's Magazine*, July 1903, 2–15.

———. *The Heart of Happy Hollow*. New York: Dodd, Mead, 1904.

————. *Li'l' Gal*. New York: Dodd, Mead, 1904.

————. "The Vindication of Jared Hargot." *Lippincott's Monthly Magazine* 73 (March 1904): 374–81.

————. *Chris'mus Is A-Comin' and Other Poems*. New York: Dodd, Mead, 1905.

————. *Howdy, Honey, Howdy*. New York: Dodd, Mead, 1905.

————. *Lyrics of Sunshine and Shadow*. New York: Dodd, Mead 1905.

————. *A Plantation Portrait*. New York: Dodd, Mead, 1905.

————. "The Way of Love." *Lippincott's Monthly Magazine* 75 (January 1905): 68–73.

————. "The Churching of Grandma Pleasant." *Lippincott's Monthly Magazine* 75 (March 1905): 337–42.

————. *Joggin' Erlong*. New York: Dodd, Mead, 1906.

————. *Fisk University News*, November 1918, 7.

————. "Sister Jackson's Superstitions." In *The Paul Laurence Dunbar Reader: A Selection of Paul Laurence Dunbar's Poetry and Prose, Including Writings Never Before Available in Book Form*, edited by Jay Martin and Gossie H. Hudson, 103–6. New York: Dodd, Mead, 1975.

————. "Jimmy Weedon's Contretemps." In Martin and Primeau, *In His Own Voice*, 238–43 (2002).

————. "Old Conju'in Joe." In Martin and Primeau, *In His Own Voice*, 219–23 (2002).

————. "A Prophesy of Fate." In Martin and Primeau, *In His Own Voice*, 250–55 (2002).

Dustin, C. W. "Paul Laurence Dunbar." *Fisk University News* 9, no. 3 (November 1918): 6–9.

Easton, William Edgar. *Christophe; a Tragedy in Prose of Imperial Haiti*. Los Angeles: Press Grafton Publishing, 1911.

————. *Dessalines*. Galveston, TX: J. W. Burson, 1893.

Eident, J. D., and Timothy Taylor. *On Prairie Winds: The Letters of J. N. Matthews and J. W. Riley*. Self-published, Lulu.com, 2015.

Elder, Arlene A. *The "Hindered Hand": Cultural Implications of Early African-American Fiction*. Westport, CT: Greenwood, 1978.

Emanuel, James A. "Racial Fire in the Poetry of Paul Laurence Dunbar." In Martin, *A Singer in the Dawn*, 75–93.

Engel, Bernard F. "Paul Laurence Dunbar's Civil War Verse." *Midwestern Miscellany* 11 (1983): 15–18.

Eskridge, Jeremiah Thomas. "The Influences of the Climate of Colorado on the Nervous System in Health and in Disease." *Denver Medical Times* 20, no. 12 (June 1901): 607–13.

————. "Some Observations during Two Years' Residence at Colorado Springs, Colorado." *Medical and Surgical Reporter* 55, no. 18 (October 30, 1886): 549.

Espenschied, Steven C. *A History of the American Steam Calliope*. New York: Vantage Press, 1986.

Eversley, Shelly Jennifer. "The Real Negro: The Question of Authenticity in Twentieth Century African American Literature." *Dissertation Abstracts International, Section A: The Humanities and Social Sciences* 59, no. 5 (1998): 1570–71.

Ewell, Barbara C., Pamela Glenn Menke, and Andrea Humphrey, eds. *Southern Local Color: Stories of Region, Race, and Gender.* Athens: University of Georgia Press, 2002.

Eyman, Henry C. "H. A. Tobey." In *Proceedings of the American Medico-Psychological Association*, 583–85. Baltimore: Lord Baltimore Press, 1909.

Fishkin, Shelley Fisher. "Race and the Politics of Memory: Mark Twain and Paul Laurence Dunbar." *Journal of American Studies* 40, no. 2 (2006): 283–309.

Flint, Allen. "Black Response to Colonel Shaw." *Phylon: A Review of Race and Culture* 45, no. 3 (1984): 210–19.

Flusche, Michael. "Paul Laurence Dunbar and the Burden of Race." *Southern Humanities Review* 11 (1977): 49–61.

Fogg, James, and John Lemuel Murray Willis, eds. *The Fogg Family of America: The Reunions of the Fogg Families . . . Addresses, Poems, Newspaper Reports and Memories.* Portland: Maine's Historical Press, 1907.

Folsom, Ed. "The Mystical Ornithologist and the Iowa Tufthunter: Two Unpublished Whitman Letters and Some Identifications." *Walt Whitman Quarterly Review* 1, no.1 (1983): 18–29.

Fossett, Judith Jackson. "1986: Paul Laurence Dunbar's Poems in Black Vernacular and 'Literary' English Earn Ambivalent Praise from William Dean Howells: *Lyrics of Lowly Life.*" In *A New Literary History of America*, edited by Greil Marcus and Werner Sollors, 425–29. Cambridge, MA: Harvard University Press, 2009.

Fox, Allan B. "Behind the Mask: Paul Laurence Dunbar's Poetry in Literary English." *Texas Quarterly* 14, no. 2 (1971): 7–19.

Frederic, Harold. *The Damnation of Theron Ware.* Chicago: Stone & Kimball, 1896.

Fronc, Jennifer. *New York Undercover: Private Surveillance in the Progressive Era.* Chicago: University of Chicago Press, 2009.

Fuller, Sara S., ed. *The Paul Laurence Dunbar Papers.* Columbus: Ohio Historical Society, 1972.

Gabbin, Joanne. "Intimate Intercessions in the Poetry of Paul Laurence Dunbar." *African American Review* 50, no. 4 (2018): 1075–79.

Gates, Henry Louis, Jr. "Dis and Dat: Dialect and the Descent." In *Afro-American Literature: The Reconstruction of Instruction*, edited by Robert Stepto and Daxter Fisher, 88–117. New York: Modern Language Association, 1969.

———. *The Signifying Monkey: A Theory of Afro-American Literary Criticism.* New York: Oxford University Press, 1988.

Gayle, Addison, Jr. "Literature as Catharsis: The Novels of Paul Laurence Dunbar." In Martin, *A Singer in the Dawn*, 139–51.

———. *Oak and Ivy: A Biography of Paul Laurence Dunbar.* Garden City, NY: Doubleday, 1971.

Gebhard, Caroline. "Inventing a 'Negro Literature': Race, Dialect, and Gender in the Early Work of Paul Laurence Dunbar, James Weldon Johnson, and Alice Dunbar-Nelson." In *Post-Bellum, Pre-Harlem: African American Literature and Culture*, edited by Barbara McCaskill and Caroline Gebhard, 162–78. New York: New York University Press, 2006.

Gentry, Thomas G. *Nests and Eggs of Birds of the United States*. Philadelphia: J. A. Wagenseller, 1882.

Gentry, Tony. *Paul Laurence Dunbar: Poet*. Los Angeles: Holloway House, 1993.

Gibson, Donald B. "Richard Wright: Aspects of His Afro-American Literary Relations." In *Critical Essays on Richard Wright*, edited by Yoshinobu Hakutani, 82–90. Boston: G. K. Hall, 1982.

Giles, James R. "Paul Laurence Dunbar." In *American Short-Story Writers, 1880–1910*, edited by Bobby Ellen Kimbel and William E. Grant, 154–59. Detroit: Thomson Gale, 1989.

Graber, Katie. "'A Strange, Weird Effect': The Fisk Jubilee Singers in the United States and England." *American Music Research Center* 14 (2004): 27–52.

Green, Jeffrey. *Samuel Coleridge-Taylor: A Musical Life*. Oxfordshire, UK: Routledge, 2016.

Griese, Noel L. *Arthur W. Page: Publisher, Public Relations Pioneer, Patriot*. Atlanta, GA: Anvil, 2001.

Griffin, Martin. "Reconciliation and Irony, 1865–1905: James Russell Lowell, Henry James, Paul Laurence Dunbar, and Ambrose Bierce." *Dissertation Abstracts International, Section A: The Humanities and Social Sciences* 63, no. 11 (2003): 3946.

Harlan, Louis R., Stuart B. Kaufman, Barbara S. Draft, and Raymond W. Smock, eds. *The Booker T. Washington Papers*. Vol. 4, *1895–98*. Urbana: University of Illinois Press, 1975.

Harrell, Willie J., Jr. "Creating a Representative Community: Identity in Paul Laurence Dunbar's *In Old Plantation Days*." In Harrell, *We Wear the Mask*, 154–69.

———. "'Nemmine. You Got Somebody Else to Ring Yo' Ol' Bell Now': Nigger Ed and the Rhetoric of Local Color Realism and Racial Protest in Dunbar's *The Fanatics*." In Harrell, *We Wear the Mask*, 242–53.

———, ed. *We Wear the Mask: Paul Laurence Dunbar and the Politics of Representative Reality*. Kent, OH: Kent State University Press, 2010.

Harris, Amy Hobbs. "'The Sole Province of the Public Reader': Elocutionist Hallie Quinn Brown's Performances of the Poetry of Paul Laurence Dunbar." *Texts, Readers, Audiences, History* 9 (2017): 36–55.

Harris, Lee O. *Interludes: Sung between the Acts in the Drama of Toil*. Indianapolis: Carlon & Hollenbeck, 1893.

Harris, Trudier. "William Dean Howells: Introduction to Paul Laurence Dunbar, *Lyrics of Lowly Life* (1896)." In *Afro-American Writers before the Harlem Renaissance*, edited by Trudier Harris and Thadious M. Davis, 306–7. Detroit: Gale, 1986.

Hawkins, William Walter. "About People We Know." *Town & Country* (Hearst Corporation) 77–78 (1921): 26.

Hay, John. *Pike Country Ballads.* Boston: James R. Osgood, 1871.

Heisel, Andrew. "What to Do with Southern Negro 'Types' in Dunbar's Hampton Volumes." *Word and Image: A Journal of Verbal/Visual Enquiry* 28, no. 3 (2012): 243–56.

Hepburn, James G. *The Author's Empty Purse and the Rise of the Literary Agent.* New York: Oxford University Press, 1968.

Holder, Stephen C. "A Man of His Times: The Fiction of Paul Lawrence Dunbar." *Midwestern Miscellany* 34 (2006): 61–68.

Honious, Ann. *What Dreams We Have: The Wright Brothers and Their Hometown of Dayton, Ohio.* Fort Washington, PA: Eastern National, 2003.

Hope, Anthony. *Captain Dieppe.* New York: Doubleday & McClure, 1900.

Howe, Edgar Watson. "Country Newspapers." *Century* 42 (May 1891): 776–83.

Howells, W. D. *The Complete Poems of Paul Laurence Dunbar.* New York: Dodd, Mead, 1918.

———. "Life and Letters." *Harper's Weekly*, June 27, 1896.

Hudson, Gossie H. "A Biography of Paul Laurence Dunbar." PhD diss., Ohio State University, 1970.

———. "The Crowded Years: Paul Laurence Dunbar in History." In Martin, *A Singer in the Dawn,* 227–42.

———. "'Emancipation,' an Unpublished Poem by Paul Laurence Dunbar." *Negro History Bulletin* 36 (1973): 41–42.

———. "Paul Laurence Dunbar: Dialect et la Negritude." *Phylon: The Atlanta University Review of Race and Culture* 34, no. 3 (1973): 236–47.

———. "Paul Laurence Dunbar: The Regional Heritage of Dayton's First Black Poet." *Antioch Review* 34 (1976): 430–40.

Hughes, Jennifer A. "The Politics of Incongruity in Paul Laurence Dunbar's *The Fanatics.*" *African American Review* 41, no. 2 (2007): 295–301.

Hurd, Myles. "Blackness and Borrowed Obscurity: Another Look at Dunbar's *The Sport of the Gods.*" *Callaloo: A Journal of African American and African Arts and Letters* 4, no. 1–3 (1981): 90–100.

Hurd, Myles Raymond. "Rhetoric versus Eloquence in the Afro-American Double Narrative: Perspectives on Audience, Ambivalence, and Ambiguity." *Dissertation Abstracts International* 46.2 (1985): 421A.

Inge, Casey. "Family Functions: Disciplinary Discourses and (De) Constructions of the 'Family' in *The Sport of the Gods.*" *Callaloo: A Journal of African American and African Arts and Letters* 20, no. 1 (1997): 226–42.

———. "'Our Family, White and Black': Revisiting the Racial Family in Turn-of-the-Century American Fiction." *Dissertation Abstracts International, Section A: The Humanities and Social Sciences* 64, no. 8 (2004): 2889.

James, Jennifer C. *A Freedom Bought with Blood: African American War Literature from the Civil War to World War II*. Chapel Hill: University of North Carolina Press, 2007.

Jarrett, Gene. "'Entirely Black Verse from Him Would Succeed': Minstrel Realism and William Dean Howells." *Nineteenth-Century Literature* 59, no. 4 (2004): 494–535.

———. "'We Must Write like the White Men': Race, Realism, and Dunbar's Anomalous First Novel." *Novel: A Forum on Fiction* 37, no. 3 (2004): 303–25.

Jarrett, Gene Andrew, and Thomas Lewis Morgan, editors. *The Complete Stories of Paul Laurence Dunbar*. Athens: Ohio University Press, 2005.

Johanningsmeier, Charles. *Fiction and the American Literary Marketplace: The Role of Newspaper Syndicates in America, 1860–1900*. Cambridge: Cambridge University Press, 1996.

Johnson, James Weldon. *Along This Way: The Autobiography of James Weldon Johnson*. New York: Viking Press, 1933.

———. Preface to *The Book of American Negro Poetry*. Edited by James Weldon Johnson. Reprint, New York: Harcourt, Brace, and World, 1959.

Jones, Christopher. "Paul Laurence Dunbar and Robert Burns: Vernacular Gateways." *Midwestern Miscellany* 34 (2006): 27–35.

Jones, Gavin. *Strange Talk: The Politics of Dialect Literature in Gilded Age America*. Berkeley: University of California Press, 1999.

Jones, Gayl. "Breaking Out of the Conventions of Dialect: Dunbar and Hurston." *Presence africaine: Revue culturelle du monde noir* [Cultural Review of the Negro World] 144 (1987): 32–46.

Julien, Claude. "Continuité doxique: Aspects sexuelles du 'problème blanc' de 'The Lynching of Jube Benson' à 'Going to Meet the Man.'" *GRAAT: Publication des groupes de recherches anglo-américaines de l'Université François Rabelais de Tours* 18 (1998): 103–14.

Kaestle, Carl F., and Janice A. Radway, eds. *A History of the Book in America*. Vol. 4, *Print in Motion: The Expansion of Publishing and Reading in the United States, 1880–1940*. Chapel Hill: University of North Carolina Press, 2009.

Keeling, John. "Paul Dunbar and the Mask of Dialect." *Southern Literary Journal* 25, no. 2 (1993): 24–38.

Kelley, Blair L. M. "Right to Ride: African American Citizenship and Protest in the Era of 'Plessy v. Ferguson.'" *African American Review* 41, no. 2 (Summer 2007): 347–56.

King, Jeannine. "Memory and Repression in Paul Laurence Dunbar's *The Sport of the Gods*." In Harrell, *We Wear the Mask*, 173–90.

Kinnamon, Keneth. "Three Black Writers and the Anthologized Canon." *American Literary Realism* 23, no. 3 (1991): 42–51.

———. "Three Black Writers and the Anthologized Canon." In *American Realism and the Canon*, edited by Tom Quirk and Gary Scharnhorst, 143–53. Newark: University of Delaware Press, 1994.

Kirk, James A. "The Sport of the Gods: Religion and Sexuality in India." *Iliff Review* 35, no. 2 (1978): 41–53.

Kountz, William J. *Billy Baxter's Letters*. Harmarville, PA: Duquesne Distributing, 1899.

Laryea, Doris Lucas. "Paul Laurence Dunbar." In *Afro-American Writers before the Harlem Renaissance*, edited by Trudier Harris and Thadious M. Davis, 106–22. Detroit: Gale, 1986.

Lee, A. Robert. "The Fiction of Paul Laurence Dunbar." *Negro American Literature Forum* 8, no. 1 (1974): 166–75.

Leuchtenmüller, Thomas. "Paul Laurence Dunbar's Overlooked Play." *African American Review* 41, no. 2 (Summer 2007): 319–26.

Lewis, Christopher. "Mama's Boys and Mothering Men: Dunbar's Deviant Masculinities." *College Literature* 46, no. 2 (2019): 311–42.

Licato, Amanda Mehsima. "Paul Laurence Dunbar's Metapoetics." *Journal of Nineteenth-Century Americanists* 7, no. 1 (Spring 2019): 131–53.

"Literary Notes." *Board of Trade Journal* 17 (1904): 553.

Long, Lisa. *Rehabilitating Bodies: Health, History, and the American Civil War*. Philadelphia: University of Pennsylvania Press, 2004.

Loranger, Carol S. "The Outcast Poetics of Paul Laurence Dunbar and Edwin Arlington Robinson." *Studies in American Naturalism* 10, no. 2 (Winter 2015): 133–49.

Loving, Thomas Jerome. *The Last Titan: A Life of Theodore Dreiser*. Berkeley: University of California Press, 2005.

Lucas, Doris M. "Patterns of Accommodation and Protest in the Fiction of Paul Laurence Dunbar." *Dissertation Abstracts International* 34 (1974).

Manweller, Mathew, ed. *Chronology of the U.S. Presidency*. Vol. 1. Santa Barbara: ABC-CLIO, 2012.

Markham, Edwin. *The Man with the Hoe and Other Poems*. New York: Doubleday & McClure, 1899.

Marsden, Steve. "Unmasking the Lynching Subject: Thomas Nelson Page, Paul Laurence Dunbar, and the Specters of American Race." In *Haunting Realities: Naturalist Gothic and American Realism*, edited by Monika Elbert and Wendy Ryden, 103–16. Tuscaloosa: University of Alabama Press, 2017.

Martin, Herbert Woodward. "Forgotten Manuscripts: 'To My Friend—Joseph S. Cotter,' by Paul Laurence Dunbar." *African American Review* 43, no. 2/3 (2009): 357–58.

———. "An Unintended Journey." *Midwestern Miscellany* 34 (2006): 93–96.

Martin, Herbert Woodward, and Ronald Primeau, eds. *In His Own Voice: The Dramatic and Other Uncollected Works of Paul Laurence Dunbar*. Athens: Ohio University Press, 2002.

Martin, Herbert Woodward, Gene Andrew Jarrett, and Ronald Primeau. *The Collected Novels of Paul Laurence Dunbar*. Athens: Ohio University Press, 2009.

Martin, Jay. "'Jump Back Honey': Paul Laurence Dunbar and the Rediscovery of American Poetical Traditions." *Bulletin of the Midwest Modern Language Association* 7, no. 1 (1974): 40–53.

———, ed. *A Singer in the Dawn: Reinterpretations of Paul Laurence Dunbar*. New York: Dodd, Mead, 1975.

Martin, Jay, and Gossie H. Hudson, eds. *The Paul Laurence Dunbar Reader: A Selection of Paul Laurence Dunbar's Poetry and Prose, Including Writings Never Before Available in Book Form*. New York: Dodd, Mead, 1975.

Matthews, G. C., and John McGovern, eds. "A Call." *The Current: Politics, Literature, Science and Art* 5. no. 120 (April 3, 1886): 222.

Matthews, James Newton. *Afterwhiles*. Indianapolis: Bobbs-Merrill, 1887.

———. *Temple Vale and Other Poems*. Chicago: Charles H. Kerr, 1888.

McClure, S. S. "My Autobiography: Progressive as Self-Made Man." *American Quarterly* 22, no. 2, part 1 (Summer 1970): 203–12.

McFarland, Marvin W., ed. *The Papers of Wilbur and Orville Wright: Including the Chanute-Wright Letters and Other Papers of Octave Chanute*. Vol. 2, *1906–1948*. New York: McGraw-Hill, 1953.

McGhee, Nancy B., and Keith L. Schall. "Portraits in Black: Illustrated Poems of Paul Laurence Dunbar." In *Stony the Road: Chapters in the History of Hampton Institute*, edited by Keith L. Schall, 63–104. Charlottesville: University of Virginia Press, 1977.

McGraw, Patricia Washington. "The Duality of Dialect and Dialogue in Dunbar." *Publications of the Arkansas Philological Association* 15, no. 1 (1989): 53–66.

Metcalf, Eugene W., Jr. "The Letters of Paul and Alice Dunbar: A Private History." *Dissertation Abstracts International* 35 (1974).

———. *Paul Laurence Dunbar: A Bibliography*. Metuchen, NJ: Scarecrow, 1975.

Miller, Ruth, and Peter J. Katopes. "Modern Beginnings: William Wells Brown, Charles Waddell Chesnutt, Martin R. Delany, Paul Laurence Dunbar, Sutton E. Griggs, Frances Ellen Watkins Harper, and Frank J. Webb." In *Black American Writers: Bibliographical Essays, I: The Beginnings through the Harlem Renaissance and Langston Hughes*, edited by M. Thomas Inge, Maurice Duke, and Jackson R. Bryer, 133–60. New York: St. Martin's, 1978.

Mink, Joanna Stephens. "Some Connections between Hardy's Blinded Bird and Dunbar's Caged Bird." *Hardy Society Journal* 2, no. 1 (2006): 30–36.

Moody's Manual of Investments: American and Foreign. New York: Moody's Investor's Service, 1919.

Moody-Turner, Shirley. "Uprooting the Folk: Paul Laurence Dunbar's Critique of the Folk Ideal." In *Black Folklore and the Politics of Racial Representation*, edited by Shirley Moody-Turner, 101–26. Oxford: University Press of Mississippi, 2013.

Morgan, Thomas Lewis. "The City as Refuge: Constructing Urban Blackness in Paul Laurence Dunbar's *The Sport of the Gods* and James Weldon Johnson's *The Autobiography of an Ex-Colored Man*." *African American Review* 38, no. 2 (Summer 2004): 213–37.

———. "'Sue' and 'A Southern Silhouette': Two Published but Uncollected Short Stories by Paul Laurence Dunbar." *American Periodicals* 27, no. 1 (2017): 95–107.

Mvuyekure, Pierre-Damien. "Paul Laurence Dunbar (1872–1906)." In *African American Authors, 1745–1945: A Bio-Bibliographical Critical Sourcebook*, edited by Emmanuel S. Nelson, 132–38. Westport, CT: Greenwood, 2000.

Nardi, Steven A. "The 'Colder Artifice': Paul Laurence Dunbar, Countee Cullen, and the Mask of Blackness." In *Behind the Masks of Modernism: Global and Transnational Perspectives*, edited by Andrew Reynolds and Bonnie Roos, 115–34. Gainesville: University Press of Florida, 2016.

"A Negro Poet: A Young Man Whose Literary Talent Shows Itself in Spite of Unfavorable Environment," *Indianapolis Journal*, October 2, 1892, 6.

Nelson, Randy F. *Almanac of American Letters*. Los Altos, California: William Kaufmann, 1981.

Nevins, Allan, ed. *The Letters and Journal of Brand Whitlock*. New York: D. Appleton-Century, 1936.

Newkirk, Pamela, ed. *Letters from Black America*. New York: Farrar, Straus and Giroux, 2009.

"The New Registrar's Office." *Alumni Quarterly and Fortnightly Notes of the University of Illinois* 1, no. 15 (December 15, 1915): 136–37.

Nichols, James Lawrence, and William Henry Crogman. *Progress of a Race: Or, The Remarkable Advancement of the American Negro*. Naperville, IL: J. J. Nichols, 1920.

Noonan, Mark. "'Jump Back, Honey, Jump Back': Reading Paul Laurence Dunbar in the Context of the Century Magazine." In Harrell, *We Wear the Mask*, 82–97.

Nurhussein, Nadia. "'On Flow'ry Beds of Ease': Paul Laurence Dunbar and the Cultivation of Dialect Poetry in the Century." *American Periodicals* 20, no. 1 (2010): 46–67.

———. *Rhetorics of Literacy: The Cultivation of American Dialect Poetry*. Columbus: Ohio State University Press, 2013.

O'Bar, Jack. *The Origins and History of the Bobbs-Merrill Company*. Occasional Papers, Graduate School of Library and Information Science. Publications Office, University of Illinois Urbana-Champaign, 1985.

Okeke-Ezigbo, Emeka. "Paul Laurence Dunbar: Straightening the Record." *College Language Association Journal* 24, no. 4 (1981): 481–96.

Okeke-Ezigbo, Felix C. "Eagle against Buzzard: The Dialect Poetry of Paul Laurence Dunbar and James Weldon Johnson." *Dissertation Abstracts International* 40 (1979): 2065A.

Oswald, Emily. "Imagining Race: Illustrating the Poems of Paul Laurence Dunbar." *Book History* 9 (2006): 213–33.

Oyen, Henry. "The Founder of 'Chautauquas': The Varied and Helpful Career of Bishop John H. Vincent." *The World's Work: A History of Our Time* 24, no. 1 (May–October 1912): 101.

Paddon, Anna R., and Sally Turner. "African Americans and the World's Columbian Exposition." *Illinois Historical Journal* 88, no. 1 (1995): 19–36.

Pawley, Thomas. "Dunbar as Playwright." *Black World* 24, no. 6 (1975): 70–79.

Peabody, Megan M. "Dunbar, Dialect, and Narrative Theory: Subverted Statements in *Lyrics of Lowly Life*." In Harrell, *We Wear the Mask*, 59–70.

Pearson, Paul M. *Paul Laurence Dunbar: A Tribute.* Berkeley: Bancroft Library, University of California, n.d.

Penn, Irvine Garland. *The Afro-American Press and Its Editors.* Springfield, MA: Wiley, 1891.

Penzl, Herbert. "Paul Laurence Dunbar's Literary Dialects." *PMLA: Publications of the Modern Language Association of America* 108, no. 1 (1993): 155–56.

Peppers, Wallace Ray. "Linguistic Variation in the Dialect Poetry of Paul Laurence Dunbar." *Dissertation Abstracts International* 40 (1979): 2639A.

Perry, Ruth Anna. "Variations on the Protest Theme in the Novels of Dunbar, Chesnutt, Johnson, and Ellison." *Dissertation Abstracts International* 41 (1980): 1599A.

Pfitzer, Gregory M. *Popular History and the Literary Marketplace, 1840–1920.* Amherst: University of Massachusetts Press, 2008.

Pfrimmer, William Wood. *Driftwood.* Buffalo, NY: Charles Wells Moulton, 1890.

———. *The Legend of Grape Island and Other Poems.* Watseka, IL: Times Democrat, 1907.

Pitcher, Geoffrey. "The Readerly Ruse: Paul Laurence Dunbar's Dialect Poetry and the Aesthetics of Authenticity." In *Voices of Power: Co-operation and Conflict in English Language and Literatures*, edited by Marc Maufort and Jean-Pierre van Noppen, 183–90. L3-Liège Language and Literature, for Belgian Association of Anglists in Higher Education. Liège, Belgium: Pagination, 1997.

Pittman, Coretta M. "Rhetorical Accountability: Paul Laurence Dunbar's Search for 'Representative' Men." In Harrell, *We Wear the Mask*, 73–81.

Pochmara, Anna. "Enslavement to Philanthropy, Freedom from Heredity: Amelia E. Johnson's and Paul Laurence Dunbar's Uses and Misuses of Sentimentalism and Naturalism." *Polish Journal for American Studies: Yearbook of the Polish Association for American Studies* 12 (Spring 2018): 113–28.

Primeau, Ronald. *Herbert Woodward Martin and the African American Tradition in Poetry.* Kent, OH: Kent State University Press, 2004.

Primeau, Ronald, and Herbert Woodward Martin. "Being a Collection of Essays on Paul Lawrence Dunbar." *Midwestern Miscellany* 34 (2006): 4–96.

Quackenbos, John Duncan. *The Illustrated History of Ancient Literature, Oriental and Classical.* New York: Harper & Brothers, 1882.

Rabban, David M. *Free Speech in Its Forgotten Years, 1870–1920.* Cambridge: Cambridge University Press, 1997.

Ramey, Lauri. "Paul Laurence Dunbar and the Spirituals." In *Black Music, Black Poetry: Blues and Jazz's Impact on African American Versification*, edited by Gordon E. Thompson, 39–54. Farnham, UK: Ashgate, 2014.

Ramsey, William M. "Dunbar's Dixie." *Southern Literary Journal* 32, no. 1 (1999): 30–45.

Raynor, Sharon D. "'Sing a Song Heroic': Paul Laurence Dunbar's Mythic and Poetic Tribute to Black Soldiers." In Harrell, *We Wear the Mask*, 32–48.

Redding, Saunders. "Portrait against Background." In Martin, *A Singer in the Dawn*, 39–44.

Reifel, August Jacob. *History of Franklin County, Indiana: Her People, Industries, and Institutions; with Biographical Sketches of Representative Citizens and Genealogical Records of Old Families*. Indianapolis: B. F. Bowen, 1915.

Revell, Peter. "Paul Laurence Dunbar." In *American Poets, 1890–1945*, 3rd series, part 1, *A–M*, edited by Peter Quartermain, 69–82. Detroit: Gale, 1987.

Revell, Peter, and David J. Nordloh. *Paul Laurence Dunbar*. Boston: Twayne, 1979.

"Review and Comment." *Business and the Bookkeeper* (Business Man's Publishing), July–December 1910, 6–7.

Riley, James Whitcomb. *Green Fields and Running Brooks*. Indianapolis: Bowe-Merrill, 1892.

———. "James Newton Matthews," *Indianapolis Journal*, November 19, 1893.

Robinson, Lillian S. "Paul Laurence Dunbar: A Credit to His Race?" *African American Review* 41, no. 2 (2007): 215–25.

Rodgers, Lawrence R. "Paul Laurence Dunbar's *The Sport of the Gods*: The Doubly Conscious World of Plantation Fiction, Migration, and Ascent." *American Literary Realism* 24, no. 3 (1992): 42–57.

Rollin, Horace J. *Yetta Segal*. New York: G. W. Dillingham, 1898.

Roman, Camille. "The Caged Bird's Song and Its (Dis)Contents." *Pacific Coast Philology* 41 (2006): 32–38.

Ronda, Margaret. "'Work and Wait Unwearying': Dunbar's Georgics." *PMLA: Publications of the Modern Language Association of America* 127, no. 4 (2012): 863–78.

Rothman, Sheila. *Living in the Shadow of Death: Tuberculosis and the Social Experience of Illness in American History*. New York: Basic Books, 1994.

Rudwick, Elliot M., and August Meier. "Black Man in the 'White City': Negroes and the Columbian Exposition, 1893." *Phylon* 26, no. 4 (4th qtr., 1965): 354–61.

Sander, Reinhard W. "Five Early Afro-American Novels." *Muse* 8 (1976): 36–41.

Sandler, Matt. "The Glamour of Paul Laurence Dunbar: Racial Uplift, Masculinity and Bohemia in the Nadir." In Harrell, *We Wear the Mask*, 98–115.

Sapirstein, Ray Julius. "'Original Rags': African American Secular Music and the Cultural Legacy of Paul Laurence Dunbar's Poetry." In *Black Music, Black Poetry: Blues and Jazz's Impact on African American Versification*, edited by Gordon E. Thompson, 19–37. Farnham, UK: Ashgate, 2014.

———. "Out from Behind the Mask: The Illustrated Poetry of Paul Laurence Dunbar and Photography at Hampton Institute." PhD diss., University of Texas at Austin, 2005.

———. "Picturing Dunbar's Lyrics." *African American Review* 41, no. 2 (Summer 2007): 327–39.

Saunders, C. C. "F. Z. S. Peregrino and the South African Spectator." *Quarterly Bulletin of the South African Library* 32 (1978): 81–90.

Savoie, John. "Dunbar, Douglass, Milton: Authorial Agon and the Integrated Canon." *College Literature* 37, no. 2 (2010): 24–47.

Scharnhorst, Gary. "From Soldier to Saint: Robert Gould Shaw and the Rhetoric of Racial Justice." *Civil War History* 34, no. 4 (December 1988): 308–22.

Scharnhorst, Gary, and Kadeshia Matthews. "'Denver Took Me into Her Arms': Paul Laurence Dunbar in Colorado, 1899–1900." *Colorado Heritage: The Journal of the Colorado Historical Society*, July/August 2011, 15–23.

Scott, William W. *History of Passaic and Its Environs*. Vol. 3. New York: Lewis Historical Publishing, 1922.

Scott-Childress, Reynolds J. "Paul Laurence Dunbar and the Project of Cultural Reconstruction." *African American Review* 41, no. 2 (Summer 2007): 367–75.

Seaton, Sandra. "'The Great Big Pahty': My Grandmother and Paul Lawrence Dunbar." *Midwestern Miscellany* 34 (2006): 85–92.

Seraile, William. *Bruce Grit: The Black Nationalist Writings of John Edward Bruce*. Knoxville: University of Tennessee Press, 2003.

Shaffer, Donald M., Jr. "Making Space(s): The Representation of Place and Identity in Black Migration Novels, 1902–1953." *Dissertation Abstracts International, Section A: The Humanities and Social Sciences* 66.7 (2006): 2581.

Shepard, Vinton R., ed. "The Case of Mr. Thatcher." *The Ohio Law Reporter: A Weekly Journal Published in the Interest of the Legal Profession in the State of Ohio* 9, no. 35 (December 4, 1911): 437–500.

Sherman, Joan R., ed. *African American Poetry of the Nineteenth Century: An Anthology*. Chicago: University of Illinois Press, 1992.

Shockley, Ann Allen. "Joseph S. Cotter, Sr.: Biographical Sketch of a Black Louisville Bard." *CLA Journal* 18, no. 3 (March 1975): 327–40.

"Shown Up by Lamb." *Mansfield (OH) News-Journal*, March 20, 1906, 6.

Simon, Myron. "Dunbar and Dialect Poetry." In Martin, *A Singer in the Dawn*, 114–34.

Sisco, Dolores V. "A Little More Than Something Else: Dunbar's Colorist Ambivalence in *The Sport of the Gods*." In Harrell, *We Wear the Mask*, 191–209.

Smethurst, James. "Paul Laurence Dunbar and the Turn of the Twentieth Century African American Dualism." *African American Review* 41, no. 2 (Summer 2007): 377–86.

Smith, Katherine Capshaw. "The Legacy of Paul Laurence Dunbar: Dialect and Racial Configuration in the Works of Silas X. Floyd and Christina Moody." *Midwestern Miscellany* 34 (2006): 36–52.

Sollors, Werner. "Was Roxy Black? Race as Stereotype in Mark Twain, Edward Windsor Kemble, and Paul Laurence Dunbar." In *Mixed Race Literature*, edited by Jonathan Brennan, 70–87. Stanford, CA: Stanford University Press, 2002.

Sonstegard, Adam. "Kemble's Figures and Dunbar's Folks: Picturing the Work of Graphic Illustration in Dunbar's Short Fiction." In Harrell, *We Wear the Mask*, 116–37.

Stoddard, Charles. "Ouida in Her Winter City." *National Magazine* 21 (March 1905): 653–59.

Story, Ralph. "Paul Laurence Dunbar: Master Player in a Fixed Game." *CLA Journal* 27, no. 1 (1983): 30–55.

Stronks, James B. "Paul Laurence Dunbar and William Dean Howells." *Ohio Historical Quarterly* 67 (1958): 95–108.

Stuart, Ruth McEnery. *Sonny: A Christmas Guest.* New York: Century, 1894.

Terry, Jennifer. "'When Dey 'Listed Colored Soldiers': Paul Laurence Dunbar's Poetic Engagement with the Civil War, Masculinity, and Violence." *African American Review* 41, no. 2 (2007): 269–75.

Thomas, Henry Wilton. *The Last Lady of Mulberry: A Story of Italian New York.* New York: D. Appleton, 1900.

Thomas, Lorenzo. "Dunbar and Degradation: *The Sport of the Gods* in Context." In *Complexions of Race: The African Atlantic,* edited by Fritz Gysin and Cynthia S. Hamilton, 159–79. Münster, Germany: LIT Verlag, 2005.

Tolson, Nancy D. "Besides Nursery Rhymes, I Learned Paul." *Midwestern Miscellany* 34 (2006): 78–84.

Toth, Emily. "A Writer, Her Reviewers, Her Markets." Chap. 9 in *Unveiling Kate Chopin.* Jackson: University Press of Mississippi, 1999.

Towns, George A. "Phylon Profile, XVI: Horace Bumstead, Atlanta University President (1888–1907)." *Phylon* 9, no. 2 (2nd qtr., 1948): 109–14.

Turner, Darwin. "Paul Laurence Dunbar: The Poet and the Myths." *College Language Association Journal* 8, no. 2 (1974): 155–71.

———. "Paul Laurence Dunbar: The Poet and the Myths." In Martin, *A Singer in the Dawn,* 59–74.

———. "Paul Laurence Dunbar: The Rejected Symbol." *Journal of Negro History* 52, no. 1 (1967): 1–13.

Turpin, Zachary. "'Twilight Is Their Child': Uncollected Poems, Letters, and a Short Story by Paul Laurence Dunbar." *Resources for American Literary Study* 40 (2019): 155–82.

Van Dyke, Henry. *Fisherman's Luck and Some Other Uncertain Things.* New York: Charles Scribner's Sons, 1899.

Vincent, John Heyl, and Lewis Miller. *The Chautauqua Movement.* Boston: Chautauqua Press, 1885.

Von Rosk, Nancy. "Coon Shows, Ragtime, and the Blues: Race, Urban Culture, and the Naturalist Vision in Paul Laurence Dunbar's *The Sport of the Gods.*" In *Twisted from the Ordinary: Essays on American Literary Naturalism,* edited by Mary E. Papke, 144–68. Knoxville: University of Tennessee Press, 2003.

Wagner, Jean. *Black Poets of the United States: From Paul Laurence Dunbar to Langston Hughes.* Urbana: University of Illinois Press, 1973.

Wakefield, John. "Paul Laurence Dunbar: 'The Scapegoat' (1904)." In *The Black American Short Story in the 20th Century: A Collection of Critical Essays,* edited by Peter Bruck, 39–51. Amsterdam: B. R. Grüner, 1977.

Ward, William S. *A Literary History of Kentucky*. Knoxville: University of Tennessee Press, 1988.

Washington, Booker T., ed. *The Negro Problem: A Series of Articles by Representative American Negroes of To-day*. New York: James Pott, 1903.

Wheat, Valerie J. "Nineteenth Century Black Dialect Poetry and Racial Pride: Candelario Obeso's *Cantos populares de mi tierra* and Paul Laurence Dunbar's *Lyrics of Lowly Life*." *Afro-Hispanic Review* 15, no. 2 (1996): 26–36.

Wiggins, Lida Keck, ed. *The Life and Works of Paul Laurence Dunbar: Containing His Complete Poetical Works, His Best Short Stories, Numerous Anecdotes and a Complete Biography of the Famous Poet*. Naperville, IL: J. L. Nichols, 1907.

Willard, Francis Elizabeth, and Mary Ashton Rice Livermore, eds. *A Woman of the Century: Fourteen Hundred-Seventy Biographical Sketches Accompanied by Portraits of Leading American Women in All Walks of Life*. Buffalo, NY: Charles Wells Moulton, 1893.

Williams, Kenny J. "The Masking of the Novelist." In Martin, *A Singer in the Dawn*, 157–207.

Wilson, Matthew. "The Advent of 'The Nigger': The Careers of Paul Laurence Dunbar, Henry O. Tanner, and Charles W. Chesnutt." *American Studies* 43, no. 1 (Spring 2002): 5–50.

———. *Whiteness in the Novels of Charles W. Chesnutt*. Jackson: University Press of Mississippi, 2004.

Witham, Barry B., ed. *Theatre in the United States, 1750–1915*. Cambridge: Cambridge University Press, 1996.

Woodson, Carter G. "James Edwin Campbell, a Forgotten Man of Letters." *Negro History Bulletin* (November 2, 1938): 11.

Young, Sandra Archer. "Coercion or Concern? Letter Writing and the Marital Woes of Paul Laurence Dunbar and Alice Moore." *CLA Journal* 54, no. 4 (June 2011): 323–36.

INDEX

Page references in italics refer to illustrations.